D1397570

Sailing on the Silver Screen

LAWRENCE SUID

Naval Institute Press   Annapolis, Maryland

SAILING ON THE SILVER SCREEN

Hollywood and the U.S. Navy

791.43658
5948s
1996

© 1996 by Lawrence Suid

All rights reserved. No part of this book may be reproduced without written
   permission from the publisher.

Library of Congress Cataloging-in-Publication Data

Suid, Lawrence H.
    Sailing on the Silver Screen: Hollywood and the U.S. Navy / Lawrence Suid.
         p.   cm.
    Includes bibliographical references and index.
    ISBN 1-55750-787-2 (cloth: alk. paper)
    1. War films—History and criticism. 2. United States. Navy.
I. Title.
PN1995.9.W3S95 1996
791.43'658—dc20

Printed in the United States of America on acid-free paper ∞

03 02 01 00 99 98 97 96   9 8 7 6 5 4 3 2

First printing

To Dolores,
without whom this book would not have been possible.

METHODIST COLLEGE LIBRARY
Fayetteville, N.C.

Contents

★

Preface

In my first book, *Guts & Glory*, I wrote a history of the making of the U.S. military image in American motion pictures. In tracing the long relationship between the armed forces and the film industry, I was also describing their mutual exploitation. Despite the book's subtitle, however, *Great American War Movies*, I could not mention every significant military film. Nor did I intend *Guts & Glory* to become a compendium of all Hollywood war stories. Instead, I selected movies about the armed services in war or peace that in a specific way contributed to the making of the military image.

I devoted much attention to the 1927 *Wings* because it was Hollywood's first major film about the Army Air Corps, received virtually unlimited assistance from the War Department, and won the first Oscar as best picture. I included *Sands of Iwo Jima,* not *Halls of Montezuma* or *Battle Cry,* because it was the first postwar Marine film and John Wayne's Sergeant Stryker remains the quintessential Marine hero. *From Here to Eternity* presented a different image of the Army to the American people, one that the service fought to keep from the screen. I spent a full chapter on *The Longest Day,* the pivotal film in the book. It ended the cycle of World War II stories and remains the model that all subsequent combat epics have imitated, and the one movie about men in battle against which to judge all other Hollywood films. Moreover, the controversies surrounding its production led to significant changes in Pentagon policies governing the process by which the military provided assistance to filmmakers.

Though I discussed *The Big Parade, What Price Glory,* and *Wings, Guts & Glory* spent very little time on the many service movies of the 1930s, however important the period became to the development of Hollywood's relationship with the armed forces. Why? Most people reading the book had not had the opportunity to see these movies. Nor has the Library of Congress become a repository for very many of these early films, so they are not readily available for scholars to view. In particular, movies about the Navy in the period before World War II received little attention, including Frank Capra's 1928 *Submarine,* the many Annapolis films of the decade, the 1937 *Submarine D-1,* and the 1941 *Dive Bomber.*

Guts & Glory did analyze most of the "classic" movies about the American military produced since the beginning of World War II. However, many significant movies about the Navy did not receive attention. *Wing and A Prayer, They Were Expendable, Bridges at Toko-ri,* and *In Harm's Way* clearly remain important to any understanding of how the Navy worked to project a positive image. Since *Guts & Glory* appeared in 1978, the Navy has received the most positive treatment of any of the military services from filmmakers in such movies as *The Final Countdown, Top Gun,* and *The Hunt for Red October.* In fact, the Navy provides a superb case study of the manner in which the armed forces formed a symbiotic relationship with Hollywood to sell themselves to the American people. In *Sailing on the Silver Screen* I tell the story of the Navy's interaction with the motion-picture industry, a relationship that began before World War I and continues to the present. Nevertheless, I have not tried to create a filmography of movies about the Navy nor mention every movie ever made about the service. Instead, this book focuses on how the Navy has used motion pictures for almost ninety years to create, maintain, and ultimately rehabilitate not only its image, but the image of the entire military establishment since the Vietnam War.

Sailing on the Silver Screen becomes military history, not of battles or great heroes but of a Navy support agency, in this case the service's public-affairs apparatus as it worked with the film industry. At the same time, in focusing on the interaction between the motion picture industry and the Navy and the products of that relationship, I have written both an institutional and cultural history. However, I have not written film history or criticism. Unlike a film historian, I have no interest in directorial style or technique, screenwriting, the history of studios, or the development of cinematic technology. Rather, I am studying movies only as the products of the interaction between the Navy and filmmakers, not unlike the weaponry that results from the service's dealings with the military-industrial complex.

Many traditional historians tend to take less seriously any book that discusses motion pictures, and even friendly historians have sometimes described me as a "film historian," whatever that connotes. However, I see film history and criticism coming more from a viewer's perceptions of the images on the screen than from a study of how the movie came into being. In contrast, I base *Sailing on the Silver Screen* primarily on original documents and interviews with people involved in the production of the motion pictures I am discussing. As a result, the book becomes a history of the making of the Navy's image in Holly-wood motion pictures, not a study of movies as art or entertainment.

I consider the quality of the films important only to the extent that people decided to see them. The reviews quoted do not serve as measures of a film's artistic merit but as documents illustrating how critics reacted to the particular film. Though reviewers may comment on the quality of a movie, their conclusions become relevant only in trying to ascertain whether the Navy succeeded in securing a product that justified its cooperation and benefited its goals. Likewise, I use the motion pictures themselves as primary documents, which I analyze in the same way any historian studies original sources. Moreover, they remain only one type of primary document from which I obtain the information to describe how the Navy worked with filmmakers to fabricate the images the service desired. I have also drawn upon documents from traditional archival sources and private collections as well as upon interviews I conducted with Navy personnel, government officials, filmmakers, and media critics. From these sources I have been able to produce a history that describes what people at the time believed they were doing, and why they were doing it, as well as what they actually did. Given this approach, *Sailing on the Silver Screen* stands as an original work of history, not a synthesis based on other material.

I believe this book makes a unique contribution to the understanding of how the Navy consciously tried to create a positive image of its people, equipment, and procedures to inform the American people of how it was protecting them from all enemies. Nevertheless, in a significant way, the Navy and the other services may have succeeded too well. Before World War II the many preparedness films had assured the nation the military was defending it against attack. Pearl Harbor exposed the falseness of that promise. After the war, drawing their inspiration from the great victories over Germany and Japan, the military and Hollywood again conspired to assure the nation the armed services would always conquer any foe. Ultimately, Vietnam gave lie to that promise.

These betrayals made the traumas of both defeats deeper and more painful, and this book details the Navy's contribution to the empty promises the military establishment made to the nation and shows how the Navy assisted filmmakers to rehabilitate the shattered images of all the armed forces. If my book provides an understanding of this myth-making and its impact on the American people, it has value.

Acknowledgments

I have only a few people to thank for their help with the research and writing of this history of the relationship between the film industry and the United States Navy. In particular, Dolores Haverstick provided support and perceptive critiques of every word and idea during the long process of turning my proposal into a completed manuscript. Without her assistance, *Sailing on the Silver Screen* would lack readability and historical insights that I believe will make it a valuable source of information on the creation of the Navy's image in motion pictures. At the same time, of course, I accept full responsibility for any errors that have crept into the text.

In *Guts & Glory*, my initial study of the Hollywood-military relationship, I acknowledged and described in detail the invaluable assistance I received from Donald Baruch, the Pentagon's liaison with the film industry for more than forty years. The information he provided me until he retired in 1989 remains the foundation on which I have based this study. Fortunately, Phil Strub, who replaced Baruch, has continued to give me access to the information I have needed to keep current with the Pentagon's cooperation with filmmakers. Even more important, Phil has followed Don's example of scrupulously refusing to ever suggest what I should say in my writing, except of course to correct factual errors.

In writing *Sailing on the Silver Screen* I have used the documents that Baruch and Strub provided, material from many archives and libraries, and the interviews I have been conducting for more than twenty years with people in the motion picture industry, the armed services, the government, and the media. As a result, I had to solicit only a few additional interviews to complete the research for this book. However, each one added significantly to important aspects of the story.

Pierre Salinger suggested a few additions to the account of the making of *PT-109*, as did the film's director, Leslie Martinson. George Stevens, Jr., and Fred Zinnemann also provided precise wording to complete the accounts of their involvement in the search for the film's director. Almost twenty years after I first contacted Capt. Colin Mackenzie, one of the technical advisers on *In Harm's Way*, we finally met for a long-delayed interview. Among other things, he saved me from embarrassment by pointing out that promotions came slowly in the pre–Pearl Harbor Navy and so I was wrong to suggest that John Wayne seemed too old to still be a captain.

While he served as director of the Navy's Public Affairs Office in Los Angeles and even after his retirement, Capt. Mike Sherman gave me valuable information about the films on which he had worked. He also arranged some key interviews that proved to be very helpful.

I would like to thank Adm. David Cooney and Jack Garrow for their continued interest and help in making the book more accurate. Marine Lt. Col. Bill Miles, one of my students at the Marine Corps Command and Staff College, as well as a former Top Gun instructor and now a good friend, carefully read and offered suggestions to make my discussion of *Top Gun* as accurate as possible. He also questioned the connection I had made between the film and the Tail Hook scandal. While he does not agree with my conclusions, his concerns caused me to look again at the references to the film's impact on the scandal.

To do this, I solicited and received information from Donald Mancuso, the Assistant Inspector General for Investigations in the Department of Defense and author of the Tail Hook Report. Although I recognize that some people in the military do not agree with the report's conclusions, I found the information Mancuso provided persuasive and I appreciate his assistance on my discussion of this very controversial subject.

As he has done for almost twenty years, Charles Silver, in the Museum of Modern Art Film Studies Center, provided me research assistance during the writing of the book, particularly in arranging for me to view two important early Navy films, the sound version of *Men Without Women* and *Hell Divers*. And, at the Library of Congress, Madeline Matz scheduled films for screening on short notice and regularly helped me track down elusive information.

The continuing support from my friends has also contributed greatly to my ability to complete the book in the face of much adversity. I can only hope that Ginny Shapiro, Jeanne Mullaney, Chuck Lieman, Gertrude Weiner, John Haugen, Charles Champlin, and Stuart Chasen know how much I appreciate their help and presence when I needed them. Likewise, I would like to thank my Aunt Marcella for her support and encouragement.

Finally, I would like to thank the Naval Institute Press for its willingness to accept my proposal and to do a book that some people might not consider naval history.

Sailing on the Silver Screen

ONE

The Early Years

For more than ninety years the U.S. armed services have provided personnel, equipment, and facilities to help in the production of movies portraying the American military in war and peace. The services believed this assistance aided their recruiting campaigns as well as their efforts to inform the public and Congress of their activities and procedures. Each military branch operated under the general guidelines that cooperation must benefit the service or remain in its best interest and not cost the taxpayer any money. Each service's approach to requests for assistance developed from its perceptions of its place in the military establishment as well as from its internal structure.

The Army has usually assisted filmmakers more readily than the other branches, recognizing that as the least glamorous service it needs all the publicity it can obtain. The Marine Corps, always concerned with threats to its existence as a separate military entity, has consciously tried to foster its image as a unique fighting force. To maintain its reputation as the first to fight in any national emergency, the Corps has cooperated only on those movies presenting the service as it perceives itself. The Air Force, both as a branch of the Army and in the post–World War II period as a separate service, has assisted movies that convey the excitement of the war in the air, either in one-to-one combat between fighter pilots or in long-range strategic-bombing missions.

While the Air Force promoted its need for airplanes, the Navy regularly cooperated with Hollywood on films it hoped would support its need for a global fleet. During the Cold War the two services carried to the motion-picture screen their debate over the merits of aircraft carriers versus heavy bombers as a first-strike nuclear force. The Navy also saw its assistance to the motion-picture industry as a means of creating an image of a glamorous military organization whose officers and enlisted men traveled to the far ends of the earth to win great victories and beautiful women.

Unlike the other services, however, the Navy did not develop a cadre of public-relations specialists until the 1960s. Instead, it assigned line officers to tours of duty in the Washington Public Information Office. Most of these officers came to their assignments with a country-club mentality, the product of their Annapolis days and subsequent careers in a small, tightly knit officer corps. They viewed the Navy as an elite organization and wanted to present that image to the nation. As a result, far more than in movies portraying the other services, Navy stories focused on officers and their singular efforts to win the war at hand or to maintain a strong peacetime presence. Those films featuring enlisted men usually portrayed the lighter side of Navy life, with ships and planes simply providing ambience.[1]

Given the concern over its image, the service was to set the standard within the military establishment for scrutinizing requests for cooperation, formulating regulations governing assistance, and supervising the production of movies. In fact, the relationship between the Navy and Hollywood originated during the infancy of the motion-picture industry, when movies changed from a novelty with a limited audience to an established and widespread part of American life.[2]

Coincidentally, changes within the Navy were making it a natural subject for cinematic stories. The service was attracting unprecedented public attention due to its new battleship fleet, its lopsided victories in the Spanish-American War, and its around-the-world cruise. Filmmakers responded quickly to this popularity. Early movies showed ships in harbors, sailors marching in parades, and prominent officers, with George Dewey, the victor at Manila Bay, the most photographed.

The Navy recognized the power of the visual image and moved to use the new medium to promote itself and its policies. Initially, the service became a producer, purchaser, subject, and censor of documentaries, newsreels, and recruiting films. Commercial dramatic movies featuring sailors or using ships and sailors as background soon followed, so the Navy Department had to decide how it wished commercial filmmakers to portray its equipment, men, and activities. Likewise, in response to an increasing number of requests to film at naval installations and aboard ships, the service began writing regulations governing cooperation with the motion-picture industry.

For the Navy, as with all of the armed services, help in recruiting has always remained as one of the primary benefits gained from assisting filmmakers. In fact, the development of the motion-picture industry during the early years of the twentieth century occurred at the very time the Navy was transforming the composition of its enlisted force. From its founding, the Navy had recruited sailors from the ports of the world. Although always somewhat dissatisfied with this polyglot force, it did not change its recruiting system until after the Spanish-American War.

Under Teddy Roosevelt, the Navy began to acquire additional, more technologically complex ships. Traditional recruiting could not supply enough men since the Navy's authorized strength nearly tripled between 1899 and 1908, to almost 39,000. Nor could seaport recruiting supply men with the needed skills. In addition, as the new Navy became a symbol of national pride, the service recognized the incongruity of relying on a foreign-born enlisted force. Consequently, to secure enough suitable recruits, the Navy Department abandoned U.S. coastal cities and foreign ports as its primary recruiting grounds.

Instead, the Navy began focusing its recruiting efforts on the nation's heartland, signing up young, white Americans. Since inland recruiting required that the Navy tell its story to a population who had little knowledge of the service, let alone of the sea, the Navy began to use film as a tool to explain the advantages of life in the service, not only to potential recruits but to their families and friends.[3]

At the 1904 St. Louis World's Fair the Navy showed about sixty Biograph Company films portraying its officers and men aboard ships in peace and war. The exhibit, which *Scientific American* described as both "instructive and spectacular," traveled the next year to the Lewis and Clark Exposition in Portland, Oregon.[4] Following up these successes, the Navy sent the movies on a recruiting tour throughout the Midwest. To add to its library, the Bureau of Navigation, which then had responsibility for personnel matters, detailed a chief electrician to photograph a variety of scenes at the Newport Naval Torpedo Station and at the New York Navy Yard. Encouraged by the results, the service took pictures of fleet exercises at Guantanamo, Cuba, the next year, and then used both movies in a traveling exhibit. Although the Navy ended the recruiting odyssey in 1908, when the films wore out, it had just begun using the visual medium to attract enlistees.

During 1907 the service had begun providing films about its activities to movie houses and to organizations such as the Navy League. Although its first ventures into production had proven successful, the Navy returned to acquiring its films from outside sources, ultimately relying on dramatic movies to spread its message. In fact, the Navy had quickly discovered it could exercise a surprising level of control over the content of these films.

As with newsreel footage shot aboard ships and on naval bases, the close supervision of dramatic movies minimized disruption at the installations and helped maintain security. At the same time, the Navy began censoring the stories to ensure they contained favorable images. Eventually, studios' requests for permission to photograph naval facilities for newsreel and fictional stories became common enough that the Navy centralized the authorization process. The 1913 edition of Naval Instructions, for example, forbade the filming of ships, stations, or equipment without the written permission of the Navy Department.[5] In 1914 the Navy provided more complete instructions in General Order 78, which required that all persons "making protracted visits" to a naval vessel secure a permit from the Bureau of Navigation. When cameramen came aboard after obtaining the required authorization, an officer was to tell them what subjects or articles they might photograph. Commanding officers of shore stations could authorize visitors to the facility or ships in the port on their own authority but had to report the visitors' names to the Bureau of Navigation. Filmmakers who used naval facilities also needed to submit copies of the movies for censorship before release. The department also reserved the right to use the film itself for noncommercial purposes.[6]

Although these regulations gave the Navy great control over privately made films, producers did not protest. Newsreels had become a popular staple of movie-house programs, and the Navy routinely granted requests for the use of its facilities. The few rejections usually involved security considerations. For example, to protect the designs of range finders and data on the range and accuracy of the fleet's guns, the Navy usually denied requests to record target practice. It also resisted filming the testing of new technology and denied requests to shoot such activities as the launching of an airplane from a battleship, the firing of antiaircraft guns, and the testing of airplane motors. Requests to show submarine launchings met quick refusal "in view of the confidential nature of all matters connected with submarines."[7] Not all of the Navy's restrictions resulted from security concerns, however. On 25 March 1915 the submarine *F-4* sank outside Honolulu Harbor, with a loss of all twenty-one men aboard. Although not objecting to the filming of the recovery operation, the Navy insisted that the newsreels "not show bodies or handling of bodies or any gruesome details" and subjected the footage to the normal censorship before release.[8]

Over the years, however, the Navy was to devote its greatest attention to the production of feature films and their portrayals of the service's men and equipment. From the Spanish-American War onward, producers made movies using actors as naval personnel. A 1902 film catalogue listed several films with a Navy setting, including the comedy *Uncle Rube's Visit to a Man-o-War,* in which Uncle Rube slips on a soft-soaped deck. Unlike documentaries, such stories utilized the service only as background for actors.

When producers first incorporated naval subjects into their features, they used the same props as in stage plays, and the result looked artificial. Realizing filming at naval facilities and aboard ship would enhance the authenticity and appeal of their stories, studios began asking local commanders for access to their bases. These requests created opportunities for the Navy to control its image on the screen. Since camera crews and actors could board naval vessels only with official permission, filmmakers had to comply with the Navy's regulations or lose the ability to create a realistic ambiance.

As a result, the Navy soon applied the same orders governing newsreels to the production of dramatic movies. Since studios initially wanted to use naval facilities only as settings for story lines, the service did not usually receive requests to photograph classified machinery or drills. Nevertheless, concerned that all movies reflect credit on it, the Navy began reviewing scripts before agreeing to provide assistance and then assigned an officer to supervise the filming. In any case, during the formative period, the relationship worked reasonably well. In 1914, for example, Pathe had no trouble securing the use of a battleship deck for a love scene in the comedy *Via Wireless,* in which an officer and young woman steal away from her mother during a visit to the ship. Unlike most of the prewar films, *Via Wireless* had a rather complicated plot centered around the development of large-caliber guns for coastal defense.

To give the production timeliness, the filmmakers used as a springboard a newsreel of President Woodrow Wilson's speech advocating strong defense. During the melodrama, the Navy's efforts to obtain the desired weapon become intertwined with the romance between a Navy lieutenant and the daughter of the manufacturer. At the end, the Navy has its gun and the officer his bride. With the Navy's help, *Via Wireless* contained footage of the Atlantic Fleet cruising, scenes aboard the battleship USS *New York* at dry dock in the Washington Navy Yard and at sea, as well as shots of naval guns being tested at Sandy Hook, New Jersey.[9]

Ultimately, the Navy began giving official support to stories requiring its active participation, allowing the Lubin Moving Picture Company to use the Newport Naval Training Station in *The Peril* and agreeing to have a torpedo boat sink a yacht the filmmakers supplied. Nevertheless, the Navy refused to cooperate on some scripts it considered unacceptable. *The Son of Nobody,* which portrayed a Naval Academy graduate as a bully and villain, did not receive assistance because the service felt the story placed "naval officers before the public in a manner that is very discreditable to them and that has no foundation in fact."[10] The Navy also refused in 1915 to cooperate with a film version of *Madame Butterfly.* As Secretary of the Navy Josephus Daniels told the Famous Players Film Corporation, "it will be impracticable to allow one of the battleships to be used to illustrate a scene in the moving picture story of Madame Butterfly. As the action of the Naval Officer in the story does not reflect credit on the Naval Service, I do not feel that I can properly do anything that will serve to make your production more convincing." Daniels's disapproval did not prevent completion of the film, which starred Mary Pickford as Cho Cho San.[11]

While not all films on naval subjects made use of the service's facilities, on occasion the Navy tried to regulate those productions as well if it felt they did not portray its men in a positive light. In most cases, the service learned of the films only after their release because the producers had not requested assistance.

Increasingly reliant on nationwide recruiting, the Navy had become sensitive to suggestions its sailors did not have a wholesome occupation. Ultimately, in late 1914 the Navy turned to the National Board of Censorship for help in preventing the release of scenes from *Neenah the Foster Mother,* which the service believed contained negative images of its personnel. Created in 1909, the private organization became part of an ongoing effort by social reformers to deal with portrayals of immorality or antisocial behavior in movies. With the cooperation of the motion-picture industry, the Board reviewed films before their release and approved those that met its guidelines. The Navy had sought the Board's assistance after a recruiting officer complained the movie showed sailors frequenting a "house of ill fame" and "dancing with women of low cast and also drinking at the bar." The officer found the Board "willing to take such steps as are practicable toward preventing the recurrence" of such scenes.

Secretary Daniels then wrote the Board for specific help, claiming that such portrayals represented "an affront to the splendid body of men themselves and to the parents and relatives of men who are honorably serving their country" and "would undoubtedly deter many self-respecting young men who see them from entering the Navy if life in it were as depicted in dissolute and immoral scenes; parents would not want their sons to enlist under such circumstances; many people would become prejudiced against the Navy and its fine and manly body of enlisted men."[12]

The Board answered that it did not have the power to exclude such scenes but said that it did issue occasional bulletins to motion-picture producers, asking their cooperation to avoid particular scenes. It had, for example, sent a letter, at the request of the New York Stock Exchange, requesting filmmakers not to represent the Exchange engaging in questionable practices. Adopting this approach, Daniels prepared one hundred copies of a letter that the Board mailed to movie producers, who responded with promises of support. Italia Film Company of America, for one, answered, "We are in sympathy with your views and will do everything possible to keep our productions free from the atmosphere described in your letter."[13]

Filmmakers were to go beyond mere promises of support, choosing to edit their pictures rather than risk antagonizing the Navy. Although Keystone Films had made *The Face on the Barroom Floor* in July 1914, well before Daniels sent his letter, it agreed to remove a scene showing a drunken sailor. In apologizing, the firm reported that it no longer employed the film's director and had posted the letter on bulletin boards, assuring the Navy the company "had made it a point of showing the bluejacket in only the best light."[14] When Daniels later complained to Universal Film that *The Human Menace* showed uniformed men drunk, a vice president of the company answered, "In view of the fact that you and your department have shown this company such unfailing courtesy at all times, it must indeed have looked like ingratitude on our part when we allowed something offensive to your department to be depicted in one of our productions. This, of course, was an oversight, but it will not happen again."[15]

The Navy had no legal basis to compel filmmakers to delete scenes it deemed undesirable. Yet when it complained to producers, it received only promises of cooperation. Letters from the filmmakers contained no hint of resentment toward the requests. With so many other parts of society seeking to influence motion pictures, producers may well have believed it advisable to acquiesce to the Navy's demands.

After the outbreak of World War I in Europe and during the period of American neutrality, the Navy continued to cooperate with film companies but took care to avoid any links with prowar messages. Comedies such as *A Submarine Pirate* provided safe settings. Released in 1915, the film benefited from the notoriety that German submarines had been receiving since the outbreak of World War I. In this instance, Syd Chaplin, Charlie's brother, co-directed and starred in the Keystone movie about a bumbling waiter's efforts to thwart the hijacking of a gold-laden liner by the inventor of a miniature submarine. Ultimately, with the help of a Navy gunboat, he defeats the pirates.

Despite the silly story, the Bureau of Navigation, the department that then dealt with requests for assistance, approved the script. As a result, the filmmakers obtained the use of a submarine, a gunboat, as well as permission to shoot in the San Diego Navy Yard—which gave the film a feeling of authenticity Chaplin could not have created on a set. In particular, the actor's antics on the submarine's deck as it plows through the water and his holding onto the periscope as the craft actually submerges stood in sharp contrast to the farce inside the boat, which Chaplin staged in the studio. Despite all the slapstick, Secretary Daniels approved the film, and the chief of the Bureau of Navigation arranged with the producers to have *Submarine Pirate* shown in all naval recruiting stations. Perhaps because of the film's authenticity, it also broke box-office records throughout the world.[16]

On his part, Secretary Daniels believed the film would encourage young men to become submariners because it presented the glamour and technology of the new weapon of war. With both parties satisfied with the results, the film helped establish closer ties between the Navy and the motion-picture industry.[17]

Of the many Navy locales filmmakers regularly used to create these images until the outbreak of World War II, the Naval Academy became one of the most popular stages for romance, comedy, and drama. Naturally, the school took great care to ensure that the completed movies conveyed "correct" stories of the process by which the Navy turned innocent young boys into officers and gentlemen. As a result, the accuracy with which such films portrayed midshipmen's experiences may be questioned.

In any case, the Academy first appeared in the 1916 war-preparedness melodrama *The Hero of Submarine D-2*. The film follows the adventures of an officer stationed at the Academy who refuses to reinstate a political boss's son who had flunked out of school. In response, the politician has the officer assigned to a submarine as commander, where he suffers serious wounds in the process of foiling a Russian plot to blow up the U.S. Fleet. The ex-midshipman, now an enlisted man, rescues his nemesis and returns to Annapolis as a hero, while the officer marries the young man's sister.

Although the film used the Academy as only one Navy locale, *Weekly Variety* thought it portrayed the school "with excellent detail."[18] With the United States in the war, the 1918 *Madame Spy* also used Annapolis as one locale for a wartime espionage movie. However, the Navy had more important things to do than help either newsreel or commercial filmmakers. Assistant Secretary of the Navy Franklin Roosevelt had to tell Pathe News that the Navy could not allow it to shoot the trials of a newly completed submarine for "certain military reasons." Moreover, since the Navy's primary combat mission, convoying ships to Europe, did not provide many dramatic stories for filmmakers to re-create, few movies featured the Navy's wartime activities.[19]

Once the war ended, however, the service again began receiving requests for assistance from producers. Some scripts, such as one for "Sons of the Sea," elicited a positive response. Secretary Daniels found the story impressive and felt that "the publicity which will be given to the work and spirit of the Navy and the opportunity for promotion offered the enlisted men will justify the cost of the assistance to be rendered." Nevertheless, the project did not reach fruition.[20]

Receiving the Navy's help on previous films did not guarantee assistance on future projects either. Writing to Secretary of the Navy Edwin Denby on 21 February 1922, William Craft first explained that he had directed two films using the Navy as background, and the service and the public had responded favorably to both. He then described his adherence to regulations in preparing to make another film set within the Navy, only to have the commander of a submarine base inform him that Navy orders prevented filmmakers from taking pictures of a submarine under way, because of an oil shortage, or from shooting inside the boat. Having spent considerable money under the assumption he would receive cooperation, Craft asked the secretary to authorize assistance so that he could proceed.[21]

The director offered "replace in kind" fuel and lubricating oil, explained that he had intended to film the interior of an older, L-class submarine, assured the secretary he had "no intention of disclosing any secrets in the pictures taken," and promised to submit the finished movie for censorship. Craft did acknowledge, "It is not absolutely necessary for me to use the interior of one of the old L-class vessels, though, it is highly desirable. In case you cannot give me this authority, I could make a 'set' of a submarine interior, but in all cases where this has been done, there has been very little resemblance to the real thing and will detract from the realism of the remainder of the film." Authenticity aside,

Craft believed the script he was submitting "will show the Navy in a good light to the public and I believe will be beneficial to the public and especially those living away from the sea-shore, who have not the privilege of seeing their Navy at first hand."[22]

Having considered advice from Navy officers, Denby advised Craft on 2 March 1922 that the service did not believe his proposed film "would show to the public the real work of the naval service or pictures which would prove beneficial either to the public or the naval service." As he pointed out, "it would appear that the Navy would be somewhat advertised as a medium in support of an anti-bootleg force. It also more or less exploits an American naval officer as a burglar. Also in the American Navy it has never been an approved policy to sink any vessel without warning, and I think this policy should hold even though the vessel were [*sic*] used by bootleggers." So Denby denied Craft's request.[23]

Ironically, despite the service's desire to use movies to promote itself, the Army won the honor of first having filmmakers exploit the glamour of its officer education when *Classmates* showcased West Point in December 1924. However, with the release of *The Midshipman* the next October, the Naval Academy began to appear regularly in Hollywood movies. Like its Army counterpart, the film relied on images of the Academy's beautiful grounds, football weekends, dances, and marching midshipmen rather than a strong plot to attract audiences. In fact, none of the Academy movies conveyed the reality of life at the Academy. Filmmakers might create dramatic tensions from a midshipman's small transgression, but never from a major cheating scandal. A midshipman and his girl might suffer through the typical cinematic trials and tribulations of young love, but the story would not show a newly commissioned officer waiting two years after graduation to get married. Seldom did a film remind audiences that Navy men took long cruises, sometimes during the arrival of babies or family crises.

A script telling a serious story about midshipmen's lives with all the warts would probably have brought a swift denial of access to the Academy. Even generally positive scripts usually elicited requests for revisions and deletions. As a result, beginning with *The Midshipman,* Naval Academy movies presented a highly sanitized version of how the service produced officers. Nevertheless, the glamour of the uniforms, the perfection of the parades, the utter sincerity and patriotism of the midshipmen, and the highly romanticized boy-girl relationships all conspired to give the Annapolis films an appeal that transcended their stories.

As the first of the many Academy movies Hollywood re-created with slight variation over the years, *The Midshipman* contained scenes audiences had never seen before, including two actual parades, the Academy's mess hall, the June Ball, and graduation, with Secretary of the Navy Wilbur giving out the diplomas. Within these activities director Christy Cabanne fashioned a story in which James, an upperclassman, falls in love with Patricia, the sister of his plebe friend, Ted. The villain, a rich civilian engaged to Patricia, arranges to get James in trouble. Following the usual misunderstandings, the villain abducts Patricia and flees aboard his yacht, with James and a Navy destroyer in pursuit. After rescuing the heroine, the midshipman graduates and marries her, Academy regulations notwithstanding.

To heighten the authenticity, the filmmakers had proposed that President Coolidge, rather than the Secretary of the Navy, hand out diplomas. Despite the propaganda value of the movie, even the government had limitations on how far it would go. Nevertheless, the Navy did allow Ramon Novarro, starring as James, to dress up as a midshipman and take his place with the graduating class and receive a diploma, albeit an unsigned one, for the camera.[24]

The intertwining of image and reality created an immediate controversy within the ranks of Academy alumni. In a letter in the *Army Navy Journal* of 13 May 1925 an alumnus contended, "The humiliating spectacle of a Secretary of the Navy presenting a fake diploma to a fake Midshipman is reprobated by practically all graduates of that institution. Such a travesty of the solemn ceremony, the crown of four years' hard work, is unpardonable." The writer argued that the Navy and its friends should boycott the "fraudulent" film and Secretary Wilbur should resign because he did not "know he is advertising a film actor and *not* the Naval Academy."[25]

Wilbur and the Navy did have their defenders. On 18 June, Arthur Barney sent the secretary a copy of a letter he proposed to submit, with Wilbur's approval, to the *Journal*. In it, he said that the condemnation of the secretary "seems to me to be unworthy of publication, except to show that we have at least one alumnus of the academy, who had forgotten those gentlemanly principles that are taught both by precept and example at the United States Naval Academy." He also said that if the secretary believed the picture presented a true portrait of Annapolis, then "criticism is unjust and above all, indiscreet." Believing that film "is our greatest educational institution," Barney said, "A good picture of the academy portraying those wonderful traditions of the school will do a great deal to win the public to our greatest national academy that is now suffering from the pangs of Public Economy as well as unjust criticism."[26] As important, Barney felt that the "publicity received from the picture will do more to promote the friendly spirit towards the Academy than anything that has been done in the past decade." Having visited Annapolis recently, he had found that most people there had voiced a "spirit of appreciation" toward the film, with "no condemnation by either officer or midshipman being heard." Therefore, he could only conclude that the alumnus had "some more or less selfish motive and certainly if he is the gentleman that an alumnus should be, he will authorize the editor to reprint the letter over his own signature and not hide in the dark under the title he has assumed to take."[27]

The Midshipman did not deserve such interest. The *New York Times* thought the film's comedy "so bright that one forgives the weakness of the story. In a longer commentary, *Weekly Variety* found the film "good propaganda for the Middies" but felt the director conveyed the spirit of Annapolis chiefly from the male characters, the situations and setting, noting that the women were "woefully weak."[28]

Variety did feel the director had "seemingly taken no liberties to send the photoplay beyond the realm of probability," and if some of the action is "exaggerated it assuredly comes within the classification of screen license." While finding the story "ordinary," the critic concluded that *The Midshipman* remained "a good picture and will be of general interest simply on the strength of the Naval Academy setting." He also felt that anytime producers wanted to make a service-academy film, "it should be financially profitable as well as a boost for the schools. The Cadets and Middies are surefire subjects, always have been and always will be."[29]

Cabanne returned to the Naval Academy in 1929, trying to replicate his earlier success. Unfortunately for him and his company, *Annapolis* became simply a pale imitation of *The Midshipman*. Pointing out that an interesting background does not in itself make a movie, the *Weekly Variety* reviewer wrote that despite the scenery, Cabanne "has turned out a pretty dull picture for the simple reason that even the Naval Academy needs to be dramatized. An industrial film company commissioned to grind on Annapolis would probably turn out a more interesting job." The critic also blamed poor acting and Cabanne's direction for the movie's deficiencies, observing, "None of the people in the plot are human or real. Only reality appears to be the building and equipment."[30]

The Naval Academy and the Navy had contributed the surroundings, but except for objecting to unflattering portrayals of its officers and men, the service had little to say about the quality of any of the scripts for which studios requested assistance. Neither the military nor filmmakers wanted to become involved with an unsuccessful movie, but producers, writers, and directors have seldom been able to judge the quality of a production until they have completed their work, if then. Consequently, over the years the military has almost never used quality as a criterion for deciding whether to assist a production. However, *Weekly Variety* had concluded, the "romance of its title and locale" ensured that *Annapolis* would have some appeal. *Salute*, appearing later the same year, differed little from this pattern, subordinating the characters to the background in which they moved, in this instance the Army-Navy football game. According to *Weekly Variety*, the marching midshipmen entering the stadium "carries a real punch to anybody that has felt the unique sensation of the game itself between the two arms of the service." The film did offer two significant historical firsts. It became the first sound movie to feature the Naval Academy and contains the first lines that John Wayne, playing a midshipman, spoke on screen.[31]

In any event, the campus, parades, and romance of the uniforms remained a sufficient raison d'être for studios to portray the Naval Academy until World

War II. While these stories seldom showed any originality, the service continued to assist filmmakers even if the benefit seemed minimal. The Navy viewed the comedic and romantic movies to which it provided assistance during the 1920s in much the same way. Often, the service chose to assist a movie such as the 1926 comedy *We're in the Navy Now* only because the producer described it as "the Navy counterpart of the Army film entitled '*Behind the Front.*'" Others like *The Fleet's In, Wings of the Fleet,* and *Let It Rain* received help simply because they showed officers and men having exciting times at sea, in the air, and on shore.[32]

Some serious, action stories did rise above Hollywood's typical fare. The Navy assisted Famous Players Lasky's "pretentious production" *The Rough Riders* not only because Teddy Roosevelt had served as Assistant Secretary of the Navy, but also because it portrayed the service's contribution to victory in the Spanish-American War. Likewise, the Navy assisted on the 1927 World War I melodrama *Convoy,* which portrayed the combined British-American defeat of a German fleet in Kiel Harbor. Nevertheless, *Weekly Variety* found the story and ersatz combat carried little weight, "leaving the picture barren of sensationalism and weary in plot."[33]

While interest in World War I was waning by 1927, the Navy continued to offer opportunities for filmmakers to create action, adventure films—even good ones! In contrast to *Convoy,* the title of Frank Capra's *Submarine* (1928) provided little indication of the film's subject. Columbia Pictures probably should have called the movie "Navy Diver" or "Submarine Rescue" since the story had very little, if anything, to do with life aboard a peacetime Navy submarine. Except for the climactic rescue effort, the filmmakers probably could have used any occupational setting for their "buddy" story of two men and the dance-hall floozie who threatens their friendship.

Jack Holt, playing master Navy diver Jack Dorgan, and Ralph Graves, as his telephone man Bob Mason, created the familiar relationship they would reprieve in Capra's *Flight* (1929) and *Dirigible* (1931). Capra immediately establishes the close friendship and interdependence of the two men during a highly realistic diving sequence set in Manila Bay. Shot in Los Angeles Harbor at San Pedro with the assistance of Navy divers and equipment, the scene shows Dorgan investigating and then preparing to destroy a sunken ship that was obstructing navigation. Aboard the diving tender, Dorgan unknowingly becomes tangled in the line guiding the time bomb to its target and finds himself following the explosive to the bottom. In a predictable but still dramatic scene, Mason dives into the sea and frees Dorgan seconds before the device goes off.

Shortly afterward the Navy inexplicably separates the friends, assigning Mason to a submarine in the far Pacific and stationing Dorgan in San Diego. There, at a dance hall, the diver meets Snuggles. Too long abroad and with too little interaction with the opposite sex, Dorgan becomes enthralled with her and quickly proposes marriage. Finding the novelty of the idea appealing, Snuggles accepts and briefly settles into domesticity.

Unfortunately for Dorgan, she cannot or will not become a typical Navy wife and soon becomes restless for the dance hall, a yen the diver cannot satisfy because of the demands of his work. When he leaves on a salvage assignment, Snuggles immediately heads to her old milieu, where she meets Mason, who has just returned from his submarine and, unable to locate his friend, is seeking companionship. Mason also becomes infatuated with Snuggles. With the Motion Picture Production Code not yet in place to prohibit on-screen adultery, the sailor and the lady embark on a torrid one-week affair.

Having no idea of his friend's changed marital status, Mason surprises the returning Dorgan at the dock, where the diver ecstatically discloses his marriage and drags his buddy home to meet his wife. Mason and Snuggles can barely hide their shock when thus confronted, and when Dorgan takes his after-action report to his superiors, Mason angrily denounces Snuggles for causing him to betray, albeit unknowingly, his best friend in the worst possible way. While Snuggles is using her wiles to calm Mason, Dorgan returns home to find them in each other's arms. Having created the requisite domestic complications, Capra turned to the film's raison d'être, the melodramatic rescue of Mason and his fellow crewmen from their submarine, which a destroyer sinks during maneuvers.

The rescue mission had its historical origins in the loss of the *S-51*, the victim of a steamer off Block Island, Rhode Island, in 1925, and of the *S-4*, which a destroyer ran over off Provincetown, Massachusetts, in 1927. Tom Eadie, the lead diver on the salvage operation to raise the *S-51*, as well as the failed effort to rescue six men trapped in the *S-4*'s torpedo room and subsequent recovery of the submarine, provided the film model for Dorgan's character. Eadie had received the Navy Cross for his work on the *S-51* and the Congressional Medal of Honor for saving the life of another diver while working on the *S-4*, and his heroics and his book, *I Like Diving,* had made him famous.

However, when filmmakers try to re-create historical events, they often lose reality. In *Submarine* the portrayal of deep-sea diving lacks plausibility, and, however dramatic, Dorgan's rescue efforts remain only Hollywood fantasy. The Navy needed nine months, including a winter pause, to bring the *S-51* to the surface from a depth of 132 feet. Public pressure, growing out of the failure to save the *S-4*'s six trapped men, forced the service to work through the winter, under appalling conditions, to bring that submarine to the surface from only one hundred feet down.

In *Submarine,* after other divers have failed to go below 250 feet in their rescue efforts, Dorgan dives to 400 feet, a depth the film acknowledges no man had ever reached, and attaches an air hose to Mason's stricken submarine. Even if a diver could have performed such a feat, the film conveniently fails to explain how a team of divers could possibly have worked regularly at such a depth to salvage the *S-44* before the men died of exposure or thirst. In one dialogue title, an admiral comments, "Now, we can raise them with pontoons." The Navy had used pontoons to salvage the *S-51* and *S-4,* but only after long struggles, in much shallower water, and without having men alive awaiting rescue. Ten years later Navy divers were able to rescue twenty-six men from the USS *Squalus* from a depth of 227 feet, but only through the use of the newly perfected McCann diving bell. Despite the impossibility of such a rescue, *Submarine* ends with Mason and Dorgan together again while Snuggles has returned to the dance hall, where she is enticing still another sailor with her well-polished come-on.

Capra's film did raise for the first time the question of why the Navy would agree to assist a submarine-disaster film, even if based on historical events. Why would the service help any film showing the failure of its officers, in this case the submarine captain who tries to surface instead of diving deeper to avoid the onrushing destroyer? Why remind the American people of the dangers of going under the sea in fragile, thin-skinned, often temperamental boats? The Navy Public Affairs Office usually objected when such stories arrived in Washington but ultimately approved most requests for assistance.

No record exists of the Navy's initial reaction to the script of *Submarine,* and Capra mentions only the help he received from the Navy after he took over from the film's original director. However, according to a 1936 memo from a Navy officer to the commandant of the 11th Naval District in San Diego, the Navy apparently had initially refused to help Capra's film. In commenting on *The Devil's Playground,* a story virtually identical to *Submarine,* including the same names for the male leads, the officer recalled that the Navy had "disapproved" assistance in the late 1920s to all submarine-disaster pictures because it did not want to become involved with stories showing doomed and dying sailors, particularly with the sinkings of the *S-51* and *S-4* still fresh in people's minds. The officer also noted that all studios except for Columbia Pictures ultimately "respected the wishes of the Navy Department by dropping their submarine pictures from their production list."[34]

In any case, Columbia Pictures did receive significant Navy help in making *Submarine.* Certainly, the images of Dorgan's unfaithful wife, his drinking, and his initial refusal to report for duty on the *S-44*'s rescue operation did not benefit the Navy. Nor did *Submarine* give possible recruits much hope of rescue if they found themselves in a situation similar to Mason's, four hundred feet below the surface. In light of the recent submarine tragedies and their potential effect on recruiting, however, the Navy had little choice but to assist a story that at least offered hope the Navy would try to rescue men trapped underseas. In truth, the film did offer some benefits. Although the captain of the *S-44* did lose his boat, he provided strong leadership for his entombed men. Mason puts aside the pain of losing his friend and bravely calms his comrades in the face of imminent death. Dorgan initially refuses to join the rescue operation out of anger toward his friend, but once he realizes that Snuggles had initiated the transgression, he acts with the highest courage to take the air hose to the *S-44*.

In broader terms, the Navy was able to get its generic message onto the motion-picture screen. During a scene showing a training maneuver, a title proclaims, "The Fleet fares forth in times of peace, with all the majesty of war, to preserve the freedom of the seas." Thus, even *Submarine* served to remind the American people that risks accompany this responsibility. It also showed that men taking this risk would "act like men" in the face of death. Finally, even if *Submarine* showed some of the Navy's warts and did not provide the most credible information about the submarine service, it offered a classic image of male-bonding within the military: join the Navy and find a friend for life.

In any case, *Submarine* became a box-office hit and established Capra as a major director. Despite the references to the Navy's submarine disasters, which *Weekly Variety* found "not entirely good judgment, either as story-telling or as propaganda," the reviewer found the film "a strong and stirring picture" because "man's fight with the forces of nature is always dramatic" and the film showed "sympathetically, the terrific odds against rescue work." The reviewer also validated the service's decision to assist the filmmakers: "The intent is plainly to demonstrate that the navy quickly and intelligently does every thing that can possible [sic] be done in such emergencies."[35]

Meanwhile, as the submarine service was receiving attention, Hollywood was discovering the visual and dramatic possibilities that stories about the Navy's air arm offered. In fact, MGM's 1929 *The Flying Fleet* became the first film to portray any of the armed services' contemporary aviation activities. The movie tells the story of five graduates of the Naval Academy, who attend the Naval Flying School together and attempt to set a long-distance-flight record from San Diego to Honolulu. Apart from the overall benefit this portrayal provided the Navy, the film contained considerable material about test-flying. It also provided the first detailed account of the trials aspiring naval aviators had to endure to win their wings.

The long overwater flight had its basis in a San Francisco–to–Honolulu record attempt by a Navy seaplane in 1925, which ended about 450 miles short of its goal. Using fabric from the wing, the crew had then sailed their aircraft to within ten miles of Kauai before a submarine rescued them. In *The Flying Fleet*, on the other hand, one of the friends spots the downed fliers, sets his own plane on fire to attract the attention of a nearby aircraft carrier, and parachutes into the sea to await rescue.

The *New York Times* thought the film contained "some splendid sequences devoted to an airplane carrier, with its marvelous deck space and the gull-like machines gliding from the vessel and swooping back home." Melodrama aside, the reviewer considered the flying scenes "so absorbing that they take precedence over the lurid pictorial story. They are something at which to marvel. The airplanes are like silver-birds on the wing, forging through the air in a wonderfully exact formation. They roll and turn as one machine, the pilots being apparently as much at home in the clouds as cavalrymen on terra firma." While other films had already portrayed the excitement of aerial combat, the reviewer felt that "nothing quite as shining or as beautiful as some of these scenes has so far been pictured in animated photography."[36]

The film's authenticity resulted not only from the full cooperation of the Navy but also from the intimate knowledge of the early development of naval aviation that Frank "Spig" Wead brought to his first screenwriting assignment. Wead, a record-setting naval aviator who had retired after suffering a disabling injury, was to become a de facto Navy publicist during a Hollywood career that spanned almost twenty years, interrupted by a return to active service during World War II.

His expertise helped make *The Flying Fleet* the prototype for the many naval aviation films the motion-picture industry made in the next sixty years. The flying sequences, rather than the plot twists and love stories, became the primary attraction of the movies and the component that made most of them highly successful at the box office. By the end of the 1920s, talking pictures were facilitating the Navy's efforts to sell the American people on the efficacy of its aircraft carriers, planes, battleships, and submarines. In the new decade, the Navy was to exploit this new cinematic technology with assistance to films that positively portrayed each of its branches.

———— ★ ————

The 1930s

The Golden Age of Navy Movies

————————

D uring the 1930s the Navy continued to view cooperation with the motion-picture industry as a means of creating an image of a glamorous organization whose officers and men traveled to the far ends of the earth. In peacetime the service projected the nation's power and provided security from attack. If war came, the Navy was prepared to win great victories. In war or peace, both officers and men expected to conquer beautiful women who swooned at the sight of a uniform. Ships, the sea, and sailors regularly served as backdrop for films of romance, comedy, music, and drama. As fascist threats increased, the service became more and more popular as a setting for films showing the military preparing to protect the nation.

While reviewing requests for assistance on these movies, the Navy regularly revised its regulations governing the process by which it extended help. Of these revisions, one of the most significant occurred in August 1931, when Secretary of the Navy David Ingalls issued a memorandum replacing the 1929 instructions covering Navy review of motion-picture screenplays. The new memorandum required studios to include a script and a statement of the type and amount of support needed with any request for cooperation. It also directed the Navy to create a Motion Picture Board to review the requests, with the director of public relations acting as recorder and handler of correspondence. The Board was to carefully consider each application and make appropriate recommendations to the Chief of Naval Operations (CNO) about whether to approve the project. The Board then had the responsibility of reviewing the completed film and advising whether to approve the production for release to the public.[1]

Under the new policy, the CNO would authorize a local commander to render help at his convenience, on a noninterference basis. The commander could choose not to provide assistance or even disagree with Washington's judgment of the project and try to reverse the decision. If a production did receive assistance, the studio had to submit the completed movie to the Board for censorship and final approval. Since officers often brought their own prejudices about motion pictures to the process, the Navy might turn down a particular story one year and approve a similar one the next. Inconsistency became the hallmark of the Navy's implementation of its policies.[2]

At the same time, the Hollywood/Navy relationship was developing into one of mutual exploitation. Often, the service gave significant assistance to a production that might contain negative images just to demonstrate new technological developments, particularly in the air and under the sea. In turn, filmmakers might agree to significant script changes that degraded dramatic tensions to ensure the Navy would provide the necessary assistance.

Despite the benefit it received, the Navy Department and officers in the field regularly found initial scripts unacceptable, and the rejection of a story usually caused a studio to kill a project. In August 1931, for example, the commanding officer of the USS *Colorado*, stationed at San Pedro, California, took exception to the script for "Summerville Number Four" after receiving authorization to cooperate on the production. Informing the CNO he had made arrangements to render Universal Pictures "all necessary assistance" to film aboard his battleship, the captain admitted he found none of the scenes "in themselves objectionable." Nevertheless, he argued that cooperation "is not justified for the reason that its release can bring no credit to the Navy and might give the public an entirely wrong impression of discipline on board ship."[3]

He pointed out that the plot focused on the efforts of a Marine bugler to smuggle a girl aboard in a seabag, while approximately two-thirds of the story portrays "the adventures of the bag. The climax of the picture occurs when the girl sits on a switch which presumably controls all activities on the ship. When she does this the anchors are let go, all boats are lowered, the turrets are fired, the whistle blows and the band marches around the quarterdeck playing 'The Stars and Stripes Forever.'" Acknowledging the picture as a slapstick comedy that "therefore might not give to an intelligent audience an erroneous impression of naval customs and discipline," the captain did not believe "it in keeping with the dignity of the Naval Service to require a United States Man of War to participate in such a farce." He concluded that "through some oversight" the Navy had failed to review the script carefully but said he would provide assistance unless otherwise ordered.[4]

Agreeing with his subordinate, the commander of the Battle Force immediately sent a message to the CNO on 16 August 1931, recommending that the Navy not undertake assistance: "To do otherwise would, I believe, cheapen the

Naval Service in the eyes of the public and bring discredit upon the Naval Service." With the message in hand, the newly constituted Motion Picture Board reconsidered the Navy's approval of "Summerville Number 4." It advised the CNO that the Navy usually helped only on feature films but, in this case, felt assistance to a comedy "is desirable, provided the picture does not bring discredit on any branch of the Government service, their uniform or personnel or those of any foreign government, and provided further, that the return to the Navy in good will and in the opportunity for censorship is commensurate with the extent of participation requested."[5]

The Board explained it had approved the script on this basis and with the "full realization of the fact that this picture was a burlesque of naval scenes." However, information from California indicated the studio now wanted more extensive assistance than originally requested, including filming aboard the *Colorado*. Although recommending the Navy limit assistance aboard the *Colorado* to one day, two Board members argued the service should honor its agreement since Universal had accepted conditions the Navy had set forth. The officers maintained that the goodwill "of this company and probably the motion picture industry is seriously involved." Furthermore, they observed that the script contained no objectionable scenes and could "never be mistaken for a serious portrayal of naval activities."[6]

In contrast, the Marine officer, new to the Board, felt that the Navy should withdraw cooperation because "the picture is an undesirable burlesque involving persons in the uniform of this Corps." Likewise, two other Navy officers on the Board recommended canceling cooperation "because the advantages to be gained in this particular case are not commensurate with the extent of cooperation required." Accepting the majority opinion, the CNO advised the Battle Fleet that the Navy "finds it necessary to cancel the authorization previously granted." With assistance revoked, Universal canceled the project.[7]

Ironically, concern about the portrayal of the nation's former enemies caused the Navy to reject Goldwyn Studios's request for assistance in June 1932 for a project entitled "U-Boat." The foreword to the synopsis of the story stated, "In times of peace we Americans are prone to forget that a big Navy is absolutely essential for the protection of ourselves, our homes and our commerce." Despite the pro-Navy message, the Board informed the CNO that the story focused on the naval wartime activities of a now-friendly government that might find some of the scenes offensive. Consequently, the Board advised the Navy not assist the production.[8]

Even before the studio had received formal notification of the rejection, Samuel Goldwyn wrote the Board that he believed the story contained "a fine bit of propaganda for the American Navy." Nevertheless, the studio submitted a revised script and requested permission to film several Navy ships, including a destroyer and submarine. The new version failed to convince the Board, which did not think the "slight changes" removed the story's objectionable features. With that, the studio conceded defeat, and the project died.[9]

While most requests for assistance had better results, Hollywood was losing interest in the Great War. To a large extent, the epics of the mid-1920s, *The Big Parade, What Price Glory,* and *Wings,* had satisfied people's appetite for serious war movies, particularly as the nation returned to an isolationist foreign policy. Perhaps more important, the Depression had caused people to lose their taste for mass carnage. While the military remained willing to assist suitable projects, limited appropriations and reduced manpower often prevented cooperation on the scale extended to earlier combat stories.[10]

The Navy faced an additional problem in helping on movies about World War I, having participated in few major battles in the "war to end all wars." As a result, if filmmakers focused on the wartime Navy, they portrayed small-scale combat in fanciful terms. The mythic mystery ships, also known as Q Ships, perfectly fitted the dramatic requirements for such stories, and Hollywood made two films in quick succession about the ersatz combat ships that masqueraded as defenseless freighters. Not meriting the expenditure of a valuable torpedo, a mystery ship hoped to lure a German U-boat to the surface to attack with its deck gun. Once a submarine appeared, the freighter would drop its camouflage and hopefully sink the U-boat before the enemy could destroy the thin-hulled "war" ship.

John Ford portrayed this small-scale combat in *The Sea Beneath,* released in early 1931, and made with full cooperation of the Navy, which staged fights, allowed shooting aboard ships, and provided men and equipment. On its part, the studio promised not to include scenes that would "discredit any branch of the Government services, their uniform, or personnel." Ford also agreed that the technical adviser could "censor on the spot, at time of taking, any scene or scenes which he may think reflects discredit on the Navy" and to submit the finished film for "final censorship of scenes, dialogue, and titles" before the studio released the movie. The studio also had to provide the Navy with two prints for showing on ships and ashore and to assure the Navy that "no personnel be required to engage in any hazardous undertaking, and that Navy material be not subject to undue risk."[11]

After screening the completed film in January 1931, the CNO informed the studio he found *The Sea Beneath* "an excellent Navy picture." He also wrote the commander in chief of the battle fleet that had assisted the production that the film "is one of the most interesting and the best submarine picture ever produced." On the other hand, the *New York Times* reviewer described *The Sea Beneath* as a "highly fictional concept of the fighting between mystery ships and submarines during the World War," observing, "It is not a picture to be taken very seriously, so far as war activities are concerned, for no mystery ship could ever have survived very long in such circumstances."[12]

Released later in the year, RKO Pictures's *Suicide Fleet,* originally titled "Mystery Ship," followed a group of friends from Brooklyn through basic training and off to war aboard an American destroyer pursuing U-boats. Their ship captures a German submarine tender, which its crew then burns. The Navy then replaces it with a similar sailing schooner masquerading as the German tender. With William Boyd, the only experienced sailor, in command of the Q-boat, the ship sets out on its "suicide" mission to discover the battle plans of the German U-boat fleet operating off Cuba.

Two submarine captains fall for the deception and come aboard the tender to discuss plans for attacking a convoy sailing from New York. However, a third U-boat commander exposes the ship's "German" captain as an impostor. When the submarine commander signals his boat to open fire, Boyd's gun crew responds, sinking two of the subs before the Q-boat goes down. A flotilla of American destroyers then arrives to depth charge the last U-boat. In approving the story for cooperation, the Navy Department had only one problem, advising the studio that the gun crew should raise the U.S. flag before opening fire on the submarines.[13]

Despite the story's rousing and patriotic climax and easy Navy approval, the commander of the Pacific Fleet Battle Force, Frank Schofield, objected to the Navy's approval of the script. He wrote to the CNO on 18 July 1931, that "cooperation will involve much inconvenience and is contrary to my judgment as to the ultimate good for the Navy." He said the requested assistance would encroach upon operations and undoubtedly take more time than scheduled and stated his belief that all assistance to commercial motion pictures had no value.[14]

According to Schofield, he considered *Shipmates,* a comedy released earlier in the year, "injurious to the Navy, in that it conveyed a very wrong impression of morale within the Navy, and of the relations between the various ranks of Naval personnel. The tone of the picture was not good." As a result, he did not want to see another movie of this kind receive Navy support. In regard to "Mystery Ship," he said the remedy "is a very severe censoring of the scenario prior to the filming of any part of the picture with Naval participation." He also suggested the Navy "withdraw from further participation" in the production of commercial feature films.[15]

Unlike its response to "Summerville Number 4," the Navy did not withdraw its approval of "Mystery Ship," but it did severely limit the amount of its assistance. In addition to providing one destroyer docked and then heading to sea with the actors aboard, the Navy deployed several destroyers steaming in front of the cameras at full speed as well as launching a few depth charges. It also loaned the filmmakers the "German" submarines for the climactic battle, even though regulations have always forbidden American men and equipment from assuming the guise of an enemy.

The assistance proved sufficient for the *Weekly Variety* to think *Suicide Fleet* had received "the full cooperation of the U.S. Navy, which put every facility at the disposal of Director Rogell." The critic also felt the film "ranks as one of the best Navy spectacles ever made. The action shots of the destroyer fleet and the German submarines carry a powerful kick, as impressive as if a newsreel cameraman had caught actual engagements during a sea battle."

In contrast, Mordaunt Hall, in the *New York Times,* had the same problems with *Suicide Fleet* as with *The Sea Below,* writing that anyone who knew something about Q Ships would find the film's "melodramatic ideas of the tricks of mystery ships very disappointing." Nevertheless, he did find the scenes in the German submarines "cleverly pictured," with the authenticity heightened by having the officers converse in German.[16]

In any event, comedies, romances, and peacetime dramatic stories received more time on the nation's movie screens than combat stories during the 1930s. Often, filmmakers had to decide which element of the story to highlight: comedy, romance, or action. At least initially, MGM touted *Hell Below* to the Navy as a serious drama about submarines. Writing to Secretary of the Navy Charles Adams on 28 September 1931, William Orr of MGM asked for approval of a script based on Cdr. Edward Ellsberg's novel *Pig Boats.* He said that before buying the book, the studio had unofficially "gathered the impression" that the Navy had liked Ellsberg's presentation of technical details about submarines. Acknowledging that the Navy had found several incidents that it most likely would not approve if included in the screenplay, Orr explained that the screenwriters had removed these probable sticking points—resulting in major changes to the plot. Orr asked the Navy to consider the prospective film and suggest any changes needed for approval.[17]

The Navy Motion Picture Board advised the CNO on 17 October that the service not extend help to the project "because the theme as a whole is degrading to the Naval uniform and is a false portrayal of the relationship which existed between the British and American Navies during the War." On the nineteenth Acting CNO W. R. Sexton asked Orr to tell the studio that the Navy "considers the picture entirely unfit for production."[18]

The studio responded with embarrassment to the rejection. Orr explained that after buying the novel, MGM had found that another company had recently made a movie so similar to Ellsberg's story that MGM had felt compelled "to get completely away from that general plot. I regret to say that in the attempt to construct a substitute story we made the mistake of submitting material which would not maintain our previous high record with the Department." Orr then asked the Navy to assign an officer to help MGM write an acceptable story and make the movie.[19] Orr also reminded the Navy that MGM had made the first motion picture about the Naval Academy and had used "precisely" the same procedures. He pointed out that this method of cooperation had produced a "highly satisfactory" result for both the Navy and the studio. He also said the studio would pay travel and living expenses during the time the officer was detailed to Los Angeles.[20]

The Director of Naval Intelligence, then the supervisor for the service's cooperation with the film industry, advised the CNO on 31 October: "It is believed that the detailing of a competent officer to assist MGM in this and other Navy pictures would result in more and better pictures and, therefore, more and better publicity for the Navy." The Director thought this assistance would also simplify the work of the Motion Picture Board since it would no longer have "to read a lot of scenarios which are totally unfit for production."[21]

However, the Director saw a significant problem with the request, believing its approval would lead other companies to make similar requests that "might eventually result in an officer or officers being regularly detailed to duty with the moving picture industry." If this happened, he said studios would have the officers "not only acting as advisers, but thinking up new ideas for pictures and writing scenarios. The Navy could hardly afford to have it known that it had officers detailed to the moving picture industry." Therefore, he recommended that the Navy deny MGM's request and suggest it retain retired and ex-officers, while still being able to obtain technical advice and criticism from the Navy.[22]

The Director, Central Division, pointed out that the CNO's 5 August 1931 memorandum on cooperation allowed filmmakers to seek technical information "informally" from the Navy to ensure that a script would be "acceptable." Since this differed completely from MGM's request to have an officer assigned to assist in the creation of the story and production of the film, he agreed with the Director of Naval Intelligence that "it would be unwise to modify our present policy and practice by thus enlarging the scope of our assistance to motion picture companies."

The Acting CNO then advised MGM that the Navy would find a "suitable retired officer" who could provide the desired assistance "and with whom you are free to make your own arrangements."[23] The studio then took nine months to complete and submit the script for "Pigboats" to the Navy. In its accompanying letter, MGM said the picture would "portray by means of an entertaining fictional story, the lives of the officers and men of the United States Navy in the submarine branch of the service during the war." Citing earlier MGM military stories, the studio said it had adhered to its "established policy of showing the actions of the characters in a manner as true to life as practicable and has made a sincere and earnest attempt at presentation of the best traditions of the U.S. Military service."[24]

After reviewing the script, the Motion Picture Board recommended on 11 August that the CNO approve cooperation if the studio removed several objectionable features. These included a deliberate violation of safety precautions leading to a gun-turret explosion; "the mutinous attitude of an officer on the bridge of a submarine necessitating members of the crew taking forcible action"; and the capture of an Austrian vessel of war, which "has no historical basis." In advising MGM of the problems, the CNO said that if the studio corrected them, the production would qualify for cooperation.[25]

The next day, MGM's Washington office told the Navy that the studio had already deleted the offensive scenes. The studio representative reaffirmed MGM's policy "of making such pictures as portray the service to advantage and feels confident that in this photoplay the features previously objected to are now in proper form." Having submitted a list of requirements, the representative requested that the service approve the script and cooperation, which the Board recommended on the thirteenth.[26]

Accepting the advice, the CNO informed MGM's vice president Louis Mayer on 20 August that the Navy would assist the production in accordance with the service's 5 August 1932 policy statement. The admiral said the Navy would inform the commanders, Battle Force, U.S. Fleet about the assistance MGM was requesting and suggested the studio confer directly with them to make the necessary arrangements. The same day, the CNO informed the Battle Force that it was "authorized and directed, at your discretion and convenience," to cooperate with MGM on the production and permit the studio's personnel to sail aboard Battle Force ships to film the required scenes.[27]

MGM made its film, now titled *Hell Below*, and submitted it for review to the Navy Board in April 1933. The film focuses on a young Navy submariner, Thomas Knowlton, who meets and falls in love with his captain's daughter, Joan. She creates the dramatic complication by not initially telling her suitor that she is married to a hopelessly crippled young aviator. The lovers enjoy a few hours of forbidden happiness, and as they are preparing to tell the husband of their desire to marry, Knowlton discovers that the aviator will regain his health. To disabuse Joan of his love, he pretends she had become only another of his many conquests. The romantic melodrama and the comedic camaraderie of the crew ashore then give way to submarine warfare. In the end, Knowlton explains his deception to his captain and dies a hero when he single-handedly closes the enemy harbor, thereby bottling up its submarine fleet.

The Navy Board found only three problems when it screened *Hell Below*. It directed the studio to delete dialogue suggesting that young officers were going ashore "for a definite immoral purpose." The Board also objected to a sequence set in Knowlton's apartment, in which the camera shows him embracing Joan, pans to burning candles, then fades out, after which follows a scene showing the candles "considerably burned down." The Navy felt this montage indicated "a lapse of time and strongly insinuating coition."[28] The Board directed the studio to cut the scene "before panning to candles to lessen the pointedness of the situation." Finally, the Board felt that the scenes in which a recruit dies behind a watertight door "are repeated so often as to be unduly oppressive" and that several of them should be deleted. MGM's Washington representative, a retired naval officer, viewed the film with the Board and made the deletions immediately, causing the Board to recommend the Navy approve the film's release.[29]

As a result of the many changes the filmmakers had to make in Commander Ellsberg's original story, *Hell Below* "curiously mingled" submarine warfare in the Adriatic, romance, and broad comedy, but the *New York Post* called it "A Spectacular Submarine Film . . . crammed with thrills for landlubber eyes." The reviewer felt the film "proves an effective pictorial representation of the undersea service, quite justifying the generous co-operation of the Navy Department and the use of Pearl Harbor, Hawaii, as a movie location." Acknowledging that earlier submarine stories served as "moderately successful exploitations of the perils and hardships of life beneath the waves," the reviewer concluded that MGM had become the first studio to make "a convincing submarine production at least to eyes inexpert in the mysteries of torpedo tubes, control-room gadgets and oxygen tanks." He also noted that *Hell Below* contained "some remarkable underwater photography. The burst of bubbles at the tail of a discharged torpedo and the explosion of depth bombs far beneath the surface are witnessed with perfect clarity."[30]

The *New York Times* showed less charity to how *Hell Below* mixed various elements, finding its transitions "from farcical doings ashore to grim sights aboard a damaged United States submersible are decidedly jarring." Still, the reviewer acknowledged that "there are scenes in the undersea craft that are extremely well pictured and so are others depicting what happens on the surface of the water." Nevertheless, he felt that "the rowdy mirth scarcely belongs to a narrative which includes sights of dying men in a submarine" and thought it "a pity" that instead of making three separate stories, "the producers indulged their fancy for combining fun and fury."[31]

This fury remains at the heart of the appeal of combat stories, whatever the service. If drowning sailors and the horrors of combat have their downside, at least in the eyes of the Navy, the struggle against death appeals to people watching the story unfold. Men may die in submarines, but more survive to recall the adventure. The very opportunity to participate in the excitement of submarine service remained the Navy's best recruiting tool.

The last major Great War Navy movie, *Hell Below* remained only one of several submarine films to receive assistance during the 1930s. Appearing in January 1930, John Ford's *Men Without Women* began the decade's exploitation of the drama inherent in peacetime submarine films and completed the transition of Navy stories from the silent to sound eras. Although Fox distributed a silent version, it was also released with a combination of titles and an understandable soundtrack, unlike *Submarine*, with its few sound effects and incomprehensible voices.

Like *Submarine*, the title *Men Without Women* provides almost no idea of the plot. The studio might well have called it "Men With Women" because the first half of the film portrays the crew of an American submarine cavorting on shore in Shanghai with assorted loose women at the world's "longest" bar. In the days before the Production Code Office's censorship, Ford could use such raunchy, double entendres as "There goes Cobb . . . the champion swordsman of the S-13!" His portrayal of sailors propositioning women in a racially demeaning manner did little to improve Americans' perceptions of Asians or women. However, the film did create an exotic image of a sailor's life—traveling to foreign ports, drinking, and whoring, all in the company of comrades in arms.

Still recovering from the tragedies of the *S-51* and *S-4*, the Navy accepted such portrayals if they might encourage enlistment in the submarine service. Despite the submarine disaster, the focus of the movie, the Navy agreed to provide a submarine and other assorted ships and to assign two technical advisers experienced in undersea operations to ensure the film's accuracy. According to then-Lt. and later Adm. John Will, he had the authority to correct errors that might slip into the script, secure needed equipment for the soundstage, and arrange to shoot aboard ships. This assistance guaranteed the finished movie would authentically depict life aboard a submarine.

In fact, Will succeeded almost too well. In the film's dramatic highlight, a destroyer runs over the submerged submarine, opening its hull and loosing an avalanche of water into the control room. The realism of the action so startled Will that he shouted, "Jesus Christ!" spoiling the soundtrack and forcing Ford to reshoot the sequence.[32]

Despite its graphic disaster, Admiral Will believed *Men Without Women* portrayed the Navy positively and had attracted young men to the submarine service. In reality, the images of the trapped men's suffering probably negated much of the appeal of travel, camaraderie, and exotic women such films were supposed to provide. Moreover, Burke, the film's only significant character, did not exactly qualify as a role model for young men considering a Navy career.

Burke has a secret he shares with no one. As the captain of a British destroyer during World War I, he indiscreetly told his girlfriend, Lady Patricia, he would be transporting "England's greatest Field Marshall" to the continent. A German submarine sank the ship, with the apparent loss of the entire crew. Realizing his return would expose his lover as a German spy, Burke maintained the fiction of his death, ultimately enlisting in the U.S. Navy. His past begins to catch up with him when Commander Weymouth, a British officer who "voted to clear the woman and damned the memory of my best friend," recognizes Burke as he is returning to his submarine.

Joining the salvage operation, Weymouth's ship locates the sunken boat, and he signs his name to the message to the crew. To keep his secret hidden and Patricia unbesmirched, Burke sacrifices his life by staying aboard the boat so that the submarine's acting commander can escape. The ensign refuses to acknowledge Burke's true identity as a band plays "Taps."

Whether Burke's sacrifice benefited the Navy, the crew's escape did help the submarine service counter the tragedies of the *S-51* and *S-4*. *Weekly Variety* felt the rescue operation, with small boats plucking each sailor from the rolling sea as he bobbed to the surface, provided "a whooping bit of flagwaving." The reviewer said the film "is almost too well done, so taut is the tension it develops. It moves forward with the quiet progress of utter naturalness, creating an illusion that binds interest and when the dramatic punch arrives the auditor is so deeply intrigued that the tragic situation is almost painful."[33]

On his part, Ford dismissed Burke's death as "one of those things." Acknowledging the tragedy in the story, he thought *Men Without Women* "was full of humor," specifically citing the antics of one sailor who bought a Chinese vase for his mother and protected it until he died aboard the submarine. The director also recalled how a bit player gave the rescue sequence its realism. When the stunt man refused to dive into a stormy sea to impersonate the submariners bobbing to the surface, a young John Wayne came forward offering to "double them all" and dove overboard.[34]

Realistic or not, Ford's film began Hollywood's portrayal of the peacetime Navy during the 1930s. Released the next year, Frank Capra's *Dirigible* used naval aviation and particularly the lighter-than-air service as a setting for another of his military buddy stories. Although the film graphically portrayed the destruction of a prized dirigible, the Navy had no reason for refusing to assist Capra since the disaster had a historical basis. More positively, another Navy airship rescues a lost exploration team at the South Pole, and the heroes receive a rousing ticker-tape reception down Broadway. Consequently, the director received all necessary assistance, including an impressive flying sequence of Navy planes and dirigibles filmed at Lakehurst, New Jersey. The service did receive a telegram from the Professional Pilots Association, however, claiming civilian pilots in San Diego "HAVE NECESSARY EQUIPMENT TO HANDLE THIS WORK AND THIS ORGANIZATION STRENUOUSLY OBJECTS TO WAR DEPARTMENT EQUIPMENT BEING USED IF COMMERCIAL PILOTS CAN HANDLE THIS WORK." In response, the CNO cited Navy policy mandating assistance to filmmakers "only in case of photoplays attempting to depict Naval Activities and only to extent necessary to insure correct pictorialization of such activities."[35]

In assisting *Hell Divers* in 1932, the Navy went even further to ensure the "correct" pictorialization of naval aviation. The *New York Times* probably best described the film: "It is a magnificently photographed production, one that includes naval air stunts and impressive 'landing' feats. It takes one through the curriculum of Uncle Sam's sailors of the air, from a naval base on land to wonderful sights of pilots bringing their machines down on the deck of the

SARATOGA. The sudden stopping of the wheels of these airplanes aroused applause from the audience."[36]

To create that reaction, the filmmakers had started with another Frank Wead story. In this case, however, his growing reputation and commitment to promoting the Navy failed to produce a scenario that pleased the service. On 22 July 1931 the CNO informed MGM that the story contained "an incorrect portrayal of the behavior of naval enlisted personnel, especially chief petty officers, while on shore in Panama. Our chief petty officers are of a very high type and they would have just cause for resentment should this picture be released in its present form." The Navy also believed that "certain scenes in this picture could affect adversely the efforts of the recruiting service to obtain the highest type of youth for enlistment in the Navy."[37]

Without question, the chief petty officer of the dive-bomber squadron and observer-gunner on an F-8C-2 Hell Diver aboard the *Saratoga* leaves something to be desired. As a twenty-year man about to retire, the CPO, played by Wallace Beery, has barely managed to avoid a dishonorable discharge on numerous occasions for his drinking and fighting. Although the CPO is a gunnery expert and a no-nonsense leader, even a father figure, when sober, the Navy had valid concerns with a story that has him leaving his post, getting thrown in jail for fighting, and missing the departure of the *Saratoga* on a training cruise. Clark Gable, playing the CPO's straight-arrow, designated heir, does counter at least some of the negative images, and the CPO's death while saving the life of his grievously wounded replacement leaves audiences remembering his sacrifice rather than his less noble antics. In truth, the Navy cared less about the dramatic story than in having its ships and planes create exciting portrayals for young men contemplating lives in the Navy.

Hell Divers did that as well as any movie to that time, and audiences would remember the scenes of carrier operations that the Navy allowed Wead and an MGM camera crew to film even before negotiations had resolved the screenplay's problems. In addition to aerial gunnery and dive-bombing sequences, the Navy also permitted the studio to show for the first time a dirigible landing aboard a carrier, albeit without revealing details of the recovery. The Navy even allowed the studio to show the *Saratoga* transiting the Panama Canal. Whatever impact these images had on audiences of the time, in the 1950s the writers of *Wings of Eagles,* Wead's cinematic biography, credited his work on *Hell Divers* and other Navy films with helping the Navy obtain congressional appropriations for additional carriers.[38]

In contrast, the service tried to avoid taking part in one of its more successful cinematic missions—killing a dangerous monster. In December 1932 the RKO Studios location manager Herb Hirst requested use of four Navy Hell Divers, stationed in Long Beach, for one day in making *King Kong.* He explained that the Eleventh Naval District commander had assured the filmmakers full cooperation if the Navy Department approved the request.[39]

Hirst also said the studio would secure insurance to cover damage and/or injury to the planes and pilots and would reimburse the Navy for the cost of operating the aircraft. RKO also agreed to conform to all the Navy's regulations covering cooperation and to submit the completed film for preview. If the Navy found any scenes objectionable, the studio would eliminate them from the final print. The CNO responded on 21 December 1932 that the script did not meet the requirements for cooperation "in that there is nothing pertaining to the Navy and use of planes as requested would compete with the civilian airplane industry." Consequently, he felt "compelled to disapprove of Naval cooperation in this project."[40]

However, the studio thwarted the Navy's rejection by requesting assistance from the commanding officer at Floyd Bennett Field on Long Island when the filmmakers went east to do location shooting. In return for $100 to the officers' mess fund and $10 to each pilot, the officer ordered four Navy biplanes to fly over New York City. According to Gen. John Winston, then a young Marine flier, he and three Navy pilots went to "jazz the Empire State Building."[41]

Winston recalled that everyone responded, "Oh, boy!" since regulations forbid planes to fly below one thousand feet over New York City. He assumed the studio had obtained permission from the authorities: "We didn't know what it was all about. They just said there was some kind of movie being made." In fact, Winston and the other pilots did not know where the filmmakers had placed the cameras. They simply made a couple of passes at the top of the skyscraper. As Winston remembered, he didn't want to run into the building, but he "got close enough to scare my observer."[42]

The mission differed little from other training assignments except for the low altitude and closeness to the building, but it provided valuable footage of Navy planes flying in formation, first peeling off, then diving at an imaginary target, then looping and attacking from the other direction. Although the filmmakers intercut twenty-eight scenes of the Navy aircraft with process shots and miniatures to create the fatal attack on Kong, most people did not hold the Navy responsible for the evil deed. As the capturer of Kong observed, "No, beauty killed the beast."[43]

In Depression times, fantasies such as *King Kong* had great appeal to audiences needing to escape from the realities of economic collapse. With the exception of a few realistic dramas like *Men Without Women, Dirigible,* and *Hell Divers,* Hollywood used the Navy and the other services most often simply as background for conventional love stories, musicals, and comedies. During the decade, Annapolis regularly became the set on which to stage such stories that illustrated the process by which young men overcome assorted obstacles on the road to becoming officers and gentlemen.

Despite the positive images in the early Annapolis films, when Hollywood next returned to Annapolis in 1933, to make *Midshipman Jack,* the filmmakers did not receive the usual blessing from the Academy superintendent. Responding to the Navy Board's approval of cooperation, the superintendent expressed serious reservations to the CNO about the value of the project, although he found only "two or three quite minor points" to revise in the Wead story. He complained "that a photoplay of better general caliber has not been proposed," pointing out the story featured a fifth-year "turn back and it is common knowledge in naval circles that men of that category are scarcely representative of the Regiment."[44]

The superintendent also "regretted that so much of the plot hinges about boy and girl relations which seems to be the natural gravitation of authors writing about the Academy." Since he believed love stories appeared less in movies about civilian colleges, he wished writers would "break away from that phase of life when they take on the Naval Academy." While acknowledging that the film would not "react unfavorably upon the Academy," he expected "the product will be somewhat mediocre" and so failed "to see wherein it can do the institution any benefit."[45]

In fact, the Academy's setting along the Severn, the uniforms, the pageantry, and naval ships made *Midshipman Jack* an Annapolis recruiting poster and a very thinly disguised documentary of plebe year. Midshipman Jack undergoes a typical rite of passage. A charismatic leader, he lacks the maturity and discipline to graduate and assume the responsibilities required of a naval officer. Although he clearly has the potential to become a fine officer, Jack had not yet achieved the ideal. Hoping that responsibility will mature him, the superintendent chooses to give him another chance as a fifth-year senior who will teach leadership to plebes. As occurs in all the Academy movies, a woman contributes to the maturing process by refusing Jack's advances until he becomes a man.

Midshipman Jack gains credibility from the extensive location shooting, including scenes inside Bancroft Hall and on the Chesapeake Bay, and provides a more detailed portrayal of the life of a midshipman than later Annapolis films, which used exteriors only to set the stage for action. Despite the superintendent's concerns, the Navy and the Academy provided full assistance to the filmmakers, who shot the band, reviews, graduation, and dances as well as having access to ships and a plane. In return, the service obtained a sympathetic film of the Academy as the maturing agent for all students.

The *New York Times* described the film as a "juvenile discussion of the gallant lads at Annapolis and the manner in which the glorious traditions of the Naval Academy are implanted in several recalcitrant students. To adopt a superior metropolitan attitude toward it would be to endow it with intentions which are alien to the producers. To note that its production is without finesse and that its story is on the inventive level of a Frank Merriwell story would be pompous and unfair." Still, the reviewer believed children "should find it satisfying." Likewise, *Weekly Variety* concluded that *Midshipman Jack* might have "interest to small town clienteles but not for the cities."[46]

Despite such reactions, Hollywood remained enamored of Annapolis and continued to produce Academy stories the rest of the decade. They told the same basic story and received the same approbations. Appearing in 1935, *Annapolis Farewell* inspired the *New York Times* critic to admit he had "long ceased wondering" where the Academy had found its midshipmen "before Hollywood took up its pious burden of glorifying it."[47]

Unlike its predecessors, *Annapolis Farewell* did not rely on a stormy rivalry for its drama. Instead, its message came from the sentimental story of a retired officer who has built part of his last ship's deck into his room as a shrine to remember his command at Manila Bay. Discovering his ship will become a gunnery-practice target, he unsuccessfully appeals for its preservation. Donning his uniform, he dies aboard the doomed ship from the shelling. The officer's funeral oration became the medium to convince the movie's midshipman hero that a Navy career will justify his efforts. The Academy gave *Annapolis Farewell* "cheerful cooperation" to create the film, and the *New York Times* found it "extremely sentimental" and "familiar in pattern," but "exceedingly well-made for all that."[48]

Appearing only two months later, *Shipmates Forever* told a typical Annapolis story about a spoiled son of a Naval Academy commandant, who would prefer to remain a popular crooner than become a midshipman and officer. Ultimately, of course, Dick Powell, as the singer, recognizes the true importance of a Navy career, becomes a hero, and wins his girl, played by Ruby Keeler. Only the presence of two of Hollywood's leading stars and the quality of the production Warner Brothers gave the film distinguished *Shipmates Forever* from other Academy stories.

In fact, the film's images of the treatment the upperclassmen administer Dick because of his arrogant disdain for the Navy as well as the rigid routine under which midshipmen lived, might make viewers wonder why anyone would want to become an officer. Women might also wonder why any girlfriend would accept the many restrictions on a midshipman's social life, including the two-year waiting period after graduation before marrying. However, if *Shipmates Forever* did not make the education process attractive, the message of patriotism and selfless devotion to the nation implicit in the hero's career choice would certainly benefit the Navy. In any case, thanks to the Navy's assistance, *Weekly Variety* said the film contained "highly interesting" views of life at the Academy and presented "the inside Navy stuff . . . in absorbing fashion." The *New York Times* thought the story routine but found "its humorous moments are many, its romantic interest not too obtrusive and it manages to be entertaining most of the way."[49]

If the film offered some interesting plot twists and good entertainment, the next Academy portrayal, *Annapolis Salute*, remained so trivial, self-centered, and exploitive that the superintendent should probably have barred the filmmakers from entering the grounds. To be sure, RKO Studios had made no representations as to the benefit the production might offer the Navy, simply requesting permission to photograph crew races on the Severn, the June Week Ball, and scenes in and around the Academy. In turn, writer/director Christy Cabanne agreed to revise the script, satisfying the Navy's minor objections to the story of a chief petty officer's son who goes to Annapolis to become the officer his father's lack of education kept him from being. However, the *New York Times* observed that it takes more than the customary parades and juvenile rivalries to make a good movie and so judged *Annapolis Salute* as "pretty feeble and uninspired."[50]

In contrast, the first of two 1937 films featuring Annapolis football may have produced "laughs and some emotional build up" but had only a secondhand connection to the Naval Academy. Appearing only a month after *Annapolis Salute,* Paramount's *Hold 'em Navy* contained a stereotypical midshipman story. Allotting the project only two and a half months from start to release, the studio considered the film of such minor importance that it did not bother to secure Navy cooperation. Instead of sending a second unit to Annapolis, Paramount asked the Secretary of the Navy only for permission "to incorporate into this production stock shots of Naval activities." The CNO had no objections to the request but informed the studio that "it will none the less be necessary for you to submit the completed picture" for review. With Navy winning the traditional football game on the last play, the service had no problem approving the film, despite the little effort Paramount put into the production.[51]

Appearing the next month, *Navy Blue and Gold* provided no new insights into the activities of midshipmen. Nevertheless, MGM made it a major production. Reviewing the studio's request for assistance, the Office of Naval Intelligence described the plot as "an entirely innocuous story of football at the Naval Academy." The Office found the script accurate, often amusing, "and not infrequently pleasantly sentimental." Unlike other Annapolis movies, however, the production did not require the Navy to stage drills, exercises, or other activities for the cameras and would use only "stock atmosphere shots" at the Academy and general scenes of midshipmen marching on Franklin Field and cheering in the stands during the Army-Navy game. Although recommending cooperation, the Office reminded the Board *Annapolis Salute* remained in production. To alleviate any concerns that this might create, the Office observed that the film would be "essentially nothing more than a football story in an Annapolis locale [which] should prove to be pleasant entertainment."[52]

The CNO asked the Academy's superintendent for his comments before deciding whether to assist the project. He responded that filmmakers needed the human interest in their movies, which caused stories to "deviate from reality and fact." Although the script provided "a fair portrayal of a phase of athletic life at the Naval Academy," he advised that "in a number of instances it strays far afield and depicts scenes and events which are either not permitted at the Naval Academy or tend to question the conduct or integrity of commissioned officers assigned to that institution."[53]

The superintendent cited a hazing scene that "might tend to create the impression that it is permitted or condoned at the Naval Academy." He said the screenwriter had promised to add a scene in which two first classmen tell the perpetrator he must resign or they will report the hazing, which he said would remove his objection. However, he recommended the Navy advise MGM to hire a technical adviser to correct other problems.[54]

When the studio received the Navy's objections, it promptly made all requested changes. In his letter informing the CNO of the revisions, William Orr, the studio representative, explained that MGM wanted the script approved immediately so that it could dispatch a film crew to Annapolis that week. Telling the CNO that he was advising MGM the Navy would require at least a week to reach its decision, Orr asked if the CNO could expedite the review. Having dealt with the Navy for more than ten years and having always enjoyed "satisfactory" relations with the service, Orr asked the CNO "to take into consideration the fact that I will pledge my company to meet, to the satisfaction of the Department, any objections that may be found in the revised script, so that if this script is found satisfactory, except for minor changes, an approval might be granted contingent upon the carrying out of this pledge."[55]

The low-key lobbying succeeded, and on 9 August the CNO informed Orr the Navy had approved the revised script of "Navy Blue and Gold." In addition, the service would also advise the Academy it had authorized assistance to the production. In his letter, the CNO noted that the revised script contained minor objections that could be corrected during filming. The cooperation ensured the Navy would find the film "unobjectionable" and approved its re-lease without revisions.[56]

Despite the required changes, the *New York Times* found *Navy Blue and Gold* "one of the more agreeable entertainments the screen has provided this season" although it had "nothing epochal about it, nothing unfamiliar, nothing soul-searching—unless an Army-Navy football game rates the adjective." Still, he said the film was "a good show, swiftly paced, capitally played and easy to sit through."[57]

The reviewer concluded that while using many ingredients from other Academy stories, the writer "by some miracle of assembly and representation, has worked them into a credible, comic, frequently touching film. The old virtues are glorified again: the good old Navy spirit, the good old Navy fight, the good old Navy girl. There are also the good old parades, the good old prayer to Tecumsah [*sic*], the good old retired seadog . . . and all the rest of the good old good olds." The reviewer even enjoyed the "warm sentimentality" and believed that as long as people like those portrayed in *Navy Blue and Gold* went to Annapolis, "we need not fear for our navy at sea or on the football field."[58]

By the end of 1937, the rise of fascism in Germany and Japan was creating a very real threat to the nation. For those people who understood the danger, images of a capable officer corps and Navy that the *New York Times* reviewer found in *Navy Blue and Gold* would naturally create a sense of security. More often, however, the Academy movies of the mid-1930s simply transported audiences to a distant and beautiful locale in which bright, good-looking boys in uniform experienced their rites of passage.

In contrast, the light romantic and comedy films of the 1930s and early 1940s required little or no material assistance from the Navy. Instead, to create a Navy ambience, filmmakers used stock footage from naval archives and only occasionally shot on location. Still, the Navy reviewed each project as though it would require full cooperation.

The Navy had rejected MGM's initial script for *Shipmates* on the ground "that it gives erroneous impressions of naval customs, discipline and procedure," while recognizing the "excellent features" of the proposed film. Consequently, the Navy accepted William Orr's offer to come to Washington to resolve any problems "with a view to finding ways and means of eliminating the objectionable features and possibly also improving the scenario from your own standpoint." Until then, the Navy advised Orr it would not authorize any assistance to the production.[59] The same day, the CNO sent a memo to the commander in chief of the Battle Fleet, advising him the Navy had authorized MGM to take pictures of exercises taking place that day. The CNO explained the Navy had disapproved the screenplay and would not release any of the footage to the public until it had approved a revised script and "censored" the completed picture.[60]

When approving the screenplay on 19 January 1931, the CNO requested detailed information about what assistance the studio would need to make the film. Mostly, the film needed stock footage that screenwriter Delmer Daves had selected in naval archives. Daves indicated that if he could not find shots of the fleet steaming into the sunset, a cameraman aboard the *California* could film it during maneuvers on the way to Panama, but he felt the filmmakers "will be well taken care of as to atmospheric background, as well as numerous closeups required, for the battle practice sequence." As a result, he did not think the studio would have to send anyone to Washington.[61]

Daves's efforts and the Navy's limited assistance enabled MGM to create a "handsome production," but the story of Jonesy, a deckhand who falls for an admiral's daughter, lacks any originality or substance. Apparently designed to elevate Robert Montgomery, as Jonesy, to stardom, *Shipmates* ends with the sailor covering himself with glory, winning the girl and an appointment to

Annapolis. Without a significant character to create, Montgomery played simply "a friendly, personable young man of no particular distinction." MGM's production assets and the few scenes of the battle fleet at sea, including night maneuvers, could not raise the film beyond the level of a "mild Spring tonic," as the *New York Times* described the effort.[62]

With an occasional exception, the other romances and comedies that followed, including *Follow the Fleet; A Girl, a Guy, and a Gob,* and *In the Navy,* received the same limited Navy assistance and enjoyed the same level of critical success. Occasionally, the service helped out even though it had declined to cooperate fully with a production, as occurred with MGM's 1935 comedy *Murder in the Fleet.* Though recognizing from the start that Spig Wead's mystery had an "entirely different nature from the usual story submitted heretofore by ourselves and other motion picture producers," the studio thought the scenario "would make a highly interesting picture and one in which all the traditions of the Navy are brought out in strikingly dramatic fashion," according to Orr's letter requesting assistance from Secretary Swanson.[63]

Despite Orr's claim and Wead's own efforts on behalf of the project, the Navy would find problems with a Navy story having "murder and bribery as the outstanding features" of the plot. After reviewing the script, the Motion Picture Board advised the CNO that it "finds the theme such that it is not suitable for naval cooperation to be extended." The story was "far from being a true portrayal of naval life and does not reflect particular credit upon the Navy." The Board also found the role played by an unknown Eastern diplomat "objectionable as it creates undue suspicion" and thought that part of the plot questioned "the integrity and loyalty of Filippino personnel." Finally, the Board said the Navy had not previously assisted "in a feature of melodramatic type."[64]

In his letter disapproving cooperation, the CNO summarized the Board's objections for Orr. He further explained that the service "has made every effort to be consistent and impartial to the various motion picture producers in confining cooperation to pictures in which naval life is depicted in a favorable nature and true to life in the Navy." The CNO believed that assistance to the proposed picture could bring justifiable criticism of the Navy "as it is manifestly outside the bounds of the normal life."[65] The CNO concluded that the film "is one that does not reflect sufficient credit to merit the cooperation desired." However, the CNO went out of his way to praise MGM's "fine spirit of cooperation" and the "splendid pictures" the studio had made with Navy assistance and wanted to make it clear that the service had not changed its basic policy on cooperation.[66]

While expressing understanding of the Navy's position, Orr defended the project, saying that MGM felt "it is a fine melodrama along the lines of the successful murder mystery stories which are now making a great appeal to the pub-

★

lic." Therefore, he wanted to know whether the Navy would object if the studio made the story without cooperation and ask if the filmmakers could take a few routine shots on the cruiser *Louisville,* similar to ones regularly taken for newsreels. He included a list of shots needed and promised that no actors would appear in any of them. Nor would the studio publicize the Navy's assistance.[67] The CNO did ultimately permit MGM to take the requested footage as long as the studio adhered to Orr's promises, but he told Orr that the Navy "reserves the right to censor" the picture before its release. After the film appeared, however, the Navy denied any cooperation, answering a citizen's letter that the scenes "showing naval vessels were very probably taken from the library of the film company."[68]

In any case, using the Navy as background for all manner of slapstick comedy and routine love stories continued up to Pearl Harbor and into the war itself. Some films, such as the 1936 *Navy Born,* contained scenes of Navy carrier operations, but the stories themselves could have occurred in any peacetime setting. However, the fact that the characters wore Navy uniforms implied that the film had actually received Navy cooperation and/or approval.

As the threat of war loomed larger, Hollywood went out of its way to avoid negative portrayals of Navy officers and men, but the service continued to express concerns about its motion-picture image. When the Bureau of Navigation received the script for *Seven Sinners* in June 1940, one of its officers observed, "If this thing is perfectly done with somebody like Vivian Leigh in the lead, and a cast as good as *Gone with the Wind,* it might get across. If it is screened with anything less than that, it will be very bad publicity for the Navy."[69]

Even though *Seven Sinners* became little more than a contemporary *La Traviata,* John Wayne and Marlene Dietrich, in the leads, did give the film a quality not usually found in such small-scale productions. Wayne's young naval officer meets and promptly falls in love with Bijou—played by Dietrich—a honky-tonk singer working at the Seven Sinners café on a South Sea island where the United States had a naval base. Despite severe warnings from his superiors to give up Bijou, the young officer decides to resign his commission to marry her. However, like Camille, Bijou selflessly renounces her true love for his own good and the good of the Navy.

The service clearly had concerns about the negative impact of a film portraying an officer who could even consider giving up his career for a lowly singer, though the young man was clearly behaving as an officer and a gentleman in wanting to marry Bijou. Moreover, once Bijou leaves his life, the officer acknowledges to his commanding officer, albeit with more than a hint of sadness, that he has put his mind at rest and is ready to go back to work. With that, he begins barking out orders to his subordinates.

By 1940, the Navy needed every officer it had in preparing to protect the nation. While the service may have provided only stock footage or limited location shooting to *Seven Sinners* and other comedies and romances, it had also been providing assistance to serious films that portrayed the Navy's new technology and weapons of war. Not all of these stories contained flattering portrayals. Nevertheless, they informed America how the Navy was preparing, or thought it was preparing, for any eventuality.

★

★

THREE

Hollywood
Prepares for War

All the dramatic films portraying the Navy in action during the 1920s and 1930s contained preparedness messages. Even the comedies and light romances included ships and sailors professionally carrying out their assignments. Each movie demonstrated to America how the Navy was acquiring weaponry and training its personnel to defend the nation against any eventuality. To the service, the threats from Japan and Germany were becoming more obvious as time passed. However, motion-picture executives had little desire to become involved with political issues, particularly Hitler's attacks against the Jews in Germany. Assimilated Jews held most of the top leadership positions in Hollywood and over the years had avoided stories that might stir up anti-Semitic attacks on Jewish control of motion-picture production. Only slowly did Hollywood begin producing serious movies about the armed services, and the stories focused on humor and romance, with the military hardware and training appearing primarily for visual excitement. Recognizing that even these films could serve as recruiting vehicles and provide information, the Navy usually approved cooperation. Often, the assistance came in the form of stock footage or permission to shoot an already scheduled training exercise.

Sometimes the Navy would appear in a subordinate role to another service, such as in *Devil Dogs of the Air*. Released in 1935, the romantic comedy featured Marine fliers Jimmy Cagney and Pat O'Brien cavorting through the air and chasing the same beautiful waitress. The Marine Corps assisted the production with planes, men, and locations, and in a grand, ten-minute documentary-like montage, the Pacific Fleet simulated a pre-assault bombardment, supporting a Marine amphibious landing south of La Jolla. With the *Saratoga* launching both Navy and Marine planes, *Devil Dogs of the Air* remains the only Hollywood film ever to show Marines flying off a carrier and serving as a component of naval aviation. Still, the film did not explain the doctrinal debate between Marine and naval aviation over their respective roles of close air support and air defense during carrier operations.

If the film focused on Marine aviation, as the superior component in the Navy Department, the Navy had responsibility for responding to an inquiry from Senator Elbert Thomas about Navy help to the movie. On 28 January 1935 Navy Secretary Claude Swanson answered that the service provided cooperation only in "rare cases" when the story featured life in the Navy. According to Swanson, the Marines and Navy assisted in "special" scenes and allowed some shooting of routine exercises.[1]

Regarding the cost to the Navy, the secretary said, the service "believed that the benefits derived by the Navy in having appropriate scenes of Naval life presented to the public in good pictures, more than compensates for the amount of work involved." Swanson claimed the expense was "negligible as the Naval background furnished is usually taken from regular routine work" and said the service had restricted filming to naval scenes the studio could not re-create, to minimize the loss of civilian employment. Finally, Swanson stressed that the Navy felt its assistance "is more than compensated by the favorable publicity value of the product."[2]

In *Devil Dogs of the Air,* the joint cooperation created images of how the Navy and the Marines working together would carry any future war to the enemy's homeland. To the *Washington Herald,* the message came across clearly: "Young American men and women, seeing the actual flying, extra-ordinary courage and skill of American war pilots, will be fired with the ambition to fly, and help conquer man's newly acquired realm, the ocean of the air." The reviewer also learned from the film "that weak as we are in the air, *weakest among important nations,* the fliers that America develops could subject any hostile air fleet to exceedingly unpleasant experiences."[3]

The reviewer provided an even better indication of the Navy's success in obtaining "favorable publicity value," observing: "Congressmen, and governors of States, seeing this picture will take pride in the marvelous efficiency of the American flier and will be humiliated by the knowledge that among the world's important nations we stand last in airplane defense."[4]

Likewise, the *New York Times* reviewer, who described himself as a "peace-loving citizen at heart" and "no admirer of the films which publicize Uncle Sam's armed forces," found the movie "distinguished by the most remarkable stunt flying and aerial photography the screen has seen in years. Even the most determined of the anti-militarists is likely to find his principles rolling under the seat when the photo-play is in the air." Apart from its entertainment value, the critic said that *Devil Dogs of the Air* was "loaded with pictorial dynamite, even if it is only an advertisement for the preparedness boys."[5]

With preparedness becoming less hypothetical, the Navy looked upon such films as the means of showing new technological advances, most particularly in undersea warfare and aviation. Although the Navy had not lost a submarine since the *S-4* sank in 1927, the service had continued to address the problem of rescuing trapped submariners. Likewise, naval aviation was developing better navigational equipment and trying to solve the problems of pilot blackout during high-speed dive-bomber attacks, with both subjects soon attracting filmmakers.

All requests for cooperation on projects that showed dying sailors and fliers would naturally create ambiguous feelings within the Navy. In particular, "The Depths Below," which portrayed the sinking of a submarine, an unfaithful wife, and an "enraged Navy husband who drowns his sorrow in drink" caused the service much discomfort. In reviewing Columbia Pictures's request, on 28 July 1936, for assistance on the movie, the senior member of the Navy Motion Picture Board advised that such images would give "the public false ideas of Navy married life and of the enlisted men of the Navy." Moreover, he felt the scene in the sunken submarine "is sure to cause unnecessary worry to the families of enlisted men in submarine service. Also the parents of young boys, who desire to enlist in the Navy, will, in a great many cases, be unwilling to consent to the enlistment of their sons." Consequently, he recommended the Navy deny the studio's request for assistance.[6]

Although the studio immediately revised the script, the changes did not eliminate "horrors of doomed and dying Navy personnel" or the master diver who "practically refuses to return to duty and go to the assistance of his doomed shipmates." Despite the detrimental effect such images might have, the CNO thought the film might help educate the public if the Navy could affect the removal of the objectionable aspects of the story. However, an officer assigned to this task quickly recognized that the script told a "practically identical" story to Frank Capra's *Submarine,* differing only in the use of dialogue rather than titles. Nevertheless, as it had done after extensive and often vitriolic negotiations the first time around, the service agreed to assist *The Devil's Playground,* the film's final name.

Ironically, neither the effort nor the addition of sound improved on Capra's original disaster story. The *New York Times* described *Devil's Playground* as a film "with a completely commonplace idea . . . treated with the detailed care and technical respect of a Hollywood superspecial. It is, in short, B product at its unimportant best." *Weekly Variety* called it an "unoriginal and familiar gob drama." If not quality, the reviewer observed that Navy assistance had provided audiences with "an extra glimpse of the fleet at sea and a mass flight of planes overhead."[7]

If *Devil's Playground* contained "fairly effective" shots of "gasping sailors trapped in the sunken sub" and good underwater camera work, the Navy needed more than images of ships and planes or a brave diver to explain the new developments in submarine rescue technology. By 1937, the Navy had perfected the Momsen escape lung and the McCann rescue chamber. To demonstrate these new devices required the service to lose two more submarines in cinematic collisions with surface ships. While the accidents may have portrayed submariners negatively, the Navy recognized the benefits from a film that provided information about the service's enhanced rescue capabilities.[8] As a result, *Submarine D-1* received virtually unlimited support from the Navy throughout its production. In contrast to Columbia's resistance to script changes, Warner Brothers had an unquestioned commitment to satisfy the service's requests. The three Warner brothers, sons of Polish immigrants, considered their movies glorifying the American military as repayment for the opportunities the nation had given them to become successful.[9]

Their commitment became clear in the letter Spig Wead included with his initial script, then titled "Submarine Story," dated 28 July 1936. Since the studio wanted to shoot scenes at the submarine base in New London and at West Coast facilities, Wead said he was planning to visit Washington to discuss the script. He assured the Navy that Warner Brothers intended "to make this as fine and creditable a picture as is possible. The studio is extremely anxious to meet the wishes of the Navy Department in every detail." He promised, "If any scenes in the script as it now stands are for any reason objectionable, I am sure that they can be eliminated or that other unobjectionable can be substituted for them." Wead also wrote that he had full authorization to represent the studio in negotiations.[10]

Wead included a note explaining that Warner Brothers understood the Navy's prohibition against civilians riding aboard submarines and against filming interior scenes, but expressed confidence the studio could make the movie without violating the regulations. He did assume the Navy would permit shooting on the deck of a submarine at anchor, docked, or tied up to a mother ship. He also hoped the Navy would allow the filmmakers to take shots of a submarine under way, submerging, and surfacing.[11]

On the other hand, he said Warner Brothers would use miniatures for the underwater scenes because the lack of space for equipment would "necessarily" require the filmmakers to re-create the inside of a submarine on a soundstage: "These sets will be sufficiently authentic in finish, size, equipment, etc., to give the audience an *impression* of reality, *but* they need reveal no detail of construction, equipment or method of operation considered confidential by the Navy Department."[12]

Wead claimed his script "displays the submarine service of our Navy in a more creditable light than any picture yet made or proposed and that it is the first one to truly reflect the training and the spirit of that service." As to its value, he said the studio believed that moviegoers remained interested in the Navy's submarine branch and so "will be grateful for being informed more fully concerning it." According to Wead, Warner Brothers had "spared no effort or expense in endeavoring to obtain a satisfactory script," and he promised that any changes the Navy requested "will gladly be made" and that the shooting schedule would cause a minimum of trouble or interference.[13]

With the studio so accommodating, the Navy readily agreed to provide assistance as long as the filmmakers showed discretion in security matters, and on 11 December 1936 the CNO authorized the relevant commands to assist Warner Brothers as needed. To this end, the CNO sent a memo on 14 May 1937 to the chief of the Bureau of Construction and Repair and to the chief of the Bureau of Engineering, advising them that the studio "very much" desired to photograph a submarine under construction. The CNO also informed the appropriate people to grant the necessary permission, subject only to "such special restrictions" necessary to "safeguard matters of military secrecy."[14]

Director Lloyd Bacon and his cameramen, assistants, and cast, including Pat O'Brien, George Brent, and Ronald Reagan, arrived in New London in late May. Having served as a naval officer during World War I and later as a reservist, Bacon easily fit into the base environment, even joining the commander on his monthly inspection, naturally with cameras running. Turning the home of the Atlantic underseas fleet into his private movie set, the director filmed the full scope of activities there, including training, boat construction, and even the launching of a completed submarine. In the years since the *S-51* and *S-4* had sailed down the Thames to disaster, the base had also become a laboratory for developing new rescue techniques, and Bacon focused his attention on the advances in submarine safety.[15]

To explain the new escape techniques, Bacon and his crew filmed at the one hundred foot training tank, put into operation in 1930. There, the Navy could simulate conditions aboard a disabled submarine at a depth of one hundred feet, with men learning to use an "artificial lung" to make their way to the surface.[16] According to submariners at New London, men could actually escape from a depth of four hundred feet without serious harm if they used the lung correctly. In fact, the lungs had become a last resort now that the service had developed a rescue bell, which Bacon's film was to portray in some detail.[17]

Back in California, Bacon, his cast, and crew spent more than three weeks in San Diego, going to sea daily on submarines, cruisers, rescue tugs, and other ships. Given the scope of the Navy's cooperation, the director had only occasional problems acquiring his footage. Once, as O'Brien was about to enter the water, sharks appeared, necessitating rescheduling of the scene. The actor faced a greater danger when the rescue buoy in which he was riding started to leak, went too far down, and then had its air hose fouled. Such mishaps produced no injuries and probably lent authenticity to the performances.[18]

Meanwhile, the studio dispatched a second unit to the Panama Canal to film two submarines transiting the waterway, and with typical movie magic, the special-effects department sank a miniature submarine at Catalina Isthmus, using a remote-control model. To help the set designers create the submarine's crew compartments on a soundstage, Warner Brothers persuaded the Navy to reverse its policy of not providing photographs of a sub's interiors. Thanks to the new CNO, William Leahy, the service selected shots of the interiors of the older "S"-type submarines, which enabled the studio to create authentic-looking sets. In constructing the "innards" of the cinematic submarine, however, the set designers did modify reality to satisfy the practical needs of filming action in confined spaces. This cinematic license had the added virtue of satisfying the Navy's security concerns since the ersatz sets would confuse a foreign nation hoping to learn American submarine secrets from the movie.[19]

In contrast, the Navy's cooperation enabled Warner Brothers to produce a pseudo-documentary detailing the training of submariners and the development of the rescue chamber. Although Ford's trapped submariners had used an early version of the Momsen Lung, *Men Without Women* had not explained its operation. The Warner Brothers film portrayed the training submariners received in the use of the lung. When the *D-1* sinks, the Navy actually received two benefits for one price: the film showed most of the crew escaping with the lung, and the new diving bell rescued a badly injured officer.

The completed film served as a recruiting vehicle as well as the medium to assure recruits and their families that while submarines might sink, they no longer had to become the death traps of earlier times. Except for the normal carping about the dull romance, reviewers found no problems with the rendering of these issues. However, the film did engender some complaints from viewers. A Chicago insurance agent wrote his senator that the Navy and the American people "are the goat" for not charging Warner Brothers for use of government facilities and suggested the studio should have paid at least $25,000, with the money going to the Navy's needs.[20] In response, the Navy told the senator that no law authorized the service to charge studios for the use of naval material in making their films. To justify free assistance, the Navy Department stated that motion pictures "which include naval scenes taken under the conditions stated, serve to stimulate greater public interest in the Navy and to assist the Government in securing desirable recruits for the naval service and that in this way it is justly recompensed for the use of naval property and facilities which may have been used in the production of such films."[21]

John Ford's *Submarine Patrol* most likely did not offer the Navy such rewards. Nor did the film contain any discernible preparedness message. Instead, the movie looked back to World War I, to Ford's own *Sea Beneath*, and to *Suicide Fleet*. Like them, *Submarine Patrol* divided its time between comedy and drama, with the humor found in the on-shore antics of the crew of green hands assigned to a wooden sub-chaser stationed in Brooklyn. The visual highlight comes in a battle between the sub-chaser and a German U-boat in the Mediterranean in 1917. However, a member of the preview audience observed, "With the passage of time, movies of the World War seem to be trying to avoid attitudes of prejudice and hate, and for this *Submarine Patrol* is commendable. Nevertheless, it does show war as a thrilling adventure, and for that reason is not to be unreservedly recommended."[22]

In fact, no film about the "splinter fleet," the name the sub-chasers had acquired, had relevance to contemporary countersubmarine warfare. Nor would the Navy have any reason to support a film about sailors lacking discipline, the hallmark of Ford's crew. Nevertheless, the Navy permitted the director to film the four wooden sub-chasers still in its arsenal, then stationed at the Naval Academy. The service found nothing wrong with the completed film and did not ask for any cuts before approving it for release.[23] If *Submarine Patrol* and the other 1930s films that combined comedy, adventure, male bonding, and occasional romance offered some benefit to the Navy, movies about naval aviation were to become the paradigm for all the preparedness films Hollywood began to produce in 1937.

At that time, President Roosevelt was still having difficulty convincing Congress and the American people of the dangers facing the nation. After his quarantine speech on 5 October 1937 and the launching of his supernavy program in January 1938, he did what he could to create images to aid recruiting and show how the U.S. military was preparing for any eventuality. In a 13 April 1938 article, *Variety* reported, "The Government is showing a more friendly attitude toward pictures since the big naval appropriations, and a closer cooperation is pledged to pictures built around the military arms of service. . . . Washington now is trying to win over picture-goers to need of adequate defense and present the U.S. show of strength."[24]

The *Army and Navy Register* described the first of these, *Wings Over Honolulu,* which appeared in mid-1937, as a story "of naval aviation in some future war." Despite its desire to have the film made, the Navy did have some problems with the initial script. The senior member of the Motion Picture Board focused his attention on the dramatic story, observing that it "smacks of and brings back most unpleasant memories of the Massie affair in Honolulu." The captain cited scenes in which officers get involved in street fights, enlisted men serve as servants for officers, officers apparently furnish their houses at taxpayers' expense, an officer's wife is portrayed as a heavy drinker who "must have her liquor," and an officer's wife tells another officer, "You'll like me—everybody does—when I'm sober." According to the captain, this dialogue would give the impression that the character "portrays the typical wife of a Naval Officer which is not true." Nowhere in the script did he "find a portrayal of the typical Navy wife, one who is a real wife and companion, the same as the typical civilian wife." Without considering whether naval aviation could provide the necessary assistance, the captain "urgently" recommended to the Board that "Naval cooperation *not* be extended."[25]

Following negotiations, the studio made all the requested changes in the script, and on 15 January the Navy informed the producer that it would provide the requested assistance at North Island in San Diego. Universal's effort to satisfy the Navy and its cooperation produced a film that "created a very favorable impression" on CNO Leahy and the officers who attended the preview.

In contrast, the film's technical adviser, future Adm. J. J. Clark, described *Wings Over Honolulu* "as a low budget affair with a terrible plot." However, the speed and efficiency with which the director shot each scene so impressed Clark that he felt the Navy could profit by copying Hollywood's procedures.[26]

Critics agreed with Clark's judgment of the film. *Weekly Variety* said it "seemed good enough to justify one more somewhat routine flight. Little that is particularly invigorating in the story and its exposition, but it is a handsome job." The *New York Times* recognized that the film focused less on planes and ships than on Navy wives, a previously neglected aspect of service life. Given the new subject, the reviewer found the film "a bit above fair rating, being gaily played, attractively mounted, and directed with surprising confidence and skill."[27]

However, by early 1939, when *Wings of the Navy* appeared, the Navy had more important concerns than romantic relationships. Containing a preparedness message, courtesy of Warner Brothers and Lloyd Bacon, the film became little more than a documentary about the training of naval aviators at Pensacola. Opening with a fly over of Arlington Cemetery by Navy planes at the dedication of a memorial to Adm. William Harrington, a fictional father of naval aviation, *Wings of the Navy* shows no subtlety in promoting the Navy's air arm. According to the studio's press guide, the admiral's career reflected "the real character and actual exploits" of Adm. W. A. Moffett, who died "gloriously but tragically" in the 1933 crash of the Navy dirigible *Akron*.[28]

The rivalry between Harrington's two sons as officers, gentlemen, fliers, and competitors for the same lady provides only a minor diversion from the almost nonstop flying sequences. At Arlington, the brothers and guests listen to the eulogy of their father's contributions to the security of the nation. The speech leaves no doubt of how the film will portray that effort: "In peacetime, men are giving up their lives to maintain and improve our greatest safeguard against war, a powerful Navy equipped with an invincible air force." The movie then demonstrates the Navy's training of men to pilot its planes, by following a class of air cadets through flight school in Pensacola.

There, the older brother, Cass, serves as a flight instructor and works on the design for a new dive-bomber, while the younger son, Jerry, learns to fly after transferring from the submarine service. When Cass suffers a crippling injury, Jerry takes over the testing of his brother's prototype plane and demonstrates its structural integrity. However, he opts to become a bomber pilot and joins a mass flight of the Navy's new Catalina long-range flying boats on a nonstop trip to Hawaii to demonstrate the plane's capability.

To ensure it would get this story right the first time, Warner Brothers sent a writer to Washington and then to Pensacola to gather information about the training of flight cadets. The effort paid off when the Navy approved the screenplay on 30 June 1938 with virtually no objections.[29] During the nine-week shooting schedule that ended on 6 September 1938, the service provided unlimited assistance both in Florida and at North Island.

According to Warner Brothers, the Navy provided 450 single-engine training and pursuit planes, 84 two-motor patrol bombers, as well as some larger planes, either on the ground or in the air. The service also gave the filmmakers access to a mock-up of the interior of one of the new Catalina bombers. Warner's public-relations department claimed the flight-training scenes would give audiences a taste of what student pilots experienced at Pensacola. It did admit, "While it is propaganda film in the sense of arousing enthusiasm for defense by air, it does not touch on the subject of actual war but, as the dedication states, glorifies men who in peace time are giving up their lives to maintain and improve our greatest safeguard against war—a powerful Navy—a powerful fighting force, the wings of the Navy."[30]

The studio had a vested interest in representing its film in patriotic terms, and the propaganda content did not seem to bother reviewers. Bosley Crowther, in the *New York Times,* thought *Wings of the Navy* "a little too pedestrian to fit the title, but then, the story is the least conspicuous part of the picture." He felt the film as a documentary "gets off the ground very nimbly, and has a good deal of value, interest and even excitement, of the purely mechanical sort, to offer to the curious." Crowther found that "the education part is so interesting" that returning to the love story created "a feeling almost akin to pain."[31]

To the average American and to Congress, the film would also help answer questions about what the Navy was doing with its appropriations. *Weekly Variety* observed, "Timely and topical in presentation of the U.S. Naval air forces and training of flyers for service, *Wings of the Navy* is a convincer to mould [*sic*] public opinion and support in favor of current Government plans for wide expansion of American air defense forces." Of course, the film also showed Germany and Japan how the U.S. Navy was preparing for any conflict, and Japan seemed to learn very well the argument for naval aviation presented in *Hell Divers, Wings Over Honolulu,* and *Wings of the Navy,* which its navy demonstrated at Pearl Harbor.[32]

As the threat to the United States increased following the outbreak of war in Europe, Hollywood continued making preparedness films about naval aviation, focusing on the development of technologies intended to help pilots do their jobs in greater safety. Released more than a year after *Wings of the Navy, Flight Command* became the first major preparedness film to appear after the beginning of hostilities in Europe. The MGM production told of the Navy's efforts to perfect a homing device to help pilots return to their airfields in bad weather. Eight years before, *Hell Divers* had illustrated the problem when Clark Gable crashed after being unable to locate the *Saratoga* during a training exercise. With war threatening, the Navy would obviously benefit from a film showing the service helping its fliers find their way home.

Like most of the Navy films of the 1930s, *Flight Command* contained a love triangle, although with a difference. Walter Pigeon, playing the squadron commander, has put the Navy and his career before his marriage, with predictable results. Arriving at North Island, Robert Taylor, playing a newly minted hot-shot pilot from Pensacola, immediately begins to fall in love with his commander's wife. After her brother dies while using the still unperfected homing beacon, Taylor provides solace for the grieving sister/lonely wife, and she begins to reciprocate his feelings. Of course, neither the Navy nor the Production Code Office would have allowed a marital split to occur. Instead, Taylor rescues Pigeon after he crashes and uses the perfected homing device to return to the fog-shrouded base for the predictable reunion of husband and wife.

Apart from its love triangle, *Flight Command* differed from other preparedness films only in its portrayal of Taylor's flagrant disregard of a direct order. As Pigeon's plane spirals down, he orders Taylor to lead their flight back to base through the foggy night, using the still-untested homing device. Instead, Taylor lands, loads the gravely injured Pigeon aboard, and only then shepherds the squadron safely home. Rather than being court-martialed for disobeying his commander and endangering the rest of the flight, Taylor becomes a hero.

In crisis situations, fighting men have often made rescue attempts in defiance of orders, and Hollywood has almost always portrayed their efforts in positive terms. However, in fostering this image with war looming, *Flight Command* ignored that Taylor was putting his squadron in harm's way, and so failed to explain the reality that commanders must sometimes sacrifice an individual for the good of the many. Why did the Navy allow the filmmakers to portray blatant disobedience of a legitimate order? To be sure, the rescue took place in peacetime and exemplified the brotherhood of warriors who refuse to abandon their comrades in arms. Nevertheless, *Flight Command* could undoubtedly have performed a greater service for the Navy and the entire military establishment by showing that it might well require far more courage to obey orders than to undertake a brave but foolhardy action.

Despite this shortcoming, *Flight Command* accomplished its intended purpose. The *New York Herald Tribune* observed, "At a time when the nation's pulse is bearing the strain of a defense-preparation marathon hitherto unknown in our history, this film about a naval air squadron is more effective psychologically than it might otherwise be." Although criticizing the love story, the review concluded that *Flight Command* "has enough excitement and authenticity about it to offset its uninspiring story." *Weekly Variety* thought the film capitalized on the "present public airmindedness of defense preparations," noting that the "aerial sequences of flight formations, target practice, landings and takeoffs from aircraft carriers are excellent and sustaining in both interest and excitement. Aerial photography is some of the best seen in years."[33]

By then, Warner Brothers had begun to turn a Frank Wead idea into the quintessential naval aviation preparedness film *Dive Bomber*. While the fictional story lacked distinction, the film gained importance because it appeared as U.S. involvement in World War II was becoming almost inevitable. In addition, the studio devoted its full resources to the production, even using color for the first time in a military movie.

As Hollywood was portraying the development and use of the Momsen Lung, the rescue bell, and an aerial homing device, Wead turned, in October 1940, to the subject of pilot blackout, which occurred in steep dives. *Wings of the Navy* had already illustrated the problem when the test pilot of Cass's plane lost consciousness during the qualification flight. While Jerry was preparing to test the second prototype, a doctor had explained the contemporary wisdom about avoiding pilot blackout, including tight belts at pressure points and yelling during the speed dive. These techniques did not completely solve the problem for naval fliers at a time when Germany was employing dive-bombing in Spain, Poland, and Holland with smashing success. The American efforts to achieve similar results naturally attracted Wead's attention. In researching the subject, he wrote to Cdr. J. R. Poppen at Pensacola for information about flight-surgeon training and work. Answering on 22 October 1940, Poppen said, "I think your idea for the motion picture is excellent. There are still a lot of people who think of a Flight Surgeon as one specially trained to sweep up after a crackup and anything which will bring to their attention our motto of 'Keep them in the air' will be very welcome." The doctor also offered Wead any help he needed.[34]

At that point Wead had two agendas, the screenplay and a desire to return to active duty despite his partial paralysis. He wrote to his friend Capt. Marc "Pete" Mitscher, then the assistant chief of the Bureau of Aeronautics, about the proposed film and the possibility of coming out of forced retirement. Answering Wead on 24 October, Mitscher first addressed Wead's new project, expressing the "hope that you can do this as we really need Pensacola advertisement at the present time, due to our extensive Aviation Cadet Program." Turning to the request to rejoin the service, Mitscher wrote that he had thought about getting Wead to come to Washington and to "direct motion picture [*sic*] of training activities that we have decided to go into. However, I feel that possibly, at the present time, it is best that you stay out there and work on your picture, particularly as you have in mind a picture that will advertise the Aviation Cadet Program, and that is what we are most interested in. . . ."[35]

To that end, Wead sent his initial story outline to Poppen in early November. Since he was traveling, his deputy assistant, Cdr. Eric Liljencrante, answered on 19 November 1940, telling Wead, "I think the thing is swell, and it certainly carries tremendous punch." He had only minor corrections since "the whole thing has a very true ring about it." He also included comments from Mitscher, who objected to the opening scene, which featured a fatal crash during a presidential review. He had suggested that Wead instead use a general naval review. He also characterized the statement that fliers need alcohol as "all rot. And certainly the inference that students drink at night before flying next day is not fact." Finally, he did not think the idea that a doctor would "conceal the fact that a pilot is a dangerous flier to the *point of the pilot's death* is very complimentary to the Medical profession."[36]

Liljencrante suggested simply eliminating the president from the review since his presence has no effect on the story, advising that the crash itself "must be kept." He agreed with Mitscher that the script should play down the use of alcohol. Liljencrante also felt the flier must still die, but the story should have him fly against all advice and after being grounded.[37]

Wead then completed the first draft of his script, then titled "Beyond the Blue Sky," and his agent sent a copy to Warner Brothers with the comment, "Frank Wead tells of the union of two tough and thrilling professions: flying and medicine, the newest thing above and below the bright blue sky. The flight surgeon is usually a pilot, too. He is responsible for the health and comfort—physical and mental—of other pilots. The flight surgeon is a research scientist. The sky is his laboratory. Pilots are his guinea pigs." He then described the story as "a combination of emotional pull and exciting action. It is, to coin a cliché, a 'picture natural.'"[38]

Wead's own note said that Mitscher and the officers in charge of Navy research had gone over the story in detail. He understood that the officers had become "enthusiastic about it, are anxious to have it made, to advertise the Navy defense training program and to show what is being done to meet the problems the story presents. So wholehearted Navy cooperation is assured in making the picture."[39]

Despite the Navy's apparent interest in the project, the studio embarked on the normal process of deciding whether to buy the script. In an interoffice memo on 3 December Walter MacEwen told Jack Warner and producer Hal Wallis that he had found the plot of "Beyond the Blue Sky" "very much in the groove" of previous military stories the studio had made. He did not think the personal story "especially good, but all of the technical data having to do with overcoming the many problems involved in high speed and high altitude flying and dive bombing is right up to the minute and provides ample opportunity for some thrilling flying sequences." He suggested that if the studio had an interest in the script, it should begin negotiations to avoid a bidding war.[40]

Since Warner Brothers had released *Wings of the Navy* earlier in the year, the studio had to decide whether a market existed for another naval aviation movie. Consequently, Warner and Wallis had Finlay McDermid make a comparison between *Wings of the Navy* and Wead's story. McDermid's work provided insights into why studios made military movies. He first acknowledged that the film and script resembled each other "in precisely the same manner that almost every service picture resembles its cousins. The primary concern of a service picture is to put over a background which is novel and thrilling to the layman, and almost inevitably it falls back on one of the simplest and surest story formulas to highlight that background."[41]

He said Warner Brothers could not "claim exclusive rights to the formula— although we've used it in at least twenty pictures; since it is equally popular on other lots and in fiction. It is used in almost any action picture which depicts an out-of-the-ordinary and dangerous occupation—shark-hunting, flying, submarining, etc." He described the formula as conflict between friends or brothers over a girl, and filmmakers played out the variations on the stage that the hazardous occupation provided.[42]

Both *Wings of the Navy* and Wead's script used the training of cadets for background color, and both had "as their biggest action moments scenes showing an airplane being tested in a power dive." However, he concluded that if Warner Brothers wanted to buy Wead's story for not too much money and use stock footage from *Wings of the Navy,* "we could probably turn out for not too much money another service picture which would have a timely exploitation value. True, its story formula would follow the pattern of its predecessor, but it would still be educationally interesting and thrilling, without being quite so expensive an investment." He also suggested the studio use the similarities in negotiating a lower purchase price.[43]

Warner Brothers bought the story, and MacEwen informed Wallis on 11 December that Wead would be coming to the studio to work on the script with all his correspondence from Washington about the story. In Hollywood, a writer often finds his or her story quickly evolves into a screenplay that bears little resemblance to the original work. In this case, the process began almost immediately when Warner Brothers changed Wead's title to "Dive Bomber," despite his objection that the Navy might consider it inadequate to the scope of the subject.[44]

In fact, after turning in his first script on 2 January 1941, Wead quickly disappeared from the scene, and Warner Brothers was to expend much time before coming up with a final script that satisfied both the studio and the Navy. As work progressed, the studio decided that *Dive Bomber* had become "a big picture with three or four complicated locations." Bob Lord, another Warner producer, told Wallis on 11 February that "if it is not beautifully organized, we are bound to make expensive mistakes." To simplify matters somewhat, the studio requested and the Navy Board agreed that the filmmakers could place the flight surgeons' school in San Diego even though surgeons actually trained at Pensacola.[45]

As shooting was beginning in March, however, Warner Brothers discovered it had a problem with the Production Code Office, which was objecting to showing rabbits in low-pressure chambers. On the twenty-fourth, Lord informed Wallis that the Office had told him that any suggestion of using rabbits in a pressure chamber would "incite wrath of the various anti-cruelty to animal organizations in the country." Even trick photography would make no difference "to the fanatic anti-vivisectionists." Lord complained, "I think this entire situation is disgusting. We are endeavoring to make a high-grade, scientific picture, showing a procedure that takes place in many laboratories all over the world."[46] He then asked Wallis to back him up in using the rabbit scenes since it would hurt the story to change the script. Lord also argued, "Unless we start fighting the many fanatic minority groups which have elected themselves to be our censors, we can never hope to make any really adult pictures. I, for one, am fed up with being dominated by a lot of old ladies."[47]

For once, filmmakers prevailed over the Code Office. *Dive Bomber* does contain a scene in which the Navy doctor and researchers place a live rabbit in a pressure chamber. Subjecting the bunny to an altitude of forty thousand feet, they find that "Elmer can take it," and Elmer's survival helped foster the film's quasidocumentary portrayal of low-pressure experiments on human volunteers. The credibility that such scenes gave *Dive Bomber* and the importance of the preparation message, not Lord's arguments, probably provided Warner Brothers with the leverage to oppose the Code Office's efforts to remove the bunny.

By March, *Dive Bomber* had come a long way from the original suggestion to produce Wead's story as a low-budget film using footage from *Wings of the Navy*. The use of Technicolor not only gave the production added significance but also enabled the studio to obtain spectacular flying scenes. Warner Brothers also demonstrated its full commitment to the film by hiring Michael Curtiz, one of the industry's leading directors, and casting three of Hollywood's top actors— Errol Flynn, Fred MacMurray, and Ralph Bellamy—in the leading roles.

From the very beginning the Navy recognized the benefits it would gain from the completed film, doing everything possible to ensure Curtiz obtained all the shots he needed. According to Lord, the service even gave the studio "as many cracks as we want at the Parade of ships in the air until we get a decent sky and clouds."[48]

With the film in post-production and the United States "in a state of national emergency," the Naval Board of Review had to approve the movie before the studio could even show the film to a preview audience. To facilitate approval,

Lord asked Poppen to attend the screening, saying, "I feel that you should be there to help me defend some of the more radical medical stuff that might shock some of the more conservative members!" Not surprisingly, given the close cooperation during production, the Navy approved *Dive Bomber* with only minor deletions on 28 July 1941.[49]

The completed film resembled Wead's "Beyond the Blue Sky" only in its focus on naval-aviation medicine and the research its doctors were doing on pilot blackout and high-altitude flying. Wead had a valid complaint about the title because the story had little to do with dive-bombing or with planes. Instead, the flight surgeons, played by Errol Flynn and Ralph Bellamy, spend most of their time searching first for the means to prevent Navy pilots from blacking out in high-speed dives and then for a way to fly at high altitude without suffering from oxygen deprivation. The film contains only a brief romantic interlude, but any potential competition between Flynn and Fred MacMurray for the girl quickly evaporates during the call to duty, and the lady goes off with a Marine.

As a result, *Dive Bomber* focused more on the Navy's preparedness for the imminent war than any of its contemporary films. It also contains the appropriate verbal messages. After successfully testing a pneumatic belt designed to eliminate blackouts during high-G maneuvers, Flynn tells Bellamy that before he put his plane into the dive, he kept thinking to himself, "There's two kinds of blackout this belt might whip, our kind and the sort they're having over London right now." During a concluding ceremony honoring the doctors, the senior surgeon assures his audience that MacMurray's death during a test of a high-altitude flight suit has helped to ensure "that the planes and pilots of this nation can more safely fly, fight and defend their country in the stratosphere."

The Navy agreed in August 1941 to lend Warner Brothers several new Douglas dive-bombers to help advertise the release of *Dive Bomber*. The service placed the planes on exhibit in principal cities, beginning in Los Angeles and New York, and installed recruiting booths beside each dive-bomber, "for it is felt that the exhibits will simultaneously promote enlistment in the Navy and arouse interest in the motion picture, which gives a complete exposition of one important part of the Navy's work."[50]

Daily Variety thought Warner Brothers had "gone far off the beaten track of the usual aviation film, far away from the glamour and glory of the fighting young chevaliers of the skies. Laid against the background of the U.S. Naval air corps, here, for the first time, is a revealing portrait of the men behind the scenes—whose duty it is to keep the pilots fit for the skies and overcome physical deficiencies—the flight surgeons." Along with the sounds of flying, *Dive Bomber* "is replete with spectacular flying scenes of a sweep and power at times almost overwhelming, but these are secondary to the drama of the grimly unrelenting warfare which the flight surgeons wage and the triumphs which emerge from their defeats. As such, *Dive Bomber* is deeply impressive and altogether fascinating. As it unfolds, the impression grows inescapably that here is being shown something of incalculable importance, something which, if war comes, may spell the difference between victory and disaster."[51]

The critic found the film "intensely absorbing, a picture which should be seen and will be thoroughly enjoyed," but he pointed out that *Dive Bomber* contains very little story: "Rather it is almost documentary, embellished pleasantly with fictional interpretation via the feud between Flight Surgeon Errol Flynn and Flight Commander Fred MacMurray." Given its subject, he concluded that the film "has the ring of powerful authenticity."[52]

Some viewers saw the movie in decidedly negative terms. E. C. Roworth wrote to Secretary of the Navy Frank Knox on 21 August, calling it "very unwise to permit the making and showing of films like *Dive Bomber*." He thought nine out of ten young men seeing it would "shy away" from becoming naval aviators for several reasons. The manner in which the film portrayed the attitudes of the officers toward the trainees gave no "indication of true friendliness but rather of unsociability, antagonism and dictatorial methods."[53] Roworth also thought *Dive Bomber* placed too much emphasis "on the fact that death in its most horrible forms is the portion, sooner or later, of each aviator." He said the film suggested that "fliers are quickly worn out, physically and mentally, after which they become helpless, useless and unwanted." Believing the Navy and the American people wanted to keep up the morale of the home front, he felt "the harsh attitudes ascribed to the officers and the cold-blooded showing of the unfavorable side of aviation cannot help but cause boys to hold back and mothers and fathers to discourage enlistment in the Navy's air arm."[54]

Writing to Secretary of the Navy Knox on 1 December, Arthur Keil voiced much the same sentiment: "If there ever was a picture shown to discourage anyone from joining the Air Corps it is the picture *Dive Bomber*." He thought it would lead every "potential draftee to stay clear of aviation" because it showed that "every aviator loses his health due to flying. Perhaps this is so, but it seems a queer time to advertise this throughout the country. If this picture was made in Germany and sent here I could see the point." Keil realized the film intended to educate the public but observed that it "sure won't get any recruits in the air service."[55]

Responding to Roworth on 26 August, Ens. Alan Brown of the Navy's Public Relations Office addressed the issues both letters raised. The service could not censor any film unless it contained secret or restricted material, and the Navy felt it had benefited from assisting *Dive Bomber*. The general reaction to the film "so far has indicated just that," but he agreed the Navy may not have given enough consideration to the negative side of the story. Still, he suggested that "should the story be what might be called 'Pollyanna,' it would not ring true and would be declared propaganda by the public." Finally, he noted that the Navy was trying to have filmmakers present the service "in the best light possible, and we hope to achieve that aim in time."[56]

"Propaganda" perfectly described *Dive Bomber* and the other preparedness films, according to isolationists throughout the country and most particularly in Congress. In a radio broadcast in St. Louis on 25 July Senator Gerald Nye (R, ND) claimed that Hollywood studios were "operating as war propaganda machines almost as if they were being directed from a single central bureau." He claimed that "for too long now, the silver screen has been flooded with picture after picture designed to rouse us to a state of war hysteria. Pictures glorifying war. Pictures telling about the grandeur and the heavenly justice of the British Empire. Pictures depicting the courage, the passion for democracy, the love of humanity, the tender solicitude for other people by the generals and trade agents and the proconsuls of Great Britain, while all the peoples who are opposed to her, including even courageous little Finland now, are drawn as coarse, bestial, brutal scoundrels." He then went on to accuse the heads of the eight major studios and their production staffs as "trying to make America punch drunk with propaganda to push her into war."[57]

Echoing Nye, Charles Lindbergh showed less circumspection in his identification of the people he considered responsible for the prowar propaganda. In Des Moines, Iowa, on 11 September 1941 the Lone Eagle told an America First rally, "The three most important groups pressing the country toward war are the British, the Jewish and the Roosevelt administration." Lindbergh thought the Jews had become particularly dangerous because of "their large ownership and influence in our motion pictures, our press, our radio and our Government."[58]

With support from Lindbergh and other isolationists both inside and outside Congress, Senate isolationists orchestrated an investigation of the film industry and its supposed pro-Allies sympathies. The hearings before a subcommittee of the Committee on Interstate Commerce convened on 10 September, with Senator D. Worth Clark (D, ID) serving as chairman. During eight days of testimony, film executives from each of the studios denied they were engaging in a prowar, pro-Allies campaign via their current productions. They all argued that Hollywood made motion pictures purely for entertainment.

Harry Warner, for one, maintained that his studio's films, including *Dive Bomber,* were "carefully prepared on the basis of factual happenings and they were not twisted to serve any ulterior purpose." He noted that "millions of average citizens have paid to see these pictures. They have enjoyed wide popularity and have been profitable to our company. In short, these pictures have been judged by the public and the judgment has been favorable." Acknowledging that his company regularly made feature films about the armed forces, he stressed his studio "needed no urging from the government and we would be ashamed if the government would have had to make such requests of us. We have produced these pictures voluntarily and proudly."[59] After eight days of sometimes raucous testimony and countercharges, the hearings recessed. With the issue still unresolved, the committee scheduled a second round of hearings to begin on 8 December.

If propaganda is defined as a means of selling people on an idea, then probably all the films the isolationists cited during the hearings contained propaganda. Though these movies told America that the armed forces were taking appropriate measures to defend the nation, *Submarine D-1, Wings of the Navy, Flight Command,* and *Dive Bomber,* as well as films featuring the Army Air Corps, such as *I Wanted Wings* and *Flight Lieutenant,* clearly did not say that the United States should come to the side of the Allies in their war against Hitler.

In hindsight, Ralph Bellamy acknowledged that *Dive Bomber* might have been "subtly stirring up a patriotic, unified sort of attitude about the war, to be ready for it when it comes along." While acting in the movie, however, he had no awareness of any propaganda intent. Although he found the low-level-flying sequences stirring and moving, he thought any preparedness message was "extremely subtle."[60]

Pearl Harbor itself gave lie to the isolationists' claim that the preparedness films were bringing the United States into the war. At the same time, the stunning success of the Japanese attack stood in stark contrast to the preparedness message that the service stood ready and able to defend the nation against any enemy. In the end, the films that the Hollywood/Navy relationship produced during the 1930s did more than entertain the American people. They undoubtedly aided recruiting and helped obtain appropriations from Congress. Unfortunately, they also lulled the nation into a false sense of security. The belief that no enemy would dare attack American territory may well have made Pearl Harbor that much more traumatic.

★

★

FOUR

The Navy Goes to War

Although Pearl Harbor traumatized the nation, the Navy began to recover immediately. With the isolationists totally discredited, Hollywood had a virtual mandate to fill its movies with enemy atrocities, negative stereotypes, and antifascist diatribes to stir up suitable hatred against the enemy. However, filmmakers still faced problems finding suitable vehicles in which to create these sentiments.

In the first months of the war, studios simply used the stories they had available. Filmmakers rewrote the endings of the few military-preparedness movies then in production, such as *To the Shores of Tripoli,* to reflect the U.S. entry into the conflict. To avoid waiting for writers to develop original screenplays for new projects, studios also resurrected World War I plots and updated them with contemporary weaponry and images of the new enemies. These early films could not provide any authentic images of combat or insights into the true nature of the war. As Hollywood settled in for the duration, however, studios began to develop scripts that drew on accounts of the early battles and the men fighting them, although many of the stories remained little more than screenwriters' flights of fancy. Even those films represented as having a historical basis combined at least some fiction with fact for reasons of security, politics, and drama.

Under the best of circumstances, filmmakers need a long period of production to turn a story into a completed movie. At this juncture they could not expect to receive significant assistance from the armed forces, who obviously had more important things to do than put their men and equipment in front of cameras.

Columbia won the race to bring a war story to the screen with a fantasy about the twenty-four hours preceding the Japanese attack on Pearl Harbor. Released in June 1942, *Submarine Raider* portrayed a hide-and-seek chase between an American submarine and one of the Japanese aircraft carriers on its way to Hawaii. The sub's captain tries fruitlessly to warn the military of the impending attack. The submarine does torpedo the Japanese carrier, which looks and maneuvers like a special-effects model, but only after its planes have launched for their attack. The authentic newsreel footage of the devastation at Pearl Harbor and a scene of a Japanese plane bombing a lifeboat clearly intended to rouse the hatred of the American people against Japan. At the same time, the submarine's sinking of the carrier fostered the idea that the Navy would lead the revenge for the sneak attack.

In contrast, RKO turned to its own film library to find the idea for *The Navy Comes Through,* which appeared in November 1942. According to the *New York Times,* the studio "floundered upon the treacherous shoals of banality" in trying to glorify the men who fought on the sea. Although the film did not rewrite history, the plot differed little from the studio's 1931 *Suicide Fleet* and follows the adventures of a Navy gun crew aboard a merchant-marine freighter in the early days of the war.[1] With the ubiquitous Pat O'Brien as the chief petty officer in command of the Navy contingent, the men battle U-boats in the North Atlantic to help ensure that war material reaches the Allies. The CPO works diligently to turn his raw crew into a well-trained fighting machine. Initially, the typically heterogeneous wartime cast, including a Cuban, a Brooklynite, a boxer, a clean-cut teenager wanting to become an officer, an Austrian, et. al., needs the help of Navy destroyers to repel the first U-boat attack. Ultimately, the chief, his men, and the Merchant Marines manage to capture a German submarine tender and turn it into a Q-boat of sorts, instead of sailing it to Ireland as a prize of war.

The ruse works well enough to trick three German submarines into coming alongside to take on supplies and sabotaged torpedoes, which explode as soon as the German craft submerge. Luck runs out when the commander of the fourth U-boat recognizes a member of the gun crew as a famous Austrian violinist, escaped from Hitler with a price on his head. The submarine launches an immediate attack with its deck gun, and a fight ensues, which a second U-boat shortly joins. With the usual carnage and appropriate tensions, the Navy gunners sink both submarines.

The Navy made its limited appearance thanks to a minute or so of stock footage. The fleet at sea, battleships, cruisers, old four-stack destroyers, and a carrier launching a plane supply the background for the opening credits and opening message. A flotilla of destroyers launch depth charges to save the merchant ship in its first encounter with a U-boat. Thousands of marching sailors and an old sailing ship provide the stage for the actors and a few live sailors during two training sequences, thanks to the magic of rear-screen projection. As background for the closing title, battleships plow through high seas, and planes appear overhead in formation.

Lacking any dramatically redeeming quality, the story itself served only as an informational and propaganda medium, beginning with the opening title: "THE NAVY COMES THROUGH has been such an established fact that it is now taken for granted. As a result we do not realize that the backbone of the Navy is not ships, planes, and submarines—BUT MEN." O'Brien's character spells this out more explicitly even before the freighter has left its dock. As soon as the men have stowed their gear, he explains to them their importance to the war effort and how the Navy and Merchant Marines were interacting to help defeat the enemy.

He first acknowledges, "I know you are all disappointed you're not on a battlewagon or a crack cruiser. But this is the hand they dealt us and we're going to play it out." Responding to a sailor's description of the freighter as a "floating pile of junk" rather than "a ship he can be proud of," the CPO says his men should take pride in their domain. He reminds them that their quarters below deck, the gun mount, and as "far as this gun can toss 'em is all Navy." He also tells his crew not to "sell the Merchant Marine short either. It's their job to get this ship across and it's our job to keep the Heinies out of their hair while they're doing it." *The Navy Comes Through* made it clear that everyone had to share the load if the nation was going to win the war.

The film also used other devices to convey its propaganda. A brief montage of the destruction of Pearl Harbor, with FDR's message to Congress providing the narrative, reminded America of how the Japanese forced the nation into war. Under a poster proclaiming, "Loose Lips Might Sink Ships," a German spy sitting in a bar across from the Brooklyn pier listens to the sailors talk about their cargo and then heads home to broadcast the information. A very young Desi Arnez, as the Cuban sailor, explains why he joined the Navy: "The United States helped make Cuba free, so I come here to free the United States." O'Brien's "We've just begun to fight" alludes to John Paul Jones's famous saying and ties all the film's messages together. While the Navy did not yet have the resources to provide even limited assistance to *The Navy Comes Through*, the film portrayed the professionalism of its men on whatever ship they might find themselves.

Following closely on the heels of RKO's production, *Stand By For Action* attempted to impart the same message, using a destroyer as the setting for both farce and serious drama and ending with a David and Goliath battle between the destroyer and a Japanese battleship—which the Americans win, of course. Although the Navy provided limited cooperation and may have received some benefit from the portrayal of its men in action, the *New York Times* would have liked "to laugh this picture off." However, "too many folks will think it serious, and that's the deplorable thing. For this is precisely the type of war-film which breeds complacency. This is the sort of mock heroics which insults our fighting men."[2]

Released the next month, *Crash Dive* created even more fanciful images of victory, this time against Germany. Thanks to permission from the Navy, Twentieth Century Fox was able to shoot virtually all of *Crash Dive* at the submarine base at New London. However, the film's portrayal of combat remained pure fantasy. Tyrone Power portrays an avid PT boat skipper who finds himself assigned as an executive officer on a submarine whose captain is played by Dana Andrews. After two cruises in the Atlantic, however, Power develops an appreciation of undersea warfare. The mandatory love triangle, in which Andrews and Power pursue Anne Baxter with differing degrees of passion, adds nothing to the story.

Within this unexceptional story, the filmmakers and the Navy combined to explain, for the first time in color, how the submarine service was training its officers and men for combat. This portrayal undoubtedly aided the recruiting of young men for the all-volunteer submarine service. However, the scenario of having American submarines fighting the war in the North Atlantic had no basis in history. Lacking German surface ships as targets, the Navy deployed virtually all its submarines to the Pacific theater from the earliest days of the war.[3]

The film's high point, the destruction of a secret German submarine base in a commando-type raid, also lacked operational plausibility. Germany had located its U-boat bases along the European coastline, not on some mysterious island somewhere in the North Atlantic. Moreover, American submariners rarely conducted commando operations.[4]

The film caused Bosley Crowther, in the *New York Times,* to wonder why he should bother criticizing the movie's antics: "*Crash Dive* is one of those films which have no more sense of reality about this war than a popular song." In regard to the commando raid, he could only observe, "to call it fantastic would be understating the case, for the sub crew . . . play commandos with a wild and vicious zeal. They blow up oil tanks, ammunition, set fire to barracks and ships and escape through a sea of flaming fuel oil, with the captain steering from the submerged bridge. Such incredible heroics have seldom been seen on the screen. It is Hollywood at its wildest. And in Technicolor, too! Oh, boy!"[5]

Such inaccuracies remained beside the point. *Crash Dive* served well as a recruiting tool. The destruction of the German submarine base, however fanciful, showed Americans beating the Nazis at a time when the country was still fighting an uphill battle in Europe.

These images of victory did not alone satisfy the filmmakers. To end the film, Power gives a heavy-handed recitation about how the Navy was leading the way in the war against the Axis. The scene dissolves to give a visual survey of

Navy ships at sea, to the strains of "Anchors Away," and Power concludes, "It isn't one branch of the service, it's all branches, and it isn't all ships. It's men. The men behind the guns of the PT boats, and the submarines, and the Coast Guard ships, and the mine layers, and the tenders, and the tankers, and the troop ships, the men that take them out and fight their way over and land them there, that's the Navy, the United States Navy."

Not all films portrayed the war at sea with such emotion. Only a month after the release of *Crash Dive* in April 1943, Lloyd Bacon's *Action in the North Atlantic* covered much the same territory as *The Navy Comes Through,* but with a more realistic approach to the conflict. In this case, the film focused on the Merchant Marine sailors themselves to salute the courage of the many sailors maintaining the sea links to the Allies.

Fresh from outsmarting the Japanese in *Across the Pacific* and the Germans in *Casablanca,* Humphrey Bogart played his usual hard-bitten persona, this time as second officer of a tanker steaming from New Jersey to the European theater. After introducing the audience to the stereotypical Hollywood crew, the film enters a U-boat as it sinks Bogart's ship. As soon as the surviving crew collects itself aboard a lifeboat, the sub surfaces and cuts the fragile craft in two, while a German officer films the scene for posterity.

During the first two years of the war, Hollywood regularly portrayed the Axis committing such atrocities, to stimulate an outburst of hatred against the nation's enemies. Bogart and most of the crew make it to a nearby raft, from which they are rescued after drifting for eleven days. Back in port, in a local bar, he meets and (following the strictures of the Production Code Office) quickly marries a singer. Despite her pleas, he rejoins his captain aboard a new Liberty Ship for a run to Murmansk, which the film details with great care. If the story seldom rises above the level of melodrama, any film in which Bogart appeared gained a significant measure of quality. *Action in the North Atlantic* also served as a vehicle for explaining the importance of supporting the Soviet Union, the dangers the German wolf packs presented to the success of that mission, and the manner in which the Navy and the Merchant Marine worked together to counter the submarine threat. In the end, Bogart sails the freighter into Murmansk after the captain is wounded during a running battle with a U-boat.

The film does contain a feel of authenticity and accuracy thanks to the limited assistance the Navy and Merchant Marine provided. Is it a docudrama? Probably not, because any film conveying the true dangers and grimness of convoy duty would probably have negatively affected the recruitment of merchant seamen. Still, *Action in the North Atlantic* did give America some understanding of the nature of the Atlantic war and the role Navy ships and gun crews were playing in getting the convoys through.

These early movies focused more on individuals than on the totality of the service's contribution to the war effort. In contrast, a destroyer became the star of *Destroyer* and the vehicle through which the Navy portrayed how its men and ships became a team to strike at the enemy. The film also became a model of the process by which a studio transformed a preparedness story into a combat movie.

Writing to the Navy on behalf of himself and producer Lou Edelman, in June 1941, Spig Wead explained that *Destroyer* would try "to create a personality out of a navy ship and to make the ship one of the main characters in the story." He proposed to begin the movie with the laying of the keel and then introduce the crew as the destroyer nears completion, picking "up the various human characters, with the dramatic problems and conflicts in their lives," so creating an interaction between the sailors and their ship. The story would then follow the destroyer from her launching, through her shakedown cruise and trials, to the troubles and difficulties she faces; "then finally in the finish [she] would come through and win her rightful place in the fleet." The sailors' stories would go side by side with the story of the destroyer "and would have their effect upon the success and failure of that ship."[6]

Wead did not elaborate on the "troubles and difficulties" the destroyer would face. When Wead wrote the Navy, the nation was not at war, although by June 1941 the United States was virtually fighting an undeclared war against Germany. Wead did not need to explain that by the time the proposed film appeared, it would undoubtedly portray the destroyer in combat. Wanting to get started on the script quickly, he expressed the hope that Edelman could visit a destroyer to talk with officers and men and, ideally, to take a brief cruise.[7]

Though Wead's concept differed little from the ideas he and other filmmakers regularly sent to the Navy, this one attracted more than the usual attention from the service, and its public-relations office began the process of providing assistance. Lt. Cdr. Stuyvesant Wright wrote to Edelman on 24 June, saying that Navy people "all appreciate the fine spirit which so many in the industry, like yourself, have shown in offering professional help and advice at a time when it is so greatly needed." Wright indicated that accommodating Edelman on a destroyer depended on operational schedules, but he was sure a research trip could be arranged.[8]

By 15 July Edelman had been able to visit the USS *Balch* at Mare Island and expected to go to sea aboard the destroyer the next week. In advising Wright of his plans, Edelman suggested that the Navy "might want to get a message to the public, which we might possibly incorporate in our picture. . . . if there is anything that the Navy would like to say, providing, of course, it can logically fit into our general scheme of things, I will be very happy to put it in."[9] Showing a pro-Navy bias, the producer then said that he had gotten "a little burnt-up today" after seeing another filmmaker "wining and dining" an Army general. He complained that "the Army seems to be getting the cream of all the effort, and I can't for the life of me figure out why the Navy Department isn't paying

METHODIST COLLEGE LIBRARY
Fayetteville, N.C.

more attention to this industry and asking the people in it to help in whatever their problems." He said Hollywood could do a great deal "to help the Navy and there is so little of it being done that I can't help but tell you how I feel about it." To him, filmmakers were supporting the Army because it "was making an effort to get it and the industry is giving more than they want."[10]

In less than two weeks the head of the Navy Recruiting Bureau sent a memo to Wright with ideas for the movie. He cited a lack of understanding among men and their parents about "how enlisted men in the Navy spend their time; the military duties of a sailor; his recreation; amount of time he spends on shore and at sea." He wanted the film to explain how sailors learned trades in the Navy that would "fit them for duties in civil life" as well as qualifying them for advancement. He also hoped it would provide "an opportunity to bring out the differences between the regular Navy and the Naval Reserve" but also show that once on duty "there is no distinction between regulars and reservists."[11]

Wright immediately sent the suggestions to Edelman, who had his cruise and was developing the treatment with Wead. On 8 September the producer advised Alan Brown, Wright's temporary replacement, "We are anxious—terribly anxious—to get it rolling because of its timeliness. . . ." To expedite the process, Edelman said he or Wead would bring the treatment to Washington to discuss it with the Navy and then "make changes immediately, so that we can go right into script feeling that all hands are pleased and satisfied."[12]

At Brown's suggestion, Edelman first sent the treatment to Washington to give the service time to read it. Despite all the Navy's help, it found significant problems that required a rewrite of the whole story. By phone and then in a letter on 13 November Brown explained to Edelman that the Motion Picture Board felt the script "presented an exaggerated and improbable picture of inefficient equipment and personnel." The service "would never knowingly place an incompetent officer or petty officer in positions of authority aboard ship, nor would it accept ships without a builder's trial run or ships which have not met specifications." For security reasons, Brown also suggested the filmmakers not include a reference to a destroyer's speed and not plan "on shooting any details of guns or fire control apparatus, as such detailed shots will not be permitted."[13]

Ultimately, Edelman received approval of his script, now titled "Destroyer Men," on 6 February 1942. By then, the Navy had more pressing concerns than cooperating on movies, no matter how beneficial their images to the service, and Brown advised Edelman "that due to the stress of the war situation and the need for ships to operate with the fleet as fighting units that active Naval cooperation will necessarily be cut to a minimum." Therefore, he requested that the producer "figure out as nearly as is humanly possible the actual scenes that you will need aboard ship." Brown did not anticipate problems in Edelman's obtaining the necessary shots of destroyers being built and launched, although the shots at sea "are the ones that are likely to cause trouble."[14]

By early April, with the production apparently on track, Brown raised the question of how Edelman intended to cast the film. Citing the Navy's letter to the heads of the major studios, in which the service stated that it would cooperate only on "A" films, Brown asked for the names of the actors and directors as soon as possible: ". . . not that we would withdraw cooperation, but merely so the final blow won't be so hard." Whether Brown's letter influenced him, Edelman cast Edward G. Robinson and Glenn Ford to star in the film.[15]

Destroyer appeared in August 1943. It remained true to Wead's original concept of focusing on how a ship and its crew work together. *Destroyer* also portrayed a man's faith in a dream. Robinson played a welder building the *John Paul Jones,* which will replace its namesake, sunk at the Battle of the Coral Sea in 1942. Having served on the old destroyer, he insists the new ship be perfect. The captain, whom Robinson had encouraged to go to Annapolis, persuades the welder to reenlist and join the new destroyer.

With his seniority, Robinson replaces Ford as the ship's chief boatswain's mate and continues his quest of perfection, thereby alienating the rest of the crew. The captain tries to convince him that mechanical perfection is not enough to win wars, explaining, the American way depends upon the emotions of human beings, upon that additional something that carried the colonists through the Revolution. Though holding up Robinson as the symbol of that "something," the captain finally demotes Robinson and returns Ford to his former position. In the end, the older sailor saves his ship after Japanese planes damage it, enabling the destroyer to ram and sink an attacking submarine. Retiring as a hero, Robinson watches the *John Paul Jones* join the Pacific Fleet.

Edelman and Wead did not completely eliminate the Navy's concern about the portrayal of poor construction. *Weekly Variety* observed that this was "likely to generate much adverse comment." In contrast, the *New York Times* observed that the film emphasized loyalty and tradition, qualities Robinson clearly represents and the Navy and the nation considered crucial during wartime. The *Times* concluded, however, that the "quality of warfare here depicted is peculiarly theatrical. The best way to take *Destroyer* is with a sizable sprinkling of salt. It is a leaky and top-heavy vessel in which Mr. Robinson serves."[16]

Destroyer did convey the message that to win the war, ships and men had to work together as a team. All subsequent wartime Navy films were to contain similar ideas, though most of the films that followed at least grounded their plots in real events. The first of these, *Destination Tokyo,* released at the very end of 1943, also became the initial movie in a trilogy using the April 1942 Doolittle Raid on Japan as their springboard.

The Warner Brothers movie improvised from the fact that a U.S. submarine had traveled to the coast of Japan to report weather conditions to the attackers. The filmmakers claimed they were attempting "to tell a factual kind of story— not a fictional exploit" about submarine warfare, drawing on incidents from several cruises in enemy waters. *Life* magazine observed that the studio had "managed to cram almost everything that has happened to the U.S. submarine service since Pearl Harbor" into 135 minutes.[17]

In a note to the "Revised Treatment" that Warner Brothers submitted to the Navy on 13 May 1943, the filmmakers explained the movie would show that submarines "are of much greater value to the Navy and the nation than simply sinkers of ships. We want them to know the high caliber of submarine officers and men, that they are skilled, well-trained, and that they can take it as well as 'dish it out.'" And unlike earlier characterizations of the enemy, *Destination Tokyo* intended "to show the Japanese as a tough adversary, an intelligent one."[18]

The scriptwriters also claimed the submarine in their film would not go "into mythical waters" and would not "sink the whole damned Jap fleet." Instead, they explained the *Copperfin* would perform its mission "quietly and well," the action would show that both the men and their ship "can take it, that a submarine can take a terrific depthcharging [*sic*] and still come home." "Most of all," the writers wanted "to show the public that the submarine service is doing a great and varied, though silent, job in this war!"[19]

In offering Cary Grant the role of the submarine's captain, director/writer Delmer Daves and producer Jerry Wald provided the actor a similar description of the film's purpose as well as its origins. In their letter of 2 June 1943, they informed Grant that the Navy had requested the film not portray the captain "as a grizzled veteran" since only young men "with particular and extraordinary gifts" became submarine commanders. They reported the Navy considered Grant to represent "the ideal type of submarine captain," and they agreed.[20] Wald and Daves also said the service had opened up its files and access to the information would ensure every incident in the film actually happened.[21]

The studio had been working on the project since February, when the Navy gave Warner Brothers clearance for the film. Apart from the official records, the filmmakers had several articles from which to draw story lines, including Hugo Bleiberg's "Prisoner on a Submarine" in the 23 March 1940 *Saturday Evening Post*. These articles had marginal value because the Navy had been reluctant to give war correspondents access to submariners for security and political reasons. Apart from concerns about operational or technical secrets, the service did not want the press to dig deeply into the problems the submarine service had been experiencing, including nonaggressive commanders, the malfunctioning and scarcity of torpedoes, and the failure to stop Japanese advances in the Philippines and at Java, Midway, and the Solomons.[22] So Daves had only two printed accounts of U.S. submarines in action when he began his research. Both described war patrols to the coast of Japan but lacked specific information about submarine operations and contained exaggerated claims of success. On the other hand, Navy records and several stories about appendectomies performed at sea by nonmedical people provided Daves with abundant material for one of the defining sequences in *Destination Tokyo*.[23]

Daves had been writing screenplays with military backgrounds for Warner Brothers since the early 1930s, and *Destination Tokyo* became his first directing assignment. He also worked on the script with novelist Steve Fisher, whom Warner Brothers had hired after he wrote a serialized novel titled *Destination Tokyo*, which *Liberty* magazine began running on 30 October 1943. When the collaboration did not produce an adequate screenplay, Daves completed an acceptable script, working with Albert Maltz.[24]

During the almost five months it took to incorporate the many submarine stories into a final screenplay, Fisher, Daves, and Maltz had to contend with Jack Warner's scrutiny, the Production Code Office's prohibitions on anything sexual, and the Navy's concerns about security and proper image. Warner tried to speed up the production, stressing the need for everyone to "know the importance of our goal." He wrote to Daves, "This being your first time at bat, I know you will put one right over the fence."[25]

On his part, the uncontestable arbitrator of moral and linguistic correctness of his time, Joseph Breen, wrote to Warner on 22 June, on behalf of the Code Office, that "the present characterization of the man, Wolf, as a man of very loose sex habits could not be approved in the finished picture. It would be acceptable to show Wolf as a 'flirtatious' type rather than the present entirely immoral characterization." He said the script portrayed Wolf as "a man of promiscuous and loose sex habits. The dialogue on this entire page should be rewritten and the business of using the 'sexy' looking doll is very questionable." Breen also reminded Warner to exercise the "usual care [to] avoid any unacceptable exposure of the persons of any of the men at any time," including scenes of the cook playing Santa Claus in his underwear and of men taking showers.[26]

In contrast, the Navy's requests for changes in the script focused on relatively minor technical matters of procedure, small security lapses, and occasional problems in the manner the screenplay intended to portray personnel. Like Joseph Breen in the Production Code Office, one officer objected to the character known as Wolf having a sexy doll aboard, observing, "In my 17 years in the Navy I have never seen a sailor with a doll aboard nor expect to in the future—This will put a bad taste in any Navy man's mouth and I should think the general public's also." In regard to the story itself, the officer found the submarine's entering Tokyo Bay by following a Japanese ship through the submarine net "only possible in the movies—too far fetched even for public to swallow—already used in *Crash Dive* and was ridiculous. Could never get out. The assignment of a modern fleet submarine to penetrate Tokyo Bay for weather data is wholly unsound."[27]

Although Warner Brothers supposedly had to accept the dictates of the Code Office and satisfy the Navy's criticisms, *Destination Tokyo* ultimately included many of the things to which Breen and the service had objected. Despite criticisms from both Breen and the Navy, Wolf had a doll aboard ship, and a "beehive" found its way into a sailor's pants; but Breen prevailed in his objection to Cookie's "Praise the Lord and pass the ammunition," even though the phrase had come into common usage after a chaplain spoke the words at Pearl Harbor.[28]

Daves also kept Tokyo Bay rather than the Japanese coast his submarine's final destination, opting for dramatic license rather than reality. Even more obvious, despite their claim to be telling a "factual kind of story," the filmmakers ignored history and submarine operations. The opening dialogue clearly sets the departure of the *Copperfin* on Christmas Eve 1942, even though Doolittle's raid actually occurred on 18 April 1942. Moreover, given the limits on the cruising ranges of U.S. submarines, the *Copperfin* would have left for Japan from Pearl Harbor, not the West Coast.

Despite these inaccuracies, Daves ultimately produced a relatively simple story with which all parties could live. The *Copperfin* sails to the Aleutians to pick up a Navy meteorologist and delivers him to the shore of Tokyo Bay to gather weather data for Doolittle's raid. Picking up the weatherman after the attack, the submarine returns to San Francisco. Within this slim framework, the *Copperfin* and her crew experience several dramatic adventures. A Japanese plane scores a direct hit on the submarine, but the bomb does not explode, and a volunteer disarms it in one of the film's most dramatic scenes. The appendectomy takes place as the *Copperfin* sits on the bottom of Tokyo Bay, and the *Copperfin* sinks a Japanese carrier—which leads to an archetypal depth-charge attack that became the model for all subsequent submarine movies about World War II.

While not the true story of a single submarine or even a completely accurate historical re-creation, most of the fictionalized incidents in *Destination Tokyo* either happened during the war or were within the realm of the possible. Bombs did strike U.S. submarines without exploding; a submarine did radio back weather information to Doolittle's raiders, but from off the Japanese coast, and probably did not contribute much to the success of the raid; American submarines did venture into Tokyo Bay, though not in the manner portrayed in the film nor so early in the war; inexperienced corpsmen performed several appendectomies in submarines during the war; and an American undersea craft did sink a Japanese carrier before the end of hostilities. But even more than the credible situations, the filmmakers' adherence to detail and concern for accuracy of procedures created a sense of reality not found in many later submarine movies.[29]

Destination Tokyo did not force audiences to suspend their disbelief to any great extent, thanks to the care Daves lavished on the film. In addition to his research in the literature, Daves lived with submariners for a week at the Mare

Island Submarine Base in San Francisco Bay. The director's attention to detail even produced an almost too realistic reproduction of still-secret radar equipment. When the Navy saw the "radar" set, it demanded to know the source of Daves's information. He mollified the Navy by explaining that he had conceived the prop from his own research and intended it to operate like an oscilloscope. Since actual radar scopes project images using an electronic sweep, the Navy was more than willing to allow the Japanese to "learn" from Daves's invention.[30]

Daves populated the *Copperfin* with the typical mixture of ethnic backgrounds and captained it with Cary Grant "as a crisp, cool and kind-hearted gent who is every bit as resourceful as he is handsome and slyly debonair." Unlike later submarine tales in which conflicts among the crew create the dramatic tensions, *Destination Tokyo* depicts a crew that is united in its effort to win the war as quickly as possible. The successful mission of the *Copperfin* undoubtedly gave a psychological boost to American morale as the war entered its third year.[31]

Destination Tokyo also contained the mandatory propaganda explaining why the United States must win the war. The cold-blooded killing of Mike, the crew's resident Irishman, by a downed Japanese pilot he tries to rescue from the sea demonstrates the enemy's perfidy. The captain then uses Mike's death to contrast American and Japanese ways: whereas Mike, a quietly religious man, bought his son roller skates, Japanese fathers give their sons daggers—"As I see it, that Jap was started on the road twenty years ago to putting a knife in Mike's back. There are lots of Mikes dying right now and a lot more Mikes will die until we wipe out a system that puts daggers in the hands of 5-year-old children." Later, an officer who was born in Japan explains that the system forces the poor farmers to sell their twelve-year-old daughters to factory owners or worse.

Whatever impact the message had, the film met with wide acclaim. After a sneak preview, a Warner Brothers executive told Warner audiences thought "we had a great picture." After screening *Destination Tokyo* on 24 November 1943, the Navy approved its release. When Warner heard the news later in the day, he sent a telegram to Secretary of the Navy Frank Knox, saying he was "delighted" that Knox had seen the film: "I feel pleased that it was so well received by you and those assembled. Trust that the public will be enlightened by the heroic deeds accomplished by the men in the silent service."[32]

Life magazine thought audiences would find *Destination Tokyo* "the most exciting motion picture about a submarine yet produced." Crowther in the *New York Times* described it as "a pippin of a picture from a purely melodramatic point of view" but warned, "Mind you, we don't say it's authentic; we don't even say it's a fair account of the way our submariners live and fight on their Far Pacific patrols. Almost every fable which has yet come out about those fellows, along with a fantastic whopper which the boys at Warners dreamed up themselves, has been crammed into the movie." He concluded that the film Warner Brothers had fashioned "in their characteristic hard-focus style, is a studiously purposeful 'epic' of the submarine service in this war."[33]

Not everyone praised *Destination Tokyo*. In a January 1944 letter to Warner Brothers, Nathaniel Clik protested the lack of "colored" or Philippine mess boys on the submarine: "It was a wonderful 'Lily White' picture. And a great morale builder for the white boys in the Navy." Acknowledging the studio had intended to boost the morale of submariners, he complained about neglecting minorities in the Navy. In contrast, a sailor on the USS *Tilefish* wrote to Jack Warner, praising the film for providing such "an authentic picture of submarines."[34]

On behalf of the Navy, Alan Brown wrote to Warner Brothers representative Bill Guthrie on 27 March, saying that *Destination Tokyo* had so impressed the submarine training people in the Bureau of Naval Personnel that "they want to make it a standard picture in the submarine schools and allied training schools." While the studio had not accepted all the Navy's requests for changes, he observed, "Despite some of the compromises with fact that were necessary, it has proved to be even more accurate than two short Navy training films made about submarines."[35]

Of all the compromises Warner Brothers made with history, submarine operations, and realism, none stood out more than the underwater scenes of the *Copperfin* in Japanese waters. Not only does the model look like a model, but any suspension of disbelief is impossible as the boat cruises barely above the ocean floor and not far below the surface. Coral reefs, mines, and seaweed shaped like seahorses do provide a visual framework for the submarine's motion. Nevertheless, watching its underwater maneuvers, audiences cannot help wondering how the *Copperfin* so easily misses the obstacles or avoids detection from above, so close does it appear to the surface.

Yet, by jamming the *Copperfin* into shallow water and placing Japanese ships within the same frame, Daves was able to heighten the tension as the submarine carries out its mission. Regardless of the Navy's claim that a submarine could penetrate Tokyo Bay and escape only "in the movies," the image of the *Copperfin* following close astern to a Japanese ship, past a mine field, and through a protective net graphically portrays the dangers the men had to endure. Once the submarine goes on the offensive, compressing the action onto a small stage emphasizes the drama even more.

After torpedoing the Japanese carrier, the *Copperfin* suffers the enemy's wrath. In the tiny space between the ocean bottom and the surface, explosions from depth charges dropped by destroyers relentlessly wrack the fragile ship, which has no place to run. Except for a momentary lapse, the men bravely wait out perhaps the most horrific depth-charging ever put on the screen, made even worse by the very closeness of the attackers and the attacked to each other on the screen.

The tensions might have become unbearable, but however well the actors try to convey the fear of dying, a sense of real doom never permeates the boat's compartments. Moreover, given the purpose of the film, audiences knew the *Copperfin* had to return home to a cheering crowd. Daves's film could not show the reality that the submarine service suffered the highest casualty rate, almost 22 percent, of any branch of the U.S. military during the war.[36]

Ironically, the film that perhaps best suggested the claustrophobia and constant threat of death inherent in service aboard submarines during World War II focused on the Marines, not the Navy. Released only a month after *Destination Tokyo, Gung Ho!* recreated the raid a Marine commando unit had made on Makin Island in August 1942. To carry the 211 marines, commanded by Col. Evans Carlson, to and from their destination, the Navy had temporarily converted two large antiquated mine-laying submarines, the *Nautilus* and *Argonaut,* into troop transports. While the marines were fighting ashore, the submarines offered support with their 5-inch guns.

Though the film changed the names of the men, including that of Maj. James Roosevelt, one of the president's sons, and enhanced, Hollywood-style, some aspects of the raid, *Gung Ho!* adhered fairly well to the facts. To make the film, Universal Studios obtained the use of two submarines to go along with the marines who assisted the actors in the battle sequences. This enabled the filmmakers to portray marines exercising on the deck of a submarine, as the men had actually done on the way to Makin Island. In a concession to dramatic license, the Navy did allow the filmmakers to create a scene in which one of the submarines resurfaces to rescue a marine left topside when the boat crash-dives to avoid incoming Japanese planes. The subsequent depth-charging and near-sinking of the submarine provide the desired tensions, particularly in the terror of the marines during the attack, but the captain's compassion is unrealistic since no military professional would jeopardize a top-secret mission to save one life. Still, the Navy benefited from the portrayal of its role in the famous raid.

In contrast to the relative accuracy of *Gung Ho!*, *The Fighting Seabees* used history only as a starting point, much like *Destination Tokyo* had. The Navy created the Seabees early in the war to serve as construction engineers to build bases and airfields on islands captured from the Japanese. Despite portraying how the new branch of the Navy performed its mission, *The Fighting Seabees* remained pure fantasy, with John Wayne, as a civilian engineer turned Navy officer, driving the story. According to Wayne, the idea for the film actually originated with a truck driver at Republic Studio who told the actor that a new organization was turning topflight construction engineers into Navy officers and warrant officers. Since Wayne didn't "have enough pull to do what I wanted to do" at that stage of his career, he advised the man to go see one of the producers, who then came to Wayne with "a great idea" for a story. Ultimately, Herbert Yates, Republic's president, told Wayne, "Duke, I've got the greatest idea that's come up so far. We're going to do a story on the fighting Seabees and put you in it."[37]

Not surprisingly, the film became little more than a Western in Navy clothes. Bosley Crowther probably said what all viewers needed to know: "Unless you're generous, you might also call it trash. For this is an old-style action drama, only topically up to date, in which a Navy lieutenant and a construction foreman are at odds on a South Pacific isle, first because of their jarring notions and second because of a girl. But, of course, the stubborn foreman finally sees the error of his views and, as the fighting chief of the Seabees, carries destruction to the Japs at Eagle Pass."[38]

Wayne thought little more of the film than Crowther did. As he recalled, Republic's writer "figured out" a story the actor considered "a good one." However, when the studio discovered the plot didn't include a girl, it ordered a rewrite that put a woman reporter on the island. According to Wayne, the addition "just took all the reality out of the picture. They really had a fine picture, kind of a lost patrol story to begin with. But it just ended up the usual type of film."[39]

The film's combat sequences did illustrate why the construction engineers had to carry weapons. The Navy gave Republic permission to shoot a Seabee training exercise at Camp Pendleton, north of San Diego, including the building of an airfield. The filmmakers then wrote the scenes into the story and cut the footage, some of which had the actors strategically placed in the action, into the film.[40] Despite this assistance, *Commonweal* observed that though the battles were "made as realistic as possible" with the help of Navy technical advisers, men who had experienced war firsthand would find flaws in the re-creations. Nevertheless, the Navy benefited from the first, and only, portrayal of the Seabees in action, and the reviewer found it "gratifying that this cinema tribute should be handled in such a straightforward, sincere manner."[41]

The Fighting Seabees had one other distinction. It became the first, and only one of two, war movies in which John Wayne dies in combat. Unlike *Sands of Iwo Jima,* in which the quintessential American fighting man gets shot in the back, in *The Fighting Seabees* he dies in glorious combat, routing the Japanese and saving the day. To the Navy, this positive image transcended the mundane plot and probably made it worth the effort.

Occurring in a fantasy film, Wayne's character's death did not cause audiences to grieve or curse the horrors of war upon leaving the theater. *The Fighting Sullivans* did not permit audiences to dismiss death as a cinematic device promoting patriotism and the war effort. Nor did it matter that the filmmakers took dramatic license in portraying the deaths of the five Sullivan brothers in the sinking of their ship during the naval battle at Guadalcanal in November 1942. Their father might go to work as he had for thirty-three years. Four of the brothers on their way to heaven might have to wait for their youngest sibling as they had to wait for him in life. Their mother might christen a destroyer *The Sullivans* in memory of her sons. But none of these images could hide the reality that all five brothers had died in combat. To be sure, many people did die in the war to protect the American way of life. But the sheer magnitude of one family's loss, however necessary the war, overrode any positive message the film might offer.

If *The Fighting Sullivans* had appeared in peacetime, the brothers' deaths might well have conveyed a powerful antiwar statement. In 1944, however, the United States was still fighting an evil enemy who gave no quarter. For the nation to survive, many men would have to die, and many families would have to suffer the ultimate sacrifice. That remained the only message *The Fighting Sullivans* offered, not any portrayal of the Navy doing its job.

In fact, *The Fighting Sullivans* had very little to do with the war itself, with combat, or with the Navy, but everything to do with the home-front war effort. The Sullivan family came to represent the values of middle America and the sacrifices the nation had to make to defeat the Axis powers. To show this, the film focused on the family and the rites of passage of the five brothers. Director Lloyd Bacon did a good job of revealing the family's "spirit of simplicity, of devotion and sentiment." The *New York Times* observed that "it so happens that there emerges in this film a simple and genuine feeling for boys and for Americans as we are. The juvenile joys of the Sullivans with their first dog, in neighborhood fights, smoking cornsilks and boating on the river have a natural, authentic appeal." The reviewer felt the film "does get down to human nature, with humor and honest sentiment."[42]

Only in the last few minutes does the Navy become a part of the story when the brothers enlist and then go off to war aboard the light cruiser *Juneau*. Even then, the Navy limited cooperation to stock footage used to create the naval battle at Guadalcanal, in which the *Juneau* was sunk. Although badly damaged during an engagement the night of 13 November 1942, the *Juneau* remained afloat. The crew managed to get it under way, and with two other crippled ships it was heading to a safe haven when the Japanese submarine *I-26* fired a salvo of torpedoes at the column. One hit the *Juneau*, which virtually disintegrated. In less than four minutes the movie shows the Sullivans aboard the ship during the battle and then trying to rescue George, the oldest brother, from sick bay. An unseen explosion occurs, and the screen goes blank. George was actually serving at his battle station when the *Juneau* exploded, and he reached a life raft with several friends. In a letter to the family, a friend later wrote that the other four boys "went down with the ship so they did not suffer. It was a sad and pathetic sight to see George looking for his brothers but to no avail." Ultimately, George died before rescuers found the survivors.[43]

The actual circumstances of the brothers' deaths was beside the point. Nor did the Navy's decision to allow the five brothers to serve together become a source of criticism. Although it had a policy of separating members of the same family in wartime, the Navy explained, the "presence of the five Sullivans aboard the U.S.S. JUNEAU was at the insistence of the brothers themselves and in contradiction to the repeated recommendations of the ship's executive officer. Serving together had been one condition of their enlistment." In fact, George had spoken for them all when he said, "And if the worst comes to the worst, why we'll have all gone down together." In the month following Pearl Harbor the nation had clearly needed patriotic symbols, and the Sullivans' request seemed made to order for the Navy. The service even waived the regulation then in force concerning the enlistment of married men with children and allowed Albert to join his four older brothers in being sworn into the Navy on 3 January 1942.[44]

In the end, the Sullivans' martyrdom was to serve the nation well in its time of need. Very soon after the loss the government requested and Mr. and Mrs. Sullivan agreed to take part in a national tour of defense plants and war bond rallies. In response to an invitation from Mrs. Roosevelt, they also visited the White House. Though the travels were emotionally and physically draining, they not only aided the war effort but served as therapy for the parents. One of the most significant of their appearances took place in April 1943, when they helped christen the USS *The Sullivans*, the first destroyer named for more than one person.[45]

The ceremony itself merged reality and fantasy for the American people, as the filmmakers used the christening as the movie's climax. An admiral explains that the parents have come "to share in the tribute to their sons, even as they shared their fighting spirit. As this ship slides down the ways, it carries with it a special armor all its own, the flaming and undaunted spirit that is the heritage of its name. The five Sullivan boys are gone. The U.S.S. THE SULLIVANS carries on. May God bless and protect this ship. May its destiny be as glorious as the name she bears."

In contrast to *The Fighting Sullivans,* Twentieth Century Fox's *A Wing and a Prayer* sought to inspire patriotism by focusing purely on the war itself, in this case on life aboard an aircraft carrier in the period leading up to the Battle of Midway. It became the only Hollywood film made during the war to dramatize the role of carriers in the defeat of Japan.

The production originated in a film treatment recounting the loss of all fifteen of the *Hornet's* torpedo planes and twenty-nine of thirty fliers at Midway. After two efforts to use Ens. G. H. Gay, the only survivor, to tell the story from his perspective, the studio gave up on "Torpedo Squadron." According to the *New York Times,* "a certain high Government official" protested the proposed story "would carry a defeatist implication." The sacrifice of fifteen planes in a few minutes certainly would not convey a positive image to the American people. Moreover, the portrayal of the subsequent torpedo bomber attacks following close behind the futile effort of the *Hornet*'s planes would not have done much to instill confidence in naval aviation. The squadron from the *Enterprise* lost ten of fourteen aircraft, while the *Yorktown* lost eight of its twelve planes. Even worse, not one torpedo hit a Japanese ship. As a result, for about one hundred seconds, the Japanese believed they had not only won the Battle of Midway, but the war itself.[46]

In less than a minute, the fortunes of war changed dramatically and irreversibly as Navy dive-bombers dropped out of the sky and inflicted mortal damage on two of the enemy's carriers. By the end of the battle, the other two Japanese carriers had met a similar fate. Obviously, the Navy would much prefer to have the victory at Midway, not the heroic but tragic story of Torpedo Squadron 8, portrayed on the screen.

Consequently, Fox spent the next several months in developing a new screenplay, and the Navy agreed to Darryl Zanuck's request to send a camera crew and a few actors aboard the USS *Yorktown* "II" during a portion of its shakedown cruise in May and June of 1943. On 26 October Jerry Cady completed a treatment titled "Wing and a Prayer," which stated in its foreword, "For military purposes, the names of men and vessels in this motion picture are fictitious, but the strategy, the essential incidents and the heroism are a matter of history." The story opened with a scene of the wreckage at Pearl Harbor, introduced the officers and men of a carrier, and followed the ship as its deceptions tricked the Japanese and led to Midway.[47]

Having decided "Wing and a Prayer" would become a major film, Zanuck, head of 20th Century Fox, involved himself with the process of turning Cady's first draft into a final, approved screenplay. In a story conference on 19 November 1943, Zanuck pointed out that the picture would not depend on plot. Instead, the filmmakers "must avoid plot, otherwise we will destroy the value of the honesty that we must maintain." To compensate, the film would have to rely on three elements: casting, dialogue, and battle sequences.[48]

Zanuck stated, "We must have characters that an audience will follow and love and root for in lieu of a story. In other words, our story is our characters." The dialogue and "the business" the characters would perform "is as vital as the casting of the characters themselves, especially the elements of comedy." Finally, the filmmakers "must adroitly take advantage of every inch" of the combat footage the studio had obtained from the Navy to create the excitement and thrill of authentic battle and arouse "genuine excitement; not melodrama so much as the feeling that our characters are actually in battle."[49]

To Zanuck, these elements "have to substitute for the conventional story that you usually find in service pictures. There is nothing new in these stories, which have been done repeatedly, and the only way this film can justify its great cost and become a distinguished, moving, and exciting document, is if we plan it that way, write it that way, and direct it that way. . . . This thing has got to stand on its own feet, and we are, therefore, first, last, and always completely at the mercy of the writer." He thought Cady had produced the best script to date, lauding in particular the prologue's question "Where is our Navy?" for providing the picture with "a new and vital impetus, a reason for being."[50]

Cady then wrote a new "Temporary Script" dated 14 December 1943, the first of several revisions, all the results of Zanuck's efforts to "keep this picture from being considered in the class of the usual service picture." On 24 January Zanuck compared Fox's project with the newly released and highly successful *Destination Tokyo* and concluded that his studio's story would have an advantage "in that the mission in *Wing and a Prayer* is a genuine, honest mission, while in *Tokyo* it was fictional. However, it was so well done that audiences no doubt accept it as factual." He also observed that no carrier movie had appeared since Pearl Harbor, whereas *Destination Tokyo* had been the second major wartime film about submarines.[51] Zanuck recognized this might not provide a real bonus, given people's perceptions: "There exists in the public mind the belief that submarine service is the most dangerous of all. Of course it is true that if a sub gets hit that's the end of it—it sinks to the bottom of the ocean. As against this, the public also regards an Aircraft Carrier as the safest place to be, because the Carrier itself looks so substantial and strong, and you do not have the feeling that people are trapped on it as in the case of a submarine. Therefore, since our story takes place on a Carrier, we do not have this element of constant menace, and we have to do whatever we can to enhance our personal plot."[52]

Zanuck suggested the film add a "melodramatic moment of danger" to the climactic battle and proposed that a submarine attack would do the trick. Feeling that *Destination Tokyo* "had great naturalness, and a great feeling of casualness," he wanted the same for *Wing and a Prayer*.[53] To accomplish this, Zanuck refined the script with his screenwriter and director Henry Hathaway. At the same time, a construction crew built a mock-up of a section of a carrier flight deck on the Fox back lot to serve as a stage for exterior scenes to match footage Hathaway had taken the previous year aboard the new *Yorktown*. In contrast to the long period needed to develop an acceptable script, the studio required only six months from the beginning of filming the last week in February to the release of *Wing and a Prayer*.[54]

The arduous effort produced a film with "Carrier X" as its hero. The story focuses on a new torpedo bomber squadron aboard a carrier cruising the western Pacific in the months before the Battle of Midway. The carrier and its escorts have orders to be seen by the enemy in widely scattered areas, but not to have its planes give battle under any circumstances. The Navy hopes this will create the impression that U.S. forces remained weak and afraid to fight.

This implausible scenario serves as the framework in which Don Ameche, the carrier's flight operations commander, attempts to instill discipline and flying skills in the young fliers led by Dana Andrews. Railing against Ameche's aloofness and strict discipline, the fliers never become likable, let alone lovable, as Zanuck had wanted. Instead, they complain about the orders and Ameche, unable to recognize their mission might have a purpose, however suicidal it appears. Nor do they understand that Ameche's knowledge of combat might help save their lives.

Still, through combat, they have matured by the Battle of Midway, where they perform heroically, contributing to the victory by sinking several Japanese ships. Some die, and the carrier suffers significant damage but continues to fight. Most important, the squadron's survivors come to appreciate Ameche's strictness, but only after he refuses to break radio silence to help one of the planes locate the carrier in a rain storm. The men listen as the plane drones back and forth in the clouds until it finally runs out of gas and crashes into the sea. Returning to the ready room, one angry pilot launches into a tirade against Ameche, just as he enters. Only then does he explain that he could not run the risk of giving the carrier's position to the enemy by signaling the lost plane and asks, "Do you think I want to dream about those three men floating around in a raft until their bodies rot?" As the air officer, he says, "I can check casualty lists and I can order more men up into the air tomorrow to become new casualties! I can refuse to endanger the lives of 3,000 men in order to save the lives of three men. I can do all those things because they're my job and I've got to do them. But to be accused of refusing to save those men because I didn't want to save them. . ." A ring of the phone stops Ameche in mid-sentence.

A destroyer has picked up the pilot and gunner. The call brings joy to the fliers, just as Ameche's outburst finally brings them an understanding of the responsibilities with which their commanders must live. In contrast to the cinematically satisfying compassion which the submarine captain showed in *Gung-Ho!*, Ameche was voicing the real dilemmas that all commanders face in sending their men into combat.

In visualizing these issues, *Wing and a Prayer* performed a valuable service for its audiences. The movie, however, offered no insights into how the Navy was actually conducting carrier operations during the war. Nor did the film in any way present an accurate account of the events leading up to the Battle of Midway or the course of the engagement itself.

Its thematic question, "Where is our Navy?" and the answer, deceiving the enemy, remained convenient cinematic fiction. During the period that *Wing and a Prayer* portrayed a lone carrier fleeing before the enemy without firing a shot, the Navy had waged an aggressive campaign against Japan with all available resources. In February, the *Enterprise* raided Kwajalein and the *Lexington* hit the Japanese held port of Rabaul on New Britain. In March, planes from the *Lexington* and the *Yorktown* attacked Japanese bases on the north coast of New Guinea. In April, the *Hornet*, with the *Enterprise* providing air support, sailed to within 668 miles of Tokyo to launch the Doolittle raid. In May, the *Lexington* and *Yorktown* led an allied force against the Japanese in the Battle of the Coral Sea, the first naval engagement in which no ship of either side sighted the other.[55]

Moreover, the film's premise that the Navy would conceive a plan that used a precious aircraft carrier as a decoy and forbid its men and planes to defend themselves lacked a modicum of believability. Military officers sometimes must issue orders that put their men in great danger, but unlike the Japanese, American leaders do not ask their men to undertake suicide missions, as the Carrier X fliers were asked to do.

Nevertheless, within the confines of *Wing and a Prayer,* the story line created dramatic conflict and held the audience's attention. More important, the film does portray life aboard an aircraft carrier in wartime with some authenticity. It also contains a scene that had never appeared in a carrier movie before and would never appear again. Using perhaps two seconds of footage the Navy supplied, the film showed the catapult launching of a bomber from the hanger deck during the height of the aerial battle.[56]

Unfortunately, the battle, created with newsreel footage and miniatures, became a generic portrayal of combat and did not resemble the actual course of events during the first day of the fighting at Midway. In particular, the film showed Carrier X's torpedo planes scoring several direct hits on the Japanese carriers even though dive-bombers had accomplished the damage. Recognizing early on that the studio would have access to a relatively limited amount of combat footage, Cady re-created a portion of the battle from the fliers' radio transmissions. As the sounds of combat are piped throughout the carrier, the film focuses on the men as they listen to the ebb and flow of the battle. The voices of the unseen fliers force audiences to imagine the details of their fighting. The technique won Cady an Oscar nomination for best original screenplay and had an impact on a future president.

During his political career, Ronald Reagan often recounted a story of a B-17 pilot, returning from a mission over Europe, who refused to leave his crippled plane after discovering a wounded crewmember had not bailed out. Instead, he told the scared boy, "Never mind, son. We'll ride it down together." According to Reagan, the pilot received the Medal of Honor posthumously for his actions. Asked to verify the story, neither the White House nor the Air Force History Office could find any evidence of such an act of heroism in Medal of Honor citations.

Ultimately, a World War II veteran provided the source of the quote, which actually had come from a torpedo bomber pilot talking to his wounded radio operator, who could not escape from their burning plane. The pilot said, "I haven't got the altitude, Mike. We'll take this ride together." Having seen *Wing and a Prayer* during the war, the veteran recognized the similarity between the film's dialogue and Reagan's quote. If the president confused image and reality, the veteran recalled that he and his friends "laughed at" the film's "corniness."[57]

In truth, *Wing and a Prayer* did combine combat sequences with soundstage action very well. It also intertwined image and reality when Dana Andrews reprimands a glory-seeking pilot, "This isn't Hollywood." Moreover, the United States did award a dozen Medals of Honor to pilots killed trying to land their planes rather than abandon wounded crewmen. Consequently, despite any corniness and its fanciful portrayal of Midway, the movie remains a credible portrayal of wartime carrier operations.

The *New York Times* acknowledged that the film did not always represent the facts "in exact proportion" but felt that Hathaway had "so skillfully woven documentary film footage into the story that it is difficult at times to spot the ending of an incident out of history and the beginning of an episode fashioned on the typewriter of Scenarist Jerome Cady." The reviewer recognized that "it still is more than likely that the development of the trap set for the Japs at Midway is, in the case of this film, more Cady than Halsey, Nimitz or King." He concluded, the film "misses out on the epic sweep of the actual Midway campaign," in contrast to the Navy's own 1943 documentary, *Battle of Midway,* which John Ford had directed. Still, providing "a good over-all glimpse of what life is like aboard a floating airfield," the film was "at once a sobering reminder of the perilous conditions under which the American Navy sailed the vast Pacific in the months immediately following Pearl Harbor and a first-rate piece of movie-making to boot."[58]

In contrast to *Wing and a Prayer, Thirty Seconds Over Tokyo,* released at the very end of 1944, had to avoid cinematic melodrama and false heroics. Based on Ted Lawson's best-selling book, the film re-created the Doolittle raid through the eyes of one pilot. Within the limits of military security, the accuracy of Lawson's recollections, and political considerations, the film portrayed real people and could not employ much dramatic license, except to protect the lives of innocent people.

As with any historical movie, the filmmakers faced the difficulty of bringing suspense to an event whose ending the audience already knew. Such quasidocumentaries as *Tora! Tora! Tora!* (1970), *Midway* (1976), and *Bridge Too Far* (1977) would all demonstrate that relatively good history without three-dimensional characterizations and dramatic tensions fails as creative art. Unlike these later historical recreations, *Thirty Seconds Over Tokyo* could offer the audience living heroes in Ted Lawson, whom Van Johnson played with boyish good humor, in Jimmy Doolittle, whom Spencer Tracy portrayed with appropriate reserve, and in the rest of the volunteers who flew on the raid.

Little of this mattered to the Navy since the movie focused on the Army Air Corps. For security reasons, the film could not even identify the *Hornet* as the carrier that transported Doolittle and his sixteen B-25 bombers to within seven hundred miles of the Japanese mainland. However, in the first script MGM sent to the War Department, the producers explained that in "dramatizing the close cooperation between the Army and the Navy without which there could have been no Tokyo raid, we seek to destroy the malingering whisper that a harmful rivalry exists between these two branches of the service."[59] Nevertheless, in tracing the mission from the training at Eglin Air Force Base near Pensacola, through the raid, to the fliers' return to the United States, the film presents the story from Lawson's perspective.[60]

If the Navy did not receive credit for conceiving the idea of launching B-25 bombers from a carrier, the film does clearly show the service's role in the mission itself. A Navy officer instructed the pilots on how to take off from a carrier and accompanied them aboard the *Hornet*. Once aboard ship, Navy personnel went out of their way to support the fliers as they prepared for the mission. Doolittle's men acknowledged the importance of that help, and the raid itself remains a paradigm of joint military operations.

Re-creating the actual launch, however, presented the filmmakers with great problems. The War Department and the Navy could not provide the planes and a carrier for MGM to use in restaging the launching of Doolittle's raiders. The studio, therefore, had to build a section of the *Hornet*'s flight deck on a sound-stage and managed to squeeze four loaned B-25s into the building.[61]

To portray the takeoffs, Buddy Gillespie, the Oscar-winning head of MGM's special-effects department, built about four-fifths of the deck of the *Hornet* on a scale of one inch to the foot. He then set the sixty-foot miniature into the studio's three-hundred-square-foot water tank. Because of its size in relationship to the tank, the miniature remained stationary. Instead, Gillespie made the carrier rise, pitch, and roll hydraulically, with pumps and wave machines moving water past the ship. He photographed miniature bombers, attached to an overhead trolley with piano wire. Special-effects men controlled the planes' "takeoffs" by means of small synchronous motors. The film editors then combined these sequences with the limited newsreel footage taken during the actual takeoffs. Gillespie did his job so well that only someone familiar with the newsreel film or having a keen eye can pick out the re-created takeoffs from the actual launchings. The Navy's contribution to the Doolittle raid ended here, and the film elicited little recognition of its actual role. Bosley Crowther, in the *New York Times*, simply said that *Thirty Seconds Over Tokyo* provided "a fitting tribute" to all the participants.[62]

By then, the nation no longer needed the kind of psychological boost that the attack on Japan had provided in April of 1942. However, in reminding the American people of the mission's audacity, the film helped fix in the collective memory the contribution Doolittle's men and the Navy had made to rallying the nation in its darkest hour.

This reminder did not go unappreciated within the Navy. Shortly after the film appeared, Secretary of the Navy James Forrestal confirmed the importance of Hollywood's portrayal of the Navy during the war when he wrote to Y. Frank Freeman, president of the Association of Motion Picture Producers, "I should like to express through you to the studio heads and producers the Navy's appreciation of the four-star performance turned in by the industry during 1944. The Navy is not only thankful for the cooperation it received but also grateful for the entertainment both in personal appearances and in pictures for overseas use, by the people of the motion picture world."[63]

Adm. Chester Nimitz agreed with this appraisal later in January. In a speech he delivered by shortwave from his Pacific headquarters to a dinner in Philadelphia honoring Bob Hope with the "Poor Richard" award, he said, "Our victories are not being won by material alone. They are being won by the high morale and the will to win of our fighting men. And these are being instilled by the men of the entertainment industry who are helping us to preserve the sense of humor and balance needed to carry on this savage fight against our enemies."[64]

By early 1945, with victory against the Axis powers virtually assured, Hollywood had drastically cut back on its production of combat movies. As a result only two Navy movies portraying combat appeared during 1945. The first, *This Man's Navy,* had about as much to do with combat as *The Fighting Sullivans.* The film featured Wallace Beery as an aging chief petty officer stationed at Lakehurst, New Jersey, with the Navy's lighter-than-air training program. The CPO ultimately ends up with his blimp in India, tracking down Japanese submarines. In the climactic scene, he and his foster son attack and sink an enemy submarine, although losing their airship. The film differs little from any number of peacetime military stories in which Beery played the same kind-hearted but blustery enlisted man in one or another of the armed services.

The second, *They Were Expendable,* told a true story about real people, albeit thinly disguised. Based on William L. White's best-seller of the same name, the film recounted the exploits of a PT-boat squadron in the Far Pacific in the first months of World War II. With orders to trade his plywood torpedo boats for time, Lt. John Bulkeley, renamed Brickley in the movie, fought a rearguard action against superior Japanese forces just after the invasion of the Philippines. Brickley, played by Robert Montgomery, and his executive officer Rusty Ryan, portrayed by John Wayne, evacuate General MacArthur from Corregidor and harass the enemy until finally expending their boats and men.

Having retired from active duty, Frank Wead returned to Hollywood to write the screenplay, and the Navy ordered John Ford to leave his outfit overseas to direct the film. The production became a labor of love and an homage to the Navy's contribution to victory. If Wayne's romance with Donna Reed's Army nurse does clash with the film's documentary-like quality, it ultimately conveyed a memorable image of separation and loss. As usual, the director took the officer's view, treating the enlisted men as if they occupied the bottom of the caste system and using their antics to supply the humor. At the same time, Ford, who knew and respected John Bulkeley, showed him as aloof from his men while equally isolated from his superiors, doing an impossible job well and refusing to give up despite impending doom.

Critic William Everson observed that *They Were Expendable,* which contained only small victories capped off by one of the great defeats in U.S. military history, the loss of the Philippines, was "an odd film indeed to make at the *close* of a war. Its sadness and melancholy hardly matched the jubilation of the period, it had little propagandist value, and yet it was still too soon for it to have real perspective on the late war—though it certainly had more than many of the similar films (*Wake Island,* etc.) made during the war."[65]

They Were Expendable did follow Hollywood's guidelines for wartime productions, providing recreation, education, and inspiration to audiences, and provided a documentary record of the wartime exploits of PT boats. While most naval officers had considered PT boats little more than pleasure craft, the plywood warships did acquit themselves well during the war. Nevertheless, they were to have no role in the postwar Navy, and so Ford's film became little more than a personal tribute to Bulkeley's exploits.[66]

To help achieve this goal, the Navy provided Ford the use of several PT boats, destroyers, and planes during location shooting, which took place south of Miami. The filmmakers re-created the wartime naval bases at Manila and Cavite. Wead worked with Ford during the filming and on occasion had to rewrite the script to fit in additional, improvised scenes. In carefully choreographing the two major torpedo-run sequences, Ford created the seagoing equivalents of one of his Western cavalry charges. His images of attack, shellfire, and flying flags became almost literal cinematic translations of wartime combat paintings. To replicate the destruction of Manila he was able to use a large brushfire on Key Biscayne.[67]

In his review, Bosley Crowther said that if the film had appeared in 1943 or 1944, rather than late 1945, it "would have been a ringing smash. For then, while the war was still with us and the wave of victory was yet to break, the national impulse toward avengement, for which it cries out, would have been supremely stirred." Instead, he concluded, it arrived "as a cinematic postscript to the martial head and passion of the last four years." Nevertheless, the film did enjoy critical acclaim. Hollywood, however, began no more combat stories for almost three years. Even so, the Navy was satisfied its wartime actions had received a full and positive portrayal from the film industry.[68]

★

FIVE

Preparing for the Cold War

T he decline in the production of military films that began in early 1945 accelerated with the end of the war. The lack of box-office interest in *They Were Expendable* as well as *A Walk in the Sun* demonstrated to Hollywood that the American people wanted to forget about combat, at least for a little while. Meanwhile, the military itself underwent a massive downsizing and a major reorganization culminating in the creation of the National Military Establishment in 1947 and the formation of the Department of Defense under the leadership of James Forrestal.

As part of the unification process, Forrestal consolidated all public-affairs operations into one office, leaving each service with a limited staff to act only in an advisory capacity and as a line of communication to the field for the Defense Department's director of public information. The reorganization also created in 1949 the Motion Picture Production Office. Under the direction of Donald Baruch, its first chief, the office underwent regular name changes. However, for the next forty years Baruch sought to follow the original mandate of his office: to direct the cooperation the military provided to the film industry. In supervising the details of assistance, Baruch had expected to put an end to the armed forces' zealous pursuit of film roles.[1]

If the world had settled into a prolonged period of peace, the downsized military would have had little reason to sell itself to the American people and to Congress. However, the Allied coalition that had defeated the Axis quickly fell apart. The Soviet blockade of Berlin in March 1948 marked the formal start of the Cold War. With the detonation of the first Russian atomic bomb in 1949, the United States entered a new period of international tensions and the threat of renewed military conflict.

Not surprisingly, after Secretary Forrestal's resignation as Secretary of Defense in March 1949, the individual services began to regain control over their public-affairs operations, a process that the outbreak of the Korean war in June 1950 further accelerated. As a result, almost from its inception, Baruch's office failed to function as originally planned, and until the early 1960s it served essentially as a conduit for requests from Hollywood to the individual services.

In this capacity, Baruch's office could recommend that a service provide assistance, could help with negotiations between a filmmaker and a service, or could refuse to approve cooperation on a film that did not benefit a particular service or the military establishment. However, Baruch could not require a service to assist a movie. Once Baruch had approved a project, he had no control over the help a service might extend. So throughout the 1950s the services had virtually a blank check to provide assistance, much as they had from the earliest days of their relationship with the film industry. Filmmakers received as much help on any movie as a service's public-affairs office in Washington and its commanders in the field decided served its best interest.

Ironically, the on-screen rivalry between the individual services began at the very time the Department of Defense was coming into being. The new Air Force led the way, with two movies about the air war over Europe appearing in 1948, but neither *Command Decision* nor *Fighter Squadron* enjoyed much success, demonstrating that Americans did not yet want to relive the recent war.

Nevertheless, in 1948 Warner Brothers put into production a script it had begun developing in March 1944—a story of carrier aviation during the war. The original idea had come to the studio from Max Miller, the author of *I Cover the Waterfront,* now a lieutenant in the Navy's Public Relations Office in Washington. With the suggestion in hand, Delmer Daves flew to Washington to discuss it with Miller, the Assistant Secretary of the Navy, and several Navy veterans of the air war in the Pacific.[2]

From his conversations came the concept of following the main character from his days aboard the *Langley,* the Navy's first carrier, through the development of naval aviation and into the war. The head of naval aviation liked the "size" of the project and said he would use his rank and position to support it. He also agreed that the film's World War II flattop should represent all carriers, as the *Copperfin* in *Destination Tokyo* had represented all submarines.[3]

Daves spent almost a day with Miller, discussing his combat experiences aboard the *Yorktown.* He had an even more valuable meeting with Cdr. Clarence McCluskey, leader of the initial dive-bomber attack on the Japanese carriers at Midway, which had turned the tide of the war. McCluskey described for Daves his Navy career from Annapolis to Midway and expressed his willingness "to do anything for us." As a result, the director concluded the flier would make an "excellent prototype for our lead" and titled his first treatment of 23 March 1944, "The Story of McCluskey."[4]

Despite now having a concept and perhaps a central character, the project lacked a unity of effort. Daves was directing *Pride of the Marines* and screening "millions" of feet of combat footage. Consequently, he relinquished the writing of the screenplay to Ranald MacDougall. Unfortunately, he proceeded so slowly that the studio concluded the war might end before it could release the film and decided to expand the story to dramatize both the history of naval aviation and World War II carrier warfare.[5]

To obtain the cooperation needed to tell this story, producer Jerry Wald met with the Navy Secretary in Los Angeles on 1 February 1945 to discuss the studio's requirements, including the use of an aircraft carrier. He explained, "We must be able to get on a carrier so we can make the scenes aboard it actual and real and not have to resort to miniatures. In other words, the Navy will have to lean backwards in their cooperation, of course, without interfering in the war effort." The secretary assured Wald this would not cause a problem since carriers sailed in and out of southern California all the time.[6]

Subsequently, Wald became obsessive in his pursuit of combat footage. He initially discussed the requirement with the secretary and later in the month wrote to the Navy's Motion Picture Section, asking it to speed up sending him combat footage. He explained that the film was to end with footage of a huge task force battering Japan. His badgering suggests that he almost believed the United States was fighting the war simply to provide Warner Brothers with film for its project. In fact, on 22 May a studio agent collecting material in Washington wrote that a "big howl" went up in the Navy's processing laboratory "about the amount of stock footage and color dupes" the studio was requesting.[7]

Wald also worked to dress the production with appropriate props and historical footage. On 23 March he wrote to the studio's Washington representative, Bill Guthrie, asking him to see about securing the use of a couple of captured Japanese planes, then at a nearby airfield. The same day, he wrote Guthrie to try to locate footage of every landing and every crash on the *Langley* from 1923 to 1925, which he said the Navy used to train carrier pilots.[8]

Although MacDougall continued to have trouble with his script, by early June he had created the raison d'être for the film. He intended to answer the question of whether the United States would commit naval suicide again once the war had ended and simply hope for peace in the face of a hostile world. In the "Forward [*sic*] and Story Outline" of 11 June he wrote, "THIS MOTION PICTURE will present this question and give this answer in dramatized form, through terms of historical facts, portrayed by actors who will be prototypes of the men in the U.S. Navy who have lived through the period which started with the destruction of a major portion of our Navy at the Washington Naval Disarmament Conference in 1921."[9] Following the stories of these men, the movie would show the public "the magnificent development of Naval Aviation in spite of the myriad of hurdles that Navy Aeronautics had to overcome: technical and research problems, economic restrictions in appropriations, the apathy of the public in peace time, political pressure and stalemates, isolationist blocks and the pressure of a certain portion of the press." The film would portray the results of the Navy's fight, the carrier task force, and MacDougall remained "convinced that an honest picture based upon sound fact and so documented (even though these facts may be disagreeable) will be far superior to fiction."[10]

Despite the sweep of the story, the Navy found problems with it, informing Wald on 25 June that everyone had overlooked the history of jeep carriers: "I feel you should consider this in terms of the final portion of the picture. We are prepared back here to provide you with any material you will require and to make suggestions as to the type of sequence which might be developed." He also reported that the Navy continued to collect footage for the studio, particularly on the *Franklin* and its struggle to survive a bomb attack off the Japanese mainland in March.[11]

Throughout the summer MacDougall continued to turn in pieces of the screen-play, apparently without recognizing that peace was about to catch up with the project. The ultimate threat to the project materialized on August 6, however, when the Enola Gay dropped the first atomic bomb on Hiroshima. Even the second bomb dropped on Nagasaki three days later and the end of the war on 14 August did not immediately halt work on the project.[12] Daves continued working on the screenplay, and on 19 September noted that he did not think atomic weapons would in any way lessen the need for the United States "to have vessels on an outer perimeter from which interceptors can be launched—we cannot wait until a rocket or an atomic bomb carrying plane reaches our shores to intercept them, so there will always be a need for an outer ring of defense."[13]

Ultimately, the definitive commentary on MacDougall's work came from Capt. and later Adm. James Thach, one of the pioneers of naval aviation and a fighter pilot who shot down six Zeros at Midway. In a long analysis of the script, dated 28 September 1945, he offered his arguments supporting aircraft carriers, which the filmmakers could use "in the final speech or wherever they will do the most good." He suggested: "As long as we need policemen on the street corner in your home town to maintain law and order we will need global police forces in peace time to maintain peace. These carriers can be moved swiftly to any area where trouble is brewing and, like a good police force, change the minds of gangster nations tempted to grab unprotected resources. This force would actually be more economical than large island installations that cannot move."[14]

While arguing the case for carriers in the atomic age, Thach prophesied they would "probably be underwater vessels that cannot be picked up by radar." He wanted to "continue the development of carriers and take advantage of every progressive scientific step along the way, we cannot wait until atomic bombs reach our shores. We must keep the perimeter defense of carriers far at sea to strike before our industries and cities are wiped out." Whatever his view of future carriers, with the war over, few people had an interest in funding a naval buildup. The military was shrinking as fast as the services could demobilize, and Hollywood was making stories about returning veterans, such as *Best Years of Our Lives,* but not about the recent war.[15]

Although Warner Brothers shelved the project, the studio allowed Wald and Daves to work on the screenplay until Hollywood decided in 1948 that war stories would again attract audiences. By then, Daves had rejected much of MacDougall's work and had a script, dated 9 July 1948, ready to send to the Navy. Responding to it on 26 July, Capt. E. M. Eller, the director of the Public Information Division, told the studio that officers who had read the script "think it is an excellent vehicle to present the history of naval aviation to the public. They are unanimous in praise of the story; although most of them had the usual thoughts about straightening out minor points." Eller did have one "important" request: "Will you bring the story up to date, suggesting through references to the 65,000 ton carrier, to carrier-operated jet aircraft, and to the new big carrier aircraft that the Fast Carrier Task Force of World War II was not the climax of naval aviation, but rather a highlight in naval aviation's continuing progress?"[16]

On 19 August the studio answered Eller, assuring him that it would emphasize the evolutionary nature of naval aviation. Capt. Harry Sears, the new director of the Public Information Division, wrote to the studio on 14 September to introduce himself and express his interest in the project. He cited some minor problems with the script that the studio should correct and said that Capt. S. G. Mitchell, the technical adviser the Navy had assigned to the film, would be available full-time during the shooting aboard a carrier for approximately thirty days and then could provide part-time help.[17] Daves completed the final script on 22 October, only three days before he began location shooting in San Diego. Despite Daves's creative differences with MacDougall's work, all of the 1945 versions, as well as Daves's final script, portray the struggle of Navy officers committed to the development of naval aviation. As the representative fictional officer, Gary Cooper flies off the first Navy carrier, the *Langley,* in the early 1920s. He so strongly advocates the need for a carrier fleet that his career is sidetracked in the 1930s. During the war, he commands a carrier and retires as an admiral, receiving a departing salute from Navy jets flying over one of the new 60,000-ton floating airfields.

The fictional story provides a framework around which the film portrays the development of naval air power. *Task Force* may lack the dramatic impact of military films that focus on people trying to survive during battle, but the combat footage, superbly integrated into the second half of the film, provides a real sense of carrier warfare. More important from the Navy's perspective, the film repeats the message that James Thach and other officers had presented to the filmmakers during the time the studio took to complete *Task Force*: Aircraft carriers won the war in the Pacific and could protect the nation against any future aggression.

Apart from the historical and combat footage, the Navy did provide material assistance to Warner Brothers. In addition to shooting several sequences ashore in San Diego, the film crew and one hundred tons of studio equipment went aboard the USS *Antietam* for twenty-four days of shooting, using the entire carrier as a set. Although the filmmakers had access to all unrestricted parts of the ship, the *Antietam* followed its normal training operations, with shooting fitted into the carrier's schedule. With the captain's permission, the ship's crew appeared as extras, performing their normal duties. As a bonus, the Navy provided an unintentional example of kamikaze warfare when antiaircraft fire hit its target and the flaming drone skimmed over the bridge and crashed into the ocean close to the *Antietam*.[18]

Famed Hollywood pilot Paul Mantz provided three antique Navy planes for the historical sequences, aboard the carrier and in the air, which Daves later integrated into the footage he had acquired. After the filming aboard the *Antietam,* which represented several carriers, including the *Saratoga, Yorktown,* and *Franklin,* the cast and crew went aboard the small escort carrier *Bairoko* to shoot the early-day *Langley* sequences. Back in Long Beach, Daves shot the movie's climactic scene in which the retiring Cooper receives the salute of the jet fly-by over the new carriers.[19]

Finally, in August 1949, five and a half years after initiating the project, Warner Brothers screened *Task Force* in Washington for the Navy. Although the service denied any role in the decision, the studio advanced the movie's release date several months to late September so that *Task Force* appeared at the height of the Navy's congressional battle with the Air Force over appropriations for bombers versus aircraft carriers.[20]

Anticipating the contemporary debate, the film's naval aviation characters argue with a newspaper publisher, senators, Army officers, and battleship admirals about the efficacy of carriers over other military hardware. In one scene, a senator observes that the service lost four carriers in the first six months of the war. In response, a Navy flier asks, "Is it your contention, Senator, that we should abandon airplanes, because they've been shot down, tanks, because they've been knocked out of action? We need to out-produce the enemy in planes, tanks, and aircraft carriers! The only thing wrong with carriers is that we don't have enough of them!" Later, Gary Cooper's character responds to a general's argument in favor of land-based bombers: "The General is right—*if* we have to take every Pacific Island enroute to Japan. But two dozen carriers are worth more than 200 enemy-held islands, anchored in one spot! Our carriers won't be anchored, they'll be fast moving islands from which we can launch fighters and bombers against the enemy wherever we choose!"

The film clearly represented the arguments of the advocates of naval aviation and was a tribute to the contribution naval aviation had made to victory in the Pacific. Of course, the Navy had been preaching to the converted in working with Warner Brothers. The studio had regularly demonstrated its commitment to a strong military. Daves had written scripts for *Shipmates, Shipmates Forever*, and *The Singing Marine* before directing *Destination Tokyo* and *Pride of the Marines*. Even before beginning work on *Task Force*, the director had developed a pro-Navy bias. In regularly traveling to Washington to do research for *Task Force*, Daves was simply continuing his close ties with the Navy.

At no time during the history of the Hollywood-Navy relationship did each party so positively exploit the other. Wald, MacDougall, and Daves eagerly sought suggestions about how best to portray the history of naval aviation and, not incidentally, to create a movie that would make money. As diligently, the Navy provided advice, information, combat footage, and ultimately men and equipment. Sometimes a fine line exists between propaganda and history. Carrier aviation had demonstrated its efficacy during the Pacific war. The Navy merely helped ensure that *Task Force* illustrated events that had occurred. Whether carrier aviation alone could have won the war remains debatable. But without carrier aviation providing air cover, the Army and the Marines could not have invaded the islands that provided the airfields from which B-29s blasted Japan into near submission and from which the Enola Gay and Bock's Car carried the atomic bombs to Hiroshima and Nagasaki.

Message aside, *Task Force* became the first major postwar film made with large-scale military assistance to bring World War II to American theaters. Using extensive Navy combat footage, the movie portrayed the reality of war in ways no special-effects men could ever hope to achieve. In the dramatic highlight of the movie, a kamikaze attack on Cooper's carrier turns the ship into a flaming wreck. Benefiting from color footage taken aboard the USS *Franklin*, the most extensively damaged U.S. ship in World War II to return to port, the filmmakers gave the audience a sense of the real horror of combat. The flaming ship was actually burning, not a skillfully done special effect. The dead men could not get up and walk away. The wounded could not wash away their burns as actors could their makeup. Consequently, *Task Force* had an emotional impact unequaled in most war films.

Despite the filmmakers' desire to also make *Task Force* historically and visually accurate, it contains some obvious bloopers. During the film's Battle of Midway sequence, Navy dive-bombers struck first, although torpedo planes actually made the initial attack on the Japanese carriers. A returning dive-bomber approaches the *Yorktown*, with one landing gear missing. The plane that crashes on deck has both wheels fully extended. Moreover, not only historians, but film critics questioned the accuracy of the movie's presentation of the evolution of naval aviation. Bosley Crowther observed, "Intra-department resistance, on the whole, was nowhere near as strong nor as obtuse in running down the airplane as it is here made to seem. . . . And certainly this picture's implication that a large aircraft carrier program was not accepted by the government until after the Battle of Midway is wrong."[21]

Nevertheless, Crowther felt that when *Task Force* reaches the World War II battles, "it springs into vivid, thrilling life. For not only has Delmer Daves, the author and director, filled it with eye-filling documentary detail but he has used combat footage generously to capture the tension of battle and the crash of disaster on carrier decks." The reviewer did pinpoint the problem that Daves had had in trying to merge history and fiction into a unified film: "Perhaps—and one can't avoid comparisons—he has not got the 'feel' of carriers as well as it was got in *The Fighting Lady,* that great documentary made during the war."[22]

Nor did Daves get it so well as the filmmakers did in putting together *Victory at Sea,* the television documentary series that encompassed the entire range of naval warfare above, below, and on the oceans in World War II. Not concerned with romance or message or the time constraints of a feature film, the series used to full advantage the same combat footage to which Daves had access. Whether this freedom enabled *Victory at Sea* to better represent naval aviation in World War II is debatable: a documentary is still a director's representation of reality, rather than reality, and so no more real than a feature film.

In any case, the Navy's arguments for building more aircraft carriers did not go unchallenged, even within the service itself, particularly when proponents of a new technology were beginning to make themselves heard. John Thach had looked in the right direction when he predicted that atomic rockets would probably come from "under water vessels that cannot be picked up by radar." However, he erred in describing these ships as carriers "of the future." In fact, while Navy aviators were testifying before Congress in favor of more carriers, submariners were pointing out the limitations of carrier-launched planes as well as the vulnerability of carriers themselves and offering missile-carrying submarines capable of delivering an atomic strike at an enemy's heartland as an alternative weapons-delivery system.[23]

Naturally, the advocates of the new technology sought to put their arguments before the American people. While the 1950 movie *The Flying Missile* contained none of the enduring images of *Task Force,* it did bring to the screen the debate over the relative merits of submarines versus aircraft carriers in the Cold War. In showing the Navy's rocket-launching submarines, *The Flying Missile* explicitly acknowledged that surface ships were vulnerable to long-range rocket attack. The film showed the Navy's efforts to install German V-1 rockets on its submarines, with absorbing technical dialogue and impressive shots of ships launching rockets. While the filmmakers shot much of the footage at the Naval Air Test Missile Center at Point Mugu, California, the fictional story set on this stage remained a hackneyed melodrama. It sagged "under the frantic behavior and facial stoicism" of Glenn Ford, who sells his vision of missile-launching submarines to his superiors in Washington. Before he succeeds, however, he suffers debilitating injuries and loses his true-blue crew chief in a test-firing accident. In the end, he returns to his boat to direct the climactic and successful launch of a rocket.[24]

The Navy apparently cared less that the missile theoretically hit an aircraft carrier than that the movie showed how a submarine could successfully launch a long-range rocket. The manner in which Ford convinces the Navy to try his idea also implies that the military had learned to consider new technology, in contrast to the opposition Billy Mitchell met when he tried to sell air power in the 1920s. Despite the demonstrated potential of submarine-launched missiles, however, carriers remained the Navy's primary attack force, and advocates of naval aviation pushed their vision of combat into movies whenever possible during the 1950s.

Attempting to duplicate the box-office appeal of *Task Force,* its first imitator, *Flat Top,* lacked the clarity and insights that distinguished Daves's film. Instead, *Flat Top* relied on spectacular aerial battle scenes and contrived dramatic tension between the characters to attract an audience. As escapist entertainment the story enjoyed a limited popularity, but as drama it lacked the power of *Task Force.*

When producer Walter Mirisch wrote to the Navy on 21 July 1950, he explained that for some time he had wanted to make a film about "the exploits of an aircraft carrier during the last war." Having come up with an idea, he asked for "an expression of the Navy's attitude" to the project since he recognized the "inestimable" value of its assistance. With the Navy's help and footage from wartime Navy documentaries such as *The Fighting Lady,* Mirisch concluded, "another great tribute can be paid to America's Naval fighting units and a splendid service motion picture can be presented to the American public."[25]

Answering for Baruch's office on 2 August, Maj. Clair Towne sent the producer the Pentagon's *Guide for Obtaining the Cooperation of the National Military Establishment (Department of Defense) on the Production of Motion Pictures.* He assured Mirisch that his office "is always ready and anxious to do everything possible to assist in the production of motion pictures that accurately portray the Services, that are in the best interests of National Defense and the public good, and that conform with the usually accepted standards of your industry with regard to propriety and dignity." Observing that film had no equal "for telling the public about the Services," he said that once the Defense Department and the Navy approved the script for assistance, the producer would have "little if any" problems in obtaining the necessary combat footage.[26] Towne did warn Mirisch that the outbreak of the Korean War might cause problems in providing physical cooperation, but that so far the Pentagon had not had to turn down requests for assistance already approved.[27]

In response, Mirisch sent Towne a brief summary of his proposed story, explaining the film would focus on a group of men stationed aboard an aircraft carrier "and by following the exploits of the carrier, portray the conditions, the problems, the heroism and the achievement of men and machines." He then requested access to a naval air station and a carrier, if possible. Although he hoped "to photograph certain aerial action as might be called for in the script," he thought he might be able to obtain the action from stock footage.[28]

Initially, the Pentagon and the Navy were willing to provide the requested cooperation. On 25 September Towne wrote Mirisch, "It goes without saying that the Departments of Defense and Navy are interested in the project, and would do everything they were able to do to make the production of your picture possible." The director of the Navy's Public Information Division, Capt. Roy Benson, advised Baruch on 28 September that it "would be delighted to see the subject picture produced. There is an urgent need for publicity concerning the Naval Aviation Cadet Program."[29]

With the promise of assistance, Mirisch set about to secure a script, and on 20 October he told Towne that his company had hired Steve Fisher, the original screenwriter for *Destination Tokyo,* and a former Navy man to prepare the story. After reading the initial effort when it arrived at the end of December, Towne advised Benson that the script was "a good starting point in the development of an acceptable story about an aircraft carrier in World War II." He acknowledged the need to make many technical corrections before the script would measure up to the required standard of accuracy and authenticity, but "it is believed that the basic story structure could be preserved."[30]

The Navy had an entirely different reaction. The Office of the CNO told Alan Brown in the Office of Information that the script "would be completely unsatisfactory." After trying to make some revisions, it realized that "the corrections that would be necessary would so destroy the continuity of the story that it would require a new and fresh start." The CNO's office particularly objected to a "psychological" portion that created "overdrawn and certainly unrealistic conflicts" between senior and junior pilots as well as between replacement pilots and the more experienced fliers. It recommended that the Navy not approve the script until the "obvious objections are corrected or deleted."[31]

Brown told Towne that a meeting between the writer and the Navy might well produce an entirely acceptable script, and Towne told Mirisch of the Navy's comments and suggestion to have the writer come to Washington to meet with "selected Navy Officers of suitable background" to help resolve the objections. Mirisch agreed that the problems could "very easily be corrected without impairing our story line and direction" but asked to have the Navy's objections forwarded to him.[32]

Mirisch was to require almost a year to produce a script the Navy would approve. Ultimately, to help meet the Navy's criticisms, he hired retired Adm. Thomas Dykers, a famed submariner, as a technical adviser, to provide "help and guidance" to the filmmakers. Dykers had served aboard a carrier during the war and after reading the current script advised Towne that he found it "still far from acceptable" but that Mirisch had "been very good about changes." He thought the Navy would find the final version "okay" since it "will appeal very strongly to the teenage kids which is actually the group the Navy should try to interest in a picture of this kind."[33]

His prediction proved accurate when Towne informed Mirisch on 5 January 1952 that although he had not received a final reaction from the Navy, "indications are that the official reception to this version is much better than anything submitted heretofore." Under the circumstances, and because the situation in Korea seemed more stable, Towne suggested the producer prepare a list of what "you figure you would need in order to make the production of an accurate and authentic picture possible." He warned that the Navy probably could not provide a carrier on the West Coast "anytime within the foreseeable future," but Towne felt "practically certain" that the Navy could make a carrier available at Pensacola.[34]

In fact, when Mirisch requested the use of a carrier in February, he found that the Navy had not made a final decision as to availability. Following a call to Baruch on the twentieth, one of the producer's aides wrote, "As you know, we have gone to considerable expense getting the script in shape so that it would be acceptable to the Navy." He pointed out that the filmmakers were "in a position where the only thing keeping us from going into production is a decision by the Navy as to when and under what conditions we can get on a carrier." He also stressed the need to do some filming aboard ship for scenes not in the archives, and he asked Baruch to expedite matters.[35]

On 13 March the Navy informed Baruch that it would allow a small film crew to go aboard the *Princeton* to photograph the needed scenes. With that hurdle cleared, Mirisch finally went into production on *Flat Top*, and on 7 July 1952 the company advised Towne that it had finished editing the movie. He also said the filmmakers thought they had "a very excellent picture." After the Navy finally screened *Flat Top* in early September, Towne told Mirisch that the Navy found the picture justified the cooperation extended and did not object to its release.[36]

In beginning work later in the year on a project that became *The Annapolis Story*, Mirisch sent Adm. Lewis Parks, the new Chief of Information, reviews of *Flat Top*, pointing out that the reaction to the film "has been uniformly excellent. . . ." Whether the movie merited the long effort required to make it may be questioned since it became simply another exposition of an aviator's life aboard a carrier in wartime, with the characters assuming stereotypical roles. In this incarnation of the aloof leader, Sterling Hayden portrayed "the taciturn commander, not a martinet but a strict disciplinarian who knows his job." He has the task of teaching his new executive officer "that a big brother attitude toward men does not develop good combat flyers." Resentment against Hayden's leadership style naturally disappears as "the logic of the skipper's methods are proven in combat." The *Hollywood Reporter* reviewer appreciated that *Flat Top* had "no false heroics, not any incredible climaxes" that convert his executive officer into a believer. Still, he found the film an "action-packed saga . . . that maintains solid interest throughout" its length with the help of "an excellent cast, attractively tinted photography and spectacular air combat shots which are skillfully and smoothly worked into the dominating feature of the story." With the focus on "lusty action" rather than the men's personal lives, as the reviewer concluded, "the result is an engrossing film that never lets down in tenseness."[37]

Daily Variety also saw *Flat Top* as a "fundamental war story" and felt that "neither the direction nor the Steve Fisher screen story rise above familiar lines." Still, the reviewer also found the film "action-packed," with the combat footage helping to "insure authenticity." He felt these images conveyed "excitement that the make-believe finds difficult to compete with and adds a tremendous wallop to the production. Dog fights between Zeroes and Navy planes, the crescendo of the carrier's protective weapons, crashing planes and bursting bombs are among the factors putting an action kick into the footage." However, he recognized that the same combat footage was used "too often."[38]

The filmmakers also repeated the opening of *Wing and a Prayer*, with its new flier ignoring a wave off when he lands for the first time aboard the flattop. As Ameche's character had done in the earlier carrier story, Hayden's immediately grounds the young pilot. While commanders must demand strict adherence to regulations and discipline wayward pilots, both plot lines ignore that during wartime, the Navy needed every available flier.

Likewise imitating *Task Force*, the opening sequence of *Flat Top* establishes a connection between the new, Korean War jet-fighter era and World War II carrier planes. The film begins in the contemporary period with Hayden in the flight-control center watching a flight of jet planes land aboard his carrier. While he tells a fellow officer that the scene reminds him of his World War II flying days, the screen dissolves to show an aircraft carrier in the Pacific in 1944, as the new squadron is landing.

The pilots' resentment of Hayden for his grounding of their comrade and for his strict training methods traces the same path as *Wing and a Prayer, Twelve O'Clock High,* and *Sands of Iwo Jima.* These cinematic clashes of wills between superiors and subordinates may lack plausibility under the wartime conditions in which they take place, but filmmakers were unwilling to sacrifice the dramatic tensions inherent in these confrontations. Instead of understanding that their commanders were simply trying to help them survive, the fliers act like spoiled children, and some die for their stubbornness. Like the other films of its ilk, *Flat Top* documents how the men's contribution to one of the climactic invasions of the war vindicates Hayden's strong leadership and training methods. Having instilled in his fliers the need to work as a team to survive in combat, Hayden can turn over command of his unit to someone younger.

Coming full circle, *Flat Top* then returns to the contemporary time to show one of Hayden's World War II fliers, now in a command position, grounding one of the new jet pilots for ignoring a wave off from the *same* landing officer, in the *same* World War II scene, that opened the film. Lack of originality notwithstanding, *Flat Top* served as the connection between the Navy's involvement in the last war and the one it was currently fighting.

The Navy and Korea

By 1952, "the police action" on the Korean peninsula had begun to provide stories that filmmakers could turn into war movies. Combat on land and in the air had quickly inspired the story of the Air Force's close air support of the Army in Howard Hughes's *One Minute to Zero* and the portrayal of the Marines' desperate retreat from the Yalu in *Retreat! Hell!*

From the start of the war the Navy had provided sea lift and coastal bombardment as well as some close air support of ground troops and interdiction of interior supply routes. While the aerial operations seemed to offer filmmakers the only possibility of dramatic stories, the two stories about the Navy's participation in the Korean War that reached the screen while fighting continued featured the submarine service, even though no submarine would fire a torpedo during the conflict.[1]

Time found *Submarine Command* little more than "a flat distillation of most of the underwater plots that Hollywood has been siphoning into movie houses for decades." Even the cruel dilemma at the heart of the film, the decision to sacrifice the lives of one or more men for the good of the many, had recently appeared in *Operation Pacific,* the first submarine story to appear since the end of World War II. In that film, John Wayne's character must leave his wounded captain on the conning tower to save the submarine, much as his character does in *Sands of Iwo Jima* when he refuses to let his unit attempt to rescue a wounded comrade in the jungle.[2]

In *Submarine Command,* on the last day of World War II, William Holden as the executive officer of the *Tiger Shark* orders the submarine to crash-dive to escape a Japanese plane, although his wounded captain and the ship's quartermaster remain on the conning tower. A hearing board and the captain's family exonerate him of any responsibility for the deaths, but Holden struggles with the burden of his actions during mundane routine of the peacetime Navy. Returning to his old submarine as its captain at the outbreak of the Korean War, Holden performs heroically while rescuing American prisoners. Although he loses his boat, his actions finally bring him peace of mind.

Submarine Command lacks unique visual or dramatic appeal. Most bluntly, the *Hollywood Citizen-News* wrote that the film "lacks imagination in writing and directing, and inspiration in the acting department. It boils down, in the final analysis, to an oft-repeated tale of fighting men. The cast is different—but everything else is the same, including the heroine being reunited at the end with her estranged mate when he finds out she's going to have a baby." Even the film's main assets, the action sequences, depict nothing "that hasn't been seen before."[3]

Unlike the submarine combat films that came before and after *Submarine Command*, its climactic rescue sequence does not contain the drama associated with attacks on enemy shipping or prolonged depth-charging. Instead, the film tried to create interest through the psychological conflict within Holden's character, and as long as it did that, Crowther in the *New York Times* felt that *Submarine Command* was "perpetually on the verge of an intriguing surprise." He described the screenplay as "a compact and levelheaded job" and the direction as "naturalistic." He also found "the ways of submariners and the atmosphere of Navy life, both afloat and ashore . . . represented with remarkable plausibility and power. In this reviewer's recollection there has never been a more solid and substantial comprehension of 'Navy' in a Hollywood fiction film, thanks to responsible direction and actuality shooting around a Navy yard."[4] As he pointed out, however, "the story goes sky high at the end in a purely theatrical blowout with the old ship in the Korean War. And also the psychological tension is completely and dismally relaxed in a blood-and-thunder adventure that has the officer recapturing his morale. It is disappointing to see a picture come so close and miss."[5]

Torpedo Alley, which appeared at the end of 1952, did not even come close, despite telling virtually the same story. Whereas *Submarine Command* had plausibility, if stale, its clone lacked credibility, even though it also received full cooperation from the submarine service. The problems began with the title, which in no way conveys the nature of the story. Moreover, its similarity to *Submarine Command,* as well as its using bits of stories from earlier submarine films, assured that *Torpedo Alley* would contain no new insights about warfare below the surface or the men who volunteered to fight in the confines of underseas craft.

Apart from the brief postwar scene that opens *Submarine Command,* the early sequences in both films are almost indistinguishable. The submarines are performing the same picket duty, rescuing downed fliers in the final hours of

World War II. In contrast to the visualization of the reason for Holden's anguish, *Torpedo Alley* never fully explains the cause of the hero's deep and paralyzing anguish, even though his guilty conscience drives the story. Mark Stevens, a famed carrier pilot whom the submarine picks out of the water with one of his crew, talks vaguely about losing his plane and men because he had frozen. Although he says he was not shot down, his crewman dies almost immediately from a bullet wound. Blaming himself, Stevens develops a guilt complex that begins to paralyze him even though he never amplifies his self-recrimination.

During the trip back to Pearl Harbor, Stevens acquires a liking for life aboard the submarine, concluding that officers do not have to assume the unique responsibility that a pilot has, which the captain refutes. In Hawaii, Stevens takes a strong interest in Dorothy Malone, a Navy nurse and long-suffering girlfriend of one of the submarine officers. With the war over, Stevens soon finds himself jobless after failing to capitalize on his fame, and he decides to rejoin the Navy as a submariner.

Stevens's schooling at New London allows the filmmakers to portray the training of submariners and the operations of undersea craft as well as any of the movies Hollywood had made at the submarine base. Unfortunately, this documentary-like portrayal and Stevens's relatively unsuccessful pursuit of Malone, now stationed at New London, constitute the only content of the film until the last few minutes set in Korean waters. Now an officer aboard a sub commanded by the captain who rescued him, Stevens volunteers to go ashore with a raiding party to blow up a railroad tunnel.

Not only does the film fail to convey any of this business with conviction, it does not explain why the Navy would accept a former pilot with obvious psychological problems, in his early thirties, as a submariner. Notwithstanding Hollywood's casting of older actors for roles aboard submarines, the undersea service has always been the bailiwick of younger men. Since the Navy and the military as a whole were undergoing a massive reduction in force during the interwar period, the submarine service would have had no reason to welcome Stevens into its ranks. At the most, the Navy would have perhaps allowed Stevens to resume flying.

The end of *Torpedo Alley* breaks the limits of dramatic license and originality when it has Stevens, another officer, and two enlisted men play raiders. *Crash Dive* had portrayed a similar, if fanciful, operation, and as a lark a submarine captain had indeed landed a raiding party on Japanese soil to blow up a railroad bridge near the close of World War II. Moreover, *Submarine Command* and the 1950 20th Century *Frogmen* had already portrayed Navy special-forces operatives specifically trained for demolition work. In the real world, submariners would deliver the frogmen to their assignments, not undertake actual raids, for which they had no training or explosives.

Consequently, the incursion lacks any plausibility. The men go ashore in broad daylight and detonate their explosives at the tunnel's mouth rather than inside where they would cause the most damage. A Korean artillery shell kills the two enlisted men as they reach their rubber life raft but does not deflate the boat. Worst of all, the captain and crew of the submarine watch the North Koreans fire all manner of weapons at the officers paddling out to sea but do not use the boat's deck gun to cover the retreat. Instead, the submarine submerges, and the captain watches the men's progress through the periscope until he finally maneuvers his boat under the raft so that the men can grab hold. In a scene imitating Syd Chaplin's ride on a conning tower in *Submarine Pilot,* the submarine carries the officers beyond the range of the North Korean guns before surfacing to complete the recovery. Aboard a Navy hospital ship for treatment of his wounds, Stevens discovers Malone serving as a nurse. Having regained his courage and sense of responsibility in combat, he now wins Malone's hand.

What benefit *Torpedo Alley* provided the Navy and the submarine service remains difficult to determine since it portrays operations outside the domain of submariners in a war in which submarines played a negligible role. Moreover, with the Navy about to enter the nuclear age, the portrayal of training and operations was about to become outdated. At the most, both submarine films made some connection between the past war and the current war, but without providing meaningful comments about the submarine service's experiences in either conflict.

In contrast, two films about naval aviation during the Korean War contained exciting images and powerful drama, while also raising serious questions about why man engaged in combat and the reason the United States became involved in Korea. *Men of the Fighting Lady* and *Bridges at Toko-ri* differed about as much in form and content as had *Submarine Command* and *Torpedo Alley,* since both came from the same writer, James Michener, who had traveled aboard an aircraft carrier off the Korean peninsula during the height of the air war and had talked with the fliers who later appeared, some with their real names lightly disguised, in the films. The problems MGM and Paramount had in bringing the movies to the screen grew out of their similar stories.

Michener had reported on his sojourn aboard the USS *Essex,* of Task Force 77, off the North Korean coast in a 10 May 1952 article in the *Saturday Evening Post* titled "The Forgotten Heroes of Korea." While the words and sentiment came from Michener, the Navy had done its job well in providing him access to the officers and men fighting the unpopular war. The author of the Pulitzer Prize–winning *Tales of the South Pacific* began his article: "We forget. Even those of us who know better forget that today, in the barren wastes of Korea, American men are dying with a heroism never surpassed in our history. Because they are so few, we forget that they contribute so much." However, of all the Americans fighting in Korea, Michener said he had "a special salute for the naval pilots who fly from our fast carriers, taking the assault to the communists over deadly seas and in the face of heavy gunfire, returning later over the dark ocean to land upon their small and heaving carrier deck." Although he considered Navy pilots no braver than Air Force pilots or Marines dug into dismal hillsides, he thought "their work is peculiar and demands an absolute kind of courage."[6]

Michener justified his belief by describing the actions of the men he had met. These included Cdr. Marshall Beebe, an ace in both World War II and the current conflict; Cdr. Paul Gray, whom the North Koreans shot down five times; and Lt. Sam Murphey, who crash-landed his plane and ran four miles with communist soldiers in hot pursuit until a helicopter finally rescued him. He described the experiences of pilots who ditched in 35-degree water, in which life expectancy is no more than twenty minutes, and survived. He also wrote about the helicopter pilots who effected the rescues as well as about officers who died in the crashes of their planes.[7]

Michener reported that the fliers of the *Essex* were coming home, but "other men like them, reserves yanked from their homes and jobs, will be coming out here on other carriers to fight this lonesome, forgotten war. And, they too, will be men far from eager for war—yet they will fight it with the same selfless courage of those who have gone before, for the same reasons. We owe them a debt we can never pay them—and above all we owe them remembrance and support."[8]

Of such stuff may come significant movies. Recognizing that, MGM wrote to Clair Towne on 19 June 1952, expressing interest in making a movie based on Michener's article: "If the reaction is favorable, we would like to register priority and request cooperation" based on an approved script. Towne responded immediately that the Navy had reviewed the story, and the "consensus is that the *Saturday Evening Post* story would provide an excellent basis for a motion picture about the Navy Carrier Force employed in the Korean conflict, and the pilots who fly our Navy aircraft." He also said the service would issue the studio a priority, pending the submission of a story outline and production plans.[9]

This became a difficult task for the studio, which initially experienced a delay in obtaining releases from the men who were to be identified by name in the movie. In addition, MGM decided to use material from a second *Saturday Evening Post* article, "The Case of the Blind Pilot." As a result, the producers requested an extension of its priority. Towne answered on the twentieth, assuring the studio the Navy would not "become too deeply involved" with any project that would conflict with MGM's priority. However, he noted that carrier aviation had generated considerable interest among other studios. Towne thought that "plenty of room" existed for more than one aviation film but said Baruch's office would protect MGM's priority "for a reasonable length of time." Still, he asked the studio to submit a story outline as soon as possible so that the Pentagon could decide on the scope of the priority.[10]

By then, MGM actually had a script, dated 19 February 1953, on the way to the Pentagon. On 11 March, Towne informed the studio that everyone had a favorable reaction to the story but cited some technical problems. In particular, he said drinking on the carrier "must be handled carefully to preclude the possibility of giving the wrong impression. Drinking aboard ship is strictly forbidden, although the medical officer may prescribe the 1/2 ounce dose of medicinal brandy as a stimulant in cases of fatigue or nerves, or whatever other condition indicates this treatment."[11]

MGM agreed to make all the requested changes, and on 5 May Towne informed the studio his office was taking steps to authorize cooperation. However, a month later the studio told the Pentagon that it was postponing production of "Panther Squadron 8," the new title of the project, until 1 October, asking for and receiving an extension of its priority.[12] Meanwhile, James Michener had taken the stories he had accumulated aboard the *Essex* and turned them into *The Bridges at Toko-ri*, a short novel about Harry Brubaker, a young lawyer from Denver, called back into the Navy to again fly jets off a carrier.

★

Despite his bitterness and griping, Brubaker becomes one of the two best pilots aboard his ship. Opening with an account of carrier launch and landing operations, Michener then describes Brubaker's ditching, rescue, and meeting with the task force admiral, who follows the actions of pilots of the age his son would have been had he not died during the Japanese attack on Pearl Harbor. The admiral's arguments to Brubaker about the necessity of U.S. involvement in the Korean War becomes Michener's opportunity to explain the unpopular conflict to the American people. Following a reunion in Japan with his wife and daughters, Brubaker returns to war and the effort to destroy the bridges at Toko-ri. Although he and his men succeed in their mission, Brubaker's plane is hit during an attack on the secondary target. He successfully crash-lands, but after North Korean bullets destroy the rescue helicopter and kill its crew, Brubaker finds himself alone in a ditch. Michener writes that at the very instant an enemy soldier fires the fatal shot, the lawyer from Denver finally understands "in some fragmentary way the purpose of his being in Korea. But the brief knowledge served no purpose, for the next instant he plunged face down into the ditch."

Random House purchased the novel, and *Life* magazine published a condensed version in its 6 July 1953 issue. In short order, four studios inquired about the Navy's willingness to assist a movie based on *Bridges at Toko-ri*. Of these, only Paramount pursued the matter. On 7 July Robert Denton, the studio's Washington representative, called Towne to discuss possible cooperation. After Towne told him the story would probably conflict with MGM's priority,

Denton advised the Pentagon that Paramount would negotiate to purchase the novel if the Navy decided that no conflict actually existed.[13]

Denton then requested a meeting with Towne and Admiral Parks to discuss the service's position on the DoD priority. After the conference, on the eighth, Parks agreed that if Baruch's office believed MGM should have protection until it had completed its film, the Navy would concur. In turn, Denton was satisfied that if Paramount bought the book, it could apply for assistance once "the way was clear."[14] As Towne summarized in a memorandum for the record, MGM was relying on the Pentagon's assurance that it had a priority on its project and "strongly believes that there is definite and serious conflict between *Bridges at Toko-ri* and their story." He noted that MGM intended to go into production in late August or early September and had its final script completed and stock footage selected. While the Pentagon would be "unable to entertain" any request for assistance on a story based on the novel from any studio, Towne concluded that *The Bridges at Toko-ri* "considered by itself, and without the element of conflict with a prior commitment, would undoubtedly be accorded a favorable reaction, and would find us agreeable to extending preliminary cooperation on the development of a screenplay, and looking toward eventual approval of the Shooting Script for cooperation on production."[15]

Once he read the *Life* version of the novel, however, Don Baruch expressed some reservations about Michener's story. In his own memorandum, on 10 July, he noted that the story contained several points "that would not be in the best interest of Defense nor the Navy to have shown in the film if & when it is made." These included the portrayal of Beer Belly, the landing signal officer (LSO), drunk at a bar, the admiral's sailing his task force too close to shore to land one last plane, a fight ashore between men of two carriers with the admiral watching, and the use of planes' props to help berth one of the carriers.[16] With little apparent concern about MGM's existing priority or story problems, Paramount almost immediately decided to purchase the screen rights for $100,000. However, in a detailed memorandum for the record on 29 July Towne summarized recent events and reiterated DoD policy as it applied to the current situation.[17]

He wrote that Baruch's office had received word that despite Admiral Parks's apparent understanding of the priorities policy, he had met with Paramount executives on his recent trip to the West Coast and agreed to allow a studio research team to take a trip aboard a carrier and perhaps do some filming at sea. Towne had also learned from one of the officers in Parks's office that an MGM executive had told the admiral that his studio had no objection to the Navy's going ahead with preliminary cooperation with Paramount. Towne noted that his office "could be relieved of its responsibility to protect MGM's priority" only if the studio would state in writing that it waived the priority. In answer to Towne's inquiry, Orville Crouch, the MGM representative in

Washington, confirmed that his studio had told Parks that the Navy could assist Paramount but emphatically added, "By all means NO! We will NOT waive our priority."[18]

Towne then told the Navy Office of Information that the service "was out of order to extend any cooperation to Paramount, either in the form of preliminary assistance or even as encouragement, until MGM's picture is completed." He also asked if the Navy had considered that "in no sense of the word" did *Bridges at Toko-ri* contain "an acceptable story as it stands" and made it clear that once Paramount submitted a script, the Pentagon would make appropriate requests for changes. Until then, he stressed that if the Navy worked with the studio in any way, it was violating DoD policy on priorities and "weakening our chances of having proper changes made in the story later on."[19]

Towne also addressed the still-sensitive issue of who was actually going to make the decisions about assistance: the Department of Defense, as envisioned under unification, or the individual services, as they had done previously. He took the Defense Department position that "it is not the function of the Navy Department, nor of the Chief of Information of the Navy, to operate with studios on consideration of motion pictures for cooperation, or on cooperation, outside the supervision of the Office of Public Information, Department of Defense." While the officers serving Parks would understand this, Towne recognized that "it is highly doubtful that this matter will be brought to his attention."[20]

Nevertheless, Towne felt strongly this should be done "because, although he is highly cooperative, and always has been, with this officer (Towne), he may unknowingly or otherwise, cause confusion and unnecessary problems, if he continues to go outside the authority of his office, on this or other projects." Parks had done more than promise studios Navy assistance during his West Coast trip. He had also discussed the possibility of creating a Navy public-affairs office in Los Angeles "similar to that now in operation illegally by the Army" so that the Navy could establish more direct contacts with the film industry.[21]

Despite opposition from Baruch's office, each service was to establish its own public-affairs operation in Los Angeles. The offices never have had authority to approve requests for cooperation. Instead, they have provided technical advice to filmmakers and acted as liaison between the studios and the Pentagon. In fact, the process by which a studio submitted its scripts and requested assistance never followed an established pattern. It sometimes asked the Los Angeles office to send the script to Baruch, submitted it through its Washington representative, or even mailed it directly to the Pentagon. After reading the script, Baruch directed it to the appropriate service or services for consideration and recommendations. Although he and the Defense Department could never force a service to assist a production, his office did have the authority to reject a service's decision to cooperate in the making of a film.

Despite Parks's discussions with Paramount and MGM, Baruch's office did retain the right to protect a studio's priority on a project. However, in the case of "Panther Squadron 8," the issue soon became moot. On 30 July Russell Holman, Paramount's Eastern Production Manager, wrote to Towne, "respectfully" requesting cooperation on the film version of Michener's novel. He said the studio planned "to produce the story as a very important feature motion picture" but that without assistance Paramount could obviously not do full justice to the "Navy achievements and heroism in the Korean War." Holman acknowledged that MGM's priority prevented the Navy from assisting Paramount until the completion of "Panther Squadron 8." However, he understood that the studio could receive earlier cooperation on some phases of production if MGM would confirm its verbal waiver in writing. He also asked for Navy comments about how to turn the novel into a screenplay the Pentagon would accept.[22]

Ultimately, MGM permitted Paramount to receive immediate Navy assistance on the condition it would not release *The Bridges at Toko-ri* until six months after the opening of "Panther Squadron 8." With that, each rendition of Michener's experiences aboard the *Essex* went its own way.[23] During the next several months MGM continued to send script revisions to the Navy and received suggestions for changes. Given the filmmakers' efforts to remain faithful to the actual events, the landing of the blind pilot aboard the carrier came under particular scrutiny. In real life, Howard Thayer had talked Ken Schecter down to a safe landing on an emergency landing strip in South Korea. Schecter had decided not to lower his landing gear—which the Navy said "was perfectly correct, as in a wheels down landing under these conditions he could have been killed by going off the runway after having landed safely." Since the script called for Schecter to land on a carrier, Navy pilots said the blinded flier "would actually be safer to come in with his landing gear down," and the film portrayed the landing this way.[24]

Did this stretch the limits of dramatic license? It clearly fictionalized an actual event, but it did capture the essence of the drama, courage, and skill that surrounded Schecter's safe landing. Otherwise, the screenplay stayed close to the stories Michener had written, even using real names for many of the characters, including Michener himself.

Finally, on 15 September Towne informed MGM that its most recent script had received a "very favorable" reaction. The Navy felt the studio had "expended great time and effort to recognize the recommendations of Departments of Defense and Navy on this project and [had] made every change which was considered necessary in order to assure the required degree of accuracy and authenticity." Consequently, he said the script qualified for all the assistance necessary to make the production possible.[25]

Producer Henry Berman later observed, "Any time you glorify a service, that's just wonderful. You can have anything they can afford to give you." In this case, "anything" included the use of two aircraft carriers and other assorted equipment and the assignment of Paul Gray, one of the heroes in Michener's article, as technical adviser. Harry Burns, author of "The Case of the Blind Pilot," and Ken Schecter also advised director Andrew Marton and the actors about Schecter's landing.[26]

First, Marton, his crew, and principal members of the cast sailed aboard the *Oriskany* from 17 to 21 August, taking shots of carrier operations and of the actors in authentic settings. Later, the company filmed aboard the *Princeton*, docked at San Diego, to complete a re-creation of a helicopter rescue of a downed pilot. Then the Navy provided jet mock-ups during the shooting of the interiors and cockpit scenes on the soundstage.[27]

In fact, the jet fighters, not the characters, became the stars of the film. Marton said he had intended this "because I loved those machines. They did marvelous things, the flying was superb." He felt the Navy loved his picture even though it had no sentimentality in it: "I went out of my way to show just hard-bitten soldiers doing a job they hated."[28]

This approach became the film's virtue as well as its shortcoming. *Men of the Fighting Lady* lacks a beginning, middle, or end, or characters with whom audiences can empathize. Instead, Marton simply portrayed the machines of war as the heroes, using the characters as straight men. Michener and the carrier's doctor, played by Louis Calhern and Walter Pigeon, respectively, provide the connections between the aerial episodes as well as the writer's messages about the war and the men who fought it.

However dramatic the combat sequences, they were clearly stock footage, and the close-ups of the fliers were created with the Navy mock-ups and rear-screen projection. Even Thayer's guiding Schecter back to the carrier lacks real tension. Just prior to the sequence, a retread veteran who wants to come out of the war with honor, but alive, dies in a spectacular crash on the carrier deck. In contrast to the suddenness of this death, audiences already know from the article or publicity that the blinded flier lands safely, not in a fiery crash. Then, from the relief over Schecter's return, the film immediately closes with images of pilots celebrating Christmas and watching a Navy-made film of family greetings, which includes one from the dead pilot's wife and three children.

All of Michener's pontifications about the pilots' bravery or his messages about the need to fight the "Forgotten War" cannot give an upbeat feeling to the ending. From the Navy's perspective, however, *Men of the Fighting Lady* contains one of the most beneficial portrayals of carrier warfare Hollywood had made. It shows the excitement of flying off and landing on a heaving deck and the courage of pilots carrying out their missions, all receiving validation from a Pulitzer Prize–winning writer.

The Navy approved the film after MGM screened *Men of the Fighting Lady* in Washington on 10 February 1954, and most critics liked the film when it finally appeared in May 1954, eleven months after the Korean police action had ended. The *New York Times* favorably compared the film to the World War II documentary *The Fighting Lady,* saying it had "the characteristics of a re-enacted documentary film, being both literal in much of its footage and genuine in its straight dramatic line." Moreover, the story had "a good solid ring of real-ism, integrity and strength," with the actors giving "stalwart and convincing" performances. He found the movie essentially "a picture of carrier operations in the day of the jet, a beautifully color-filmed document of Navy fliers as they are today," it was "graphic and thrilling" and could "sit very proudly along-side *Battleground* and *Thirty Seconds Over Tokyo,*" two of MGM's classic war stories.[29]

The *Los Angeles Times* thought the film's facts overshadowed "fiction in its drama and suspense," with "histrionics" at a minimum, giving *Men of the Fighting Lady* "the documentary realistic touch that such a story needs. Yet there are tension, humor and pathos enough for the best fictional piece." The *Los Angeles Mirror* agreed the jet planes outperformed the actors, and com-pared to the "absorbing action scenes the disjointed story winds up as filler material, giving the actors little to work with other than the gadgets on their Mae Wests."[30]

In contrast, *Bridges at Toko-ri* uses virtually the same settings and combat incidents only as a background for the story of Harry Brubaker, who finds him-self fighting a war that he does not understand and does not want to fight. After reading the novel, George Seaton, one of the film's producers, told his partner, Bill Perlberg, that it would make "a very, very good picture." Perlberg agreed, and they had the studio buy it, not knowing then or later about the conflict with MGM's production.[31]

According to Seaton, the story attracted him because of the admiral's last speech. Knowing that Brubaker has died, the admiral muses, "Why is America lucky enough to have such men? They leave this tiny ship and fly against the enemy. Then they must seek the ship, lost somewhere on the sea. And when they find it, they have to land upon its pitching deck. Where did we get such men?" Seaton also appreciated the meaning of Brubaker's death: "The ironic ending which the exhibitors said we shouldn't do at all. I said this man has got to die in two inches of mud. The exhibitors said that you can't kill the hero. Well, we killed the hero because I think in a way it was an anti-war picture. I've always been anti-war."[32]

Despite the death, the Navy considered the film as a whole beneficial because of its portrayal of carrier aviation. But the producers still faced problems in securing Navy cooperation. On 5 August 1953, responding to Russell Holman's request for a Pentagon critique of the story, Towne enumerated parts of the book "which will have to be carefully handled in order to assure an acceptable

First Draft Script" and explained the problems both he and Baruch had previously pinpointed. He said the studio would need "care and consideration" in writing the script, but "there are no problems that are insurmountable. There are undoubtedly many solutions to each of the objectionable situations discussed with the one exception being that of the problem of Beer Barrel." Towne also said that his office and the Navy would discuss the project at any time and "suggest and recommend" revisions so that full cooperation could begin when the time came.[33]

The time had already come. Paramount had not waited to resolve the conflict with MGM before beginning to turn Michener's novel into a motion picture. With sparse character development or detailed exposition, the novel differed little from a cinematic treatment, and within two weeks screenwriter Valentine Davies transferred Michener's terse prose into an initial script. After receiving the MGM waiver, producer William Perlberg boarded the *Oriskany* at Alameda with a special studio unit for a five-day cruise to make plans for filming the story. Then on 8 September Paramount announced that Mark Robson would direct the film, with William Holden starring as Brubaker.[34]

Despite the research trip aboard the *Oriskany,* Paramount could not receive any cooperation until the Navy and the Defense Department had read and approved a final screenplay. On 14 October Bob Denton sent Towne the script, notes and related correspondence, a list of the studio's needs, and a formal request for permission to shoot background footage in and around Japan the next month. Since Holden had another commitment in the near future, Denton said that the studio wanted to start the background shooting in Japan in November and then do the principal filming at Paramount and around San Diego, beginning on 4 January 1954. He pointed out that MGM had given its waiver to help "ease Paramount's production problems," and the studio had agreed not to release *Bridges at Toko-ri* until six months after *Men of the Fighting Lady* had appeared.[35]

Denton then explained that the enclosed script did not include the modifications the writer would make after his research trip aboard the *Oriskany,* and an enclosed memo itemized "specific details which we know to be incorrect." He recognized that the assistance Paramount was requesting might change "where some scenes cannot be done one way there are always other devices that we can use. Naturally we will in general adhere to the availability and dictates of the Navy forces we work with while in Japan and surrounding waters." Denton then asked for suggestions, claiming, "*The Bridges at Toko-ri* will be one of Paramount's most important productions, and we can give you the assurance that our producers, directors, players and production crews intend to cooperate in a willing and highly effective manner so that we may bring in a picture that will be a credit to all concerned."[36]

The Pentagon had received or would receive few requests for assistance so audacious in their scope and so demanding for such immediate action as Denton's letter on behalf of Paramount. Until this request and accompanying material arrived, neither Baruch's office nor the Navy had so much as seen a script. Yet Paramount wanted to start shooting in Japan on 16 November. Moreover, the studio's idea of "background shooting" encompassed the use at sea of "a Carrier Task Force consisting of 2 Essex type carriers, 2 cruisers, 1 battleship and 14 destroyers." Recognizing that he may not have gotten things quite right, Frank Caffey, the production manager, asked that the Navy furnish the correct number of ships for that type of operation: "This is a carrier force supposedly engaged in the bombing of North Korea."[37]

To Paramount, the request probably made sense, since the filmmakers were eschewing the use of stock footage in favor of shooting all aerial and carrier scenes live. The balance of the studio's needs showed the same degree of restraint. Caffey said the crew would "confine our actual operations at sea to the deck of one carrier . . . together with one destroyer where transfer is made in breeches buoy between the carrier and the destroyer." He requested twelve Banshee jets and twelve propeller planes engaged in deck activities, takeoffs, and landings, as well as two rescue helicopters and a third helicopter to serve as a camera platform.[38]

Caffey did not request the Navy actually ditch a fighter, saying this would be done in miniature at the studio. Likewise, Paramount's special-effects department would create in miniature the attack on the bridges at Toko-ri and the crash-landing of Brubaker's plane in a rice field. However, the technical adviser, Marshall Beebe, Michener's guide during his time aboard the *Essex* and one of the heroes of his magazine piece, did locate a wrecked jet and arranged to have it transported to Thousand Oaks, California, for the filming of Brubaker's last stand.[39]

Caffey's list sounds almost as if he believed the postwar Navy existed only to re-create the Korean War for Paramount. In addition, for the aerial shots of the Banshees, traveling in formation and peeling off to dive, the production manager expected the Navy to furnish a camera plane capable of keeping up with the jets and said Paramount would "appreciate any help the Navy could give us in flying our equipment in Navy cargo planes."[40] Caffey also indicated that he would like to use men from the carrier to double for the actors and to film them doing their assigned duties during landings and takeoffs. He could limit the number of his crew aboard the carrier if he "would receive assistance when at sea in getting our cameras and equipment around the decks . . . and that a group of Navy personnel could be continuously assigned for that purpose."[41]

Assistance in the Far East was only the first phase of the cooperation Paramount expected. Back in California, during the thirty-day shooting schedule, Caffey envisioned spending two "continuous" weeks at sea aboard a carrier out of San Diego. He requested a carrier of the same class as used off Japan:

"This carrier would need to be carrying the same complement and type of planes as established on the carrier in Japanese waters." He intended to bring along a crew of seventy men and all their equipment. Again, he would need to make some aerial shots of the Banshees and wanted the Navy to supply a plane "fast enough to be used as a photographic ship." He also said it "will be necessary to change certain of the numbers and markings of the carrier used at San Diego to match those of the carrier used in Japan." Finally, if the company failed to satisfactorily complete the helicopter-rescue scene in Japanese waters, he would want the Navy to stage the operation off San Diego.[42]

Towne forwarded the material with an accompanying memo to the Chief of Information's office on 16 October and requested confirmation "to *us in writing*" that the matter of MGM's priority waiver had been resolved. Before acting on the request to operate aboard a carrier task force, Towne also said the Navy had to provide all comments about the script, "recommendations and/or objections in not more than ten days from this date." Moreover, only if Paramount agreed to comply with all requests for changes would the Pentagon consider "the feasibility of the proposed trip to Japanese waters. This trip, of course, would be at Paramount's expense, via commercial transportation, for both personnel and equipment."[43]

He then asked Slade Cutter to scrutinize the request for assistance "carefully," pointing out that some of the requirements "are completely unreasonable and impossible; others are not in accordance with established policies pertaining to the cooperation which may be extended on the production of commercial motion pictures. The whole must be considered from the standpoint of the situation in existence now and possibly in existence in the Far East at the time that the cooperation will have to be extended." Towne also suggested that the Navy meet with Baruch's office to discuss the entire project as soon as it had reviewed the material.[44]

Meanwhile, *Bridges at Toko-ri* had become a best-seller, and Seaton's willingness to accommodate the service became clear in the revised screenplay Denton submitted on 22 October, with the comment that it "incorporates many of the changes suggested to us by your office."[45] Then, on the twenty-seventh, Denton informed Towne that MGM was putting its waiver in writing for the Pentagon, and two days later the conflict in projects was resolved once and for all. More important, he said the studio was shortening its request for assistance: "We would now like, if possible, two days' aerial shots of a Task Force in operation; then, one carrier and two destroyers for eleven days at sea, or for whatever reasonable period of time such ships could be spared from their regular assignments; two carriers for the windmill dockside sequence at a Naval Base in Japan for a maximum of two days, plus the straight aerial shots mentioned in our original list. . . ."[46]

Writing to Denton on 2 November, Towne said that all concerned considered the revised screenplay "an improvement" that showed the studio had given "careful consideration" to his letter of 5 August. Several of the "sensitive" areas had become "entirely acceptable, while in certain other cases, additional attention will be required." To solve the remaining problems, Towne enclosed a list of the Navy's comments and recommendations for the studio's action and said the Navy assumed "these comments will receive due attention and that appropriate revisions will be made in the script."[47]

He added that the Navy had sent dispatches to the appropriate Far East commands, describing the required assistance and asking for comments on the ability to cooperate with the filmmakers. In the meantime, Towne explained, the basic principle governing all assistance was "that there will be no action filmed in Korea which could just as well have been shot on the West Coast. Filming in Korean waters will involve more personnel and more units of the fleet than is necessary if the scene can just as well be shot with less, or in waters outside San Diego." Everything followed from this premise, including the number of ships used and the actions portrayed.[48]

In regard to the ocean rescue, Towne said Paramount would have to stage the sequence on the West Coast with studio stunt men. The Navy would provide the helicopters, but the studio would have to provide the camera aircraft. Likewise, the Navy would supply the Banshees for the flight scenes, but on the West Coast, not in Japan, and Paramount would have the responsibility for obtaining the camera plane. On the other hand, he agreed, "filming of routine activity aboard the carrier is entirely in order and is exactly the kind of material, a requirement for which justifies our permitting the production crew to proceed to the Far East."[49]

Addressing the Navy's major concern, the portrayal of Beer Barrel, the carrier's landing signal officer, Towne pointed out that "there is no reason to believe that any air group would have to rely on a man who, by his own admission, requires a can of beer 'sloshing around in his belly' to bring the planes back aboard." Beer Barrel's drinking ashore and sneaking beer aboard his ship "is understandable, but his drinking to get himself in condition to perform his duties is out." Although Michener and the script described him as weighing 250 pounds, the Navy stressed that all LSOs "must be qualified and active Naval Aviators and obesity is not tolerated."[50]

Towne further said the Navy would assist on the sequence showing propeller planes assisting the docking of the carrier, "providing this situation occurs during the stay of the production crew in the area. This maneuver will not be staged by the Navy solely for the cameras." In any event, Towne said the filmmakers could obtain close-ups of the propeller aircraft tied down to the deck "without undue difficulty, and long shots of the carrier being warped in probably would not show the aircraft on deck anyway." However, he stressed the film must explain that the use of propeller blades to aid in docking was "an emergency measure and will not be engaged in otherwise."[51]

Towne then said that the studio would have to reimburse the government at established rates for the transportation of equipment, billeting of the crew, and feeding of the film company aboard ship. The Navy would not assign personnel aboard ship or at naval establishments ashore to help the production crew. The studio could hire off-duty personnel, but "such additional duty will have to be voluntary and by mutual agreement with the personnel involved."[52]

In response to Towne's letter and the Navy's comments, Denton submitted a final, revised script, dated 4 November 1953, to Towne on 12 November. He said it contained much rewriting in accordance with the suggested corrections, particularly in regard to the characters of Beer Barrel and Mike Forney, the irreverent rescue-helicopter pilot. The LSO still drinks and smuggles beer onto the carrier, but he does not get drunk to do his job, does not weigh 250 pounds, and almost looks as if he could pilot an airplane. Forney still disdains all officers, except the fliers who trust him to save their lives, but he shows less hostility toward his superiors in the film than in the novel. Toning down Forney's persona removed the explanation for the pilot's transfer from the carrier. However, the changes persuaded the Navy to approve assistance to Paramount.[53]

The studio received sufficient assistance to portray carrier operations with reasonable authenticity and to create beautiful and exciting flying sequences. Although *Bridges at Toko-ri* may have lacked the documentary realism the combat footage provided *Men of the Fighting Lady*, it gained dramatic impact from its story. If *The Bridges at Toko-ri* used the jets only as background in the portrayal of men trying to survive in a hostile setting, the film benefited the Navy by showing the contribution its carriers made during the Korean War. The movie itself also validated the nation's involvement in the unpopular conflict. After ditching and being rescued, Brubaker receives a lecture from the admiral on why he is again fighting: "All through history, men have had to fight the wrong war at the wrong place. But that's the one thing they're stuck with. . . . A jet pilot does his job with all he's got because he is here. It's as simple as that. Militarily, this war is a tragedy. But if we pulled out they'd take Japan, Indo-China, the Philippines. Where would you have us take our stand? At the Mississippi?"

Ironically, by the time *Bridges at Toko-ri* appeared in late December 1954, the Korean War was quickly becoming a bad memory, and Michener's defense of its necessity seemed beside the point. Instead, as Seaton had said, the film made a clear statement about the futility of war. Having helped knock out the bridges at Toko-ri, Brubaker crash-lands his damaged plane behind enemy lines and seeks shelter in a muddy ditch. Despite Forney's efforts to extricate him, Brubaker and his would-be rescuers die in a gun battle with the North Korean soldiers. Unlike those of other cinematic heroes, however, Brubaker's death offers no spiritual uplift. The image of Brubaker lying face up in the mud, with his executioner standing above him, produced a feeling the Korean War had been a tragedy, Michener's writings notwithstanding.

The Bridges at Toko-ri provided no answer to the admiral's final question, "Where do we find such men?" Instead, Brubaker's death suggested that war has no redeeming features and so made the first anti-war statement in a Navy movie. After seeing the movie, Michener himself agreed: "The great and terrible tragedy of war had come through." Still, the movie did not denigrate the bravery of the American fighting man who did his job to the best of his ability, whether or not he agreed with the conflict. As a result, the Navy could ignore the anti-war images and love the portrayal of carrier warfare and the dedication of its men.[54]

Both messages live side by side, neither distracting from the other, thanks to the filmmakers' commitment to the story. During the editing process they cut out Brubaker's explanation of his decision to fly the dangerous mission: "Sometimes you look courage right in the face—the face of another man. That does something to you, something you can't put into words. That's why I have to go." The *Saturday Review* called it "a tribute to the honesty of the film-makers that this piece of empty heroics, which must ring false from the screen, is no longer in the picture." Instead, Brubaker simply takes off to attack the bridges.[55]

The reviewer also thought the image of Brubaker dead in the ditch impressed the "image of sacrifice upon the memory. This clean and purposeful hewing to the spirit of the film lifts *Bridges at Toko-ri* far above the men-at-war stereotype it could easily have been." The difference "is in the development, which has been purged of untruth." The heroics "are in what men do, not in what they say," and the Navy's assistance allowed the director to show what the fliers do: "The fascination and danger of carrier flying are shown so beautifully that it is enormously satisfying to hear the admiral's period to the piece, as he says with wonder and sorrow, 'Where do we find such men?'"[56]

Reaching the same conclusion about the merits of the film, Crowther in the *New York Times* started with the hardware, calling it the "best stuff" in the picture. "The conception of how the Navy performed in the Korean war, so far as its rendering of air support to the ground forces was concerned, is vividly and movingly developed in this punctilious film. Respect for the heroic effort is immediately inspired." However, the filmmakers "have been as meticulous and authentic" in portraying Michener's "poignant story" of Brubaker, his wife, and his comrades as they were in showing the Navy in action: "They have cast the film to perfection and seen that it is played with rare restraint." Crowther also said the movie did not seek to answer the questions it posed: "Its purpose simply is to show the human and professional resolution, organization and sacrifice that prosecution of the war required. And it has fulfilled this purpose in a truly efficient and moving way. One of the best of modern war pictures is *Bridges at Toko-Ri*."[57]

In contrast, *An Annapolis Story* has only two distinctive features. It became the last movie to portray life at the Naval Academy and did so in color. Even so, like *Flat Top,* it remains simply another product of Walter Mirisch's low-budget school of filmmaking. When the producer first approached the Pentagon in August 1952, he said the film would "concern itself with a cross-section of life at the U.S. Naval Academy. It will touch upon as many of the traditional and social events as possible, including graduation, the Ring Dance, summer cruise, etc."

The story focused on an older Academy instructor and a member of the first class, who had come to Annapolis "as a result of his fine record as an enlisted man in the Fleet," with their conflict having "its roots in their dissimilar attitudes." Naturally, they fall for the same lady, and their rivalry runs through the story. Ending up aboard the same ship off Korea, the men reconcile after "realizing that they represent two types of men, equally important, without which we would never have the greatest Navy in the world."[58]

Although the Pentagon found the basic idea acceptable, Towne advised Mirisch on 5 September that aspects of it "will probably not be acceptable." However, he said the Navy would provide constructive criticism and suggestions to help him "determine the feasibility of going ahead with the project along lines which will eventually qualify it for the cooperation needed on production." On his part, Academy superintendent C. Turner Joy objected to the antagonism between the protagonists: "It is difficult to conceive that areas of conflict in such a situation could be presented in either spoken or visual form in such a manner as to be considered typical of or in harmony with the discipline and traditions of the Naval Academy."

Joy believed that "such a theme is not 'The Annapolis Story' and therefore lies the principal objection to the rough story outline." Moreover, he said that "The" in the title "implies an historical and documentary film and not the development of personal conflict between an instructor and a young midshipman receiving his basic education and indoctrination in the rudiments of the naval profession." Consequently, he rejected Mirisch's story.[59]

Even when Mirisch screened his film in the Pentagon as an untitled "color production," in early February 1955, he had not yet come up with an acceptable title to satisfy the Academy's concern over the "The." Only after the Pentagon approved the film on 9 February did Mirisch change "The" to "An," which won quick Navy approval. By then, he also had received complaints that the film no longer focused on Academy life, but on the brothers' careers at Pensacola and in Korea. As a result, it also suffered in comparison to the recent carrier films.

Ultimately, the producer needed more than two years to create a suitable script and complete production, using battle footage and a rehash of earlier Navy movies to tell a trite story of two brothers who compete at the Academy, for a girl, during flight school, and in the air over Korea. Mirisch was so committed to the project that he did not even send director Don Siegel to Annapolis to shoot background scenes. Back in Hollywood, Siegel simply put his actors in front of rear-screen projections of the Academy activities, which a second unit film crew had taken.[60]

By shortening the Korean portions of the film, Mirisch eliminated the possible conflict with the earlier carrier movies. Still, the Pensacola and Korean War sequences lessened the truth in advertising of the film's title, whether with "The" or "An." In any case, *An Annapolis Story* remained simply a cut-and-paste movie created with a few location shots of the Academy, stock footage of carrier operations, and some combat footage. The acting and dialogue remained mundane, if not outright bad. Perhaps worst, the filmmakers showed their lack of respect for viewer intelligence by mixing World War II and Korean War aerial-combat footage. Audiences did not need aircraft-identification training to notice that when one brother attacks a North Korean MiG, a World War II Japanese plane crashes into the water.

However, the *New York Times* said that people who still liked Academy or Korean War films would find *An Annapolis Story* a "perfectly legitimate little recruiting poster for our Naval Academy" filled with "wholesome, scrubbed-looking young people." The critic also noted that "it's hard to imagine these bounding, entirely harmonious lads ever emerging as realistic defenders of their country in war or peace." As a result, the movie remained "the Rover Boys every step of the way, in this old-fashioned, innocuous and pointedly utopian gold-brick of a picture."[61]

Did such a film benefit the Navy in the mid-1950s? Admiral Joy's lack of enthusiasm suggests that if Annapolis had ever needed to recruit midshipmen, it no longer had a shortage of men wanting a free education. Moreover, after the release of *Men of the Fighting Lady* and *Bridges at Toko-ri,* people fully understood the effectiveness of carrier operations. With only generic combat footage, some from the wrong war, *An Annapolis Story* had nothing to add to the portrayal. Nor did its oft-repeated rites-of-passage story provide new insights into the reasons why young men sought out a military education and career.[62]

Harold Lloyd, in his first feature film, *A Sailor-Made Man* (1921), joins the Navy to win the hand of his girl, with the service becoming the place for a young man to experience his rite of passage.

On the parade ground in *The Midshipman* (1925), the first of several films to capitalize on the romantic image of the United States Naval Academy. The star, Ramon Novarro, was allowed to participate in graduation ceremonies for the filming of the conclusion.

John Mack Brown as a plebe in *Annapolis* (1929), a less-than-successful attempt to portray Academy life.

The first sound movie to feature the Naval Academy, *Salute* (1929) uses romantic entanglements and the Army-Navy rivalry to provide drama.

MUSEUM OF MODERN ART/FILM STILLS ARCHIVES.

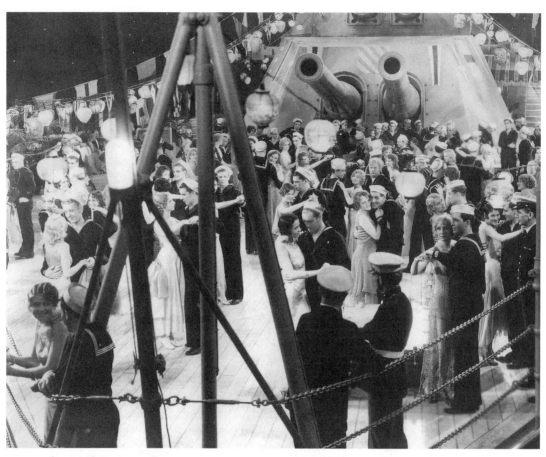

In *Hit the Deck* (1930), the Navy served only as a background prop for an early Hollywood effort to bring musical comedy to the screen. MUSEUM OF MODERN ART/FILM STILLS ARCHIVES.

Midshipman Jack (1933) gains credibility from the extensive location shooting, including scenes shot inside Bancroft Hall and others shot on the Chesapeake Bay. Although it received largely negative reviews, the film does provide a more detailed portrayal of the life of a midshipman than other Naval Academy movies.

In *Annapolis Salute* (1937), one of the least-inspired films about life at the Naval Academy, the plot again centers on a romance. Even the title is borrowed from the earlier *Salute*.

MUSEUM OF MODERN ART/FILM STILLS ARCHIVES.

P.688-40

Ruby Keeler and Dick Powell in *Shipmates Forever* (1935). A continuation of the coming-of-age theme in Annapolis films, the movie is distinguished by its emphasis on patriotism and selfless devotion to duty. MUSEUM OF MODERN ART/FILM STILLS ARCHIVES.

Navy Blue and Gold (1937), a major MGM release featuring James Stuart, Robert Young, and Lionel Barrymore, synthesizes the thematic concerns of earlier Annapolis movies, with the plot revolving around the Army-Navy football game. Museum of Modern Art/Film Stills Archives.

Chief Boatswain's Mate Edward G. Robinson antagonizes Glenn Ford and the rest of his destroyer's crew with his demands for perfection in *Destroyer* (1943). MUSEUM OF MODERN ART/FILM STILLS ARCHIVES.

Director Delmer Daves (seated, center), producer Jerry Wald (seated, right), and actor John Garfield (seated, left) during the filming of *Destination Tokyo* (1943). Though not historically accurate, *Destination Tokyo* was the most realistic submarine movie yet to appear on the screen. DELMER DAVES PAPERS, STANFORD UNIVERSITY LIBRARIES (M192/16/7).

A Navy crew performs for cameras during the filming of *Crash Dive* (1943) at the submarine base at New London, Connecticut. FRED FREEMAN COLLECTION.

Gary Cooper in *Task Force* (1949), an epic tale of the development of naval aviation. Warner Brothers advanced the movie's release date several months so that *Task Force* would appear at the height of the Navy's congressional battle with the Air Force over appropriations for bombers versus aircraft carriers.

Museum of Modern Art/Film Stills Archives.

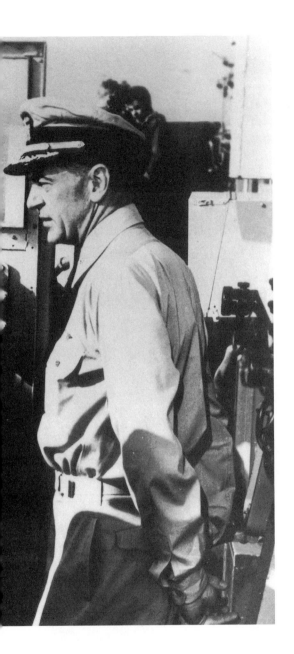

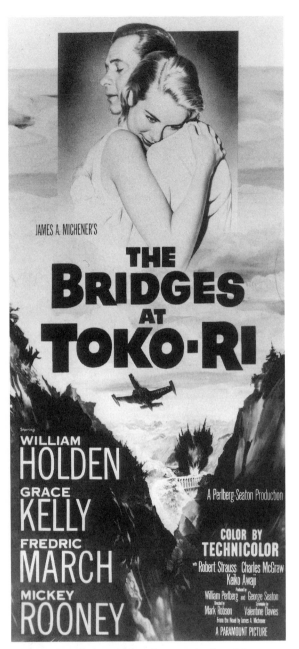

Promotional poster for the movie that *New York Times* reviewer Bosley Crowther called "one of the best of modern war pictures." The Navy's cooperation in the making of the film allowed for its authenticity and exciting flying sequences; the film, in turn, provided the Navy with a public demonstration of the contributions made by its carriers to the Korean War.

MUSEUM OF MODERN ART/FILM STILLS ARCHIVES.

Van Johnson, portraying Cdr. Harry Burns, the Korean War jet pilot who talks a blinded flier down to a safe landing aboard their carrier in *Men of the Fighting Lady* (1954). MUSEUM OF MODERN ART/FILM STILLS ARCHIVES.

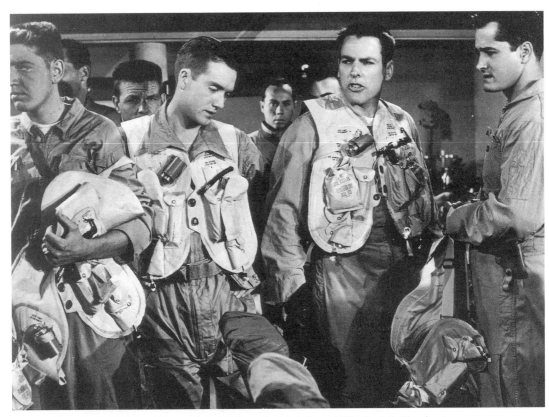

An Annapolis Story (1955), with John Derek (right) and Kevin McCarthy (center right). A low-budget compilation of Annapolis backdrops and stock World War II and Korean War footage, the film did little to enhance the Academy's or the filmmakers's reputations. It remains the last movie to focus on life at the Naval Academy.

Robert Mitchum plots his next move in his confrontation with the captain of a German submarine (played by Curt Jurgens) in *The Enemy Below* (1957), the first Hollywood movie to give a human and humane personality to the enemy.
MUSEUM OF MODERN ART/FILM STILLS ARCHIVES.

Burt Lancaster and Clark Gable confront each other in *Run Silent, Run Deep* (1958), probably the most realistic of the World War II submarine films that enjoyed great popularity during the 1950s.

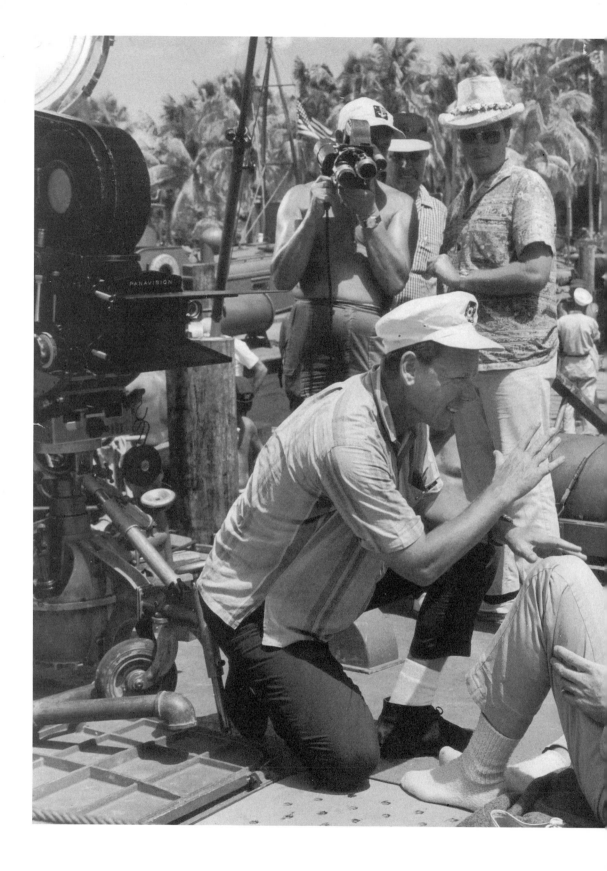

Director Leslie H. Martinson and
Cliff Robertson, who portrays a
young John Kennedy waging war in
a torpedo boat in *PT-109* (1963),
a film that Warner Brothers could
justify only because it featured the
incumbent president.

Leslie Martinson directing Robert
Culp in a dockside scene during
location shooting of *PT-109*.

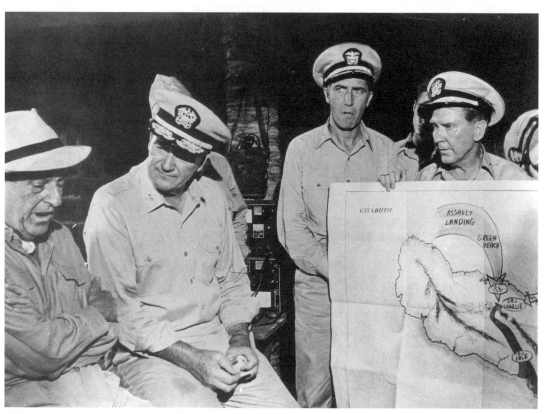

John Wayne, shown here with Franchot Tone, Patrick O'Neil, and Burgess Meredith, as a Navy captain and later admiral in Otto Preminger's *In Harm's Way* (1965), a sweeping, if deadened, recreation of the early days of the Pacific conflict. MUSEUM OF MODERN ART/FILM STILLS ARCHIVES.

Otto Preminger and Capt. Colin Mackenzie discuss a scene aboard a submarine during filming of *In Harm's Way*.

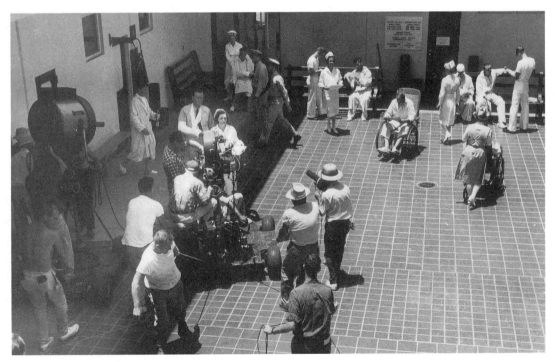

Shooting a hospital scene for *In Harm's Way*.

Director David Green discusses a scene with
Charlton Heston on the set of *Gray Lady
Down* (1979). The making of the film, which
is about an attempt to rescue the crew of a
sunken nuclear submarine, was supported by
the Navy after a lengthy review-and-revision
process. The Navy finally decided that it was
better to cooperate than to have the film made
without any input from the Navy. UNIVERSAL CITY
STUDIOS, INC.

Producer Harve Bennett aboard USS *Ranger* during making of *Star Trek IV* (1986). Following the success of *Top Gun*, the Navy was more willing to cooperate on projects that at a minimum showed Navy personnel performing in a professional manner.

Director John Milius receives advice during the filming of *Flight of the Intruder* (1991) aboard the USS *Independence*. Set during the Vietnam War, the movie emphasizes the commitment of the Navy's officers and the effectiveness of its machines, not the politics of the conflict.

On the Surface in World War II

Whether Michener's arguments for the necessity of fighting in Korea convinced many people, the movies based on his writings could not portray the war as a glorious success. Most people were to blame the politicians, rather than the military, for the American failure to win an outright victory. Consequently, the armed services suffered little damage to their images, in contrast to the savaging of their prestige and honor that the Vietnam War was to cause. Nevertheless, the Korean War could never serve Hollywood as a model for positive portrayals of the American military, as World War II had.

After all, Gen. George Patton had said, "Americans love a winner and will not tolerate a loser. Americans play to win all the time. I wouldn't give a hoot in hell for a man who lost and laughed. That's why Americans have never lost, and will never lose a war, because the very thought of losing is hateful to Americans." Consequently, the glorious victories against Germany and Japan, not the standoff with the Communist Chinese and North Koreans, provided filmmakers with an endless variety of combat stories to turn into exciting recreations of World War II combat.

During the same period the military, in peacetime repose, served as a stage for all manner of comedy, romance, and noncombat adventure. The Navy in particular became the setting for many films that had no connection to the service except that the actors wore uniforms approximating the real thing. Most of these "Navy" men impersonated enlisted sailors because the service usually frowned on portraying officers in slapstick comedy or silly farce. Officers and gentlemen simply did not do the things shown in the 1951 *Let's Go Navy,* a stereotypical Hollywood B comedy.

Aimed at a very young male audience, the film shows the Bowery Boys enlisting in the Navy in an attempt to find two crooks who wore uniforms when robbing them of money they had raised for charity. The Navy was simply one more setting for the Boys' slapstick routines. With the entire story shot on a soundstage, the studio had no reason to go through the process of asking for assistance. The few seconds of battleships and guns firing undoubtedly came from stock newsreel shots.

The Navy would have found no basis for cooperation given the film's portrayal of officers and the Boys' shenanigans aboard ship. The filmmakers hired a retired naval officer as a technical adviser to attain a modicum of authenticity in the sleeping arrangements of the enlisted men and in their speech. However, the inaccurate rendering of life aboard ship suggests that the officer had little influence on the director during production. Ironically, *Let's Go Navy* undoubtedly benefited the service. For young, naive men, the lax discipline, the fun and games aboard ship, and the beautiful, scantily clad (for that day) girl doing a hula for the boys suggested that Navy life offered more excitement than a civilian job.

Like *Let's Go Navy*, the 1952 *A Girl in Every Port* used the Navy only as a stage for Groucho Marx. The filmmakers shot the shipboard scenes on a soundstage, and the art director made no effort to create even the slightest sense of authenticity. The film did not even use actual footage of Navy ships to produce a modicum of authenticity. Still, the Navy benefited from the portrayal of adventure and romance.

Big Jim McLean, a Cold War melodrama, requested some very limited assistance in the form of stock footage of the battleship *Arizona* in motion. In his letter to Towne, Robert Fellows explained that after the company had started shooting on location in Honolulu, he found the story "could be better told by the inclusion of some Navy personnel" and wanted to shoot a few scenes at Pearl Harbor.[1]

At another time, obtaining assistance without a prior request might have caused the Navy and Baruch's office to lodge a strong objection with the filmmakers. However, the House Un-American Activities Committee was cooperating on the production, which starred John Wayne, then in the process of creating his heroic image. Towne responded that the Pentagon had given permission to his agent to obtain the shot of the *Arizona* and that the script "has been considered to justify the limited cooperation which you have already obtained."[2]

Such stories, as well as later comedies like *Don't Give Up the Ship, Francis in the Navy,* and *Don't Go Near the Water,* received little or no assistance and provided limited benefit to the Navy by keeping images of the service in front of the American people. In contrast, movies that reminded the nation how the Navy had fought the last war received assistance from the Pentagon and the Navy.

The submariners and naval aviators carried their intramural battles for funding from Congress to movie houses across the country. Likewise, both branches of the Navy argued in Congress and on motion-picture screens for their respective weapons systems against the advocates of heavy bombers. The Navy's surface fleet, particularly battleship officers, had relatively little to sell in the aftermath of World War II. The United States built no additional battleships, and Hollywood did not feature a dreadnought in any movie until *Under Seige* in 1993, when terrorists kidnapped the USS *Missouri* as it was heading back into retirement. Nevertheless, during the 1950s filmmakers created many stories about how the Navy had fought and helped win the victory on and near the surface.

Most of the movies contained familiar elements: the commander who imposes strong discipline on his men, the happy-go-lucky enlisted sailors, the cruelty of war, and usually death to one or more of the central characters. Only occasionally did Hollywood produce a story out of the norm and cause the Navy difficulty in dealing with an unflattering portrayal of its men. More often, the Navy reacted positively to scripts, either initially or after the service made clear what it expected the movie to show. The Navy prevailed over appreciative filmmakers in virtually every instance and received a story that provided some benefit.

Frogmen became a valuable informational vehicle, revealing to the American people for the first time the contribution a new type of fighter had made to winning World War II. The Navy did show some reluctance to have the story told. In answer to an inquiry from a retired officer about available stock footage, the service's Public Information Office wrote, "Official Navy library footage of Underwater Demolition Teams (UDTs) is practically non-existent, nor have we been able to locate any edited film on the subject." The Office also explained that most of the organization's wartime activities remained classified, but the two reports about UDTs in the Atlantic and Pacific during the war could be used only within the Navy Department.[3]

Inquiries later in the year from Leo Morrison, an independent filmmaker, led to an August meeting in Baruch's office with the producer and writer, James Cross, and a subsequent visit to the UDT training facility in Coronado. Then on 21 November Morrison called Baruch's office to tell him that he had interested Darryl Zanuck in the story, but he wanted to secure Pentagon cooperation before committing 20th Century Fox to the project. Baruch's office advised the studio it would give it a priority for ninety days to develop a plan to make the film. Although he disappeared once the studio acquired the idea, Cross set the tone of the production in his treatment of 12 December. In addition to being previously untouched in film, as he noted, "by deed and action, under the worst possible circumstances, these men played a large part in most of the small victories that led to the ultimate great victory."[4] Sam Engle, the film's producer, on 20 February 1950 met with Assistant Secretary of the Navy John Kroehler, who gave the studio "his blessings and assistance in the project." He suggested assigning deEarle Logsdon, a retired lieutenant commander, then a civilian lawyer in the office of the Navy's Judge Advocate General, to act as technical adviser for the production. According to Towne, Kroehler was interested because he had been "one of the powers behind the original development of UDT right from the start, and carried on thru the war."[5]

Apart from the usual problems of creating a suitable story, Engle had to deal with the secret nature of the UDT mission and methods. Even before the studio delivered a final script, the Navy did agree to cooperate on the production. In a memo to the Eleventh Naval District on 1 May 1950, the Director of Public Relations explained that the service "is particularly interested in seeing that the activities of the underwater demolition teams during World War II are shown in a truthful manner to the public." And he asked that "informational assistance, physical cooperation and guidance be rendered within the limits of security, the availability of personnel and material, without interfering with the military program and at no cost to the government."[6]

With the screenplay going through revision after revision, Darryl Zanuck finally became involved in the production on 1 July, writing to the producer that he saw the story "loaded with excitement, suspense and possibilities for thrilling underwater melodrama." However, he had concerns about the "overall character structure of the drama." Just having an original story about a branch of the military Hollywood had not yet explored "does not however prevent us from telling a sound story. The present story when you forget all of the comedy, suspense and excitement is a standard, formula service story, the usual undisciplined tough guy who does his job well and dies at the finish." Movies had portrayed this character "in one variation or another in practically every service story starting with *To the Shores of Tripoli*." He did not object "to the character himself even though he is completely formula and stereotyped—if there is some other character conflict in the story or something of a *deep nature* to take it away from *Sands of Iwo Jima*, etc., etc."[7]

Zanuck did not expect the writer "to come up with anything as profound and deeply moving as *Twelve O'Clock High*, which was a solid character study, but certainly we must have something with more depth to it than this outline reveals if it is going to stand up with *American Guerrilla in the Philippines* and *Halls of Montezuma*. I am afraid that even with good comedy and wonderful excitement and marvelous underwater stuff we will still be classified as just another routine service story."[8]

As with *Wing and a Prayer*, Zanuck demonstrated a keen astuteness about the nature and appeal of war movies and an understanding of the difference between art and mundane entertainment. After dissecting the characters, he reiterated that he would not object to any of them "if we could find some new slant to them or if something dramatically emotional developed between them."

He then said that the characters should develop throughout a film. In contrast, the current story "is devoid of heroics in spite of the fact that they do a very heroic thing in capturing the first Japanese prisoners. The whole emphasis has been away from heroics, thus it is honest, realistic and tough—as different from the ordinary service story as *Twelve O'Clock High* is from *Iwo Jima*." Citing the recent fighting in Korea, he said, "War is today becoming a reality again. Sure there is comedy in it, but it is ironic comedy, and it will not be won by fabulous tough guys but by seasoned disciplined men who hate the job they are doing but have to do it."[9]

Despite Zanuck's suggestions, the filmmakers continued to have problems creating a satisfactory screenplay. Even a new writer and the arrival of Adm. Thomas Dykers as technical adviser did not produce immediate results. As late as 6 November, when the studio submitted a formal request for cooperation, it said it expected to revise the accompanying script, dated 3 November 1950, after the Navy made suggestions or corrections. Shooting was scheduled to begin by 27 November, and the studio told Towne it would like to meet with the Navy to "effect technical corrections and obtain approval" of the script. This proved unnecessary since the Navy approved the script with only one modification, the toning down of one character.[10]

Like *Flying Missile*, *Frogmen* does portray a new and important branch of the Navy for the American people. However, as Zanuck feared, the film fails to create original characters performing a different story. Worse, since 90 percent of the story takes place on or below the surface, the film is a pseudo-documentary, showing how frogmen performed their missions and perhaps interesting people in the new technology that spawned the new sport of scuba diving. Director Lloyd Bacon believed another distinguishing feature was the final scene in which frogmen blow up a Japanese submarine base in a huge explosion lasting sixty-two seconds. He recalled, "I have made eight pictures with a war background, but none of the others contained a sequence with so much concentrated fireworks and all the trimmings. When you see it on the screen it practically blasts you out of your seat."[11]

In truth, the story has little power to move audiences. The underwater-demolition team's new commander, played by Richard Widmark, tries to enforce strict discipline and alienates his men, who fondly remember their former easygoing commander. Twentieth Century had done the same story, much better, the year before in *Twelve O'Clock High*. As the *Saturday Review of Literature* pointed out, the story itself is never the movie's center of attention but is "simply an excuse to send the cameras below the waterline for some of the most remarkable and occasionally the most beautiful shots in a long time. You readily forget the ordinariness of the story in the extraordinary grace of young men swimming through the watery half-light as if in slow motion, placing their charges of TNT, stringing the long connecting fuses, delicately cutting their way through a Japanese anti-submarine net. It's fascinating, exciting stuff, and the sound-man has ingeniously matched the novelty of these visuals with the muted, half-roar of cannon and the spatter of small-arms fire as heard by the men below the surface."[12]

This served to justify the film for the *New York Times:* "The dauntless swimmers who are fearlessly led by Richard Widmark and Dana Andrews perform incredible feats. But the straight demonstration of their techniques as literal one-man submarines is utterly fascinating, and thus the picture is too." Such images undoubtedly inspired young male viewers to consider the challenge the elite underwater-demolition service offered. Certainly this benefited the Navy and justified its assistance.[13]

In contrast, the 1952 *Okinawa* contained nothing new either in its story or its images of war. The almost invisible plot revolves around a gun crew on a destroyer on picket duty off Okinawa during World War II. The stock characters bitch and complain during lulls in the fighting, but once in battle they perform heroically. Actually, the story serves only as a framework for the combat footage of destroyers forming a ring around the vulnerable carriers supporting the last major amphibious assault of World War II. By 1952, however, people had seen most of the footage, and without a legitimate story to tie the sequences together, *Okinawa* offers little to recommend it. *Weekly Variety* probably said it best: "As a war drama, Columbia has a minor league effort in *Okinawa*. Put together with little imagination, it's slated as secondary material."[14] For the Navy, however, the images of Japanese planes tumbling from the sky provided sufficient benefit to justify lending a few ships and access to its film vaults.

For dramatic stories about interesting people, Hollywood turned to the veterans of World War II, who had begun putting their experiences onto paper. James Jones, Leon Uris, and Herman Wouk, among many others, wrote novels containing characters about whom a reader might care. *From Here to Eternity, Battle Cry,* and *The Caine Mutiny* all became movies portraying the military and war with some realism and passion.

While the novels captured military life, and their authenticity helped make them instant critical and popular successes, each contained images that did not flatter the services, particularly officers. Used to receiving positive scripts or ones they could modify appropriately, the public-affairs offices of each military branch struggled to a greater or lesser extent with the filmmakers to achieve a mutually satisfying screenplay. From the studio's perspective, the novels had pre-sold the movies they would produce, and to change the plots might well weaken the films. The process of turning the great war novels into possibly great war movies sometimes became as dramatic as the combat stories themselves.

Whereas the Army had major problems with *From Here to Eternity,* the Navy had only two areas of concern with *The Caine Mutiny*. It objected to the word "mutiny" in the book's title, claiming the service had never had a mutiny.

Likewise it found Captain Queeg, the World War II equivalent of Captain Bligh, offensive to and derogatory of its officer corps. Consequently, Stanley Kramer, the film's producer, needed more than eighteen months of intense negotiation to resolve the problems and obtain assistance.

Aware of the potential problems in Wouk's novel, Warner Brothers asked its Washington representative to submit a synopsis of *The Caine Mutiny* to the Defense Department in April 1951 for an official reaction about Navy assistance on the film. Answering for the Navy and the Pentagon, Towne said the "consensus of opinion of all concerned is that the development of a screenplay which could be considered acceptable for official cooperation would be a difficult, if not impossible, task for any writer to achieve."[15]

He explained that everyone felt the plot contained a "combination of extremes, both as to characterizations and situations. . . . Neither the characters portrayed, nor the situation that they became involved in would have been tolerated in the Navy for long." He also noted that the "resolution of conflicts is accomplished after such a lapse of time as to be of no value in redeeming the service, or in offsetting the derogatory and very harmful sequences through which one must wade during the major part of the story."[16] Although the story itself contained many factual errors, he said the Department of Defense would not now "offer constructive criticism in the interests of accuracy and authenticity . . . in view of the nonacceptability of the overall story line." Attempting to disabuse the studio from undertaking the project, Towne concluded, "We do not desire to offer any hope of our being able to work anything out on this project, as far as eventual approval of cooperation of Departments of Defense and Navy are concerned."[17]

Ironically, Herman Wouk always considered himself a Navy man. He had even sought technical advice from the service while working on the novel. In contrast to *From Here to Eternity*, *The Caine Mutiny* contained no physical brutality, no whorehouses, no adultery, and no profanity. In an introductory note, Wouk commented on his style: "The general obscenity and blasphemy of shipboard talk have gone almost wholly unrecorded. This good-humored billingsgate is largely monotonous and not significant, mere verbal punctuation of a sort, and its appearance in print annoys some readers." Moreover, Wouk did not paint an unflattering portrait of the Navy as a whole, and until the service suggested otherwise, he believed he had written a complimentary story.

Despite the title, *The Caine Mutiny* focuses not on a "mutiny" but on Willie Keith, one of the war's ninety-day wonders. He has joined the minesweeper *Caine* as a newly commissioned ensign after graduating from Princeton and Officer Candidate School. Aboard the *Caine*, during the war in the South Pacific, Willie matures from a pompous and affected mama's boy to a man who ultimately becomes the ship's last captain. The reader observes Captain Queeg and the "mutiny" from Willie's viewpoint. An unwilling participant in the takeover of the *Caine,* he finally reaches manhood as a result of his actions when a kamikaze hits the ship in the closing days of the war.

Although the mutiny and court-martial become the dramatic focus of the novel, the significance of *The Caine Mutiny* as a war story lies in Wouk's portrayal of life on a minesweeper during wartime. He successfully re-created the experiences of men living in close proximity aboard ship, facing danger together for extended periods. Many Navy men have testified to having served under officers like Queeg, except for his extreme behavior and breakdown. Moreover, many high-ranking officers have agreed that Lieutenant Maryk's takeover of the *Caine* during the typhoon was legitimate under the circumstances Wouk created.[18]

These opinions notwithstanding, the title itself prompted most of the Navy's opposition. Adm. James Shaw, the film's technical adviser, later observed, "I hazard a guess that if the book had been named 'The Caine Incident,' minus that inflammatory word 'Mutiny,' Navy cooperation would have been obtained speedily." From Wouk's first discussion of his proposed book with the Navy's Public Information Office in 1948, however, the service stated that it had never had a mutiny aboard any of its ships.[19]

History does not support this contention. Before beginning his assignment, Shaw researched the subject and uncovered several incidents aboard Navy ships that clearly qualify as mutinies. Perhaps the most famous of these occurred aboard the brig *Somers* in 1842, when the ship's captain hung Midn. Philip Spencer for mutiny. His execution caused a sensation since his father was Secretary of War. The Navy tried the captain for murder, but the court acquitted him, justifying his claim that he had put down a mutiny.[20]

Whether Spencer actually mutinied, the Navy seldom demanded historical accuracy in films, as *Destination Tokyo* and *Wing and a Prayer* demonstrated. Instead, the service used plausibility as the determining factor, with dramatic license giving filmmakers some flexibility. In military comedies, even plausibility often went by the board.[21]

Plausible or not, *The Caine Mutiny* obviously reminded many naval officers of *Mutiny on the Bounty* and Fletcher Christian setting Captain Bligh adrift in a rowboat. Nothing so dramatic happens on the *Caine.* Wouk himself wrote, "It was not a mutiny in the old-time sense, of course, with flashing of cutlasses, a captain in chains, and desperate soldiers turning outlaws. After all, it happened in 1944 in the United States Navy." Wouk also explained when he first came to the Navy for assistance that the mutiny was a "mutiny of the mind," not of arms.

While most Navy men seemed to understand this distinction, they did not necessarily trust the American viewing public to do the same. Wouk reinforced this concern when he focused on the mutiny in greater detail in *The Caine Mutiny Court Martial.*[22]

When inquiries from Warner Brothers and other studios about possible cooperation met a stone wall in the spring of 1951, they decided not to pursue the
project. Then Stanley Kramer, a young, independent producer, took an option
on the screen rights to *The Caine Mutiny*. By the summer of 1951 Kramer had
a financial and distribution arrangement with Columbia pictures as well as a
reputation for refusing to compromise his artistic and creative principles.
Kramer himself conceded, "I was known as somewhat of a 'rebel' to the military establishment and to the government sources with whom I dealt. If I
weren't a 'rebel' then I was considered a radical, a man who was dealing in
extremes and in bothersome material."[23]

His 1950 film, *The Men*, had focused in a serious and controversial manner
on hospitalized World War II paraplegic veterans. By showing the public how
the government rehabilitated seriously wounded servicemen, Kramer's film had
significant informational value and benefited the armed forces. However, his
earlier *Home of the Brave* (1949) portrayed the abuse of a Negro soldier by his
fellow GIs during wartime and helped establish Kramer's controversial reputation. Consequently, the Navy anticipated trouble as soon as he began to develop a screenplay based on *The Caine Mutiny*.[24]

In contrast, Kramer claimed he saw Wouk's book simply as "a very broad-
based novel of the Navy. It's really a cross section of Navy life on a mine
sweeper in the Pacific—officers and men and the crazy Queeg." The Navy naturally found little benefit in having one of its officers characterized as "crazy,"
irrespective of the mutiny problem. Slade Cutter, director of the Navy's Public
Information Division, said he received orders "to drag the Navy's feet, so to
speak, as long as possible to delay the inevitable and to get the script cleaned up
as much as I could."[25]

Kramer did start off on the wrong foot with his selection of Stanley Roberts to
write the screenplay. According to Cutter, talking with Roberts was "like talking
to Baby Snooks. My pride in the Navy was something absolutely impossible for
him to comprehend or accept. He thought I was silly, unrealistic, irrational, and
the possessor of that worst of all impediments to progress—the military mind,
whatever that is." Roberts had an even more serious deficiency from the Navy's
perspective. In the Red Scare that swept Hollywood in the late 1940s and early
1950s, he had been accused of having ties to the Communist Party. Whatever
the truth of these charges, Cutter said the Navy Office of Information gave
them credence, and this "had no small part in the dragging feet operation."[26]

However, Kramer made his most serious mistake in his efforts to win Navy
assistance when he decided to approach the Navy directly, which amounted to
entering a lion's den unarmed. Both Baruch and Ray Bell, Columbia's Washington representative, attributed most of the producer's problems to his refusal to
follow regular military channels in requesting cooperation. According to Bell,
Kramer believed that on the strength of his reputation as a filmmaker, he could

"probably obtain better and quicker cooperation from the Pentagon than working through me."[27]

Again, the producer saw the situation differently, wanting no lobbyist who believed in compromising to obtain military help. This "more adamant viewpoint," with which Kramer admitted he approached the military, perhaps as much as the book itself, caused the eighteen months of on-again, off-again negotiations, sometimes in the Pentagon, sometimes publicly in the media, before he obtained assistance.[28]

Kramer tried to keep as much control over the script as he could, while willing to make some concessions to the Navy. In one early effort to capture the flavor of the novel and perhaps curry favor with the service, Kramer hired Wouk to work with Roberts. As soon as the author realized the depth of the Navy's feelings about not wanting his book transferred to the screen, he urged Kramer not to make the movie and offered to return the money he had received for the film rights. The producer responded with a "scathing" letter, calling the author "some sort of jellyfish."[29]

When Roberts completed his initial script and Kramer sent it to the Navy for consideration, the service found its worst fears fulfilled. Slade Cutter recalled that the "enlisted men were worse than bums, and the admiral was a stupid stuffed shirt." He conceded that it would have ruined "the picture to attempt to portray the 'Caine' as anything but a 'honey barge.' And we didn't object to that. The problem was that there was no indication that the rest of the Navy wasn't as bad as the 'Caine.'" To rectify this omission, the service encouraged Kramer to make it clear that the *Caine* and Queeg were aberrations.[30]

At the same time, the producer faced pressure from Harry Cohen to satisfy the Navy since Columbia's financial arrangement on the project gave it some control over the size of Kramer's budget. He did, of course, have the option of eschewing Navy assistance and making a small, "interior" film, focused on the court-martial itself, as Wouk had done with his play.[31] He could also have resorted to miniatures, special effects, and combat footage for the exterior sequences, as other filmmakers had done when they couldn't obtain real ships. However, Bell noted that by 1954, when *The Caine Mutiny* appeared, filmmaking "had matured to the point where you could no longer phony something and feel that it was creditable to sophisticated audiences."[32]

Kramer also explained that the story occurred in the "massive environment of the U.S. Navy at war," which required large-scale military assistance to recreate. Not to obtain this cooperation and make the film "on a smaller scale would be to rob it of its value." Therefore, he pursued the Navy more resolutely than the service dragged its feet. Surrendering to Cohen's importuning, Kramer did seek Bell's help in Washington and ultimately "jumped the chain of command" by requesting a meeting with the Secretary of the Navy to passionately plead for assistance.[33]

Ironically, the meeting became only a formality, although the Chief of Information, Adm. Lewis Parks, was bitterly opposing Kramer's efforts to secure cooperation. In fact, most naval men had enjoyed Wouk's novel and only wanted the movie version to be as authentic as possible. After reading the book, even the CNO, Adm. W. M. Fechteler, conceded, "It's a hell of a yarn." He simply wondered how Wouk in just two years at sea as a reserve officer had observed "all the screwballs I have known in my thirty years in the Navy." So, when Parks went to see Fechteler about Kramer's impending visit with the Secretary, the CNO told him, "You had no business refusing cooperation in the first place."[34] Parks recalled that Fechteler never had discussed the film with him before and his comment "pulled the rug right out from under me after all this time." Recognizing that he had lost the fight, Parks salvaged what he could. After Kramer's meeting with the Navy Secretary, which now served only to formalize Fechteler's pronouncement, Parks told the producer that the approval did not "mean that you are going to get any extra help from me, because I don't agree with it."[35]

Rather than allowing Kramer to use his own technical adviser, Parks assigned James Shaw, an active-duty officer with experience on ships similar to the *Caine,* to serve as the official Navy representative on the film. During his six-month assignment, Shaw worked with writer Michael Blankfort on revising Roberts's script, arranged for Navy assistance at Pearl Harbor and San Francisco, and ensured accuracy in the portrayal of procedures.[36]

Despite Kramer's travails obtaining assistance, director Edward Dmytryk received "total" cooperation during the making of the film. In Hawaii, for example, the Navy put all its dockside derricks into operation simultaneously for one of Dmytryk's shots. The Navy also provided attack boats, marines, a carrier, and two destroyer-minesweepers (one in Pearl Harbor and one in San Francisco) to play the *Caine.* The service did not allow Kramer to acknowledge its cooperation, but the producer did include a title stating "The dedication of this film is simple: To the United States Navy."[37]

By working with Kramer and assigning one of its best officers to serve as technical adviser, the Navy expected that it would gain a more positive cinematic image. Writing to Ray Bell in September 1953, Admiral Parks said, "I am still hopeful that *The Caine Mutiny,* although it will show the seamy side of the Navy, also will include some decency and good and thereby be a good movie reflecting credit upon the armed services and the people in uniform." Perhaps because their expectations had been so low, naval officers were enthusiastic about the way Kramer had handled the story when they saw the finished film at a Pentagon screening in January 1954.[38]

In a formal letter of approval, the Department of Defense Public Affairs Office stated, "We consider that Columbia Pictures fulfilled its obligations to the Department of Defense in bringing *The Caine Mutiny* to the screen in such a commendable manner." On behalf of the Pentagon, Baruch wrote to Kramer, "We do want you to know, officially, that we believe you faithfully carried out your assurance to produce *The Caine Mutiny* in a manner which would be in the best interest of the Department of Defense. We consider the job well done, and will look forward to working with you in the future."[39]

In fact, the film they praised did not stray far from Wouk's book. The author himself "thought it was a poor adaptation of my work." However, any artist has difficulty seeing his work altered, and filmmaking necessarily demands liberties be taken in translating a lengthy book to the screen. Except for the differences in the presentation of Queeg's actions as a naval officer and the rationalization of the mutiny, however, the film does adhere closely to the novel.[40]

The portrayal of Captain Queeg does illustrate how the military manages to improve its image in any film it assists. Although Wouk's book and Kramer's film treat Queeg ambiguously, both the character and the Navy fare significantly better in the film than in the novel. Wouk reduced Queeg to virtual insanity and then half-heartedly tried to save him. After the court-martial, Barney Greenwald, the lawyer for Maryk (whom the Navy tries for mutiny), unsuccessfully rationalizes Queeg's breakdown by suggesting that he helped guard the country during the 1930s, when most Americans ignored the Navy and its dedicated men. One literary critic observed, "Queeg is a goddamn maniac," and Wouk's justification had validity only if he had showed that "Queeg worked himself down to the elbows for six years on this tin can in the North Atlantic and therefore he was crazy." Consequently, in Wouk's version, the reader concludes that Queeg became mentally ill and the Navy carelessly allowed a potentially dangerous man to command a ship.[41]

In contrast, the film portrays Queeg as an obviously disturbed man who performs in an increasingly irrational manner. Most Navy men have acknowledged that Maryk has real justification for taking over the *Caine,* given the events leading up to the crisis during the typhoon. Greenwald's post-trial cinematic defense of Queeg focuses on the conflict between a regular Navy officer and civilians turned sailors. In confronting the officers of the *Caine* after Maryk's acquittal, the lawyer blames them for Queeg's mental illness. When Willie points out that Queeg actually endangered the *Caine,* Greenwald retorts, "He didn't endanger anybody's life, you did, all of you. You're a fine bunch of officers!" When reminded that he had argued during the trial that Queeg had "cracked" during the storm, the lawyer responds that the captain had come to his officers for help, and they had turned him down: "You didn't approve of his conduct as an officer. He wasn't worthy of your loyalty, so you turned on him. You ragged him. You made up songs about him. If you had given him the loyalty he needed, do you think the whole issue would have come up in the typhoon?"

When Maryk agrees with Greenwald, Willie realizes that the officers really had committed mutiny. Greenwald continues, "Ah. You're learning Willie.

You're learning you don't work with a captain because of the way he parts his hair. You work with him because he has the job." Thus, the film shows Queeg as disturbed as in the book, but as Greenwald points out, "He couldn't help himself." This breakdown of a dedicated regular Navy officer came not from within, but from civilian warriors, and clearly the Navy would prefer Kramer's Queeg to Wouk's petty tyrant.

Kramer knew that he had improved Queeg's character only to win Navy cooperation. In his pitch to the Secretary of the Navy, he had said, "Fellows, you just aren't acquainted with dramatics. You cannot make white unless you make black. . . . Look, Captain Queeg was an officer who had battle fatigue and was going off his rocker. He did these things. Why did he do them? He did them perhaps because some of his officers were not patient enough with him and did not realize he was a sick man." To win cooperation, Kramer promised to show "simply that Queeg was an officer in the Navy who had gone off his rocker." Later, Kramer conceded that the ending he devised "was immoral," and he became convinced that Maryk "should have taken over command."[42]

The success of the Navy and the Defense Department in modifying Captain Queeg's behavior probably had little effect on the public's perception of the Navy. They knew perfectly well that the service did not usually staff its ships and bases with unstable officers. The United States could never have won the war if many Queegs had captained Navy ships. Audiences also realized that Michener's admirals or *Task Force*'s Gary Cooper did not command all the Navy's carriers. In fact, James Jones believed that the military might well benefit more from realistic portrayals like *From Here to Eternity* than the more typical, sanitized war films. He suggested that audiences recognize a falsely positive image as pure propaganda and reject it out of hand.[43]

Whether *The Caine Mutiny* actually benefited the Navy, its struggles with Kramer showed that if a filmmaker wanted assistance, he would find a way to get it. Even *Mister Roberts,* in which Jimmy Cagney's paranoid senior officer battles Henry Fonda's Lt. (j.g.) Roberts, ultimately received full cooperation. Initially, Baruch did not see how the Navy could assist the filmmakers, given the nature of the captain's character in the original play, since he "is far from being the type of man the Navy should want to admit to." Likewise, Towne concluded "that there is only a remote possibility of the Navy being able to assist this production with a freighter for the background filming. In addition, the story, as it stands now, holds little possibility of being able to qualify for cooperation."[44]

Following discussions within the Defense Department and the Navy about the proposed film, Towne wrote to the studio's Washington representative on 30 September, saying that the attitude of all concerned parties "is sympathetic but skeptical. Nothing would please us better than to be able to find justification for extending the cooperation which is presumed to be necessary in order to make production possible." However, "the character of the ship captain would undoubtedly be the first stumbling block on the road toward eventual approval" of assistance. The story had "other objectionable characteristics of course, not the least of which is the basic character of Mister Roberts himself."[45]

Baruch's office did not close the door to assistance, and over the winter, Warner Brothers and producer Leland Hayward went ahead with the development of a screenplay. The studio also cast Cagney and Fonda as the main characters. Selecting John Ford to direct the film virtually ensured that the Navy would agree to cooperate, given the director's work during the war and his making of *They Were Expendable.* After the script arrived at the end of May 1954, Baruch had changed his opinion, finding the "script [is] handled quite well, basically story is good. . . . cannot object too much to something that has been played to thousands of people and no objections have been logged against the characters. . . . The Captain is still a type the Navy wouldn't be proud of and probably under certain Pub. Info leadership would not want to have done. . . ."[46]

After reading the script, the Navy Chief of Information informed Baruch's office he wanted to take a personal interest in the production, and on 15 June 1954 the Navy agreed to cooperate with Warner Brothers. As a result of the assistance, the Navy had no objections to the film when the studio screened it in the Pentagon on 19 April 1955. The *New York Times* found *Mr. Roberts* "strikingly superior entertainment." Even though the movie contained the play's struggles between Mr. Roberts and the captain that had worried Baruch and Towne, it also showed Roberts's unselfish sacrifice for his men and the final tragic achievement of his goal. Mr. Roberts's death may convey the downside of war much as Brubaker's did in *Bridges at Toko-ri,* but as the reviewer pointed out, the film "is loaded to the gunwhales and with screamingly funny scenes which, in several instances, are visual improvements on the play." Perhaps for this reason the movie probably benefited the Navy.[47]

During the rest of the decade none of the movies portraying the surface Navy was to present the service with any significant problems. *Away All Boats,* for one, told a straightforward combat story. Based on Kenneth Dodson's best-selling novel, the movie focused on the actions of a new attack transport that goes into battle, with Jeff Chandler, an Annapolis graduate, commanding the customary Hollywood complement of inexperienced sailors. The Navy's willingness to let Universal Studios film the largest amphibious maneuvers in its history gave the otherwise unexceptional movie whatever appeal it had.

The two hundred ships and ten thousand Marines who staged the landing at Vieques Island off Puerto Rico enabled the filmmakers to create a movie that showed the contribution of amphibious assault ships to winning World War II but lacked much dramatic impact. As *Time* pointed out, the "characters are so simply drawn that it might have been more convenient to hang labels about their necks," starting with Jeff Chandler as "the Good, Grey Commander." Still, with the help of combat footage and the Marine assault, the film "brought vividly to life" the island landings, the combat, and the kamikaze attacks on the task force.[48]

Appearing the next year, *The Enemy Below* also contained dramatic battle sequences. However, the interaction between the two leading characters, who meet only in the final scenes, made it a classic movie about World War II. In as simple a plot as any filmmaker could create, Robert Mitchum plays a destroyer captain patrolling in the South Atlantic who wages war against Curt Jurgens, who plays a German submarine captain. Having just taken command of his ship, and with a peacetime background as a freighter captain, Mitchum's character must not only fight the unseen enemy but quickly win the confidence of his crew. In contrast, as a career officer, Jurgens's character has the respect and perhaps even love of his men, who realize they are fighting in a lost war, for a cause in which many of them no longer believe, if they ever did.

Once the destroyer comes across the submarine, the film becomes a battle of wits between the two captains, who quickly come to respect the abilities of the other. Their fight evolves into a kind of chess game as they trick and bluff each other, each making brilliant moves as well as careless mistakes. Ultimately, depth charges force the sub to the surface, where Jurgens manages to torpedo the destroyer. In turn, Mitchum rams the submarine with his sinking ship.

The two tired warriors salute each other's skill from afar and then, aboard an American destroyer that has rescued the survivors, bury their dead and philosophize about the nature of their struggle. As well as the movie renders the simple story, *The Enemy Below* distinguishes itself for the manner in which it portrays America's former enemy. During the war, films had contained images of Germans and Japanese as vile enemies who fired on helpless airmen as they dangled from parachutes or cut lifeboats in two. Since the Navy waged its war from a distance, movies about the war at sea only occasionally carried such propaganda messages. In *Destination Tokyo*, for one, the Japanese pilot shot down by the *Copperfin* stabs to death the sailor trying to rescue him. However, by 1944 the fliers preparing to bomb Japan in *Thirty Seconds Over Tokyo* do not hate the Japanese people, only the leaders.

By then, most people realized the United States was going to win the war, and at least some officials within the government had concluded that the Soviet Union would become America's enemy in peacetime and the United States would need allies in this new struggle. So the postwar movies reflected the reality of the Cold War, and none of the movies about the war contained the early wartime images of the nation's former enemies. Hitler and the Japanese warlords, not the average soldier or civilian, became the scapegoats. Nowhere did Hollywood portray the Holocaust or the buck-toothed Japanese smiling as he killed American soldiers or sailors in cold blood.

★

The Enemy Below contains perhaps the final comment about how the world had changed. Jurgens's character receives sympathetic treatment, making it clear to his executive officer that he has no use for the government in power. As a professional military man, he is only doing the job for which he has trained, but the war has tired him out, and he no longer has the stomach for combat. Nevertheless, he fights and fights well, as any warrior must. His duel with Mitchum, which neither man wins, suggests that nobility exists among warriors.

The Enemy Below made it easy for viewers to forget the true nature of Hitler's Germany, but the Navy had no problem with this because the enemy had become the ally against a new and even more evil foe. At the same time, *The Enemy Below* presented life aboard a destroyer in wartime with as much, if not more, realism than any movie Hollywood had ever made. To help the filmmakers create this authenticity, the Navy relieved a destroyer captain from his command and assigned him to work with screenwriter Wendall Mayes and director Dick Powell.[49]

Initially, the captain provided Mayes with information for the combat sequences and about the sonar, maneuvers, and dialogue. Then, during filming at the studio and in Hawaii, the technical adviser and Herb Hetu, the Navy's liaison officer to the filmmakers at Pearl Harbor, ensured that the movie would accurately portray how the crews on both ships would work out the maneuvering and combat problems. Mayes said they wanted audiences to say, "Hey, those guys really know what they're doing up there."[50]

To film the exterior scenes aboard the destroyer at sea, the Navy provided a ship for an extended period. The service even fired two training torpedoes at the destroyer to create the scene in which Mitchum's character outguesses Jurgens's by turning his ship at the last minute to avoid being hit. The filmmakers shot the sequence from the air to show the torpedoes straddling the destroyer. In contrast to such realism, Twentieth Century Fox used miniatures to film the scenes of the destroyer's ramming the submarine. While the difference between the live-action and special-effects photography becomes obvious, the latter sequence passes by so rapidly that it distracts only marginally from the realism of the rest of the movie.[51]

Of course, the ships serve only as the stage for the man-to-man combat. *Time* described the confrontation as "the best game of poker a man could ever hope to kibitz . . . Dick Powell, whose direction is far more exciting than his crooning ever was, plays it to a fare-thee-well." Stanley Kaufman in *The New Republic* wrote, "Sheer excitement is distilled by means of the acute camera work, the literate dialogue . . . and solid performances. . . ." Edwin Schallert, in the *Los Angeles Times,* thought that the philosophical conversations about the grimness of war and the understanding that develops between the two captains make *The Enemy Below* more than "just another war feature, even though as a study of battle, it is one of the most compelling." He thought the film lacks "any sop whatsoever of romantic appeal. But that it is so honest in its treatment of its subject that the respect it evokes compensates for any lack of the customary entertainment attraction."[52]

Not all movies about World War II in which the Navy appears lacks "entertainment value." The service assisted *South Pacific,* one of the most successful Broadway musicals of all time. Without that heritage, the Navy would have asked for significant revisions. Even so, the service told Baruch that it desired some of the portrayals of its personnel "toned down and presented in better taste." To 20th Century, Baruch pointed out, "Probably if this was a navy subject, there would be numerous suggestions for changes, however it has been considered by the Marine Corps and the Navy with the realization that it was a successful musical which was seen by thousands of people and apparently no adverse reactions have been registered with the Services."[53]

On the other hand, *The Gallant Hours* carries the lack of "entertainment value" to its logical extreme, becoming little more than a dry history lesson about the battle for Guadalcanal. In fact, this portrayal of Adm. William "Bull" Halsey's leadership and skill in winning the battle contains no images of combat at all—undoubtedly the first time Hollywood ever made a war movie without the war. Structurally, the film resembles the duel between the Mitchum and Jurgens characters in *The Enemy Below.* However, though *The Gallant Hours* portrays Isoroku Yamamoto with intelligence, even speaking his own language, screenwriters Beirne Lay Jr. and Frank Gilroy focused on Halsey during the four weeks from 18 October 1942, when he takes command of the South Pacific Force and Area, to the victory in the Naval Battle of Guadalcanal on 15 November. Concentrating on Halsey's planning, staff, and subordinate commanders, *The Gallant Hours* presents a one-sided portrayal of the events. Yamamoto remains a two-dimensional character, even though James T. Gotto, who plays the admiral and advised director Robert Montgomery on technical matters, actually had served on Yamamoto's staff.[54]

Newsweek probably provided the most succinct analysis of the film. Although praising Cagney's "restrained and intelligent" performance, the reviewer complained that *The Gallant Hours* "completely misses the boat" as a naval biography. The film skims over the details that made the decisions difficult and interesting and shows almost no actual battle. "As for creating individual characters," the writer concluded that the movie "simply decorates its personnel with a few superficial traits (the admiral didn't like to take his immunization shots) and calls it a day." As a result, he concluded that *The Gallant Hours* contains a "loose, tritely handled series of episodes." The two-word summary: "Empty vessel."[55]

James Cagney did eschew his usual outgoing, sometimes out-of-control characterization, giving Halsey a quiet, sensitive, and restrained portrayal. In focusing entirely on Halsey's quiet determination and his facility for inspiring confidence and devotion in the men around him, the film attempts to explain his leadership qualities and the way he became a hero in his own time. Cagney explained, "My hardest chore in playing Adm. Halsey was to keep James Cagney from coming through. That would have been disastrous. Halsey had no unusual mannerisms and (director) Bob Montgomery and I felt that inserting any or emphasizing gestures would be theatrical. So we avoided any attempts at character details."[56]

Montgomery, who produced as well as directed the film, adhered strictly to a documentary approach in telling his story. He wanted the film to show what happens in the minds of responsible men: "What we want to say is that leadership includes certain qualities. Of course our primary function is to entertain. The trick is to get the audience to say, later on, 'Oh, I see!'"[57]

Jesse Zunser of *Cue* found *The Gallant Hours* "impressive" as history but said that as drama the movie "is overlong, over-talky, over-narrated and tedious. It also completely lacks naval action—which is remarkable in any seagoing saga, in peace or war, and is virtually a celluloid extension of the printed page, overloaded with annotations, footnotes, glossary and an impossible script."[58]

Unfortunately, footnotes, annotations, and a glossary do not always make accurate history. Some people might dismiss the movie's errors as insignificant or as simply dramatic license, but they do raise the issue of the film's credibility. Although perhaps a minor point, Halsey replaced Admiral Ghormley on 18 October, not 16 October as the movie shows. Far more important: the filmmakers changed history to create a dramatic climax, the end of Halsey's duel with Yamamoto.

Having issued his historic order "Attack—repeat—attack!" to initiate the Naval Battle of Guadalcanal on 12 November 1942, Halsey listens to the sounds of combat for three days. Then receiving word that Yamamoto will be traveling on an inspection trip, he orders the Army Air Corps to shoot down the admiral's plane. On the fifteenth, as he and his staff await word of the success of the mission, they learn that the Japanese fleet is retreating. At that moment, they also learn that Yamamoto has been shot down. Only one problem exists with this scenario: Yamamoto did not actually die until 18 April 1943.

Does moving up the date five months destroy the film's credibility? If the filmmakers changed the date of one of the most significant events of the war, could viewers believe the dialogue and chronology of anything else in the film? Does dramatic license excuse the compression of history? After all, Halsey did order the Army to shoot down Yamamoto. The admiral did die.

In the end, *The Gallant Hours* does provide at least a reasonably accurate portrayal of one of the great officers in U.S. naval history as well as an explanation of how Halsey won a major victory that helped seal Japan's fate. The inaccuracies did not bother the Navy, which did not demand stricter adherence to the facts in return for giving the filmmakers a few planes and ships. In addition to the reverent story of Halsey, the Navy received a picture glorifying the officers and men, dead and alive, who made the victory at Guadalcanal possible. Moreover, the film provided a fitting capstone to Hollywood's efforts since the end of the war to show the Navy's contribution to the defeat of Germany and Japan.

★

★

EIGHT

Submarines versus Aircraft Carriers

During the 1950s, filmmakers had by no means neglected the contributions submariners and naval aviators had made to victory in World War II. On the way to exploiting the Korean War market, *Submarine Command* and *Torpedo Alley* had portrayed one of the submarine service's most appreciated jobs in the war against Japan, the rescue of downed aviators. *Flying Missile* had illustrated how submariners were putting knowledge gained from the last conflict into practice to fight the Cold War. At the end of the decade, *On the Beach* was to use a submarine to portray where such technology and weapons of war might take civilization.

Appearing on an average of more than one a year, virtually all other movies of the 1950s about submarines relived the real, as well as sometimes the imagined, heroics of the men who fought the war against Japan under the Pacific Ocean. Not surprisingly, the films became redundant and their plots almost indistinguishable.

Practical reasons encouraged Hollywood to so regularly return to undersea-combat stories. They did not cost much to make, relatively speaking. Given the small crews that manned submarines, studios did not have to issue large casting calls. Sets did not require much effort or imagination to construct and might even be borrowed in whole or part from previous productions or other studios. In addition, when Chief of Information Adm. Lewis Parks, a famed World War II submariner, visited Hollywood in July 1952, he urged filmmakers to make more movies about the Navy, promising its full cooperation. Studios readily understood the virtue of including a submarine story or two in their schedules.[1]

From a dramatic point of view, as Darryl Zanuck had observed during the writing of *Wing and a Prayer*, the threat of accident and death exists every time a submarine submerges, a World War I–vintage pigboat or a state-of-the-art nuclear-powered submarine. In combat, danger from enemy attacks creates another level of dramatic tension. The throbbing of destroyers' propellers, the ticking of depth charges as they sink, the scrape of mine cables, the confined spaces—all combine to attract audiences who want to share vicariously the thrills that draw men into the submarine service.

While the submarine service demonstrated a particular willingness to assist stories about its men and ships, the benefit it received from these 1950s movies remains questionable. It believed the movies became an excellent recruiting tool for the service's all-volunteer force. Moreover, the price of providing the requested assistance was small, usually no more than a single submarine and a destroyer or two for a few days of exterior shooting. Submerging and surfacing cost no more if done in front of camera crews and produced the same training.

From the end of World War II onward, however, no American submarine would fire a torpedo in anger. Diesel-powered attack submarines were rapidly becoming antiques by the late 1950s as the Navy acquired a nuclear submarine fleet that rendered World War II training methods and tactics obsolete. At best, Hollywood's portrayal of submarine combat against Japan provided a vague rendering of history and the generic excitement of undersea warfare, rather than information about the contemporary submarine service.

Still, the drama of World War II fought under the sea held an endless fascination for filmmakers. Once such visually exciting films as *Task Force, Twelve O'Clock High,* and *Sands of Iwo Jima* had demonstrated that World War II films would attract large audiences, the floodgates opened on the making of stories about each of the services. Warner Brothers became the first studio to schedule a submarine story set in World War II when it began work on *Operation Pacific* in conjunction with John Wayne's production company.

To find material for a suitable story, the studio bought a set of Navy Battle Reports, and the research department made a compilation of submarine actions in the Pacific to assist screenwriter George Waggner. Waggner went to Washington in early November 1949 to discuss the project with the Defense Department and the Navy. After his visit, John Horton in Baruch's office wrote to Waggner on 18 November that the proposed film "is of great interest to us" and that the Pentagon stood "ready to serve you as we may to facilitate and aid this progress." Wayne, who would star in the film, wrote to thank Horton for the assistance Waggner had received. He also said that the filmmakers felt the story line the writer had discussed "will lend itself to making a picture of which we can all be proud."[2]

Attached to his initial screenplay, dated 3 February 1950, Waggner noted that the personal story was wholly fictitious, but the incidents had actually happened, as recorded in the Navy Department's patrol reports. Based on input from Warner Brothers, with which Wayne had a distribution agreement, Waggner prepared a second draft of the screenplay dated 21 April 1950, which the studio forwarded to the Navy for comments and approval.[3]

On 22 May Towne sent George Dorsey, the Warner Brothers Washington representative, the Pentagon's rather unfavorable reaction: "Generally speaking, the present treatment of the submarine story is thought to be weak and inadequate compared to the tremendous possibilities offered by the subject of World War II submarines and submariners." Furthermore, the service found it "a bit disappointing that Warners have chosen to subordinate the dramatic impact of possibly hundreds of heroic exploits which are a matter of record . . . for a weak romantic story."[4]

Towne added that the Navy did find well-written the portrayal of the submarine captain's sacrificing his life by ordering his ship to crash-dive. However, the portrayal of the submarine's rescue of nuns and children, also based on a real incident, was not "nearly as dramatic as the hundreds of actual cases where submariners went in to shore right under the guns of shore batteries to rescue downed aviators" or other military personnel. The Navy "strongly" suggested the studio give "serious thought to eliminating some of the weak incidental sequences of this story, and take advantage of the tremendous dramatic value of actual submarine exploits in the war in the Pacific. It is believed that a greater story and motion picture would result."[5] Despite these concerns, the Navy desired to have the story completed, and believing Warner Brothers would seriously consider making changes in the script, Towne advised the studio that the Pentagon was ready to provide full cooperation. Nevertheless, he made it clear that some "corrections will have to be made, in addition to any changes which the studio feels should be made in the structure of the story to bring it closer to the one the Departments of Defense and Navy expected to see."[6]

To achieve this, Warner Brothers hired retired Adm. Charles Lockwood, a famed submariner, to help Waggner revise the script. Lockwood had found the story "highly exciting," but in a detailed memo to production manager Bill Guthrie on 8 June 1950 he suggested numerous changes and additions, beginning with the idea that some funny stories might help. Lockwood also hoped that the filmmakers would have the submarine sink a capital ship: "There were plenty of such sinkings. . . . They were an important part of the submarine contribution to victory." The admiral then offered a detailed analysis of the entire script, focusing on technical details and command decisions.[7]

Unfortunately, the Navy found significant problems with the revised script that Towne received on 2 August 1950. On 10 August the service informed Baruch's office that it disapproved of the script, which introduced a plot line about the failure of American torpedoes during World War II. The service objected "to the critical manner in which the story is presented. It borders on being vindictive. It presents the Navy in an undignified and unkind light." The Public Relations Office acknowledged "that some torpedoes were faulty. However, we do not wish to create an impression that these faulty torpedoes resulted from deliberate culpability or inefficiency on the part of persons in the Navy."[8] Feeling the script created this impression, the office said it did not "wish to air publicly any strong grievances submariners may have against those people furnishing them with torpedoes later found to be faulty."

The service then "recommended that the script be rewritten to remove our objections and to tell the story in more subdued manner not reflecting discredit upon the Navy." The Navy suggested scenes showing the failure of some torpedoes, the realization that a problem existed, the formation of a team to find the problem, and the solution. Throughout the sequence, "submariners should naturally be irked at their ill luck but still determined to play an important part in finding out what was wrong. A more sympathetic attitude on the part of the submariners is required in the script."[9]

The next day, Towne informed Dorsey that the Navy found "that some major changes have been made in the treatment since we approved the first draft. The changes have resulted in a presentation of the problem of faulty torpedoes in a very critical and vindictive manner, and is likely to give an impression of a state of discipline that would in time of war be inimical to a proper performance of the military mission." Towne assured Dorsey that the Navy had "no basic objection to laying bare the problem of faulty torpedoes. There is objection to the manner in which the problem is attacked. If the approach to the problem is constructive instead of destructive, and if it can be handled in a manner that will not bring discredit on the Navy, but will instead result in determining the solution to the problem, the story will likely be approved."[10]

Dorsey immediately sent a telegram to Guthrie, saying that the Navy had withdrawn its approval because of the "faulty torpedo sequences." In response, Lou Edelman called Towne, who explained that, as written, the script showed the officers complaining about the faulty torpedoes as a bunch of soreheads. Edelman conceded the point, and the two men agreed to change a scene in which an officer blows his top in front of the admiral. In the new version, the officer vents his anger, the admiral stops him cold, the officer "profusely apologizes," and the admiral, "getting back the respect due his rank and position graciously accepts the abject apology tendered." The changed script implied that the "discipline of the Navy must be upheld at all costs."[11] In regard to the faulty torpedoes, the producer explained that inserting the plot line had given the story a significance it had not enjoyed previously. Towne agreed but reminded Edelman the Navy had solved the problem during the war and the contemporary torpedoes performed with complete reliability. After further discussion Towne promised Edelman full cooperation once the filmmakers had a script with "the vindictiveness eliminated."[12]

With this quickly done, Warner Brothers began filming *Operation Pacific* at sea aboard the USS *Thunder* at the end of September 1950. The studio also built a huge mock-up of the submarine on a soundstage for sequences impossible to shoot at sea. The resulting movie follows the officers and men of the *Thunderfish* on its patrols in enemy waters, with all the requisite submarine actions, with the problem of the defective torpedoes providing the distinguishing ingredient.

The dramatic high point of the story comes when Wayne's character orders the *Thunderfish* to submerge to avoid an attack, leaving the boat's mortally wounded captain, Ward Bond, on the conning tower. Although he has made the correct decision, he earns the animus of Bond's Navy pilot brother. In the end, Wayne's character solves the problem of the defective torpedoes, becomes the captain of the submarine, blunts the attack of a Japanese armada, and rescues Bond's brother after he has to bail out during battle.

In truth, *Operation Pacific* seemed to focus as much on Wayne's courting his ex-wife, played by Patricia Neal, as on submarine warfare. Such dialogue as his question about her boyfriend, "When you kiss him, do you get that old zing?" brought scorn from the *New Yorker*. Worse, the action at sea caused the critic to conclude, "I would hesitate to trust the Weehawken ferry to the hands of the gentleman, and I'm afraid the lady makes an unlikely Lorelei."[13]

To the Navy, the romance was secondary to the portrayal of the submarine force. The revelation of the torpedo problem did little to help the service's image, particularly since most people had not known about the flawed weaponry. Nevertheless, *Operation Pacific* illustrated that the Navy did ultimately correct the fault and how the submarine service contributed more than its share to the overall victory in the Pacific. It also left Hollywood with little new to include in subsequent submarine tales since the film contained a little bit of everything U.S. submarines had encountered during the war. Consequently, subsequent undersea films simply imitated *Operation Pacific*.

The 1957 *Hellcats of the Navy*, in which Ronald Reagan met his future First Lady, might actually have qualified as a comedy if the filmmakers had not played the story straight. In one of his two combat roles, Reagan, as the submarine captain, must capture a Japanese mine, which is virtually undetectable on sonar, so that experts can study it. In 1944, the film's setting, the Navy was trying to get close enough to Japan's shore to destroy its vital shipping lines. During the cruise, Reagan's character must leave behind a frogman, his rival for the hand of the character played by Nancy, to escape from a Japanese attack.

The film uses this "dilemma" to raise real questions of command responsibility between a captain and his executive officer, with the former trying to explain that promotion comes to those who have the ability to make hard decisions quickly and well. Ultimately, the executive officer has to make the same decision and leaves his captain on the surface. Reagan's character survives, but his second in command has experienced the weight of command decisions and so becomes a better officer.

Hellcats of the Navy does derive a sense of authenticity from the appearance in name, if not in actual person, of Adm. Chester Nimitz, who delivers a foreword about the actual operation he supervised during the war, which served as the genesis of the film. Nevertheless, *Weekly Variety* noted, "This succeeds as far as the fighting is concerned, but cannot make real the unoriginal screen story the screenwriter concocted from the original book. . . . The underwater fighting is laced with a formula plot which at times gets awfully trite, but results are still okay for the general, dual-bill situation." Conceding some suspense in the minefield charting operation, the reviewer suggested that the script "plies a hackneyed course dealing with problems of command that will sacrifice one man to save many and the resentment that such action causes. A romantic angle is plastered to the carcass of the plot and means little."[14]

Despite the failure of the film as drama, the Navy found a way to benefit from its involvement in the production. By supporting the film's premiere at New London, the submarine service was able to put on a show for the press. One of the journalists in attendance, Charles S. Aaronson, "came away from the base an astonishingly articulate proponent of things Navy, submarines in particular, and submarine personnel in special particular." He also thought that "such films as *Hellcats of the Navy* serve, in this view, a greater service nationwide than entertainment merely. They offer to a generally lethargic populace a keen, objectively favorable presentation of the kind of thing these defenders do, most often at serious risk, to protect us, especially when the chips are down."[15]

In addition to submarine rides, the Navy provided a three-hour cruise, a cocktail party at the officers' club with a large number of senior officers, a brief ceremony before the screening, and then the film. Aaronson reported on life aboard a sub, including the bruises, and was awed by the efficiency of operation and brightness of the sailors: "This kind of promotional effort is of extraordinary value, to a motion picture, to the motion picture industry, and in significant degree to the nation as a whole and its vital defense system."[16]

Not all submarine movies received or needed such a promotion. One of the few that did rise above mediocrity, *Run Silent, Run Deep*, helped keep the genre alive. Appearing early in 1958, the highly praised adaptation of Capt. Edward Beach's popular novel of the same name contained many of the elements common to the earlier submarine films, as well as its one unique element, the captain's obsessive efforts to develop a "down the throat" shot, which he hopes to use to avenge the sinking of his previous boat. However, the film focused on the conflict between the captain and his troubled executive officer, played by two of Hollywood's leading stars, Clark Gable and Burt Lancaster.

Ironically, this interaction was the weakest element in the book, at least according to Delmer Daves, who critiqued the novel for its cinematic potential. He found the story strong on naval incident and detail but lacking "in personality developments, human relations,—what we call the 'personal' story." As a result, he felt any film based on the novel needed to develop the conflict between the captain and his executive officer very carefully.[17]

Not only did the screenwriter do that, but the filmmakers also received substantially more material assistance from the Navy than Daves had had for *Destination Tokyo*. This cooperation and a highly detailed studio mock-up of a submarine's interior gave the movie a better visual sense of life aboard a World War II submarine than any previous story. The filmmakers actually built their mock-up with the same dimensions as actual submarines.[18]

However, many of the incidents leave the audience confused or incredulous. In the film's opening sequence, a Japanese destroyer attacks a U.S. submarine and sinks it with depth charges. Yet its captain somehow finds his way onto a life raft, avoids capture in Japanese waters, and makes his way in short order back to Pearl Harbor. The story itself is built on the premise that a Japanese submarine is torpedoing American craft while both are submerged. Historically, on both sides, submarines destroyed their counterparts when they found them cruising on the surface. Former submariners do not deny the possibility of a successful attack on a submerged boat but consider it a remote occurrence. Likewise conceding that submarines could torpedo an attacking destroyer with a straight-on bow shot as shown in the movie, submariners said it rarely happened.[19]

Despite such lapses of plausibility, *Run Silent, Run Deep* resembles a documentary, focusing on techniques of attack and command decisions. The *New York Times* praised the film more for its skillful filmmaking that did not "waste movement, time or words." Crowther said tension became the key to the action and resulted from screenwriter John Gay's keeping his script "efficiently rigged" and from Robert Wise's direction. He also thought Gable gave a fine performance as the captain, "fierce, self-confident and self-contained," and Lancaster was "impressively punctilious as the troubled 'exec.'"[20]

The next silent-service film, *Torpedo Run* drew on historical events, including a submarine captain's having to sink a Japanese merchant ship carrying his wife and children, and a submarine's sinking of one of the aircraft carriers that launched planes against Pearl Harbor. It also showed the actual loss of a submarine and the manner in which the crew escaped. The filmmakers chose to build larger-than-life sets, in which the crew, with Glenn Ford again playing a sub commander, performed their duties while their captain attempts to track down the carrier with Ahab-like myopia.

Like most obsessions, the captain's leads to tragedy. When he finds the carrier, he discovers the Japanese are using a merchant freighter as a defensive shield. Although Submarine Command in Pearl Harbor has informed him the freighter is carrying 1,400 American dependents captured in the Philippines, including his wife and child, Ford attacks anyway. Although he fires only two torpedoes in a narrow spread rather than the normal six, he misses his target and hits the freighter. Through the periscope he sees a few survivors in the water, whom the Japanese destroyers are using as bait.

Ford has no choice but to leave, much as John Wayne's and William Holden's characters left their captains and Ronald Reagan's abandoned the frogman. *Torpedo Run* does differ from other submarine movies in actually portraying the stress that command decision creates, in much the way *Twelve O'Clock High* showed the breakdown of Gregory Peck's character. The film also reinforces the need for complete honesty in military men by including a scene in which Ernest Borgnine, as the submarine's executive officer, tells Ford that he will have to report that Ford slept for more than a day after sinking the merchant ship. Somewhat implausibly, Submarine Fleet allows Ford one more chance to track down the carrier, and Borgnine's character temporarily gives up a chance to captain his own boat to help the effort, which proves successful.

As with all the films receiving assistance from the submarine service, *Torpedo Run* does contain a good portrayal of life aboard subs in wartime. It also has a unique portrayal of a combined operation, showing a British submariner aboard, both learning from the Americans and giving help based on his own experiences. In addition to showing the questionable ability of torpedoes to blast a hole in a sub net, the film also portrays for the first time the use of the Mortenson escape lung in combat, with the resulting drama as the men struggle to escape from a flooded sub.

By the time *Torpedo Run* appeared in October 1958, authenticity could no longer sustain dramatic tensions. Audiences could predict when the depth charges would fall and who would live or die. In the *New York Times*, Crowther observed that the film offered nothing "new or unconventional. . . . Stereotypes of pig-boat fighting that were stale in *Destination Tokyo* are played and replayed in this picture as if they were freshly inspired. Periscopes are looked through, torpedoes are fired at ships, orders to 'Take her down!' are shouted and depth-charge attacks are endured." The film "is also played in a highly hackneyed fashion and often faked with preposterous miniatures." Worse, shooting the movie in color and CinemaScope "only makes more apparent the toy-like look of those miniatures."[21]

The descent to mediocrity continued with the totally forgettable *Submarine Seahawk,* which appeared in January 1959. Put together with some stock footage, some sets from more expensive productions, and a few miniatures, the film goes along on a patrol with an inexperienced captain and his dissatisfied crew. He ultimately wins over his men when his plans lead to the destruction of a large portion of the Japanese fleet. *Weekly Variety* thought the film succeeds "when it sticks to the tension-building sequences of the sub stalking the enemy. . . . Its [*sic*] been done before, but its [*sic*] still engrossing." The movie weakens when it follows the men ashore "or when it explores some of the human relationships of the crew members. An unstable Navy officer who attempts to take over the sub's command the first time his two superiors are absent from the bridge is strongly incredible."[22]

Certainly more credible, *Up Periscope*, which appeared the next month, returned to the mundane. The film has a rigid captain, a frogman on a secret mission, a clash of officers, a successful raid, and a return to port with all hands happy. Nevertheless, *The Hollywood Reporter* felt the film had "enough new structural gimmicks to make it fresh and unusual." Acknowledging the few moments of tension, A. H. Weiler, in the *New York Times*, concluded that *Up Periscope* "sails a movie course that is not particularly exciting. The bravery shown here is no longer unsung."[23]

Appearing in October 1959, *Battle of the Coral Sea* only reinforced the fact that filmmakers were running out of ways to portray submarines in action. The movie had virtually nothing to do with that early 1942 battle. Submarines did conduct reconnaissance missions, which serves as the story's springboard, and the Japanese did capture submariners, including the crews of the *Perch* and *Sculpin*. Beyond such historical incidents, however, *The Battle of the Coral Sea* has no connection with reality.

No record exists of Japanese frogmen forcing an American submarine to the surface with mines or a captured crew being imprisoned on a remote island, as the movie portrays. Such implausibilities only set the stage for the Americans' equally unrealistic escape, which is the excuse for a gigantic shoot-out and massive explosions, more reminiscent of a low-budget wartime film than a retrospective submarine story.

Despite the absurdity of the plot, the Navy did allow the filmmakers access to facilities and ships in San Diego, including a submarine, a destroyer escort, and tugs. The assistance did little to improve the quality of the story or benefit the service beyond suggesting that its men would show bravery and ingenuity in the face of adversity. According to *Weekly Variety, Battle of the Coral Sea* had "no unique value" but did have "an appearance that surpasses its budget."[24]

Ironically, after nearly a decade of making so many similar underseas-combat films, Hollywood was to end its love affair with the submarine service with a movie that bears little resemblance to any of the previous stories. Perhaps reflecting the distance from the war itself, Universal Pictures approached the Pentagon in January 1957 for cooperation on a comedy about the misadventures of a pink submarine. Writing to Baruch, George Dorsey, the studio's Washington agent, promised *Operation Petticoat* "would be a credit to the submarine service."[25]

Without reference to the story's humorous nature, the Navy advised Baruch's office that the treatment contained several incidents from its own *U.S. Submarine Operations in World War II*. Citing some inaccuracies in the treatment, the service concluded that the story "seems to have possibilities, but it needs considerable technical cleaning up, particularly by someone who has served in an S-boat." Wallace Marley, writing for Baruch, told the studio that the office had recently reviewed a television script that, like *Operation Petticoat*, portrayed a submarine evacuating nurses from Corregidor. However, the "action in the two stories is quite different," and he believed the television program would air long before Universal's film. Marley also indicated the office would consider cooperation when it received a final script.[26]

Cary Grant's reprise of his submarine-captain role from *Destination Tokyo* provided the only common ingredient between *Operation Petticoat* and all the movies about underseas combat in the Pacific. Despite its comedic format, however, the writer had based the story on actual incidents, albeit ones happening to several submarines. The pinkish *Seadragon* had actually sailed from the Philippines because the Japanese attack caught it undergoing repairs. Several submarines did evacuate people from Corregidor in the days before the island finally surrendered on 6 May 1942. The *Spearfish*, with James Dempsey in command, was the last boat to put into the island, where it picked up twenty-five passengers, including twelve Army nurses and the wife of a naval officer, the night of 3 May, thus becoming the actual inspiration for the movie.[27]

In *Operation Petticoat*, Grant's character wants to take his submarine out of dry dock and into action when the war breaks out. When he cannot find enough of either white or red lead undercoating paint, he combines the two and ends up with a pinkish hue. After a Japanese air attack blows up the stock of regulation gray outer paint, he has to depart with a pink submarine. The screenplay made the events logical enough for the Navy to agree to provide the World War II submarine *Balao* and then allow the filmmakers to paint it pink at the appropriate time. Producer Robert Arthur admitted, "We blushed when we asked for it and almost fainted when the Navy said okay."[28]

The submarine simply serves as the stage on which Army nurses coexist with sailors during the escape from the advancing Japanese in the first days of the war. Writing to Dorsey in June 1958, Arthur recognized the need for "a fresh approach" to the subject in light of all the other submarine movies already released or in production. He explained that he intended to "relate *Operation Petticoat* in the broadest possible comedy terms with the underlying drama inherent in the basic situation." This approach would enable the film "to avoid the familiar cliche character relationships generally used in service stories, such as the conflict between skipper and exec officer" or a young officer's rite of passage "through a heroic death, etc." Having women aboard the boat provided the uniqueness of *Operation Petticoat* and gave the filmmakers endless opportunities for comedy, limited only by the still-existing Production Code.[29]

When it read the script in July 1958, the Army objected to the use of its nurses "in a 'slap stick' comedy type of supporting role. Such a portrayal of the serious professional women who were forced down in Mindanao would not be taken lightly by these women, their friends, and families." The service felt the public "is a bit tired of this kind of so-called entertainment. There has [*sic*] been too many comedy type movies portraying Army nurses in a similar setting which gave a false interpretation of the majority of professional nurses practicing in the Army Medical Service. We may know the difference but the public does not and it is to the public we look for support in obtaining professional nurses for the Army Nurse Corps."[30]

In informing Dorsey on 21 July 1958 of the Army's reaction, Marley said Baruch's office felt that "with a word of caution to the studio, they can develop an acceptable screen play that will reflect credit to the Army Nurse Corps and also have the situation comedy and entertainment value desired." Ultimately, the studio satisfied the Army and Navy and received the assistance it needed. After the studio screened the film in the Pentagon on 14 September 1959, Baruch wrote the producer that all military observers "unanimously declared it a success." He also assured Arthur, who had attended the screening, that the "laughs were genuine, and everyone present thoroughly enjoyed the picture. However, beneath all the good fun and jokes, the story shows the wonderful ingenuity and spirit of a crew to keep the ship afloat and in the battle." He hoped the Pentagon's reaction would not prove misleading and the film would "keep audiences around the world laughing for a long time."[31] Although Arthur requested permission to use Baruch's comments in advertisements, the Pentagon found such use "inappropriate." Given Bosley Crowther's reaction, the studio undoubtedly regretted the decision. The reviewer found *Operation Petticoat* "repetitious and a trifle monotonous" and blamed the problem "on the self-intoxication of the writers and Director Blake Edwards. They were evidently rendered more giggly by the gags than is the audience. The situation is not sufficient for extension over two hours despite the personableness of the actors and the prettiness of the color film."[32]

Such criticism notwithstanding, *Operation Petticoat* became a big hit thanks to the continuing appeal of Cary Grant, the appearance of the then-popular Tony Curtis as the submarine's executive officer, and the presence of the five nurses aboard the boat. From the Navy's perspective, the sight gags and double entendres were secondary to the opportunity to convey images of the lighter side of life aboard submarines after so many grim portrayals of wartime combat. Nor did it hurt for Grant's and Curtis's characters to end up marrying two of the nurses.

By the time *Operation Petticoat* appeared at the end of 1959, World War II was fast becoming ancient history, and the Navy had very few submarines of that vintage still on the active list. More important, the service no longer needed stories about the bravery of its men in World War II, since such images had relatively little value as recruiting posters. Therefore, a pink submarine had the distinction of making the last wartime cruise on the silver screen.

Meanwhile, Hollywood had continued making carrier stories, set both in peacetime and during war. While *Bridges at Toko-ri* had portrayed the downside of carrier warfare, the flying sequences still had appeal, and the three naval aviation films of the mid-fifties offered more of the same. However, they also shared powerful images of death and destruction in battle, and each purported to tell a true story. Two focused on crippled aviators returning to active duty, while the third provided a documentary-like account of the USS *Franklin*, the most heavily damaged U.S. ship to return to port.

Ironically, the two most realistic movies, *The Eternal Sea*, appearing in 1955, and *Battle Stations*, released the next year, enjoyed almost no success and have seldom even appeared on late-night television or cable. Undoubtedly, their unrelenting grimness doomed them to a quick demise. Yet each in its own way conveyed the courage of men in combat as well as, if not better than, any of the more popular aviation stories that Hollywood produced after World War II.

The Eternal Sea follows the struggle of John Hoskins, a famed carrier pilot, to stay in the Navy after suffering a devastating injury on the eve of achieving his life's goal of becoming the captain of an aircraft carrier. In one moment he loses a leg and the USS *Princeton* to Japanese attackers. Recuperating in the hospital at the Philadelphia Naval Base, he watches the construction of the new *Princeton* from his window. In the face of disbelief and flat-out opposition from all sides, including his long-suffering wife, Hoskins invokes a little-known regulation stating that the Navy cannot retire an officer or enlisted member wounded in combat if the person wishes to remain in the service.

Hoskins receives command of the *Princeton*, from which he wages an ultimately successful campaign to fly jets off carriers, and he returns to the cockpit to demonstrate the feasibility of his theory. Having made vice admiral, he turns down another promotion to work on improving the Navy's air-transportation capacity after seeing how men wounded in the Korean War had suffered on their way back to Hawaii.

Despite its inspirational images, *The Eternal Sea* failed to attract audiences. The film's intense seriousness contributed to its lack of box-office success, but Hoskins's own personality, at least the one Sterling Hayden creates, does little to increase the movie's appeal. The flier has little humor and shows almost no sensitivity for his wife and children. His whole life revolves around his career and an obsession for command, certainly not an endearing quality. Nevertheless, his story deserved to be told. His courage and perseverance are the stuff of naval legend, and today's carriers stand as his legacy.

Despite its equally legendary subject, *Battle Stations* never became more than a thinly disguised account of the *Franklin*'s last cruise. The filmmakers do not identify the carrier and change the names of the actual men, who become only generic cinematic characters. Moreover, viewers had seen all the same footage of the destruction one Japanese bomber had wrought, either in *Task Force* or in *Victory at Sea*. Nevertheless, *Battle Stations* did accurately recreate virtually every detail of the courageous struggle of the crew to save their ship.

The daily log of the *Franklin* supplied the entries for the cinematic carrier's journey from the West Coast to a spot fifty or so miles off the coast of Japan in March 1945. The attack of the single Japanese bomber matches the actual event to the minute. Finally, the crew's frantic and ultimately successful efforts to save the ship as well as its voyage back to the Brooklyn Naval Shipyard follow closely what actually happened, with the actual heroes easily recognizable to anyone who knows the story.

In black and white rather than color, *Battle Stations* not only re-creates history but explains better than any other carrier movie the actual workings of the ship, thanks to a top-to-bottom tour the new chaplain receives. Except for some early humor and one interaction between the ship's captain and a rear gunner, the portrayal of the travails of the carrier remains too grim to qualify as entertainment. The successful efforts of the young enlisted man to have his pilot returned to flight status attest to the realism of the film and stand in stark contrast to the implausible grounding of fliers in *Wing and a Prayer* and *Flat Top*. This refusal to fictionalize the story as much as the use of the previously seen footage combined to doom the movie to a quick demise.

In contrast, *Wings of Eagles* and its subject, Frank "Spig" Wead, enjoyed the good fortune of having John Ford direct and John Wayne star as the tragic hero. In the guise of Wead's fictionalized biography, *Wings of Eagles* also told the history of aircraft carriers and presented the ultimate argument that they represented the backbone of the fleet, the "spearpoint of battle" for the Navy. Appearing in 1957, the film not only showed how the carriers performed their mission, but the process by which the service had worked with Hollywood to get "the public on our side. Getting them to help us out with the money men in Congress."[33]

Wead undoubtedly deserved a serious cinematic portrayal. After graduating from the Naval Academy in 1916 and serving aboard a minesweeper in hostile waters during World War I, he became one of the Navy's early aviators. He commanded one of the first torpedo-plane squadrons as well as the first squadron of planes to operate from an American aircraft carrier. At one time he held five world records in naval aviation and led the Navy squadron that won the Snyder Cup in Paris in 1925. The next year, at the height of his career, Wead fell at home, becoming partially paralyzed and confined to a hospital bed.[34]

While undergoing a painful and long rehabilitation, he began writing articles for aviation trade journals and then fiction for pulp magazines. He later recalled, "I didn't know any writers, so I had to work out things for myself. I found that first, one must learn story construction, like an architect. Then add the suspense and emotion according to one's own feelings for the characters involved." Ultimately, he graduated to writing for the stage and motion pictures, including the play *Ceiling Zero*, which he adapted for the screen after he arrived in Hollywood in 1928. While he wrote many stories about the military and aviation, his Navy movies, including *Flying Fleet, Dirigible, Hell Divers, Midshipman Jack, Dive Bomber,* and *Destroyer,* undoubtedly gave Wead his greatest satisfaction.[35]

Despite his limited mobility and age, Wead managed to talk his way back to active duty after Pearl Harbor, serving first in the Navy's War Room in Washington. He later supervised new carrier groups at Quansett, Rhode Island, and after being promoted to commander became planning officer at Pearl Harbor in the office of the Staff of Commander Air Force, Pacific Fleet. Ultimately, he experienced combat firsthand, serving aboard a carrier during the invasion of the Marshalls, the first attack against Truk, and the battle for the Marianas. For his service in combat, the Navy awarded him the Legion of Merit. He retired to Hollywood in 1944, where he wrote *They Were Expendable* for his long-time friend John Ford before dying in 1947.[36]

Of such stuff do great film directors such as Ford make heroic epics. Since he had contributed so much to the Navy's efforts to sell itself to the American people, any story based on Wead's life should have had an immediate appeal to the service. However, the first two attempts to develop the project in Hollywood led nowhere. Kenneth MacKenna, working at MGM on a third effort, and retired Adm. John Dale Price, a friend of Wead's from their days at Annapolis, informed Baruch in November 1954 that "the material so far written does not live up to the possibilities of the inspiring story of Wead's life, nor does it conform to the true traditions of the Naval Service." However, with Price's advice and collaboration, MacKenna indicated that a new treatment of Wead's life would do "justice to both Wead and the Navy."[37]

During the next eight months MacKenna kept Baruch informed of his progress in developing a satisfactory story. When the screenplay finally arrived in September 1955, it still contained numerous errors, particularly in setting people and events in the incorrect time. In response to the critique by the Navy's Historical Section, the studio submitted a revised script, which it said incorporated all the recommendations. The Navy believed the screenplay would "make an interesting motion picture," but the Chief of Information told Baruch that the story still contained historical inaccuracies. Since the service perceived the film as "a fictional drama," it said it saw no value in attempting to correct the errors. Still, the office told Baruch that it had no objection to extending full cooperation to the production.[38]

Informing MGM's Washington representative of the decision, Baruch did request the deletion of a Navy pilot's comment, "Headline grabbing stunt—Army every time." He also asked that the filmmakers consider eliminating a fight scene because many movies "have sequences of Service personnel fighting in public and the over-all impression is becoming unfavorable. In this case, there does not appear to be any inherent story point to the actual fight." Indicating that the technical adviser could make minor corrections during the production, Baruch asked MGM for a list of requirements, including those for location shooting aboard a carrier.[39]

The Navy agreed to allow Admiral Price to act as technical adviser even though active-duty officers usually served in that capacity and so had more leverage in securing accurate portrayals. However, the Navy recognized the possible conflict of interest, particularly since the revised script that the service received in March 1956 still contained the problems Baruch had mentioned to the studio in November. As a result, the Chief of Information asked Baruch to request that "minor script changes be made throughout to eliminate the appearance that the principal character and his wife are in a constant pre-alcoholic state with the impression that this is typical Navy conduct."[40]

Admiral Price himself addressed the Navy's concerns in a letter to the Office of Information, suggesting minor revisions. In particular, he asked whether the service would withdraw its objection to the fight scene if Wead would take "the sting" out of the action by reminiscing later in the film, "Oh, those are the forgotten days; twenty years ago—those things don't happen any more. The Services have learned to fight as a team, not each other." The Navy found the proposed changes agreeable, since the service's primary concern was with images of planes and combat.[41]

With this in mind, the Navy provided full assistance in the making of *The Wings of Eagles,* with only the availability of a carrier and airplanes where and when the studio needed them causing minor problems. The production became a labor of love for Ford, Wayne, Price, and screenwriter William Wister Haines, all of whom had been close friends with Wead. Although the movie suggests Wead died of a heart attack resulting from the effort he expended during his time in combat, he actually died in Hollywood, in Ford's arms.[42]

The director should have hewed closer to the truth, for the film ends with Wayne ignominiously dangling from a breeches buoy as he transfers from his aircraft carrier to a waiting destroyer and so to retirement. Although Ford was paying personal homage to his friend, the film fails to elicit much compassion for a man who experienced the height of success as a flier and writer as well as the depth of despair as a cripple forced to use a wheelchair and later crutches. Instead of becoming a sympathetic, courageous man struggling to recover from a tragic accident, Wayne's Wead changes from a self-centered egotist who has abandoned his wife and children for the excitement of naval aviation to a self-pitying invalid who refuses to have anything to do with his family. Even after becoming a successful screenwriter, the cinematic Wead abandons his only attempt to reconcile with his wife and returns to the Navy after Pearl Harbor.

Given the fictional form Ford used to tell Wead's story, audiences have no way of separating reality from illusion, and perhaps no film biography more deserves the disclaimer that any resemblance between the characters and actual people is purely coincidental.[43] *Wings of Eagles* had more serious problems.

Newsweek observed that Wead's struggle to overcome paralysis "may sound like realism with a vengeance; it has to be seen to be disbelieved." Likewise, the *New York Times* film critic wrote, "Like many affectionate tributes, this one comes more from the heart than from the head—or, at least, from that cerebral area where great motion pictures are conceived. The life of Spig Wead, while full of daring and a remarkable fortitude, was not one to delude a Hollywood veteran into thinking it meat for a deep biography."[44]

The Navy did not care about such criticisms, being concerned only with its image in general and, in this case, with the image of naval aviation. However, *Wings of Eagles* elicited some decidedly negative reactions. Dick French, for one, wrote to the Secretary of Defense "Complaint Dept." that he wanted the military to know that if the country "is or ever was in the hands of a drunken Navy typified by broken families and godless conduct as expressed in *Wings of Eagles,* I would certainly be ashamed to admit it." He suggested that the Pentagon "count the times in the film that liquor is portrayed as 'normal' and 'regular' as well as references to child abandonment, wayward fatherhood and selfish motherhood." French concluded, "I was ashamed of the picture, but more so of our Government for letting its proud name be connected with it." He said his wife and children "for once" agreed with him and signed the letter "An irate Republican."[45]

In reply, Baruch told French that John Ford had described *Wings of Eagles* as a tender-tough account of an extraordinary pioneer Navy flier and writer and, above all, a brave man. According to Baruch, the military saw the film's early scenes as "marked by rowdy male humor, but the most deeply felt and moving portion of the story is that part where Wead attempts against medical advice to overcome his paralysis. . . . a brusque combination of comedy and tragedy." He thought the producer and director "deserve a great deal of credit, because there was so much which had to be included and so much which could only be presented obliquely." Given the time in which Wead lived, Baruch felt French's "objections can be rationalized."[46]

Although the Pentagon might rationalize the negative images, the film contained few positive images to benefit the Navy. *Task Force* had covered much of the same history, perhaps in a more pedantic manner but certainly with more visual excitement in the combat scenes. In contrast, *Wings of Eagles* compressed World War II into a brief and incoherent montage of a generic battle. As a result, Ford's film added little if anything to people's knowledge of naval aviation, let alone providing a true appreciation of Spig Wead, the flier and screenwriter, whose own work had ironically already done everything for the Navy that it might have expected from his cinematic biography.

The nuclear submarines, supercarriers, jet planes, and missile-launching surface ships that Congress was by then funding became a better legacy for Wead than *Wings of Eagles.* From Hollywood's perspective, any benefit its motion pictures featuring the Navy had brought the service over the years remained secondary to the profits they earned the studios. For practical reasons, filmmakers had created stories on which the Navy would agree to cooperate. By the end of the decade, however, audiences were becoming tired of the traditional portrayals. Moreover, the old studio system was giving way to independent producers with no commitment to the old ways of doing business with the Pentagon. As a result, the Hollywood/Navy relationship that had worked so well for almost fifty years was beginning to come under considerable stress.

★

NINE

World War II Again and the Bomb

A lthough the Navy had helped establish the guidelines regulating cooperation with Hollywood, the service was an innocent bystander when
the relationship came under attack in 1961. Ironically, the problem
arose during the production of one of the very great movies about men at war.
Not only did the armed services provide full assistance to *The Longest Day,* but
the film contained only the most positive images of the U.S. armed forces.
Nevertheless, due to political considerations beyond the control of the individual services, the free and easy process of doing business with Hollywood almost
came to an end.

The controversy began far from the scene of the crime. On 7 September
1961, during the height of the Berlin Wall crisis, Jack Paar, the host of NBC's
"Tonight" show, traveled to one of the border crossings where several confrontations had recently occurred. Seven Army officers and about fifty men in
seven jeeps arrived and took up positions in front of Paar's cameras. The Army
later explained that it had simply permitted Paar to film a changeover of units.[1]

By the next day, news of Paar's visit to the border crossing had reached
Washington, where it caused an immediate outcry in the Senate. Majority Whip
Hubert Humphrey commented that the government had more important things
to do than "provide a backdrop for television shows." Senator Clifford Case suggested that "the practice of making facilities of the defense establishment available for any private ownership, for commercialization and commercial profit, is
one to be examined and should be permitted only in a situation in which their
use would not in any way endanger the security of the United States." Even
though the 8 September issue of *Time* had described how the Army was assisting

149

producer Darryl Zanuck in making *The Longest Day,* the film did not enter into the discussion, and the Senate lost interest after the Army announced it had taken disciplinary action against two officers.[2]

Unfortunately, David Brinkley made the connection when he defended his network colleague on his evening news broadcast. Then, Assistant Secretary of Defense for Public Affairs Arthur Sylvester expressed his reservations about Pentagon cooperation with the film industry: "I have grave doubts whether this sort of thing is a proper use for military equipment and manpower. It looks to me like a skunk in the military garden party." He questioned the Army's assistance to Zanuck while it was complaining about a manpower shortage. Sylvester further noted, "Zanuck isn't paying for any of the time our troops put in or for the equipment."[3]

To protect the White House and the Secretary of Defense, Sylvester launched an examination that ultimately led to a new set of regulations governing military cooperation. The Navy contributed to the controversy at the end of January 1962 when a sailor died while preparing explosives for use in filming *No Man is an Island,* which was receiving limited assistance. Although the man had taken leave to work on the movie, Congressman Walter Norblad declared that filmmakers should hire their own extras and employ civilian experts for dangerous special effects.[4]

Ironically, the Navy had been involved with few films at the beginning of the decade. In 1960 Delmer Daves had received courtesy assistance to shoot a few brief scenes at the submarine base in New London for the melodramatic *Parrish.* Although the film has nothing to do with the service except to give Parrish a place in which to mature, the Navy did receive good publicity from his nuclear submarine's cruise to the North Pole. The service also provided the ships from which soldiers and marines re-created the landings in *The Longest Day.*[5]

In contrast, *No Man is an Island* focuses entirely on a Navy man, George Tweed, who had refused to surrender to the Japanese when they overran Guam at the beginning of the war. Instead, Tweed stayed alive for three years with the help of the Guamanian people. From his hideout, Tweed broadcast news of the war's progress with a makeshift radio until the American invasion force arrived. Then he escaped with information that helped the Navy soften up the Japanese defenses. Despite this positive image of a Navy man, the sailor's death during the production forced the Pentagon to justify the studio's use of a destroyer and a few sailors. Baruch explained, the script "closed with the unmistakable impression that Tweed's actions and information contributed to the successful attack on Guam. His refusal to surrender himself or his men are embodied in the present-day Code of Conduct."[6]

The filmmakers had requested assistance during the summer of 1961, before the controversy over cooperation began, and had not encountered any significant problems. After the Navy read the script, the Office of Information advised

Baruch the story qualified for limited cooperation, indicating, however, that the producers should substantiate the claim that the film was "based on the official records of the U.S. Navy." Due to current Japanese-American relations, it also recommended that the filmmakers eliminate or play down the torture scenes in the script.[7] Baruch's office conveyed the Navy's reaction and the decision to provide limited assistance to the producers, also objecting to the use of the term "gooks" because it did not reflect America's present relations with the Japanese or Guamanians: "Although the use of the term is a historical fact of World War II, we have been successful in prevailing upon producers to tone down certain vernacular references to a former enemy when the latter is now a strong ally."[8]

The producers agreed to play down or eliminate terror and torture, explaining that they had intended to "portray the Japanese military of 1941–45 not as terrorists but simply as professionals, doing their jobs in the manner prescribed by their ruling hierarchy of the time. It will be our endeavor [*sic*] at all times to play them correctly and impersonally as possible within that frame of reference—in other words, as being businesslike, harressed [*sic*] by the pressure of the mounting counter-attack, but never with the overt sadism of, for example, *Bridge Over the River Kwai*." They also tried to justify the use of "gook" for "dramatic effect."[9]

The argument fell on deaf ears, with the Navy advising Baruch, "While we do not deny the term was used by members of the Navy, we feel no benefit can be gained by portraying Americans who have no regard for the sensitivities of other people." Baruch then wrote the producers: "In our ever-increasing responsibility for maintaining a mutual friendship and respect among people of foreign lands, the use of disparaging terms to identify ethnic, national or religious groups is inimical to our national interest, particularly in motion pictures sanctioned by Government cooperation."[10]

The filmmakers eliminated "gook," and the Navy approved assistance. Though the controversy over military assistance to filmmakers had begun by then, the Navy provided a destroyer, some personnel, and other limited help. In return, the Navy gained a positive portrayal, but requested that the company remove the acknowledgment of the Navy's cooperation "in light of circumstances involving the death of a Serviceman during production and the attendant publicity."[11]

Despite such assistance, filmmakers remained concerned about Sylvester's intentions and new regulations. Consequently, the Motion Picture Association (MPA) solicited Senator Humphrey to write to Sylvester in mid-June 1962 about the status of his examination. Sylvester responded that he understood "the benefits of cooperating with the film industry to more fully inform the American public of the activities of the Department of Defense" and cited the criteria that filmmakers would have to meet to now receive cooperation. These included the requirement that the film be of high enough quality to ensure success at the box office, the need to assure safety for service members working on the productions, and the requirement that assistance not interfere with the military's operational readiness.[12]

Sylvester then told Humphrey that his office had already developed new guidelines to ensure filmmakers met these criteria and would "serve the best interests of the taxpayers and the nation." He also assured the senator the new guidelines would not prevent assistance to filmmakers, and said his office had recently approved help for *A Gathering of Eagles* and *PT-109*. In fact, neither of these examples actually proved Sylvester's assertion. Air Force Chief of Staff General Curtis LeMay had taken a personal hand in securing cooperation for the movie about the Strategic Air Command after learning that Sylvester had rejected Universal Pictures's request for assistance. LeMay simply wrote to Sylvester, saying that the Air Force wanted the film made, and almost immediately after his aide delivered the memo, Sylvester reversed his decision.[13]

Nor does Sylvester's claim that his office had recently approved assistance to *PT-109* provide a credible proof his new guidelines worked. In the pre-Sylvester era, the Navy would have routinely agreed to assist similar, but fictional, stories, given their innocuous nature and the limited help needed. However, if high dramatic quality figured as a criterion in deciding whether to cooperate on the production, Sylvester should probably have denied Warner Brothers's request for help.

Lewis Milestone, the movie's original director and one of Hollywood's most respected filmmakers, thought the script contained a lot of "cornball jokes" and was "just another adventure story." He claimed that if the script had focused on a fictional hero, the studio would have abandoned it: ". . . why bother? We've got better stories than this." Perhaps. But *PT-109* had one virtue: it portrayed President John Kennedy.[14]

Unfortunately, this unique attribute also created the film's problem. The hero had to remain a two-dimensional character. It could not contain a romantic interlude and could not show a man with human fallacies. After all, President Kennedy would be running for reelection soon after the film's projected release date. None of this ultimately mattered to Warner Brothers. Unless the president chose to object, Sylvester was going to approve assistance irrespective of his new guidelines.

On his part, once Jack Warner, a long-time friend of the Democratic Party, had read Robert Donovan's book *PT-109* and decided he wanted to make the movie, little doubt existed that the studio would receive Navy assistance. While naturally taking a keen interest in the making of *PT-109*, the White House wanted to avoid any hint of impropriety. To this end, on 6 January 1962, Pierre Salinger, the President's press secretary, advised Secretary of the Navy Fred Korth, "The White House has no objection to the Navy's participation, but we want to make it very clear that the Navy should not extend a single bit more cooperation to this movie than it would to any movie in which it determined that the interests of the Navy as a fighting Service were involved." Salinger suggested the Navy review its recent assistance "to determine the level of cooperation extended to those movies and that the assistance to Warner Brothers in this venture be kept in conformity to this past record."[15]

In fact, Warner Brothers had far less problem obtaining needed assistance than in selecting a director and a star. On both matters, the White House became intimately involved. Initially, the studio considered hiring Raoul Walsh, who had directed such military classics as *What Price Glory, Operation Burma, Fighter Squadron,* and *Battle Cry.* However, he was nearing the end of his career, and his most recent effort, *Marines, Let's Go!,* had failed badly. George Stevens Jr., whom Edward R. Murrow had appointed director of the Motion Picture Service at the U.S. Information Agency, had seen the film just before coming to Washington and described it as "an embarrassing piece with Marines roughing up little Japanese innkeepers."[16]

When President Kennedy first met with Stevens, he expressed concern about how *PT-109* would turn out and had Salinger quickly call Stevens back to the White House to discuss the film. Stevens, the son of the Oscar-winning director, told Salinger that he had come to the USIA to make movies to inform people in other countries about the United States. He warned the press secretary that if Warner Brothers produced a coarse *Marines, Let's Go!* type of film about the president, "it's going to undercut what I've come to Washington to do."[17]

Salinger then asked how to determine Walsh's competence, and Stevens suggested they screen *Marines, Let's Go!* To his dismay, when he came to the White House to watch the movie, he discovered that Salinger had not seen a film in six months and, worse, soon realized that Salinger "was enjoying himself immensely." Stevens thought to himself, "Jesus, what have I gotten myself into. . . . I'm over here saying they should watch Walsh's film and make a judgment and Pierre is obviously going to like this thing just fine." While trying to figure out what to do, Stevens said a tall figure came into the screening room and sat down in a rocking chair to watch. As if things could not get worse, the film started to get better.[18]

After ten minutes, Kennedy turned to Salinger, told him to stop the screening, and said, "Tell Jack Warner to go fuck himself." Stevens thought his emphatic comment spoke well for Kennedy's "instincts." However, his intervention brought down the wrath of Jack Warner and producer Brian Foy, who later told Salinger, "Look, you can't let Stevens tell us how to make an exploitation picture." Nevertheless, Stevens did continue to help the White House to find a director with whom to entrust Kennedy's wartime heroics. Among others, he talked with two of the greatest Hollywood directors, Fred Zinnemann and John Huston.[19]

In a memo to Salinger, Stevens wrote that Zinnemann said he would make every effort to be available to direct the film because "he agrees that it is an extremely important and very sensitive undertaking." Zinnemann later could not "recall the exact words, but thinks that he was probably just being courteous, as he had no desire to get involved in political propaganda." In any case, Stevens closed his memo to Salinger by pointing out that people will believe *PT-109* "represents to some degree, the thinking of the President. If it is made by one of America's leading film makers [*sic*] it will in the very least illustrate good judgment and the best intent. This will carry with it the opportunity for excellence."[20]

Ultimately, Jack Warner telegraphed Salinger on 22 March 1962 that he had selected Lewis Milestone, who had to his credit such military classics as *All Quiet on the Western Front* and *A Walk in the Sun* to direct *PT-109*. He also said "it [was] imperative" they meet that weekend when Salinger came to Los Angeles in order "to resolve other problems," including the matter of who would portray Kennedy in the movie. The President had expressed a desire to have Warren Beatty play him. However, Foy told Salinger he considered the actor "mixed-up," and if he were to receive the role, Kennedy would appear as "mixed-up."[21]

Despite the producer's opinion, Kennedy told Salinger to meet with Beatty while in California. The actor said he would very much like to undertake the part but told Salinger he saw "no future" for the picture with Foy producing it. In the end, the studio tested several actors and sent the results to the White House, where Salinger and Kennedy finally selected Cliff Robertson for the part.[22]

With the director and actor finally in place, Warner wrote to Kennedy on 11 June, saying he was personally "attending to the production of this picture to the utmost of my ability." He assured the President that the completed movie "will be worth all the effort we are expending, and it is my aim to see that this picture will have the same quality as the most important motion picture with which I have ever been associated." However, while in Florida filming on location, Milestone disagreed, voicing his complaints about the quality of the script. Warner immediately fired the director, explaining to Salinger that Milestone had been "directing the picture at too slow a pace."[23]

Robertson and the new director, Leslie Martinson, who had worked mainly in television, took exception to Warner's representation, saying the filming had been progressing satisfactorily. Martinson considered Milestone one of Hollywood's great directors but did take issue with his judgment of the story, considering it "an exceptional episode in a young man's life." He described the film as a dramatic account of survival and a "tremendous saga," which portrayed a man, his wisdom, bravery, and determination to save his crew.[24]

At the same time, Martinson recognized the problem of not being able to develop Kennedy's character fully and having to "deemphasize" some of the events, due to the constraints of filmmaking. He pointed out that the Japanese destroyer had actually cut *PT-109* in half at midnight, but he staged the scene at dawn, thereby shortening Kennedy's time in the water before he finally swam for help at 4:00 in the afternoon. The director claimed that if he had more accurately conformed the sequence to the actual events, people might not have believed the truth of Kennedy's efforts to save his crew.[25]

Dramatic license aside, *Newsweek* was to describe the script as "agonizingly bad." At one point, Kennedy responds to the fact that no officer wants *PT-109* due to its beat-up condition: "It may take some work, but I'd like to give it a try." When a wounded sailor says he wants to repair motors if he survives the war, Kennedy answers coyly, "I'm not much on dry-land motors. I'll find something else to do." Donovan denied including anything remotely resembling these exchanges in his book. However, he observed, "To make a movie, they have to invent dialogue. I do sympathize with their problem."[26]

Less generously, one of the actors observed, "The only thing the film needs is right at the end somebody ought to look at Kennedy and say, 'You know, that kid ought to be President someday.'" Glumly recognizing the nature of the script with which he had to work, Robertson said, "I'm like a painter who is given three pots of paint and told to come up with twelve colors." In response, Martinson acknowledged that the actor had a difficult job but claimed the script made Robertson's Kennedy believable and the role helped his career.[27]

Apart from any script problems, Bosley Crowther in the *New York Times* found the film "highly colored, synthetic and without the feel of truth. Too much of it was obviously shot on sound stages and in the studio tank." In fact, Martinson said he shot only one scene on a studio set because of time constraints and called it "a tragic thing." For the most part, the director maintained he created a "perfect" reproduction of Talagai in the Florida Keys.[28]

The limited assistance Martinson received from the Navy satisfied Sylvester's criterion that the military provide cooperation only on a non-interference basis. Since the Navy no longer had any World War II vintage PT-boats, Warner Brothers constructed reasonable facsimiles. The studio requested use of about one hundred sailors and a few ships and planes for a short time, but the Pentagon had to reduce even this limited request. While the controversies surrounding the making of *The Longest Day* figured into the decision, White House fears of Republican criticism and the Cuban Missile Crisis contributed to the Pentagon's action.

Ultimately, the Navy provided less than a dozen sailors and rejected the studio's request for planes, but did lend a destroyer, six other ships, and some equipment. As a result, Warner Brothers had to hire off-duty sailors and rent the needed aircraft. However, most likely no amount of assistance would have improved the quality of *PT-109*, which despite Martinson's efforts resembled a dull campaign propaganda film more than a Hollywood commercial release.[29]

Not surprisingly, Salinger liked the completed film, while recognizing it became one of the greatest bombs Warner Brothers ever produced. According to his press secretary, the President "was not very excited by it . . . he was not crazy about it." The film has become a staple on cable television, but it found an appreciative audience in Europe, particularly in France, where Salinger said a television round-table on the film in the mid-1970s became "a huge success."[30]

Regardless of the film's dramatic or visual quality, however, *PT-109* lacked any images that could significantly benefit the Navy. It had no PT-boats in its inventory. The portrayal of a young officer having a Japanese destroyer split his plywood craft in two certainly did not provide much comfort to young men thinking of enlisting in the service or to parents sending their loved ones to sea. Nor did the fact that the lieutenant shamelessly used his wartime heroics to further his political ambitions say much for the value of a Navy career. From Hollywood's perspective, the cooperation the Navy gave to *PT-109* did little to convince studio executives that Sylvester's reexamination of the Hollywood/Pentagon relationship would not negatively impact future requests for assistance. Before committing significant money to stories requiring extensive help from the armed services, studios would need to see how the armed services responded to scripts not affected by political considerations or the desires of Curtis LeMay. Shortly after Sylvester wrote to Senator Humphrey, Kenneth Clark, executive vice president of the Motion Picture Association, observed that the industry would manage to work things out, "but cooperation will be more difficult in the future than in the past. The old easy, informal ways are over."[31]

As if to reinforce that impression, in October 1962 Sylvester repeated his belief that the "United States military can't be rented by anyone. They are not going to be turned over to motion pictures indiscriminately." His office would continue to provide assistance, but he stressed that in the future he wanted "all Hollywood requirements spelled out in advance. And whether the training is necessary or merely make-believe, we don't want to be put in the position of writing to any parent that 'your son was killed in making a picture.'"[32]

To that end, the regulations he issued in January 1964 imposed tighter control over cooperation. The new policy did not in any way stop military assistance to filmmakers, but Sylvester said that now "they got it on our terms," and the new DoD Instruction allowed for "less ordering stuff all around and more precise definition beforehand of what cooperation was to involve. It was not a case in which we just went whish, come take anything you want."[33]

The new policy had the immediate effect of greatly reducing the number of films made with military assistance. Following the release of *PT-109* in 1963, the Navy provided significant cooperation to only one film during the rest of Sylvester's tenure in the Pentagon, which lasted until 1967. Moreover, his policies had relatively little impact on the making of *In Harm's Way*, Otto Preminger's epic of the war in the Pacific. Preminger thrived on challenging any rules that prevented him from exercising his artistic freedom. Having successfully battled the Hollywood studio system, the Catholic Legion of Decency, and the Production Code Office, the producer/director would have obtained assistance regardless of the policies.

Based on James Bassett's novel, the movie followed the vicissitudes of Capt. and later Adm. Rockwell Torrey through the early months of the Pacific war. Torrey, played by John Wayne, loses two ships, a leg, and his estranged son in combat, but wins a major battle, command of a task force, and Patricia Neal, as a Navy nurse. She and Wayne reprieve their *Operation Pacific* love affair, and although they look well-worn fourteen years later, the intensity of their courtship threatens to become the film's focal point. Ultimately, Wayne tears himself away from his on-shore activities long enough to help the Navy win its first victory of the war, albeit in a fictional, generic battle.

Despite an uplifting ending and Wayne's presence, the film offers little benefit for the Navy. Apart from a graphic portrayal of Pearl Harbor, Torrey's alcoholic executive officer, played by Kirk Douglas, and his wife embarrass the service. After making a fool of herself at the officers' club, the wife cuckolds her husband with an Air Corps pilot before conveniently becoming a victim of a Japanese strafing attack. When Douglas's officer receives the news, he drowns himself in self-pity and alcohol before raping Torrey's son's girlfriend. Undertaking a crucial, if implausible reconnaissance mission, he dies bravely, but without redemption, since Torrey refuses to recommend him for a medal. Still, the Navy loaned Preminger a few ships and men and allowed the director to restage a portion of the attack on Pearl Harbor within the port area itself.[34]

While the Navy gained little from this help, Preminger's interest in making *In Harm's Way* remains equally inexplicable. The director acknowledged it represented "a big step away from most of the films I have made so far. I try not to repeat myself too much, in other words not to fall into a formula way of making pictures, not to make pictures in just one category." Although he found Bassett's story "interesting" and a good role for Wayne, he did not make the movie to glorify war: "I would never have it that because I am completely against war."[35]

Nor did he consider combat films different from any action movies: "Whether it is a Western or a war film, there's a lot of action. You have undoubtedly some scenes where people fight and kill each other, where people run or drive fast tanks, ships. In *In Harm's Way,* all those models chased each other like mad. But it has no moral or ethical defense. It is in no way important intellectually that it is a war film. Whatever the film is about, if it includes some war scenes or is about war, it is another chase." To Preminger, the chase went back to silent films and the "basic motion picture thing that one man runs after the other and whoever can run faster kills the other."[36]

Not surprisingly, given the director's perceptions, *In Harm's Way* stretched the limits of dramatic license. Marines parachute into combat, which never happened in World War II. Torrey risks capture when he accompanies the "para-marines" to the drop zone, despite having devised the battle plan. The larger than usual cinematic models still look like models as they sail on the studio's "sea." Nor does the climactic battle or very much else relating to combat convey any sense of reality.

Ironically, Capt. C. J. Mackenzie, one of the technical advisers, said Preminger "was very anxious to make this picture very authentic and depended upon me to watch this end of it." Unfortunately, the director's concern with authenticity had to do, not with historical reality, but with "phraseology used, uniforms, haircuts, etc." Still, Mackenzie believed the movie had "mutual advantage" for both parties, with the director having "a great deal of respect for the Navy and he was very anxious to make a picture which showed the Navy in good light."[37]

More important for the service, in Torrey, John Wayne created one more image of the quintessential American fighting man. He discussed his portrayal with Mackenzie every day, and once, when the technical adviser criticized him for acting like a cowboy, Wayne angrily responded, "If I am going to be a naval officer, I want to be the best naval officer there is." As a result, his studied portrayal of Torrey as a dedicated officer and leader provides the film's only positive portrayal of the Navy in the first months of the war.[38]

The filmmakers' good intentions did elicit praise for *In Harm's Way*. *Weekly Variety* said it contained "a full, lusty slice of life in a time of extreme stress," which Preminger had "artfully guided so that incidents of adultery, rape, suicide, opportunism and stupidity in high command—not to overlook a couple of pungent but typically salty expressions—come across naturally, making their intended impression without battering the audience. This film is as good an example as any of what by now is an old Hollywood adage, 'It's not what you do, but the way that you do it.'"[39]

Time felt that with "half a dozen plots to juggle, Preminger keeps all of them interesting for at least two of the three hours spent *In Harm's Way*." Still, the reviewer found it "marred by wearisome repetition and by a climactic confused sea battle between miniature U.S. and Japanese fleets. But even toy battleships do not seriously impede the progress of a slick, fast-moving entertainment aswarm with characters who seem quick-witted, courageous, and just enough larger than life to justify another skirmish in the tired old Pacific." However, the *Los Angeles Times* probably best captured the film's problems: "From a quiet fade-out scene at the end the screen cuts to the cast of characters superimposed on raging waves and culminating loudly in the burst of an atom bomb. Preminger may have been making a last-ditch attempt at significance here, but I am afraid most people will already be half-way out of the theater by this time."[40]

To Sylvester, *In Harm's Way* showed his regulations were working. Preminger had tried to bypass the new policy by asking James Bassett, who had worked on Richard Nixon's 1960 presidential campaign, to see if Nixon would call President Kennedy to find out "if we can use the Navy to shoot our picture." When that failed, he went through normal channels and paid for any help he received as the new guidelines required. The director emphasized that he reimbursed the Navy for its time: "I remember very well, there was never the taxpayers' money involved."[41]

The new requirements may have given impetus to Hollywood's move away from combat movies, but America's changing attitudes toward the armed forces during the 1960s also influenced the content of military films. By 1962, audiences had less interest in reliving past military glories. President Kennedy had proclaimed a new era of peace, the Cold War was apparently thawing, and the Soviet Union was negotiating a nuclear-test-ban treaty with the United States. Despite the Bay of Pigs, the Berlin Crisis, the Missile Crisis, and a minor war in Southeast Asia, military preparedness seemed less important than it had during the 1950s, when nuclear war posed an omnipresent threat. In the midst of this semi-peaceful interlude, World War II and Korea seemed inappropriate topics for film.

Of course, the fear of nuclear holocaust continued in the early 1960s. The military still talked of new weapons, of intercontinental ballistic missiles to replace long-range bombers, of nuclear submarines and aircraft carriers. Despite the talk of a thaw, the Pentagon was conducting business as usual. The contradictions, as well as the growing distance from the earlier wars, created a new atmosphere, one in which it became possible to voice subtle criticism of the military in films. In Hollywood, the defenders of the traditional relationship between the film industry and the military—Louis B. Mayer, Harry Cohen, Harry and Jack Warner—were disappearing from positions of authority. Only Darryl Zanuck retained his power throughout the early 1960s. Television was ending the old studio system, and bankers and conglomerates were taking over Hollywood. The new filmmakers had more concern about financial returns than positive military images and so showed a willingness to invest in potentially profitable projects regardless of the Pentagon's reaction. Often the new generation of independent producers had no contact with or commitment to the traditional relationship, and nothing remained sacred. Film became simply a medium for creating drama. Neither the Production Code's view of sex and the family nor the military's view of its own infallibility enjoyed respect.

Hollywood had no overriding reason to challenge the image of the U.S. military as all-conquering, its leadership as always correct, and its troops as brave, competent fighters. Nevertheless, the Bay of Pigs fiasco and the Cuban Missile Crisis had caused the nation to question some basic assumptions about the armed forces' abilities. Perhaps remembering the unfulfilled promises of the pre–World War II preparedness films, people showed less willingness to accept images similar to those the military had put into the Cold War movies of the 1950s.

The thirteen days in October 1962 during which the United States and the Soviet Union came to the brink of nuclear war forcibly reminded America of the dangers the Bomb posed to the future of mankind. Having lived for more than fifteen years under the tensions of a peace maintained through the threat of nuclear destruction, people were ready to look at the negative side of the Bomb. In fact, Hollywood had begun to question the efficacy of the nuclear-arms race even before President Kennedy forced Nikita Khrushchev to blink, when Stanley Kramer brought Nevil Shute's 1957 best-seller *On the Beach* to the screen in 1959.

Shute told a simple, straightforward science-fiction story about the aftermath of an unexplained nuclear war, which produced a cloud of radioactive dust that has blanketed the northern hemisphere and killed the entire population. Now the cloud is slowly spreading south. In Australia, Cdr. Dwight Towers, the crew of the American nuclear submarine *Scorpian,* and the civilian population await death. Sent to investigate an indecipherable signal emanating from the coast of Washington State, the *Scorpian*'s crew discovers that the wind was causing a Coke bottle resting on a telegraph key to tap the mysterious signals and confirms that no one remains alive. By the time the submarine returns to Australia, death from radiation sickness is imminent, and Towers takes his ship to sea for its last dive.

To Kramer, the nuclear scientist's explanation of the holocaust "was something I felt deeply then—and now." In the movie, Fred Astaire, as the scientist, recounts what happened: "The war started when people accepted the idiotic principle that peace can be maintained by arranging to defend themselves with weapons they couldn't possibly use without committing suicide. . . . Some poor bloke probably looked at a radar screen and thought he saw something; . . . he knew that if he hesitated one-thousandth of a second his own country would be wiped off the map, and so he pushed a button . . . and the world went crazy."[42]

To portray the results of this craziness, Kramer focused on a few Australians as they faced death. To create his movie, he needed a few shots of a submarine cruising on the surface as well as access to an American nuclear boat so that his art director could build interior sets for the scenes aboard ship. Kramer's production designer Rudolph Sternad wrote to Baruch's office on 28 May 1958, requesting permission to film an "Atomic Type Submarine" docked in Melbourne, making a run into and out of the harbor there, as well as a submersion and surfacing in open waters. He also requested research help for the construction of a mock-up of the interiors of a submarine on a soundstage in Melbourne. In addition, he asked about borrowing obsolete equipment such as a periscope unit.[43]

This request for limited courtesy assistance evoked an immediate and angry response from the Navy Office of Information to Baruch: "It is difficult to perceive how cooperation in this production could in any way enhance the U.S. Naval Service of the Department of Defense. . . . Any service cooperation on such a movie would only serve to dignify the story and add an official blessing to the possibility of such an impending disaster."[44]

The United States Information Agency had a similar response, telling Baruch that "at this time this film with its utterly pessimistic outlook and message does not deserve any cooperation in connection with its production. . . . [the] entire theme is negative to say the least, and frankly there appears to be a tendency to 'blame America' in much of its presentation." Not feeling the film "could conceivably advance the interests of the United States," the USIA did not wish to become associated with it "in any way."[45]

Given this reaction, Baruch advised Sternad on 1 July that the request "is not favorably considered for government assistance" since the Pentagon felt "it does not meet the basic stipulation of Defense policy for cooperation, 'in the best interest of national defense and the public good.'" Nevertheless, he said the Navy would furnish some informational assistance. For the record, he added that the service would not have been able to provide a nuclear submarine in Australia or at sea "in other waters" during the period Kramer would be filming.[46]

Sternad then requested as many photographs as possible of the interior of a nuclear submarine as well as unclassified exterior shots of the superstructure. In light of the unavailability of a boat, he asked if the Navy had black-and-white stock footage of an atomic submarine that Kramer could use. Baruch's office did send Sternad eighteen Navy photographs and told him that the service "will be happy to make a minimum quantity" of film available.[47]

Kramer then came to Washington on 25 August to meet directly with Pentagon and USIA officials. He helped his cause by bringing with him Adm. Charles Lockwood, his technical adviser. As a result, the Pentagon agreed to allow the director to make shots of a nuclear submarine submerging and surfacing, and the USIA withdrew its objection to government involvement.[48]

In the meeting, Lockwood said he understood that an American submarine would be visiting Australia while Kramer would be filming. Although the Defense Department pleaded ignorance, it agreed to allow Kramer to make some unclassified scenes aboard a submarine if one did show up. In turn, Kramer agreed to make "such changes that were mutually agreed on by the Navy and himself to remove the pessimistic slant of the novel on 'utter annihilation' which might be unfavorably interpreted."[49]

Baruch's office then briefed Navy Chief of Information Adm. C. C. Kirkpatrick, who agreed that the Defense Department was handling the project correctly. However, on 20 October Kirkpatrick told Baruch that after "careful consideration, it has been definitely determined that the motion picture *On the Beach* would not serve any beneficial purpose for the Navy, and cooperation should not be extended by the Navy for its production." Although the Navy had already given Kramer the promised photographs and had allowed him to take pictures aboard the USS *Sargo,* Kirkpatrick told Baruch that the Navy "does not wish to be further identified with this production."[50]

Kirkpatrick's decision had as much effect as Admiral Parks's refusal to cooperate with Kramer on *The Caine Mutiny.* On 23 October Kramer met with Chief of Naval Operations Arleigh Burke to discuss the situation. To receive the help he needed, Kramer agreed to incorporate Burke's "philosophy" into the script, and on 29 October Kirkpatrick informed Baruch he was canceling his 20 October decision.[51] Baruch told Kramer on 4 November that the service had not put the philosophy "on paper, as yet, but, meanwhile, there is no reason for you to be concerned about cooperation." He said the Navy would release the footage Kramer's representative had selected and make arrangements to provide an appropriate submarine for the director's use in Hawaiian waters.[52]

Baruch also reminded Kramer that the Navy expected him to change the script to the Navy's "satisfaction. The philosophy will be the basic matter for re-write." Although the service expected to review the revised script, the Navy would not delay providing the submarine. He also told Kramer that he might want to acknowledge cooperation in the titles and the Navy's assistance "justifies it anticipating thirty 16mm prints for use on board ships where no admissions are charged."[53]

Admiral Burke did not worry about the portrayal of the Navy itself in *On the Beach.* In the memo delineating his philosophy, the CNO said the Navy was supporting the film out of "responsibility for the effect which the film will have on the public. It is assumed that our support gives us some voice in the script. It is important that we use this lever in the national interest." Burke believed the film would create "revulsion against the use of nuclear weapons of any kind and a possible sense of defeatism with respect to the use of armed force as an instrument of national policy." If this happened, it could "seriously reduce the resolution of the American public to take the risks at lower levels of conflict which their security demands. A certain amount of this is inevitable, but the damage will be reduced if the script undertakes to show how the war might have been avoided."[54]

Burke then gave Kramer three ideas. First, the film should explain that the West should have developed the concept of limited war, to prevent being "stampeded into inordinate reaction (general war) because they had no other way of dealing with a deteriorating situation." Second, the Communists should bear primary responsibility for the war. Third, the film must explain that the major powers should have made their nuclear strike forces invulnerable: "Instantaneous response of U.S. retaliatory forces had been rationalized as a virtue when it was really an unfortunate necessity to avoid pre-emptive enemy action." Burke felt the movie could be highly successful, both at the box office and in the national interest, and suggested the Navy continue working with Kramer "with a view to furthering both these objectives."[55]

Although Burke forwarded his philosophy directly to Kramer's technical adviser, the Pentagon's Office of Security Review and the USIA found it "unsatisfactory material to pass on to the producer." Baruch later recalled that he decided to "not dispute" Burke's views. However much or little of the CNO's philosophy Kramer incorporated into *On the Beach*, the film could not in any way serve U.S. national interests.[56] Like the novel, its message was a simple and final warning to the world. Mankind has failed. The human race has committed suicide. Civilization has come to an end. In the novel, the few remaining Australians take poison, and the American submarine vanishes into the mist on the way to its final voyage. Watching its departure, Moira, who could never make Towers forget his wife and children "alive" back in Connecticut, also, in Shute's words, "put the tablets in her mouth and swallowed them down with a mouthful of brandy."[57]

Despite all his good intentions, Kramer chose to dilute the unmitigated grimness of Shute's reality. Instead of the Shute's ending or even the empty streets in the film's penultimate scene, *On the Beach* closes with an upbeat message. A Salvation Army banner proclaiming, "It is not too late . . . Brother," fills the screen, even though the film has already made it perfectly clear that time has run out for Man.[58]

The false optimism aside, *On the Beach* became one of the most discussed and thought-provoking films of the decade, generating the first serious discussion of the value of the Bomb. Its dramatic power resulted from juxtaposing human stupidity with courage and nobility. All of the characters, civilian and military alike, have become victims of the madness to which they somehow, contributed, knowingly or unknowingly. Now they must accept responsibility for their collective actions or inactions. In Gregory Peck, as the submarine captain, and Ava Gardner, as the girl who does make him forget his wife, these elements of innocence and guilt come together, with no apparent character flaws, and thus even more tragic.[59] In fact, the Navy could point to Peck's submarine captain with pride as a perfect officer and role model. His crew also performs in an exemplary manner, voting, at the end, to go home rather than remain alive on shore for a few more days. Nevertheless, after screening the film, the Department of Defense requested that Kramer not include a title crediting the Navy for its assistance, to avoid "any possible misunderstanding in regard to Government endorsement" of its contents.[60]

After all the vacillation about assisting Kramer, the Navy had ended up giving him only the informational photographs, a limited amount of stock footage, and a submarine sailing under the Golden Gate Bridge. The Navy had agreed to route a nuclear submarine to Australia for Kramer, but the USS *Segundo* arrived too late to star in the movie. By then, Kramer had used the British submarine HMS *Andrew,* with its sailors dressed as Americans.[61] Of course, the submarine remained only a prop in a film that Kramer hoped would alert the world to the reality that the Bomb might be the destroyer, not preserver, of the world.

If Kramer needed support for his position, a nuclear submarine captain told him: "Young fella, you think too much about this H-bomb thing. Millions of people might be killed but it's not the end of the world." Kramer's film suggested the opposite, that the Bomb could destroy all civilization and so *On the Beach,* not the Vietnam War, marked the real beginning, albeit in a very limited way, of a greater scrutiny of the U.S. military establishment by the mass media and the cultural community.[62]

In fact, anti-Bomb movies became the medium for making antimilitary statements during the 1960s. The Bomb's potential to destroy all of modern civilization suggested that its dangers might well outweigh its military benefits. In criticizing this particular weapons system, filmmakers could comment on the horrors of war without attacking the necessity of having a strong military establishment. Using the impersonal Bomb as a symbolic scapegoat also avoided the risk that the excitement in combat movies would mute any antiwar feelings arising from scenes of battlefield horror.

Of course, many people, especially those in the military, did not accept disarmament as a viable alternative. Fletcher Knebel and Charles Bailey used the military's dissatisfaction with a crisis-initiated disarmament treaty as the starting point for their novel *Seven Days in May,* published in 1962, which details a plot by a popular chairman of the Joint Chiefs of Staff and his cronies to stage a coup.

While Hollywood wanted to turn the best-seller into a movie, and Columbia Pictures obtained an option on the novel, the military considered *Seven Days in May* a travesty. Arthur Sylvester, then developing his policies on cooperation with Hollywood, told Ray Bell, still Columbia's Washington representative, that any movie based on the book would never receive Defense Department assistance. Bell felt that Sylvester had read the novel as a depiction of an ineffective government and asked Pierre Salinger to read the novel as a personal favor.[63] After the President's press secretary finished it, Bell told him about Columbia's problems with the Pentagon and asked if he thought the book was detrimental to the country. "Hell, no!" said Salinger. He could see "absolutely" nothing that would hurt the military and thought that a few revisions in the script would create a strong document, showing that a plot to overthrow the President would undoubtedly be nipped in the bud, as Knebel and Bailey demonstrated in the book. Consequently he met with Bell and Sylvester at the White House to explore the possibility of military assistance to the film. Afterward, Bell thought Sylvester might have modified his position, but before he could request assistance, Columbia dropped its option.[64]

Edward Lewis and Kirk Douglas then acquired the rights and set out to make the film. Lewis said in October 1962 that he "anticipated noncooperation and stumbling blocks from the Pentagon" but expected the executive branch would be in favor of the movie. He planned to make it anyway, believing "it is important that we have the strength to see that such a problem exists and meet it; this is a patriotic film."[65]

President Kennedy apparently agreed. According to his aide, Ted Sorensen, Kennedy enjoyed the book and joked that he knew a couple of generals who "might wish" to take over the country. With Kennedy's approval, director John Frankenheimer and his assistants toured the White House so they could accurately reproduce the living quarters and the Oval Office. The director later received permission to film entrance and exit scenes at the White House and stage a riot in front of the mansion. Ironically, Frankenheimer created his demonstration two days after the initialing of the 1963 Nuclear Test Ban Treaty in Moscow, and police had to move real pickets aside for the fictional riot.[66]

Frankenheimer did not follow up Bell's efforts to obtain military assistance "because we knew we wouldn't get it." The filmmakers did ask to visit the office of Gen. Maxwell Taylor, then Chairman of the Joint Chiefs of Staff, but the Defense Department made permission contingent on the submission of a script. While refusal preserved the director's creative freedom, it also caused problems with visual authenticity in scenes involving military locales and equipment, particularly aboard an aircraft carrier.[67]

The Navy would undoubtedly not have approved even courtesy assistance, script or no script, given the manner in which the story portrays one of its highest-ranking officers. In the film, the President's aide visits the commander of the Sixth Fleet aboard a carrier in the Mediterranean to ascertain his knowledge of the coup. Although the admiral denies participating in the conspiracy, he signs a letter admitting he knew about the plot and had failed to report it. However, when the aide dies in a plane crash while returning to Washington, the admiral lies to the President about the incriminating letter.

This portrayal clearly tarnished the Navy's image, but the manner in which Frankenheimer created the scene left the Navy red-faced. Going to San Diego in May 1963 with a camera crew and Martin Balsam, who played the aide, Lewis and Frankenheimer called the executive officer of North Island Naval Air Station and asked to shoot a scene of a boat crossing the harbor from the quay wall. The officer agreed since the filmmakers would not be using any Navy equipment and provided an escort to accompany them.[68]

After shooting the scene, Lewis requested permission to go aboard the USS *Kitty Hawk* to film the same scene from the higher vantage point of the flight deck. The carrier's duty officer granted permission, assuming the escort officer had cleared the project through the necessary channels. When Frankenheimer completed the shot, he asked if he could photograph Balsam disembarking from the small boat and walking along the bow of the carrier. Then Lewis asked for and received permission to shoot Balsam, accompanied by the escort, crossing the flight deck and entering the carrier's island. Before leaving the carrier, Frankenheimer also shot another scene utilizing two sailors as extras and filmed the small boat approaching from a lower angle.[69]

In advising the Motion Picture Association what had happened, Baruch said the Pentagon believed Lewis had "acted unethically in obtaining cooperation" in San Diego and claimed that the producer "was fully aware of our policy covering the assistance on such productions but took the calculated risk that someone in the field might be unaware of the policy and from a seemingly innocent request involved the Navy in a situation that is embarrassing." Baruch asked the Association to take appropriate action.[70]

Lewis denied the allegation. He explained that the request to shoot aboard the ship was "a simple, unplotted, natural location request" made so that "the wishes of the director could be fulfilled." Lewis said he had given the ship's office all the information about his project: the name of the book, the studio involved, the stars, and the director. Since *Seven Days in May* had been a bestseller for over a year, he assumed the officer would have known its subject matter. Lewis also questioned the Defense Department's contention that he was "fully aware" of its policy governing assistance, because he had never discussed cooperation with the Pentagon. He did concede that the Pentagon had no obligation to assist projects with which it did not agree.[71]

The Navy's involuntary assistance did give *Seven Days in May* authentic visuals in which to tell the story of an attempted coup. It also lent authenticity to the film's comments about the mood of the country in the mid-1960s. President Lyman sadly notes that the coup had nothing to do with the military's lust for power but resulted from the growing anxieties of the nuclear age. Fear, not General Scott, was the true enemy. In an observation equally appropriate to the earlier anti-Bomb films *Dr. Strangelove* and *Fail Safe,* President Lyman suggests that the Bomb "happens to have killed man's faith in his ability to influence what happens to him"—an assessment clearly not within CNO Burke's philosophy.

Continuing the anti-Bomb theme, *The Bedford Incident* uses an obsessed ship's captain to look at the military's control over nuclear weapons. Like Ahab and Queeg before him, Captain Finlander of the *Bedford,* as played by Richard Widmark, loses touch with reality as he pursues an elusive Russian submarine. Although unexplained, the captain's obsessed chase grows out of his antipathy to Communism as well as the pressure of commanding nuclear weapons directed against the enemy. Having detected the Russian submarine in Greenland's territorial waters, Finlander continues his tracking even after the enemy has returned to international waters and apparent safety. No longer involved in just another Cold War confrontation, he feels compelled to force the Russian submarine to the surface and ignores all orders to break off the hunt. The film ends with the accidental triggering of nuclear weapons. On the bridge, Finlander explains that he does not intend to attack first: "The *Bedford* will never fire first. But if he fires one, I'll fire one!" The weapons officer, hearing only "fire one," presses the button. Picking up the sound of the missile entering the sea, the Soviet submarine fires its torpedoes. Suddenly realizing where his obsession has taken him, Finlander refuses to take evasive measures. The resulting explosion destroys both the hunter and his prey.

To create this story, producer/director James Harris and screenwriter James Poe did take a five-day cruise aboard a destroyer, courtesy of the Navy. They also met in November 1963 with officials at the Pentagon and incorporated their suggestions into the script. The screenplay then went to an admiral who made technical corrections in the depictions of Navy operations and dialogue. Poe took the script back to the Pentagon in June 1964, at which point the Defense Department and the Navy objected for the first time to the script's cataclysmic ending.[72]

Officials said they did not want an atomic explosion implied in the ASROC firing, even though the missile's nuclear capability had become public information. The Navy also objected to Finlander's passivity after the Soviet launch, feeling his "calm stoic acceptance of termination is apt to be misinterpreted by the public." To motivate the captain's zealous pursuit of the Russian submarine, officials suggested the craft "exhibit an unusual and strange device" and that the film "introduce the strong possibility that the Russian submarine's torpedoes are armed with nuclear warheads," then not part of the script. Finally, the Pentagon wanted Finlander to state clearly, "Only if the enemy fires first will we fire."[73]

Poe incorporated the suggestions into his revised script of 14 June, which he then sent to Harris, Richard Widmark, and Ray Bell. Harris and Widmark refused to accept the Pentagon's version of the ending. Harris thought the message of accidental nuclear warfare "worth saying again and again." Since the Pentagon and State Department did not want an American movie to show the U.S. Navy provoking a nuclear incident, the Department of Defense rejected the filmmaker's request for a destroyer and other assistance.[74]

Harris had anticipated the Pentagon's refusal, planning in August to "either use models, miniatures, and process, or fake it with some other kind of destroyer" if necessary. The deadlock with the Pentagon forced him to resort to these expedients. Since he had intended to make the film in England anyway, Harris was able to obtain a British destroyer and helicopter for his opening sequence, in which Sidney Poitier, playing an American journalist, arrives aboard the *Bedford* to research a story on Captain Finlander and the new Navy. The British also allowed the company to shoot establishing shots with a miniature American-type destroyer in its model-test basin on Malta. The shipboard sequences were then done on a mock-up of a destroyer built in a studio in England.[75]

Harris and Widmark also hired Capt. James D. Ferguson, a recently retired Navy officer, as technical adviser. Ferguson himself said that neither the Pentagon's refusal to assist the film nor the film's ending bothered him, but he acknowledged that the climax "was stretching things pretty far. . . . It probably could happen, but it would be really far-fetched."[76] According to Ferguson, a captain would not normally be in a position to have his words misinterpreted, but he acknowledged that the film did not portray a normal situation. Ferguson believed that the whole point of the story was that Finlander "was driving himself nuts." Harris thought the story could be more accurately described as Finlander's "driving everyone else nuts," which caused the weapons officer's misinterpretation.[77]

Captain Ferguson did not believe that forcibly removing Finlander offered a viable solution. He thought that Maryk acted correctly in removing Queeg but considered the situation on the *Bedford* differed completely. Finlander's irrational behavior began only during the submarine chase, while he was on the bridge, where a captain has complete control. While Ferguson always considered the story implausible, he tried to make the film "look like it could happen" by modifying the script and correcting procedures and dialogue.[78]

While Harris accepted these changes, he had to resort to use of a British destroyer and helicopter to represent American counterparts. As Ferguson noted, when the helicopter delivers Poitier to the ship, "you can see it is a British ship. All Navy men will notice it . . . but the only people who would know are those familiar with ships and helicopters." By opening the film with a live shot, Harris was able to establish a sense of reality, which then allowed him to use models and mock-ups without much loss of authenticity.[79]

Bell thought the filmmakers "did turn out a very credible picture. They maintained the authenticity." He said the Pentagon failed to understand that most people believe what they see on the screen and would conclude that the military had given assistance, whether it had or not. Ferguson believed that the audience would become "so engrossed in the action that they don't care whether it is real or not." He thought the movie "had a feel of authenticity even if it wasn't 'real!'"[80] Harris believed that striving for authenticity should serve only to support the drama and the issues with which the film was dealing. If glaring errors exist in the illusion of authenticity, it can jeopardize the audience's willingness to accept the more important parts of the film. Still, the director believed authenticity for its own sake became merely an exercise having little relation to film as an art form.[81]

The Bedford Incident relies less on visual authenticity than on story and dialogue for dramatic impact. Ironically, the buildup of tensions during Finlander's pursuit of the Russian submarine obscures the intended message. Finlander becomes a Queeg clone, and his mental deterioration, like Queeg's, becomes the heart of the story. Despite Harris's hope that his movie would warn people of the possibility of an accidental nuclear confrontation, audiences become more involved with one man's irrationality than with mankind's irrational reliance on the bomb to preserve the peace. Moreover, the destruction of the two ships would have occurred even if it had resulted from conventional weapons.

The presentation of nuclear weapons in *The Bedford Incident* and the other anti-Bomb films beginning with *On the Beach* differed greatly from the manner in which Hollywood had presented the Bomb in the Cold War Air Force films. While each story required a significant suspension of disbelief, collectively they conveyed not only anti-Bomb but also broader antiwar statements.

Given the Cold War mentality of the 1960s, these anti-Bomb movies challenged the prevailing opinion that the U.S. military could do no wrong. Of course, the Navy found little benefit in assisting serious-minded cautionary tales that showed admirals approving a coup against the U.S. government or ship captains waging war against the enemy in peacetime. However, the service could still comfortably cooperate on conventional potboilers set in the traditional Cold War confrontations between East and West.

Ice Station Zebra seldom rises above its genre and, with the exception of its portrayal of life aboard a nuclear submarine, lacked a story that audiences can follow. Based on Allistair MacLean's novel, the film follows Rock Hudson as he captains his ship toward Ice Station Zebra somewhere near the North Pole, supposedly to rescue a group of scientists after an accident. In fact, the American ship and passengers are trying to beat the Russians to the base to recover secret photographs from an errant Soviet spy satellite. Or something like that.

The filmmakers requested the typical requirements, a submarine cruising on the surface, diving, and reappearing, as well as help in creating the interior ship scenes. MGM's military liaison man sent Paddy Chayefsky's script to the Pentagon in March 1965, asking permission for the screenwriter to visit an atomic submarine "to clarify some of the scenes in the script which you will notice have been written without benefit of any knowledge concerning underwater craft, atomic or otherwise."[82]

Not surprisingly, the Pentagon rejected the request, citing the character portrayals, the story line, and an "unfair distortion of military life." The Defense Department believed any film based on the original script would "damage the reputation of the Navy and its personnel." The objectionable scenes included the showing of a pornographic film on the submarine. The studio did not help itself by dispatching a person to San Diego, where he managed to get aboard a submarine under the guise of doing research for a forthcoming movie, without first obtaining permission and security clearances.[83]

Producer Martin Ransohoff responded to the rejection by saying he would make the movie with or without the Navy's assistance. He also disagreed with the service's interpretation of the screenplay: "I feel that the script Paddy Chayefsky has come up with . . . is a favorable, not unfavorable, treatment of our Navy. If the brass will read our script more carefully I think they will agree." Nevertheless, Ransohoff had the screenplay rewritten. In submitting it on 7 May 1965, MGM said it had "taken cognizance of your remarks from your letter of 2 April 1965 and have attempted to rectify any reasons for non-cooperation by the Departments of Defense and Navy."[84]

When it did not get a response to its revised script, MGM on 2 June asked its Washington representative to ascertain the status of the story and then observed: "As you probably know, Mr. Ransohoff will go ahead with the production, cooperation or not. Of course if cooperation is afforded us the Navy and DOD will then have control over what we do with the story. Without any assistance from the military, then naturally, anything can happen."[85]

Of course, nothing did happen, since the Navy ultimately agreed to provide the requested assistance, and in August 1967 the filmmakers went to San Diego for four days of shooting at the submarine base and aboard the USS *Ronquil* docked, cruising, and diving. Director John Sturgis even mounted cameras on the submarine to acquire some underwater footage. With Navy help, the studio then constructed the interior of the *Tigerfish* in six sections on a soundstage. Mounted on hydraulic rockers, the set could tip to a twenty-three-degree angle to simulate the submarine's diving and surfacing.[86]

In return for this relatively minor assistance, the Navy received a documentary-like portrayal of nuclear-submarine operations, as well as a visual reminder of the dangers of going beneath the sea. Although the film plods along, the crew's professionalism in saving the sub from a saboteur provides at least some compensation for the portrayal of the dangers of submarine life. Perhaps conveying the quality of the story best, one sailor shouts, "She's slowing fast." With an incomprehensible ending, in which neither the Americans nor the Soviets obtain the photographs, *Ice Station Zebra* is a mundane Cold War film, more reflective of the 1950s than the 1960s. The Navy and the filmmakers remained serenely oblivious to the real war in Vietnam. But by the time *Ice Station Zebra* appeared, Hollywood would not be able to ignore the war for much longer, although it made the effort by looking back to World War II one more time.

TEN

Tora! Tora! Tora! and Vietnam

Until Vietnam entered the American consciousness in the mid-1960s, the Navy was willing to provide limited assistance to even the silliest comedies, such as Disney's 1966 *Lt. Robin Crusoe.* The film simply retells Defoe's classic, with Dick Van Dyke playing a Navy pilot who parachutes from his burning jet fighter while on "a routine mission" somewhere in the far Pacific. Before being rescued, he cavorts with the natives, most particularly Nancy Kwan. To this farce, the Navy loaned shots of a Navy jet and a carrier deck, with the crew standing at attention when Van Dyke returns to civilization by helicopter. If the film did little for the Navy's image, it did keep the service in front of the American people.

Even with the war becoming a concern, the Navy provided courtesy assistance to John Boorman's 1968 *Hell in the Pacific,* an allegory set on an island in the Pacific in World War II. Given the film's commentary about men at war, the filmmakers should not have expected any more than the few photographs the Navy forwarded. In contrast, *The Private Navy of Sgt. O'Farrell,* also set in World War II, presented no problems to the Navy, particularly with Bob Hope in the starring role. Although the filmmakers found it impossible to satisfy the Navy's request to incorporate something about the contemporary Navy in the story, they agreed to produce a ten-minute short, with Bob Hope as the commentator, showing the "modern Navy in the manner which you requested."[1]

As the Vietnam War became more controversial, however, Hollywood showed less interest in making war films. Not surprisingly, the one major movie to which the Navy provided major assistance during the Vietnam era featured an earlier war. With excessive hyperbole, even for them, ad writers called *Tora!*

Tora! Tora! "The Most Spectacular Film Ever Made." The headline writers for the *New York Times* review probably described it more accurately: "Tora-ble, Tora-ble, Tora-ble." Seldom had a studio spent so much money—at least $25 million—and received so little in return.[2] Darryl Zanuck and Twentieth Century Fox adopted the style and scale of *The Longest Day* in an attempt to duplicate its box-office success. To re-create Pearl Harbor, *Tora! Tora! Tora!* crosscut between the two sides as they moved to war. The title came from "Tora," Japanese for tiger, the code word used to notify the carriers that the attackers had achieved surprise and the raid could go forward as planned.

The film's pseudo-documentary style and close attention to historical accuracy fails to create any dramatic tension as events lead up to Sunday morning. The characters seem to be marking time, waiting for the movie's highlight—sweeping destruction portrayed in vivid color, designed to attract audiences. *The Longest Day* ultimately overcame this dramatic problem because it portrays D-Day authentically, dramatizes a glorious victory, and has believable characters. Despite four years of effort, the filmmakers could not give *Tora! Tora! Tora!* the same illusions of reality. Nor could they disguise the fact that the movie depicts the Japanese killing American men, sinking American ships, and destroying American planes and facilities, with virtually no American response.

Why would Americans want to be reminded of such a day? Before the filming began, producer Darryl Zanuck explained, "Audiences may not think they are waiting for *Tora! Tora! Tora!* but audiences never know what they want until it's put in front of them. *Tora! Tora! Tora!* will say something about today." When the film became embroiled in controversy during production, Zanuck took out full-page advertisements in the *New York Times* and *Washington Post* to further explain his portrayal. He wrote that he hoped his film would "arouse the American public to the necessity for preparedness in this acute missile age where a sneak attack could occur at any moment. You cannot arouse the public by showing films where Americans always win and where we are invincible. You can only remind the public by revealing to them how we once thought we were invincible but suffered a sneak attack in which practically half our fleet was lost." *Tora! Tora! Tora!* was not "merely a movie but an accurate and dramatic slice of history that should never have occurred but did occur, and the purpose of producing this film is to remind the public of the tragedy that happened to us and to ensure that it will never happen again."[3]

Meanwhile, Zanuck's son Richard, vice president in charge of production at 20th Century Fox, was expounding on the studio's philosophy in other terms: "We go for idea pictures which contain a lot of entertainment. We don't get involved with the message pictures or anything very preachy. We don't try to do anything terribly intellectual—that can be dangerous." For the most part, he said, Fox made "sheer entertainment pictures," compared with those of other studios.[4]

Elmo Williams, the producer of *Tora! Tora! Tora!,* also rebutted Darryl Zanuck's claims of social significance: "There is only one reason why studios make films and that is to make money. Nothing else." He did suggest that film-makers have social consciences: "We are concerned with telling stories fairly and presenting the truth as much as we can, especially in the case of films that require cooperation of a government agency."[5]

The failure of *Tora! Tora! Tora!* had nothing to do with its accuracy. Even though the film shows the U.S. military's greatest defeat to that time, Williams said that no one in Washington asked him to "play anything down." The film's portrayal of Pearl Harbor adheres to the 1960s' interpretation of the events that led up to 7 December and the reasons for the military's lack of preparedness. Twentieth Century based the screenplay on two contemporary books about Pearl Harbor, Ladislas Farago's *The Broken Seal* and Gordon Prange's *Tora, Tora, Tora*. When Fox first circulated *The Broken Seal* (the story of the break-ing of the Japanese code) throughout the studio, readers found the Pearl Harbor section of the book the most exciting. However, the production received its pri-mary impetus when Fox acquired Prange's best-selling book shortly after it appeared in Japan in 1966.[6]

If developing a screenplay that fairly portrayed both sides and yet did not "take years" to tell required great effort, turning the script into a movie seemed an insurmountable task. One producer initially offered the project turned it down, asking, "Do you want to bury me?" Elmo Williams finally received the job, largely because of his success in handling the production logistics for such military films as *The Longest Day* and *The Blue Max*. His early career as a film editor and his work on *High Noon,* for which he won an Oscar, gave him the expertise necessary to supervise the editing of a long, complex movie. In fact, he had to edit into one movie two separate productions: one from Japan, por-traying the Japanese side of the story, and one shot mostly in Hawaii, recreat-ing the attack.[7]

To bring order to the project, Williams took "a very simple approach . . . I used the Japanese point of view, the airman's point of view because it allowed me to use miniatures and to get around the problem of ships and planes that no longer existed, things we couldn't build." However, actual filming had to take place at Pearl Harbor, if the recreation of 7 December was to have any sense of authenticity. In July 1967 Williams and director Richard Fleischer went to Hawaii with Pentagon approval to scout the necessary locations. They could not use Hickam Field, now Honolulu's airport, but found Ford Island and other airfields and military areas involved in the attack available.[8]

Of necessity, Williams resorted to miniatures for establishing shots of the Japanese fleet on the open sea and the American ships berthed at Pearl Harbor. He also managed to create reasonable facsimiles of a few major ships, on which to shoot on-board sequences. In Japan, the studio built full-size replicas of parts of the Japanese battleship *Nagato* and aircraft carrier *Akagi*. In Hawaii, Twentieth Century Fox built a replica of the aft half of the *Arizona* on two barges close to where the original battleship had been moored on 7 December. The mock-up also represented other battleships at Pearl Harbor that day and was constructed so that it could be "destroyed" during shooting. The cost of the replicas and miniatures came to $3.5 million.[9]

To recreate 7 December itself, Williams required operable aircraft. Only a handful of airworthy Japanese planes, vintage 1941, still existed, and the producer needed an entire air force. The existing aircraft lacked spare parts and the reliability to withstand the many hours of strenuous flying the script demanded. So he ruled out using original Japanese planes and decided to remodel American planes to resemble the Japanese aircraft.[10]

Hollywood had already used disguised American planes in its combat films. American AT-6s had portrayed Zeros, although they bore only a slight resemblance to the Japanese planes. AT-6s were also rebuilt, with varying degrees of difficulty, to approximate Japanese Kate torpedo-bombers and Val dive-bombers. In *Tora! Tora! Tora!*, AT-6s substituted for all three aircraft. Williams also had to come up with two flyable and two "taxiable" P-40s, five flyable B-17s, and one flyable PBY, as well as nonflyable derelicts and mock-ups of all three American planes, to be destroyed during the attack. The cost of the air operations came to $2.5 million.[11]

All of this reconstruction and disguising was necessary because the U.S. military had no ships, planes, or equipment dating from Pearl Harbor. Nevertheless, 20th Century could not have made *Tora! Tora! Tora!* without the Pentagon's assistance. Williams secured approval to use military facilities in Hawaii, subject to the usual requirements of safety and noninterference with regular activities. He also needed a few active and inactive ships in Pearl Harbor, men, and, most important, access to an aircraft carrier to film the Japanese takeoffs and landings. To ensure this assistance, Fox kept Baruch informed of the progress of the project from its inception in September 1966. The Pentagon had provided information, stock footage, and comments on several versions of the script. In July 1967 Williams submitted a revised screenplay, and with only minor requests for changes relating to technical and historical accuracy the Pentagon approved it in mid-September.[12]

Williams praised the military for going along with a film about its most humiliating defeat: "After all, what is a defeat? Sometimes you've got to lose a little battle to win a big one." Fleischer thought the military's assistance showed its willingness to accept a necessary evil: "I think it was just one of these things where they had no choice because they're damned if they do and damned it they don't. I think they would have been more damned if they hadn't cooperated because then there would have been the accusation that they had something to hide and something to cover up."[13]

The Navy explained its decision to cooperate in more positive terms. J. M. Hession, the director of the service's Los Angeles Public Affairs Office, recommended cooperation to the Chief of Information because "the July 1967 script is apparently an accurate document of the events leading up to the Japanese attack on Pearl Harbor. It is in the best interests of the Navy that this film be completed in order that it may impress the public with the importance of seapower and the necessity of maintaining a strong Navy."[14]

In October 1968, during the debate over whether to allow the filmmakers to stage takeoffs and landings on a carrier, R. M. Koontz, the Navy's Director of Media Relations, told the Chief of Information: "This film can and should be an accurate portrayal of a vital moment in our history. . . . Additionally, despite the fact that it was a Japanese Carrier Task Force, it will be a most effective and dramatic portrayal of a resoundingly successful carrier task force operation." Williams and Fleischer agreed that the positive image of a successful carrier raid figured in the Navy's decision to cooperate. Moreover, as Fleischer pointed out, the film showed the bravery of the men under attack. Still, he conceded, "I don't know if there is any great positive value in the whole film for the Navy." However, he thought the Navy had no choice but to cooperate.[15]

Although the Pentagon had approved the revised script in September 1967, it did not formally agree to cooperate until it received the final corrected screenplay in February 1968. Mindful of the legacy of Arthur Sylvester, who had left office in early 1967, the military carefully analyzed all of Fox's requirements. In his 1967 memo to the Chief of Information, Captain Hession had suggested that the Navy assist "only on those sequences portraying American Navy forces, and then only within reasonable limits for sequences requiring the utilization of ships and aircraft, so that operational efficiency will not be impaired." Throughout the production, both the studio and the Pentagon tried to avoid any hint of impropriety that might trigger a controversy like the one concerning *The Longest Day*. Ultimately, the General Accounting Office ruled that all military cooperation on the film had followed the guidelines set forth in Sylvester's 1964 regulations and that the studio had paid all the costs it had caused.[16]

The only significant problem that arose between the studio and the Pentagon dealt with using an aircraft carrier to stage the takeoffs and landings of the Japanese attack force. In approving cooperation on 2 February 1968, Daniel Henkin, Deputy Assistant Secretary of Defense for Public Affairs, told the studio that the landing of studio aircraft remained under consideration and suggested that "it would be best to consider an alternate plan."[17]

With filming finally scheduled to begin in late 1968, Fox requested in August 1968 use of the *Valley Forge* to stage landings and takeoffs. The Pentagon replied to Ellen McDonnell, the studio's Washington representative, that although it had given the request "every consideration," it had "determined that such use of an operational carrier cannot be authorized under the provisions of current Department of Defense Instruction."[18]

The Pentagon explained that since the carrier would represent a Japanese ship, the Pentagon could assist only on a courtesy basis, rather than provide the normal cooperation. Such help as requested would involve "improper utilization of manpower and equipment" even if the studio could afford the cost of a carrier and crew for the period needed. In fact, the safety issue became the heart of the matter: "Flight deck crews perform demanding and hazardous duties under the best conditions, and to require them to work with old equipment with which they are unfamiliar would add unacceptable risks for them and the pilots." The Pentagon did explain that the rejection did not preclude filming nonflying sequences aboard an available carrier on a noninterference, no-special-arrangement basis.[19]

Although Williams had built a mock carrier in Japan, he still needed a carrier for filming the launch and return of his reconstructed planes. Consequently, he flew to Washington on 5 September to discuss the situation with Henkin. This led to almost two months of spirited debate within the Pentagon. The Navy wanted to allow Fox to stage its landings and takeoffs, but the Defense Department Public Affairs Office expressed strong concern about the danger and the uproar that would result if a Navy man were killed or injured during filming.[20] Navy commands at all levels stated that the takeoffs and landings were "feasible," and on 11 October the Chief of Information told Phil Goulding, the Assistant Secretary of Defense for Public Affairs, that the Navy "strongly recommended" it be permitted to provide a carrier for the filming.[21]

Goulding's main concern focused on the possible danger of the flight operations to the carrier's crew. Having spent some time on carriers as a journalist and as a government official, Goulding had found them "really terrifyingly dangerous places. The idea of crews, who were accustomed to dealing with jets taking off and landing, being put in a situation where they would be dealing with propeller-driven planes I thought was scary." He also believed "very, very strongly" that men did not join the Navy to take part in Hollywood films. He did not see how the government could "explain to the family of the kid who backed into a propeller and lost his head what he was doing in the service of his country." Goulding's staff reinforced his concern, telling him that "cooperation would be difficult to defend from a noninterference standpoint or if there should be an accident involving injury or death."[22]

Koontz had anticipated continued resistance and gave the Navy answers to potential Defense Department objections. Since the carrier was involved in a "precedent-setting way," Koontz expected Goulding's office "to say no and base it on safety considerations determined by non-professional, non-aviation, and non-Navy personnel." He rejected the argument about the propriety of a U.S. carrier's representing an enemy ship, citing the many instances in which

American men and equipment had depicted enemy forces. He also said the refusal of a carrier for *Tora! Tora! Tora!* would establish a precedent for disapproving cooperation on a film about the Battle of Midway, a glorious Navy victory, then in the early stages of development.[23]

The intra-Pentagon debate became more complicated when Jack Valenti, president of the Motion Picture Association, brought the weight of the film industry to bear. When Zanuck requested help, Valenti wrote letters on 3 October to both Goulding and Secretary of Defense Clark Clifford in support of Fox's request. He asked Goulding to help in "making sure that this request is granted" and wrote to Clifford, "I may need your help." Citing "some minor resistance" in the Pentagon, Valenti said that he wanted the Secretary "to know this in case this request gets to your level."[24]

In providing Clifford possible responses to the military's objections, Valenti argued that American military personnel and equipment had long been permitted to represent enemy men and armaments. He then recounted the measures Fox was taking to ensure the safety of the flying sequences. He also noted that the studio had already spent $5 million on the project and expected to spend more than $20 million: "I need not point out the catastrophic consequence to a major motion picture from the denial by the Defense Department in this instance."[25]

Valenti's arguments did not sway Goulding. In a long memo to Clifford on 24 October he repeated his opposition to Fox's request. He acknowledged the Navy's reasons for cooperating on the film: it would help recruiting, serve as a historical document, evoke a patriotic response, and remind people of the need for strong armed forces to deter or defend against unexpected military attack. Nevertheless, he argued, "I have yet to see a reason why a U. S. carrier steaming at taxpayers' expense should represent a Japanese ship." Goulding advised Clifford that Williams had informally sacrificed the need for carrier landings, "which represent the greatest danger," and would settle for filming only take-offs. However, Goulding rejected the compromise, saying no possible benefit to the military justified the risk.[26]

Clifford, of course, had more important things on his mind, and he turned the matter over to his deputy, Paul Nitze. A former Secretary of the Navy, Nitze quickly decided in favor of the Navy, believing the film would help the Navy: "I thought we would be better off with the film being made than not being made even though there were risks involved." He said the issue "was whether or not to accept these risks, whether the benefits would be greater than the risks. I felt the benefits would be greater."[27]

Twentieth Century and the Navy did not, however, win a complete victory. Clifford accepted Nitze's decision but specifically ruled out any carrier landings. Even so, Williams and Fleischer were able to obtain the footage they needed. At the end of November, thirty carrier-qualified naval aviators on authorized leave or inactive duty convened at El Toro Marine Base south of Los Angeles to familiarize themselves with the reconstructed aircraft and to practice Japanese-type formation flying. On 1 December the Navy loaded thirty planes aboard the USS *Yorktown,* docked at the naval air station in San Diego, and it departed on a regularly scheduled training exercise off the California coast.[28]

During the first two days aboard, the filmmakers and pilots rehearsed the takeoffs, and Capt. George Watkins, the Navy's technical adviser for the carrier operation, re-created the landing of Air Group Commander Fuchida's Zero aboard a Japanese carrier. Since the studio planes could not actually land, the director filmed Watkins taking off in the Zero and then making a touch-and-go landing. Williams later created the landing in the editing room. On the fourth, under the supervision of Cdr. Ed Stafford, the overall technical adviser, and Watkins, the other twenty-nine planes took off in the dawn light, went into their formations, and did a flyby of the carrier, as Japanese planes had done in 1941. Despite the Pentagon's concerns, everything went smoothly, and Fleischer and Williams got all the carrier shots they needed.[29]

On the screen, the carrier sequences convey authentic excitement, as well as showing the beauty and grace of planes taking off from a carrier into the morning light. Likewise, the flying scenes done in Hawaii and over Pearl Harbor recreate the shock of the sudden appearance of Japanese planes. In particular, the film comes alive when Japanese aircraft surround a civilian biplane out for an early morning flight. The scene combines humor with foreboding, and as long as the movie follows the planes over Hawaii and into Pearl Harbor, *Tora! Tora! Tora!* maintains a strong sense of reality.

The carefully constructed full-size mock-ups of the Japanese ships as well as of the *Arizona* add visual realism to the film. In fact, some of the Navy ships are less believable than the *Arizona* mock-up because they dated from after Pearl Harbor. The staged explosions at Pearl Harbor seem realistic because the filmmakers used actual locales and original buildings, even blowing up an old hangar the military had scheduled for demolition. The destruction of the *Arizona,* taking only thirty seconds of screen time, became the visual climax of the movie. Generally speaking, these fireworks seemed more realistic than most cinematic explosions. However, the illusion of reality collapses when the filmmakers cut from live action to special-effects shots and miniatures, photographed in the lake on the Fox Ranch near Los Angeles. The miniatures and painted backdrops look like miniatures and painted backdrops, and the viewer cannot possibly pretend otherwise.

Williams and 20th Century Fox do not deserve criticism for their effort. The studio spent millions of dollars building the miniatures, which were as accurate as the art and special-effects departments could make them. The filmmakers simply faced an impossible task in matching the stunning live aerial shots over Pearl Harbor with the miniatures. Likewise, with the explosions of the miniatures and the destruction in Hawaii of the P-40 mock-ups looked like special effects and fiberglass models.

Since the filmmakers intended the scenes of havoc as the core of the film, their shortcomings vitiated the success of the flying sequences and the destruction of the *Arizona*. The real problem, however, lay in the film's impotent drama. In *The Longest Day*, history and drama merge. The actors become historical figures, real people with whom the audience can empathize. Through them, the film portrays a human story. In *Tora! Tora! Tora!* people and their actions remained secondary to the exploding bombs, ships, planes, and other instruments of war, "toys" the director moved around for his cameras.

The actors never become more than wooden caricatures, simply reading their lines. Admiral Kimmel, the commander of Pearl Harbor, who narrowly escaped a bullet, remarks in the film: "It would have been merciful if it had killed me." If the explosions, mock-ups, miniatures, and actual ships and planes were better integrated, the lack of realistic characters might pass with less notice. However, all the construction, special effects, and military assistance never meshed. Consequently, *Tora! Tora! Tora!* fails as drama and entertainment, even though it re-creates history with reasonable accuracy.

However, the film could not exonerate the American military for its lack of preparedness or the government for its failure to alert Hawaii in time to meet the attack. As a pseudo-historical documentary, *Tora! Tora! Tora!* shows the ironies and errors that produced Pearl Harbor, the bureaucracy and blind tradition that amplified each mistake beyond calculation. It also explains the Japanese intentions and portrays the attack as a brilliant military operation skillfully planned—a far cry from the image of the Japanese in Hollywood films of the war and early postwar years.

Although no single person emerges as the American scapegoat, and no heroes appear, the film does portray American bravery under fire and the can-do attitude that has typified the majority of American war movies. Moreover, the audience of the time knew the U.S. military won the war. As Admiral Yamamoto, the commander of the attack, observed, Pearl Harbor served only to "waken a sleeping giant." The movie's closing image suggests American determination to fight back, validating the Pentagon's decision to help in its production. However, given the military's situation in Vietnam in 1970, even a glorious World War II victory, presented in a better showcase than *Tora! Tora! Tora!*, would have had a difficult time improving the image of the U.S. armed services.

The film's failure at the box office is readily explicable. Vincent Canby's review, which had inspired the "Tora-ble, Tora-ble, Tora-ble" headline, says it all: "From the moment you read the ads for *Tora! Tora! Tora!* ("The Most Spectacular Film Ever Made!"), you are aware that you're in the presence of a film possessed by a lack of imagination so singular that it amounts to a death wish. As it turns out, this poverty of fancy has gripped not only the advertising copywriters but just about everyone connected with the film, from the directors and writers and cameramen on down to the uncredited artists who painted some terrible Pearl Harbor backdrops, which, from time to time, are seen through office windows and look like old Orpheum circuit scenic drops against which jugglers used to perform."[30]

According to Canby, *Tora! Tora! Tora!* fails because it adheres too strictly to its goal of re-creating history, thereby eschewing "the prerogatives of fiction, or what it understands to be the prerogatives of fiction." He pointed out that movies of re-created history such as *A Night to Remember, Is Paris Burning?* and *Tora! Tora! Tora!* overlook "one elementary principle of film esthetics, that is, that every movie is fiction, whether it is a newsreel shot in Vietnam, a Stanley Kramer exploration of some contemporary gut-issue, or a cartoon by the Disney people. The very act of recording an event on film transforms the event into fiction, which has its own rules and its own reality." Despite good intentions, he said that *Tora! Tora! Tora!* "purports to tell nothing but the truth" and yet "winds up as castrated fiction." In regard to the production itself, Canby pinpointed two crucial problems.

The characters never acquire life, and the Japanese and American components of the movie never merge. As a result, the audience is presented with "two different movies." In the end, Canby suggested that the film's failure centers on its aspirations: "*Tora! Tora! Tora!* aspires to dramatize history in terms of event rather than people and it just may be that there is more of what Pearl Harbor was all about in fiction films such as Fred Zinnemann's *From Here to Eternity* and as the *Variety* review pointed out, Raoul Walsh's *The Revolt of Mamie Stover* than in all the extravagant posturing in this sort of historical mock-up."[31]

If *Tora! Tora! Tora!* failed as drama, it did succeed in rekindling the controversy over military cooperation with filmmakers even though the technical adviser had ensured that Fox had paid all costs. Nevertheless, after a serviceman wrote to *Sixty Minutes*, complaining about Pentagon assistance to the production, producer Bill Brown went to Hawaii, ostensibly to do a feature on the re-creation of Pearl Harbor. On the 13 May 1969 broadcast, however, Mike Wallace raised questions about the decision to provide the carrier, about its use to transport the studio's planes to Hawaii after the launch sequence, and about the Navy's assistance to the company at Pearl Harbor. He ended, "Should the taxpayer, and the serviceman, help to subsidize the undertaking?"[32]

Brown later admitted to "subterfuge" in misleading the Navy and the filmmakers on the focus of his story. He also acknowledged that even before beginning his research, he had decided the studio was exploiting the Navy and taxpayers. With his mind made up, he refused to accept the Navy's claim that the *Yorktown*, which transported the studio's planes to Hawaii, had been scheduled to stop there en route to recovering an Apollo spacecraft. Nor did he believe the studio had agreed beforehand to pay all costs: "I still am not convinced that was so."[33]

Even minimal research would have confirmed the Navy's explanation. The week the planes arrived in Hawaii, newspapers reported Fox was paying commercial freight rates for the carrier transportation. Ultimately, congressional and General Accounting Office investigations confirmed that assistance to the studio had followed Pentagon guidelines. At the time of the broadcast, however, *Sixty Minutes* had not yet become an established tradition, and the controversy the *"Tora! Tora! Tora!"* segment stirred up helped make the program a success.[34]

Coming at a time when Congress and the press were attacking the military because of Vietnam, the *Sixty Minutes* program triggered a wave of congressional criticism reminiscent of the uproar surrounding the making of *The Longest Day*. The renewed controversy raised filmmakers' fears of additional red tape and more congressional criticism of large-scale Pentagon assistance to other war movies. Likewise, the Defense Department became even more cautious in considering requests that required a major expenditure of time and personnel. As a result of these issues, the financial failure of *Tora! Tora! Tora!*, and the growing antimilitary sentiment in the country, Hollywood stopped making films about World War II.

In truth, Hollywood's disenchantment with World War II had begun in 1964 with the release of *The Americanization of Emily*. Most people had accepted the necessity of World War II, and whatever adverse impact combat had had on individual soldiers, Hollywood had always portrayed them as leading the United States to triumph over a barbaric enemy. Not until almost twenty years after the end of the war did a filmmaker suggest that a person should perhaps not make such sacrifices, even for the good of the country. Unfortunately for the Navy, a Navy officer became the mouthpiece for such heresy.

The Americanization of Emily became the first major Hollywood production to portray an American serviceman proudly professing the virtues of cowardice, and many reviewers reacted with stunned outrage. One critic described the film as "so hypocritical—because it dares to call itself funny—so callous, so cruel, and so crass, that it provokes only anger and a feeling of resentment that we, as Americans, have allowed ourselves the 'luxury' of permitting such encroachment against our very heritage as it were."[35]

The Americanization of Emily undoubtedly lacks evenness and presents its message too verbosely, but with satire, slapstick, and serious drama, the film questions the glorification of war and ridicules the idea that to die for one's country is a positive good. Starting with William Bradford Huie's novel of the same name, Paddy Chayefsky used a rather conventional love story to reexamine the glorification of war. Director Arthur Hiller said Chayefsky used "savage comedy with brash and irreverent situations," rather than traditional drama, to make his antiwar statement.[36]

The biggest change Chayefsky made in transferring the book to the screen was turning the hero, Charlie Madison, played by James Garner, into a professed coward, a "charming churl whose principle it is to be without principle." Madison, a junior Navy officer in pre–D-Day London, serves as a "dog-robber," procuring luxuries—from liquor to food to women—for his boss, an admiral planning the invasion, in return for the security of a safe position. In the course of events, Madison meets an American-hating English war widow, played by Julie Andrews in her first nonsinging and probably best screen role.[37]

Mixing charm with his philosophy of cowardice, Madison woos Emily by taking advantage of her bitterness over her husband's death. He tells her, "I preach cowardice. Through cowardice we shall all be saved . . . If everybody obeyed their natural impulse and ran like rabbits at the first shot, I don't see how we could possibly get to the second shot." He talks about the unreasonableness of waiting to be killed "all because there's a madman in Berlin, a homicidal paranoid in Moscow, a manic buffoon in Rome, and a group of obsessed generals in Tokyo." Garner forgets that if he and everyone else ran away, the "paranoids" and "buffoons" would happily take over. Nonetheless, his philosophy suggests that to eliminate war, people might "get rid of the goodness and virtue" they usually attribute to combat.

The widow's response? "I am glad you are yellow. It is your most important asset, being a coward. Every man I ever loved was a hero and all I got was death." Ironically, as Garner wins the battle for Emily's love, his admiral's brainstorm thwarts his efforts to stay alive: the first dead man on Omaha Beach should be a sailor so that the Navy can show it has no peer for bravery among the services. In a scene of comic irony, Madison finds himself forced onto the beach at gunpoint ahead of the assault force. At this juncture, the filmmakers conspire to save him. Initially reported dead, he reappears in England as a wounded hero, and after first refusing, he agrees to return to the United States to take part in a victory-bond drive.

This traditional heroic ending notwithstanding, *The Americanization of Emily* stirred up wrathful criticism not only in the media but among preview viewers. According to the director, he even lost a few friends "because their heroic vision of the goodness, virtue, and nobility of war has been tarnished" by the movie's disrespect for the traditional American view of combat. Hiller even attended the first public screening in New York to hear reactions from an actual audience. He found many people "hopping mad."[38]

One viewer considered it "a pretty deadly joke making a comedy episode out of the D-Day landing and having laughs at the expense of an admiral who had a breakdown." Others objected to the film's messages: that there is no virtue nor goodness in war; that death in war isn't noble; that women who wear their widow's weeds like nuns help to perpetuate the very wars that gave birth to their sorrows; that men who die in war are probably victims of the glamorization of war. The consensus was that the film perverted American institutions and misrepresented human foibles. Many viewers felt it should never have been made.[39]

In response, Hiller suggested that dead heroes are simply dead men and could have achieved more by living as cowards. He emphatically believed that "a wild, satiric, cynical comedy" was the way to comment "on the lunacy of the attributes we attach to war. . . . Goodness and virtue and nobility are so out of place in the context of war that satiric laughter is the only logical response." Still, he acknowledged that *The Americanization of Emily* does not ridicule those who have to go to war, nor argue that all wars are bad, nor say that there aren't times when lives must be sacrificed for good cause. The film, he said, shows "war for what it is, a barbaric, inhuman act of man—a miserable hell. It says one thing we can do toward eliminating war from our world is to get rid of the goodness and virtue we attribute to war. Be grieved by death, but not proud of it. Stop naming streets after generals, stop erecting statues. It says stop applauding death—stop celebrating war. These celebrations are helping to perpetuate circumstances in our world that will bring our heroes, again and again, into situations where they must give their lives." War is not a fraud, but the fraud "is in the virtue and goodness we attribute to war. If you glorify war you create a climate for more wars."[40]

★

In 1964 the Navy did not find Madison's Navy officer very funny, let alone acknowledge the possible existence of officers resembling Madison. Realizing this, the producer did not even bother to seek the limited military assistance he needed for the brief Omaha Beach sequence. Predictably, the Navy discouraged the film's distribution to base theaters because the "story and characterizations do not present the Navy accurately."[41]

Ironically, Madison ultimately accepts his hero's mantle in the best tradition of the American fighting man. Bowing to his love for Emily, he seems to embrace her argument that "war isn't a fraud. . . . It's very real. . . . We shall never get rid of war by pretending it's unreal. It's the virtue of war that's a fraud. Not war itself. It's the valor and the self-sacrifice and the goodness of war that need the exposing. And here you are being brave and self-sacrificing and positively clanking with moral fervor, perpetuating the very things you detest, merely to do the right thing." But what is doing the "right thing" in this instance—telling the truth about what happened on Omaha Beach, or letting "God worry about the truth" and knowing the "momentary fact" of his love for Emily?

Emily herself accepts society's traditional values. When she first meets Madison, she does not "want oranges, or eggs, or soapflakes, either. Don't show me how profitable it would be to fall in love with you. . . . Don't Americanize me!" While she had initially found Madison's cowardice a virtue, she now finds it a failing if it means he will go to prison for telling the truth about Omaha Beach. Having become Americanized, Emily wants her man home even if he must play the false hero. If the final sequence weakens the film's message, it does so with such rapidity, so close to the end, that most viewers miss the transformations completely, or find them so ambiguous that they ignore the switches but still appreciate the movie's pacifism.

According to Bosley Crowther in the *New York Times*, the film was "a spinning comedy that says more for basic pacifism than a fistful of intellectual tracts. . . . It gets off some of the wildest, brashest, and funniest situations and cracks at the lunacy of warfare that have popped from the screen in quite some time." Despite the praise, the film's then-unique message and the ambiguity of its apparent change in direction initially caused it to have indifferent success at the box office.[42]

Not until the rise of the antiwar movement of the late 1960s did *The Americanization of Emily* find its place as a cult film voicing the ideals of the Vietnam War protesters. More than any other contemporary film, it addressed the antiwar generation's disillusionment with the armed forces and the growing realization that the U.S. military could no longer sweep all enemies before it. It became a quintessential non-Vietnam Vietnam movie, containing one fundamental idea with which war protesters readily identified: it was better to be a live coward than a dead hero. During the period a significant segment of the population adopted this philosophy and came to reject the long-standing notion that the highest calling a person could have was to die for his or her country.[43]

In fact, Hollywood had already warned the nation about the dangers of American involvement in Vietnam in the under-appreciated 1966 *The Sand Pebbles*. Set in China in 1925, the Robert Wise film gave a view of Navy life during the interwar years different from the romantic musicals, comedies, and dramatic stories the motion-picture industry had turned out contemporaneously. From the Navy's perspective, the movie does contain positive images of its men doing their jobs in difficult times, with little appreciation from the nation.

Like *The Americanization of Emily,* however, *The Sand Pebbles* probably said more about the current war in Southeast Asia than the period it ostensibly portrays. Unfortunately, most Americans ignored the film's allusions to the rapidly expanding conflict in Vietnam. On his part, Bosley Crowther had said in his review that the film would have less appeal to audiences as historical romance than "as a weird sort of hint of what has happened and is happening in Vietnam. . . . Broad, ocher Oriental rivers spreading among gray-green hills and cut by a shallow-draft gunboat flying the American flag; old cities crowded with people, yellow faces in black blouses and student caps, peasants toiling slowly in rice paddies—in these we sense a realm of present peril."[44]

Crowther compared the shock of the gunboat's captain when rebellious Chinese challenge his prestige and power to "the reverberating tremors of our own national shock and dismay when we found ourselves grimly confronted with a more recent Oriental responsibility. In the ire and resentment of his crewmen as they have to take on the task of fetching American citizens out of the bristling hinterland, we feel the tightening muscles and the quivering nerves of American men in Vietnam. And in the open suspicion and frank withdrawal of the focal 'China sailor' in this case, we catch the current vibrations of antagonism towards our present jam."[45]

These images do exist in the texture of *The Sand Pebbles*. However, not enough people recognized the similarities between the Chinese civil war in which the sailors of "Sand Pebbles" found themselves and the growing American involvement in Vietnam to make a serious effort to change government policy. Consequently, the "jam" escalated into a full-blown crisis.

The more controversial U.S. involvement in Vietnam became, of course, the less interest filmmakers had in portraying it. In fact, the Navy was the only service filmmakers even considered using as a setting for major home-front military stories before the war ended. Although naval aviation contributed to the destruction of Vietnam and the Navy's riverboat patrols received television coverage, Navy personnel did not usually get directly involved in ground combat, and the service did not suffer the media attention My Lai brought to the Army or Khe Sanh to the Marines. As a result, the war seemed to damage the Navy's image less than that of the other services.

★

Recognizing this, filmmakers submitted requests for assistance on two major peacetime Navy stories, but the service did not demonstrate any particular enthusiasm over this "honor" and adamantly refused to cooperate with the producers of *Cinderella Liberty* and *The Last Detail*. Vietnam contributed to the Navy's perception of the scripts and suspicion of the manner in which the filmmakers intended to portray the service, but the stories do convey the impression that military regulations count for little, that sailors spend their time drinking and womanizing, and that their language consists primarily of four-letter words.

Together, the films created a strikingly different portrait of life in the contemporary Navy than had the peacetime films of the 1930s or the innumerable musicals and comedies of the 1940s and 1950s. These new films also suggested that the discipline and patriotism shown in combat films such as *They Were Expendable*, *Task Force*, and *Tora! Tora! Tora!* had become obsolete. Both movies showed that the Navy still offered an interesting environment in which a young man could spend a few years with unusual but friendly companions. The movies may not have had the informational value the regulations governing cooperation stipulated, but they did not necessarily hurt and probably helped recruiting—always a goal of the services in cinematic portrayals.

Appearing at the end of 1973, *Cinderella Liberty* required some shots on a Navy base and aboard a ship. In seeking assistance, producer-director Mark Rydell initially took his script to the Navy's Los Angeles Public Affairs Office. The story of an affair between a sailor, played by James Caan, and a prostitute, played by Marsha Mason, obviously left something to be desired from the Navy's viewpoint. The screenplay also included inaccuracies in Navy procedures as well as a good deal of profanity. Finally, the ending, which showed the sailor apparently deserting the service, would have been so repugnant to the Navy that it alone would have precluded cooperation despite the mitigating circumstances. Caan's character only switches places with a retired, but competent, sailor so he can find a home for the prostitute's son after she disappears.

Ironically, the desertion did not become an issue during Rydell's initial discussions with the Navy in Los Angeles or later in Washington. Focusing on the script's other problems, Rydell and lower-level Navy officers revised the story until Baruch's office and the Navy's Public Affairs Office gave the producer/director tentative approval for limited cooperation. At that point, top Navy brass demanded further revisions that would have totally changed the character of the film. Despite additional changes, the Navy Chief of Information refused to approve cooperation, believing the script contained an implicit antimilitary statement.[46]

Baruch himself thought the Navy had not acted in good faith, saying that in revising the script, Rydell had made a great improvement, and that a film based on that version would not have been detrimental to the Navy, especially if a project officer had overseen the appearance and actions of the characters. Given the limits of his position, Baruch's only option would have been to ask the Assistant Secretary of Defense for Public Affairs to order the Navy to cooperate. He had not done this in twenty-four years of serving as the conduit between the Pentagon and Hollywood. *Cinderella Liberty* did not present a reason to break precedent since he had not had direct involvement in the project because Rydell needed assistance only from the Navy.[47]

The director felt he had more than fulfilled his end of the negotiations and believed he had solid grounds for appealing the decision to higher Navy authority and contacted Jack Valenti for help. While Valenti did call the Navy, he had no desire to challenge the Navy, agreeing with its position on the script. Consequently, unlike his efforts on behalf of *Tora! Tora! Tora!*, he simply told Rydell to rent a ship.[48]

Despite his refusal to intercede, Valenti believed the military should not base its decision simply "on whether or not they liked the director or the star of the story." Instead, he thought "the government should cooperate on the making of a film if it is not a costly thing for the government and is not going to interrupt training. . . ." The film's limited requirements clearly fell into this framework, and Baruch, for one, felt Valenti could have reversed the decision if he had tried because Rydell "had shown good faith, was led down the primrose path, and had wasted time and money doing what the Navy asked, only to be told that it was useless!"[49]

In any case, Rydell returned to his original script, obtained additional financial backing from Twentieth Century Fox, and made the film without Navy cooperation. Whether the earthy language, unconventional love story, and desertion projected a realistic or negative image of the service, *Cinderella Liberty* did not show the Navy as it would have liked the American people to see it. Since there were no positive-military-image films being released, the essentially irreverent images in Rydell's film, as well as in *The Last Detail,* furnished the only fictional picture of the service during the early 1970s.[50]

Producer Gerald Ayres's request for assistance on *The Last Detail* experienced a similar fate. The movie followed the odyssey of two Navy MPs detailed to escort a young prisoner from the Norfolk, Virginia, naval base to the Navy prison in Portsmouth, New Hampshire. The youth, about to serve eight years for attempting to steal $40 from a charity box, is a big, pitiful slob, and the two Navy MPs initiate him into manhood through a series of drinking bouts and a sexual encounter. The film establishes a texture and tone of military realism in its first three minutes, when the audience hears a string of obscenities uttered with dazzling speed. Jack Nicholson's character expresses extreme pride in his nickname, "Badass," while the characters played by Otis Young and Randy Quaid trade lines such as "Tell the M.A. to go fuck himself," "I ain't going on no shit detail," and "You're a lucky son of a bitch." Even its mild (by contemporary standards) words, such as "crap," "bastard," and "badass," would have gotten the film banned by the Production Code fifteen years earlier.

The Navy's reaction to the script and the producer's efforts to obtain even limited military assistance illustrate the service's extreme sensitivity about its image during the early 1970s. After visiting Norfolk in early August 1972, Ayres called Baruch to discuss the project and the process of obtaining cooperation. In his letter accompanying the script, he explained he had found that the way "the Navy has responded to a changing society is impressive and should be noted in the film." With revisions he intended to make in the screenplay as a result of his research trip, Ayres thought the film "will be a credit to the Navy." He requested minimal cooperation, since the movie would require only a few days of shooting on the naval base. Ayres could fake the Navy facilities if he didn't receive assistance but said, "Given the extraordinary showcase appearance of the Norfolk base, that could be a shame."[51]

After reading the screenplay, Baruch called and recommended that Ayres not submit it to the Navy. He explained that the script created a poor image of the Navy by showing the prisoner participating in various escapades with his escorts. Ayres expressed a willingness to delete some of the profanity and discuss correcting any inaccuracies. He then wrote, "I sincerely hope that the Navy understands that I am as anxious to cooperate with them as to receive their cooperation."[52]

Despite Ayres's willingness to negotiate, the Navy decided it could find "no benefit" in assisting the film. Its Information Office felt that "no minor modification of the script can produce an acceptable film for the Navy." After failing to change the Navy's mind by phone, Ayres wrote to Bob Manning, the civilian motion-picture officer in the Navy Office of Information, noting that he did not consider himself "irresponsible in the representation of reality nor in any way hostile to our armed forces."[53]

He stressed he was trying "to show a human drama with a Navy background" and wanted "cooperation, advice and support to make the script all the more accurate and, as a consequence, all the more effective." He had offered "to make script changes in accordance with your advice. If you found portions of the screenplay unsympathetic or unreal with regard to the Navy, I wanted to come to discuss those portions with you." He expressed "shock" at the Navy's suggestion that he save his airplane fare by not bothering to come to Washington to discuss the script. He repeated his offer to be cooperative in return for assistance: "You seem to feel my script is so far from pleasing the Navy that I would, to use your words, 'have no plot left by the time you altered your script sufficiently to get our cooperation.' I would appreciate further explanation of this, if it is possible for you to set it down for me."[54]

Acknowledging that his characters broke some regulations, the producer pointed out that characters in most films that received military assistance did so: "We can both list them. This rule breaking is shown in a mostly humorous light. On the more serious side of our story, the petty officers strictly adhere to orders and turn over their prisoner as ordered. In the course of these actions, they show themselves first and foremost to be humane and compassionate." Ayres refused to believe that the Navy "would not want men in positions of leadership who are humane and compassionate. Our times are too much in need of such men."[55]

Jack Garrow, director of the Navy's Production Services Division, responded to Ayres's contentions on 19 October, assuring him that the Navy would discuss the film with him. However, he said Manning "was very correct in informing you that it is very unlikely we could arrive at a mutually agreeable script without emasculating the premise of your story." Garrow claimed that Manning was trying to help, not hinder, the producer.[56]

Conceding the story "may make an entertaining R-rated film," Garrow repeated that the service did "not consider the action of the film in the best interests of the Navy, or for that matter a reasonable occurrence within today's Navy." While finding the escorts "sympathetic in their own fashion and somewhat enthusiastic about the Navy," Garrow said their characters perpetuated "a false derogatory stereotype." While the Navy probably would not assist on such a portrayal, he expressed a willingness to discuss the matter further.[57]

Instead, Ayres, his coproducer Lester Persky, a Navy veteran, and his director Hal Ashby made the film without cooperation. Persky had become involved with the project because he "knew" the script "had the ring of truth." Ashby reinforced this authenticity by taking some exterior shots of the entrance to the Portsmouth Naval Base. He was so successful in creating the illusion of being on the base that the completed film fooled even Navy officers.[58]

Adm. John Will, for one, the technical adviser for *Men Without Women,* accepted the word of a film critic he had trusted and went to see the movie. Although he walked out after ten minutes, he concluded that the Navy had assisted in the making of the film "because I recognized shots at the Fifth Naval District." The apparent cooperation made him angry since he believed the film would hurt Navy recruiting: "Any mother who sees this picture would never allow a son of hers to join the Navy or have anything to do with it."[59] In fact, the movie so distorted Navy procedures that its story was implausible to anyone familiar with Navy regulations and activities. Although the Navy had assisted on even more implausible comedies, as Ayres had reminded Manning, the average viewer with no frame of reference might think *The Last Detail* showed the Navy as it was.

Inaccurate or not, the humor and good-natured friendship that developed among the three main characters probably did more good than harm to the Navy. In contrast to the Navy leadership's refusal to assist the production, the Navy's lower-echelon public affairs officers recognized what these new portrayals of servicemen represented. The staffs believed they should discuss all projects with producers and writers who came to the Pentagon for assistance. By working with these filmmakers, the officers reasoned, they might be able to temper the extreme characterizations and produce more balanced images. So strongly did Garrow feel that the Navy should have cooperated with Rydell, particularly after the Public Affairs Office had reached an agreement on a revised screenplay, that he actually considered resigning from the Navy. Instead, he later became Chief of Information, presiding over cooperation to *Top Gun,* the film that completed the rehabilitation of the military's image so badly tarnished by Vietnam.[60]

In any event, the Navy was to escape the worst images of the Vietnam War that had appeared in the media. Television news had most often simply showed Navy jets roaring off and landing on aircraft carriers, with combat footage limited to the planes' bombs exploding against an invisible enemy. Likewise, the Navy avoided negative portrayals in most of the anti-Vietnam movies of the 1970s. Even in *Apocalypse Now,* the defining Vietnam film of the decade, the Navy, although having a highly visible role, did not receive the brunt of Francis Coppola's negative portrayal.

The Navy was never involved in Coppola's efforts to obtain assistance from the Defense Department. Objecting most particularly to Willard's instructions to "terminate" Kurtz, the Army and the Defense Department rejected all of Coppola's importunings, including his final one in February 1977. With filming almost completed, he wrote directly to President Carter, saying, "I need some modicum of cooperation or entire government will appear ridiculous to American and world public. . . . This film tries its best to help America put Vietnam behind us, which we must do so we can go on to a positive future."

Except for Paramount Pictures's request in the making of *Bridges at Toko-ri,* the Pentagon had never received an application so audacious in its scope or so demanding of immediate action. It fared no better than Coppola's earlier efforts to obtain Pentagon assistance.[61]

Whether the completed film made the United States look ridiculous or helped put Vietnam to rest is highly debatable. Television and the print media had done a thorough job of exposing the true nature of the military's actions in Southeast Asia, and only the Gulf War finally put the ghost of Vietnam in its proper place. On his part, Coppola certainly did not show much sympathy for the Navy. A Navy river patrol boat serves as the unifying image of his story, carrying Captain Willard upstream on his search for renegade Colonel Kurtz. The boat's crew did not provide a positive image of the service, given the men's lack of discipline, pot smoking, and indiscriminate firing on peasants and tigers. However, *Apocalypse Now* is essentially an Army movie, and probably few people realized Willard was making his excursion complements of the Navy.

In fact, the service appeared in only four films of the post-Vietnam era that did not contain antiwar rhetoric. The 1979 made-for-television *When Hell Was in Session* and the 1987 *In Love and War* recounted the long imprisonment of Admirals Jeremiah Denton and James Stockdale and the manner in which their wives kept the faith until they returned. The 1987 feature film *The Hanoi Hilton* covered much the same terrain but in a semifictional format. However, all three stories presented a good-image/bad-image problem to the Navy.

Without exception, the officers represented their service with the highest level of fortitude and ingenuity as they struggled to survive their seemingly endless ordeals. Even the most radical anti-Vietnam protesters would have a difficult time criticizing the POWs, in light of the manner in which the filmmakers portrayed them. On the other hand, nothing could mask the reality that as the officers entered the Hanoi Hilton, they faced long years of privation. Admiral Stockdale, for one, was to spend seven and a half years in the North Vietnamese prison. Nor could the aviator's do anything to mitigate the horror of the situation in which they found themselves. Perhaps worst of all, the films portrayed the wives as the true victims of war. Their husbands had chosen to become pilots and understood the risks of their profession. While the women had chosen to marry Navy men, they could not have anticipated all of the difficulties.

Despite these negative images, the Navy could not in all good conscience object to the stories or to providing the limited assistance the filmmakers needed to show their heroes aboard an aircraft carrier or during a flight operation. Nevertheless, the Navy did have a specific problem with *In Love and War,* even though the nation had awarded Admiral Stockdale the Congressional Medal of Honor for the manner in which he had conducted himself in prison. Based on the book he and his wife wrote after his return, the film opens with then-Commander Stockdale flying air cover the night of the purported North

Vietnamese attack on American ships patrolling in the Gulf of Tonkin. In response to word that the enemy was firing on the task force, Stockdale radios back that he can see no attack, a position he has maintained since his return from captivity. The official U.S. position has always been that the attack did take place, thereby justifying the Gulf of Tonkin Resolution. The Navy would have a problem permitting filming aboard a carrier or even authorizing the company to obtain stock Navy footage for a movie showing a contrary interpretation of history.[62]

Baruch informed Assistant Secretary of Defense for Public Affairs Robert Sims that Navy Chief of Information Garrow did not object to the portrayal and wanted to provide assistance, if the filmmakers would revise some passages "that may divulge intelligence material." In addition, Baruch told Sims he had discussed the matter with the Pentagon Internal Security Affairs Office, the DoD historian, and the Office of the Joint Chiefs of Staff (JCS). Based on their concerns, he said he had informed producer John Avnet that the Pentagon could not approve assistance "because of the controversial 'truth' that the Stockdales espouse."[63]

Although Avnet had then offered to include a screen title stating that the film expressed one man's opinion, Baruch told Sims that the JCS and ISA "reiterated their negative reactions." Baruch went on to explain that Avnet had requested Baruch bring the matter to the secretary's attention but advised Sims that in his opinion the film "could add substantial fuel for questioning Presidential authority on taking certain military actions." For this reason, Baruch believed "official association with the project is not in the best interest of DoD." Sims agreed: "Don't see how we can cooperate—not in interest of DoD or USG."[64]

Baruch then advised Avnet that the Pentagon could not approve the screenplay or provide assistance "even with your proposed legend about the picture being based on one man's opinion. The attack and the Tonkin Gulf Resolution remain on the record and nothing has been found officially or released to otherwise refute them." Avnet, who had produced the highly acclaimed television series *Call to Glory*, did not give up. He approached the Defense Intelligence Agency and even the CIA for help in changing the Pentagon's position, offering to change the script to satisfy concerns about security matters.[65]

Avnet also called Sims directly and then made a written request to obtain archival footage of jet planes, destroyers, and carrier operations. He explained that the "minimal cooperation would certainly allow us to put a finer movie on screen and we would appreciate it very much if you could allow this to happen." Ultimately, Sims authorized the use of stock footage because Avnet had incorporated some of the requested changes into the script, but "we are unable to provide further assistance on the picture."[66]

The Navy had been willing to give the footage because of the esteem in which it held Stockdale. For Sims, however, the changes became the relevant factor even though he also had tremendous respect for Stockdale: "They don't make more authentic heroes." Consequently, he would have ignored the Pentagon's concerns about Stockdale's opinion about the Tonkin Gulf Incident "in a blink of an eye, had this been the crucial issue." However, Sims learned from reliable sources about fears the movie "would inadvertently reveal prisoner of war tradecraft that was still being taught," and it was felt this might endanger future American prisoners. Sims said that Avnet recognized the problem and agreed to changes that protected intelligence methods. The Tonkin Gulf sequence itself opened the film and passed very quickly. Few people probably recognized the significance of Stockdale's account, seeing only a grim and sad movie containing one of the most positive portrayals of a naval officer ever made. Sims found the film "inspirational" and did nothing to accidentally endanger captured American servicemen.

In contrast, the 1984 *Purple Hearts* uses the Vietnam War and combat only as the stage on which to tell a traditional love story, in this case between Ken Wahl as a Navy doctor and Cheryl Ladd as a nurse. The scenario did not differ from military romances Hollywood had set in all other American wars, with the combat, created with limited military assistance, serving only as an obstacle to the consummation of the relationship. The film never even bothers to explain that a Navy doctor would accompany a Marine mission because the service believes that every leatherneck must fight, which doctors cannot do. Even though the doctor acquitted himself well under fire, World War II and peacetime, not Vietnam, remained the stage on which the Navy continued to perform for filmmakers in the years following the end of the war in Southeast Asia.[67]

ELEVEN

A Return to Normalcy

T he reestablishment of the Hollywood/Pentagon relationship in the post-Vietnam era began with two disaster films that had nothing to do with the military. The Air Force contributed to *Airport 1975*, providing the helicopter that lowered Charlton Heston into a disabled 747 jet. In *Towering Inferno*, the Navy supplied the helicopters that helped rescue people from a burning skyscraper. Although one of the helicopters hits the building and explodes in a ball of flame, Bill Graves, the director of the Navy's Los Angeles Public Affairs Office, described it to the Chief of Information as "just one more catastrophe in a continuing series that leaves the to-be-rescued group a little concerned and depressed with their state."[1]

The Navy felt it would garner "excellent 'public relations' exposure in what promises to be one of the box office biggies of the coming season." According to Graves, the filmmakers "handled well" the Navy's presence in the story even though a line about Navy pilots being the best qualified to fly under adverse conditions did not make it to the screen. Graves felt the Navy men "look good, act well and have short haircuts" and said that the second helicopter "executes some superb airmanship" and the crew remained "very professional and obviously fearless" in helping save lives.[2] Such images represented a radical change from James Garner's cowardly officer and Jack Nicholson's foul-mouthed Navy escort. However, to show Navy men performing their real jobs—protecting the nation in wars the public perceived as necessary—filmmakers returned to a World War II setting because for them Vietnam was clearly not an appropriate locale.

193

Walter Mirisch became the first producer to do so when he decided to make a film about the Battle of Midway. Having already made *Flat Top* and *The Annapolis Story,* Mirisch felt drawn to naval aviation. Conceiving his project as a tribute to the American Bicentennial, he saw the story of the first major American victory in World War II as symbolizing the nation's spirit and will to triumph in the face of great odds.[3]

As *Wing and a Prayer* had suggested in a highly fictionalized manner thirty years earlier, the Battle of Midway became the turning point in the Pacific Theater. There, in June 1942, American forces facing a superior Japanese force sank four enemy aircraft carriers and emerged victorious. From that time onward, U.S. strength continued to grow while Japan was unable to mount another offensive equal to that of Midway.

When Mirisch submitted five copies of the screenplay, then titled "Battle," to the Defense Department on 6 November 1974, he indicated he would require Pentagon assistance to make the film. He wanted to use the USS *Lexington,* based at Pensacola, for both interior and exterior settings. Remembering the controversies about staging landings and takeoffs for *Tora! Tora! Tora!,* Mirisch made it clear he was not asking to use the one World War II aircraft carrier still on active duty for any flying sequences. Neither the Navy nor the Defense Department would have anticipated any problems with the story or Mirisch in light of his earlier naval films. Unlike *Tora! Tora! Tora!, Midway* would reveal no unprepared military leaders, no unchallenged attacks, no victorious enemy.[4]

In his reaction to the script on 19 December 1974, the head of Navy Aviation Periodicals and History wrote to the Navy's Chief of Information that the film "could be useful in recruiting efforts as part of the Bicentennial and as an adjunct to the Sea-Air Operations Hall of the new Air and Space Museum which will focus on carriers." The captain of the *Lexington* told the Navy Department that he could provide the requested assistance but considered it "impossible to provide services on a strict non-interference basis. There will be inevitable loss of deck time at sea and working time in port." Nevertheless, on 30 December 1974 the Navy informed Baruch's office that "cooperation is both feasible and in the best interests of the service."[5]

With approval in hand, the film company traveled to Pensacola Naval Air Station in May 1975, where the cast and crew spent several days shooting aboard the *Lexington* dockside. Then the company and two World War II F4F Navy fighters Mirisch had rented spent a week on the carrier during one of its regular training cruises, filming exterior and interior sequences. Even though the two planes had flown to Pensacola from Texas and Illinois, neither the Navy nor the producer raised the possibility of flying the planes onto or off the *Lexington.* Instead, director Jack Smight used the aircraft solely as props for the actors. With only two planes, Smight had to stage his shots carefully to create the illusion of a full flight or hanger deck. As a result, the footage could not convey the carrier's imposing dimensions or create much visual authenticity.

The problem of replicating life aboard the carrier during the Battle of Midway paled when compared with Mirisch's task of re-creating the actual battle between the two major naval task forces. Apart from the carrier and locations in and around the naval air station, the Navy could not provide material assistance, given the paucity of World War II ships and equipment. Fortunately for the producer, the two fleets had never come within sight of each other at Midway, and Mirisch was able to re-create the air-to-sea battle with Navy combat and gun-camera footage. He also acquired some of the bombing sequences from *Thirty Seconds Over Tokyo* and *Tora! Tora! Tora!* and used miniatures and mock-ups.

Unfortunately, the actual combat footage did not provide *Midway* with an authentic sense of aerial warfare. Blowing up the 16mm film to 35mm CinemaScope proportions cut off the bottom and top of the frame. Mirisch thought this produced "a much more exciting effect" because it placed the viewer in the center of the picture and made the action "much more dramatic than it was originally." Even so, audiences easily recognize the combat footage by its deep blue cast and grainy quality.[6]

In fact, many of the Navy combat scenes postdated the Battle of Midway. One spectacular and often-used crash sequence, in which an F6F Hellcat returning to its carrier breaks in two while landing, actually occurred in October 1944 during the Battle of Leyte Gulf. The film's climactic plane crash played even looser with aviation history, showing a Korean War–vintage jet plane, not a World War II dive-bomber, slamming onto a carrier deck. Admitting he simply needed one more spectacular crash, the film editor acknowledged he did not realize the plane's identity.[7]

Only plane enthusiasts, military historians, and World War II veterans would notice these flaws or the repetition of shots, which the filmmakers attempted to disguise by reversing the film from left to right. Much of the movie's box-office success resulted from people who went to see the battle sequences irrespective of their chronological accuracy. Young viewers either had not seen the original footage and combat documentaries from which Mirisch borrowed the battle scenes or had found them unimpressive on a small television screen, and the Sensurround sound system gave a new dimension to the images, even if the sound track did not always synchronize with the action.

Mirisch had intended *Midway* to be more than a series of World War II combat clips enhanced with technological gimmicks. He had aspired to create a dramatic story to remind the American people of "a most prideful" event in American history. The film does succeed as history as well as any Hollywood release has ever done, but as with *Tora! Tora! Tora!*, *Midway* fails as drama. The two films suffer the same basic problem. The historical figures fail to become living people with whom the audience can empathize. Only Henry Fonda, who plays Admiral Nimitz, successfully captures the essence of the man: a commander who has grown accustomed to the isolation that comes with the responsibility of four stars. The other Americans are all rumpled, informal, and skilled in the art of war. The Japanese, led by Toshiro Mifune as Admiral Yamamoto, are more formal and stoic throughout, as if resigned to their defeats. The filmmakers treat both sides with an evenhandedness that refuses to explore the abilities and decisions of the combatants, and the film attributes the American victory to luck. No one makes a major mistake or even voices serious fears about the outcome of the battle, and this lack of emotionalism dissipates any sense of tension.

Recognizing the problem of creating drama within the framework of historical events, Mirisch chose to graft a fictional character onto the story. Capt. Matt Garth, whom Charlton Heston plays in his bigger-than-life style, finds himself at the center of events throughout the film. As Vincent Canby observed in the *New York Times,* Garth's character might "have been stolen from some terrible movie made shortly after World War II." Garth's son, also a Navy flier, informs his father that he has fallen in love with a Japanese-American girl, interned in Hawaii with her family.[8] The Romeo and Juliet story provides some of the most ludicrous dialogue to appear in any Hollywood movie:

> Son: "Dad, I've fallen in love with a Japanese girl. I want to marry her. Dad, I need your help."
> Garth: "I damn well guess you do, Tiger."

The romance draws on every cliché found in a Hollywood war movie. Although the girl is willing to give up her man for the good of his career and his country, she waits for him as any good serviceman's woman does and welcomes him home, eager to love him despite the terrible burns he has suffered. Meanwhile, Garth the elder stands around looking grim about both the romance and the impending battle. Heston never makes him any less wooden than the historical figures with whom he mingles, and the character simply accentuates the film's lifelessness in everything except the Navy's combat footage. In the end, Garth dies after leading the final attack on the Japanese fleet—perhaps because Mirisch had one more fiery crash left in the editing room—and few people care.

Why did a movie containing two-dimensional characters and purloined visual images, telling a story about a distant battle, attract such interest at a time when the armed services were still recovering from the trauma of Vietnam? Realizing that his film did not succeed because of its creative merits, Mirisch thought it rode the wave of nostalgia then in evidence in the United States. He said that World War II was becoming romanticized, and its generation wanted to relive the time when a united country had fought a so-called good war. Mirisch said he was not attempting to help the nation forget Vietnam by portraying a great victory from an earlier war. To him, *Midway* simply helped young people learn about World War II and the major turning point in the war against Japan.[9]

Vincent Canby was less charitable in his review: "*Midway* is a kamikaze attack against one of the greatest sea battles of modern times. The battle—history—survives while the movie blows up harmlessly in a confusion of familiar old newsreel footage, idiotic fiction war movie clichés, and a series of wooden-faced performances by almost a dozen male stars, some of whom appear so briefly that recognizing them is like taking a World War II aircraft-identification test."[10] Canby also had an unkind word about the Sensurround system that used low-frequency signals to re-create the sense of battle, noting that though the system worked with *Earthquake,* here it simply annoyed the ears.

However, the film showed the Navy in the best possible light. It reminded the American people of the service's proud heritage. Its combat sequences also showed once again that war, directed against a proper enemy, is exciting and that victory can stir up patriotism.

Frank McCarthy had no such altruistic purpose in making *MacArthur,* hoping simply to duplicate the artistic and box-office success he had had with *Patton.*[11] Although it was an "Army" film, the Navy did provide a few men and ships as background. Despite this limited, courtesy cooperation, the Navy Chief of Information Adm. David Cooney had problems with the manner in which the script portrayed the service. In particular, he expressed concern about the portrayal of the 1944 meeting at Pearl Harbor of Adm. Chester Nimitz, President Roosevelt, and General MacArthur.[12] Conceding that he was a "persnickety historian" and the Navy was "a tough bunch to satisfy," he did not "want any movie-goer to get the erroneous impression that Admiral Nimitz was an obstacle to the liberation of the Philippines." Cooney said Navy records indicated that Nimitz had expected MacArthur to retake the Philippines while the Pacific Fleet established control of the Formosan Straits. Cooney also questioned the accuracy of other scenes and asked McCarthy to either provide citations to support the actions and dialogue or delete the sequences.[13]

In fact, apart from a few Navy ships used to produce the necessary images of war, McCarthy used the Navy's assistance primarily to re-create the Japanese surrender on the *Missouri,* the only historic artifact to appear in the movie. The Navy merely turned the ship around at its mooring at Bremerton, Washington, to enable the filmmakers to shoot the scene with the sea, rather than the city, in the background. McCarthy and the studio returned the deck to an approximation of its appearance in September 1945. They also recruited off-duty sailors to provide the audience for the signing of the treaty and refurbished two cabins used for interior filming.[14]

The filmmakers also received Navy permission to shoot aboard the USS *Baltimore* at the San Diego Naval Base to re-create Roosevelt's meeting with MacArthur, Halsey, and Nimitz at Pearl Harbor. Finally, to stage MacArthur's evacuation from Corregidor, the Navy allowed McCarthy to modify two PTF boats from its Coastal River Division 12 based at Coronado to resemble World War II PT boats, and to use a third boat as a camera platform. The scenes of

★

naval flotillas supporting World War II landings and the invasion at Inchon came from combat footage.[15]

However limited the assistance, *Towering Inferno, Midway*, and *MacArthur* signaled that the service was again willing to help filmmakers on projects portraying it in a reasonable light. So when the script for *Airport '77* arrived in the Navy Department, the Navy saw the request for cooperation as proof that Hollywood was again feeling comfortable about working with the Pentagon. More important, the Navy saw the film as an opportunity to show its men and equipment working competently, albeit in a nonmilitary setting.

Another in the series of disaster stories that had replaced war movies in the 1970s, *Airport '77* would offer the Navy the chance to demonstrate its new underwater-rescue equipment. A privately owned 747 jet filled with the stereotypical collection of passengers and a priceless art collection ends up on the ocean floor in the Bermuda Triangle. At the penultimate moment, Navy divers attach flotation gear to the 747's fuselage and bring it to the surface. Unlike earlier underwater-rescue stories, the Navy highlights its ability to save trapped people without the embarrassment of losing one of its submarines.[16] To film the operation, the cast and crew traveled to San Diego in September 1976 for two weeks of shooting. The director filmed sequences aboard the USS *Cayuga* and at the Navy Coordination Center. The Navy also provided helicopters, frogmen, a Navy landing field, as well as search-and-rescue aircraft.[17]

The service soon had another chance to demonstrate this equipment and underwater-rescue techniques in more detail, but unfortunately in a story requiring the Navy to save the crew of a sunken nuclear submarine. The service had been fending off the project since 1971, when it first received an inquiry about assistance to a project based on David Lavalle's novel *Event 1000*. If submariners did not show much enthusiasm, the Navy's Public Affairs Office saw in the proposed film a half-filled cup, not a half-empty one. As *Tora! Tora! Tora!* demonstrated the value of aircraft carriers, the Navy saw the story as an opportunity to show how it could rescue trapped submariners.

Apart from the Navy's reluctance to become involved in the project, the difficulties of transferring the novel to the screen resulted from the war among several filmmakers for the rights to, and then credit for, the script. In the fall of 1971 both Frank Rosenberg, then at Avco Embassy Pictures, and ABC Pictures asked the Navy about the prospects of receiving assistance. Although the service agreed to provide research help and even a cruise aboard a nuclear submarine, the project followed a tortuous path before going into production.

The original novel portrays the plight of a U.S. nuclear submarine that collides with a freighter off the East Coast and sinks to a depth somewhat below the limits of the rescue equipment then available. Bing Crosby Productions (BCP), which acquired the rights to the novel in early 1973, hired Rosenberg to write and produce the film. In a letter to Baruch, the company said the plot would focus on "the actions and reactions of the survivors below and the rescue force above—with special emphasis on the commander of the rescue operation. We intend to depict the modern Navy, weaving into the film many of the recent innovations in the field of human relations and would hope that the finished product will be an incentive for naval recruiting."[18]

Despite such a worthy goal, after some initial discussions, Rosenberg ran into a wall of silence from the submarine service in San Diego. After investigating the problem, Baruch discovered that the refusal to cooperate "was just another way that the Sub people were making it difficult because the Admiral doesn't like the story." Ultimately, the writer/producer did complete and submit a script to Baruch on 10 July 1973, asking for a reply within two weeks, which the submarine service ignored. Finally, in mid-August the Information Office discussed with Baruch a proposed memo that the Chief of Information planned to send Rosenberg.

In it, the Navy said it could not recommend Pentagon assistance "based on the script as presently written" but thought that with major modifications Rosenberg might come up with a story that benefited the service: "The film could show the public the immense effort the Navy has expended in equipping submarines and in planning and developing rescue systems and salvage assets for a disabled submarine event. Further, the film should depict the tremendous reaction and marshalling of assets such a disaster would generate. It is believed this could be done without reducing the suspense or impact of the story." The Navy then enumerated the "inaccuracies and innuendoes which obviously would not enhance recruitment for the Navy and especially for the submarine service."[19]

The Navy objected to the script's picture of a Navy unprepared for such an emergency and apparently unconcerned about the trapped men. The script also failed to show all the rescue and survival aids available to the submarine and to depict the massive search effort that the Navy would mount. Most important, the service disliked the portrayal of the trapped sailors: "The detail of the crew's plight inside the submarine may be designed to make the film interesting and perhaps macabrely fascinating to the audience. However, the psychological effect of many viewers could well be detrimental to submarine recruiting efforts." In particular, the Navy complained that the script showed one of the submersible rescue craft finding in its floodlights the body of the captain who had been trapped on the bridge, nineteen men dying in a fire after being trapped on the bottom for some time, and several men dying of pulmonary problems.[20]

When Baruch told Rosenberg of the Navy's objections, the producer/writer agreed to make changes and scheduled a meeting with the Navy on 21 August 1973. After the discussion, Rosenberg sent the service a letter of understanding about the revisions he would make. However, on 18 September the Navy told Baruch that it did not recommend assistance: "After extensive review of the script and subsequent memoranda, as well as taking into account the great amount of military assistance which would apparently be required, it has been determined that providing cooperation would not significantly benefit the Department of Defense as delineated in the DoD instruction governing cooperation."[21]

By then, Rosenberg had told Baruch that BCP had decided to make the film without cooperation. In relaying the Navy's decision, Baruch acknowledged that Rosenberg had "no obligation now to consider any of our story recommendations," but he did hope that the producer would "retain the legend about the present day capability of the Navy to rescue personnel from submarines."[22]

In reality, Rosenberg had little chance to make the film without Pentagon support. The producer acknowledged as much when he told Baruch the next November that BCP remained very much interested in making "Event 1000" and asked that the Pentagon reconsider the matter of cooperation, agreeing "to make reasonable changes in the screenplay in order to obtain the necessary assistance." He listed seven reasons why the film would benefit the Navy and "encourage men to join a proud Navy and have pride in themselves as well," including giving it a "more visible profile and, thereby, give our citizens—and especially the new Congress—a sympathetic look at a modern Navy that many people are aware of in only the vaguest way." Specifically, the film would show "that at enormous cost, the Navy had developed a deep-water submergence vehicle that is capable of rescuing men at almost any depth."[23]

The Navy remained unimpressed, despite a suggestion from Norm Hatch, Baruch's immediate superior, that Rosenberg "should be given the opportunity to discuss with the Navy possible changes which could make the screenplay acceptable." The Office of Information told Baruch's office, "The positive objectives that Mr. Rosenberg outlined in his letter do not alter the very thorough review given to this project by cognizant offices of the Navy upon which the Navy position was developed." Accordingly, the Office remained reluctant to encourage the producer in any way "because we do not believe that the scope of revision required would be satisfactory to Mr. Rosenberg." The Navy also told Baruch that since it could not "identify any basis for reconsideration at this time it is recommended that no further action be taken unless there is some new and substantial proposal." Consequently, Baruch wrote the producer, "It is regrettable that a workable solution for continuing discussions has not materialized. It is apparent that the Navy feels most negatively about the story of 'Event 1000.'"[24]

Although Rosenberg abandoned the project, the story refused to disappear. Eleven months later director Robert Aldrich submitted a script about a nuclear-submarine disaster, entitled "Gray Lady Down," to the Pentagon. The Navy had the same reaction to it as it had to Rosenberg's effort, which was not surprising since Baruch described the scripts as "virtually identical." He told the service the Pentagon had "a moral obligation" to give Rosenberg another chance to produce the movie if it found Aldrich's script more acceptable. It did not, and the negative reaction ended Aldrich's interest in making the film.[25]

The story surfaced one more time a month later when Walter and Marvin Mirisch acquired the screenplay for their company. According to Marvin Mirisch, the William Morris Agency had brought in the script, and liking the story, his company had bought it.[26] The Mirisch acquisition of the property immeasurably improved the prospects of its being made. The two brothers had a long relationship with the Pentagon, going back to the early 1950s, when they had produced *Flat Top* and *The Annapolis Story.* More recently, they had made *Thousand Plane Raid* in 1969 and were then in the process of completing *Midway.* Working out of Universal Studios gave the brothers additional credibility with the Defense Department and the Navy.[27]

Recognizing that the script did contain inaccuracies, the Mirischs immediately had Universal's Washington representative, John Horton, request the Navy's comments on the previous script. On 16 January 1976 Baruch forwarded the Navy's December 1975 review of the "Gray Lady Down script." He also said he had previously told Aldrich and Rosenberg that if an acceptable screenplay could be developed from the story, "we considered there was a moral obligation on our part to give Rosenberg the option of trying another approach to 'Event 1000' since the properties are so similar."[28]

In Los Angeles, Marvin Mirisch had talked with Cdr. Bill Graves in the Navy's Information Office about meeting to discuss how to make the script acceptable. Graves, who had worked on the earlier versions, concluded, "If anyone will make a submarine picture acceptable to the Navy, it will be Mirisch." When Baruch heard about the meeting, he called the Navy's Information Office in the Pentagon, which told Graves to cancel the meeting. From Baruch's perspective, a "meeting with [the] producer suggesting changes would be [a] tacit indication the revised script would be approved."[29]

Nevertheless, Graves did meet with Mirisch on 23 January and told the producer that the Navy would not cooperate with the script as it stood. He suggested the brothers look for another vehicle if they wanted to do a movie on submarines or deep-sea rescue. Mirisch persisted, and Graves offered to keep his door open if they needed technical information during rewriting. According to Marvin Mirisch, the company set out to revise the script on the basis of the Navy's comments and its own judgment that some of the action was too melodramatic. For example, Jim Whittaker, the company's new screenwriter, took out the military/civilian clash and the involvement of a Soviet nuclear submarine in the rescue operation.[30]

With the Mirischs producing the film, the Navy quickly modified its position on providing assistance. When Baruch learned of the change from John Horton, he wrote in a memo for record, "This is contrary to the 'party line' I had been told earlier." In confirming the change the next day, Baruch learned that the Navy had said it would review a revised script if the filmmakers deleted such objectionable items as the Russian participation in the rescue and the loss of the submarine's captain. Baruch then called Rosenberg to tell him of the Navy's new position, explaining that the Pentagon would consider a rewrite of his screenplay "if he wanted to cut out those same elements in his project." Although the producer no longer had an interest in making the film, he began legal action seeking remedies for the loss of his story and ultimately received suitable remuneration and a screen credit for his adaptation of the novel.[31]

In any event, when the Mirischs sent Whittaker's first effort to the Navy in April 1976, it met the same fate as earlier scripts. The Office found the new version "essentially the same script" the Navy had turned down in December 1975, and the reviewing officer advised Adm. David Cooney, the new Chief of Information, that the screenplay "must be disapproved. The only decision we have to make is whether or not to encourage another major rewrite. (I recommend against any further encouragement.) It is a compelling drama, but I have searched in vain for any justification for cooperation. I can find nothing positive about the Navy throughout this script." The officer also observed that despite technical advice from a submariner, the writer "continues to show a complete lack of understanding of submarines. He continues all previous errors in terminology, ship types, and other details covered by the numerous and specific notations we made in the first draft."[32]

Although the filmmakers continued their research, Bill Gray, assigned to the project as production manager after his work on *Midway,* advised Graves that the Mirischs were having second thoughts about making the movie. In addition to concerns about having enough money to do the film right, the studio was worried about the possibility of an expensive settlement with Rosenberg. Admiral Cooney's 25 May letter to Walter Mirisch added to the gloom.[33] Cooney wrote that he was "disappointed to find that the basis of many of the Navy's original objections still exists in the script." He dissected the story's springboard, pointing out that "there is no logical reason for the submarine to surface in the middle of the night so far out to sea, and the circumstances surrounding the actual collision are most unlikely. These events are a preamble to further scenes in the script which either give a false impression of some aspect of naval service or highlight possible hazards of serving in a submarine." The use of an explosive charge to right the submarine, Cooney observed, is "so unrealistic that it does nothing to counteract, in the minds of the audience, the hazard of an impossible rescue situation. The possibility of a sinking with no chance of escape will seem realistic to the audience, but the final escape sequence of events will not."[34]

Cooney also objected that other parts of the script "will do harm to the Navy. The bickering between the two key naval officers throughout the rescue attempt certainly does the Navy no good, and it is totally unrealistic. Nor does having whiskey aboard the submarine, which is also unrealistic." Citing the many technical inconsistencies, Cooney concluded, "There is much that must be done to the basic script before the Navy can lend its assistance in production." Although his staff would continue to provide technical advice, he warned that "a basic rewrite will not solve the problem."[35]

Cooney's letter apparently inspired the company. On 15 June Graves wrote to the Chief of Information, "'Gray Lady' is giving one last try. A very significant rewrite of the entire story will be in your office by Thursday." Graves also reported that he had been working on a daily basis with Marvin Mirisch and Whittaker, had made calls to submariners to obtain technical advice. He also said the new story would have no incompetence or failures by Navy personnel, no Navy equipment failure, and no accidental loss of life or injury to the submarine's crew as a result of the sinking. He also promised, "No panic, no fires, no illegal liquor, no sailors stumbling over each other, no yelling, no crying—just officers and men reacting as they have been trained."[36]

According to Graves, the filmmakers had agreed to delete the use of explosives to right the submarine, tone down the conflict between the two officers, and, most important, demonstrate the unique capabilities of the DSRV. He then wrote, "I think we have a workable script, assuming the basic premise of the sunken submarine and the problems encountered in its rescue are not on automatic stop." He also told Cooney that many "sunken submarine stories" were making the rounds in Hollywood, and sooner or later someone would make one: "If there is to be such a submarine story, I would certainly rather do it with Mirisch and Universal than anyone else in Hollywood. They are known entities, with whom I have some influence."[37]

The Mirischs had apparently decided to make the movie whether or not the Navy provided help, for Graves told Cooney that production was to begin the day after Labor Day. His postscript suggested how much the producers apparently wanted Navy help: "Mirisch has accepted our proposal that a crawl run at the end of the film saying something like this. 'The U.S. Navy's DSRV shown in this film is today a reality and on constant alert. It is equipped and ready to rescue men in submarines of any nation and at any depth in all of the world's ocean area in which submarines operate.'"[38]

The filmmakers did not actually deliver the revised script until 2 July, when Horton brought it to Baruch, who in turn forwarded it to the Navy. After reading it, the Assistant Deputy Chief of Naval Operations (Submarine Warfare) told Cooney, "The script overall is very pro-Navy." However, he said some technical inaccuracies remained, and while insignificant, he felt they detracted from "the realistic flavor that the author attempts to portray." In addition to suggesting corrections, he noted, "Despite the many improbabilities, am sure my kids would enjoy the show and OP-02 sees no reason why the Navy shouldn't support."[39]

In helping the Mirischs reach this point, Graves had followed the philosophy held by the public-affairs officers of the other services. If Hollywood was going to make a movie about a submarine disaster, the Navy had more to gain by supporting the production than ignoring it, even though the service might have serious reservations about the portrayal. As a result, with the submarine service's opinion in hand, the Navy completed its review of the script, and on 16 July Cooney told Baruch that the service would cooperate with Mirisch in *Gray Lady Down* if the studio accepted additional revisions to the 15 June script. He said the producers also had to agree that "any differences encountered in portraying the U.S. Navy will be resolved by the on-scene technical advisor or Navy Information Office representative."[40]

In return, the filmmakers received use of a nuclear submarine, a submersible, Navy rescue ships, equipment, and sailors to serve as extras. Without such help, no filmmaker could have created a submarine movie with the authenticity that surfeited *Gray Lady Down*. Nevertheless, the question remains whether the effort to obtain a screenplay that satisfied both parties ultimately created a film that benefited either side.

Following screening of the film in the Pentagon, on 23 November 1977, Baruch told the studio representative, "It was the consensus of opinion that it was an excellent example of assistance being of mutual benefit to the producer and DoD. The Navy cooperation showed up especially well and contributed greatly to the factual and visual impact of the film." Baruch's praise for a movie that did little for the Navy's image illustrates how the service was coming to accept the reality that in the post-Vietnam era, military stories would contain less laudatory portrayals than during the golden years of the Hollywood-Navy relationship.[41]

From the service's perspective, of course, any deviation from the norm aboard a submarine—a collision or sinking, a personality conflict among the officers that interferes with operations, the launch of a nuclear strike—is an aberration. The Navy would prefer any movie about its nuclear submarines show only an uneventful six-month cruise. However, creating drama from the mundane presents a severe challenge to screenwriters. In attempting to come up with just such a story for a made-for-television movie, producer Peter Greenberg went to Hawaii with his screenwriter in June 1983 to research life aboard a submarine. Saying he did not want to make the typical disaster story, Greenberg suggested to a Navy public-affairs officer at Pearl Harbor that he might make the ship's captain a pacifist and/or the executive officer a homosexual. The filmmakers did get a ride aboard a nuclear sub, but they never did make their movie.[42]

In contrast, the producers of *The Fifth Missile,* based on the novel *The Gold Crew,* were able to sell a far-fetched submarine melodrama to NBC television. The film told a story of strange happenings occurring aboard a Trident-class submarine when a toxin contained in the paint used in a refit of the ship causes an adverse reaction among the crew and almost triggers a nuclear strike. According to David Soul, who played the submarine's captain, his character's strength became his weakness during the crisis: "Therein was his frailty. When the going got tough on this ship, his malleability, his humanness was tested and he cracked. He's sort of like Capt. Queeg." The Navy turned down the request for cooperation, and the producers had to reproduce the topside of a Trident and use an Italian navy base at Taranto as a set.[43]

Clearly, the images in *Gray Lady Down* validated the early concerns the Navy had expressed about supporting a submarine-disaster movie. Although the film did give the service the opportunity to demonstrate its submarine-rescue equipment, all the finessing of dialogue and actions could not deny that a U.S. submarine had collided with another ship on the open sea. Collisions do happen and ships do sink or run aground despite having the most technologically advanced guidance systems. Ironically, as Charles Champlin observed in his review of *Gray Lady Down,* the failure to use such systems may have caused the disaster: "One sharp-eyed science major in the crowd noted with alarm that the navigator was calculating the position with a *slide rule.* Everyone knows that slide rule companies are going bankrupt right and left, left behind by the new pocket calculators of which every schoolchild has one. (The year of the accident is not clear; maybe it was BC.)"[44]

Accidents occur for inexplicable reasons. Assisting a movie using such an event as its springboard could not be in the Navy's best interest. While the Mirischs undoubtedly empathized with the Navy's position, the producers faced the same situation as Max Youngstein, who had to negotiate with the Air Force for assistance to make *Fail Safe.* If he accepted the service's contention that the U.S. Fail Safe system was infallible, he had no movie. However much the Navy tried to limit the dying, the graphically depicted drowning of the submarine's executive officer and the loss of most of the crew were essential to the drama and to any box-office success the film might enjoy.

Despite his best efforts, Graves, who served as the technical consultant during filming, could not tone down the dramatic conflict between the submarine's captain and his executive officer, the portrayal of which the Navy had always criticized. Likewise, the film portrays bitter disagreement between the senior officers conducting the rescue operation. Worse, the argument takes place in full view of the crew aboard one of the rescue ships. Differences of opinion do occur between honorable people, especially during times of crisis, but the Navy believes that officers should not disagree in public or in front of enlisted men, and certainly not on a motion-picture screen.[45]

The Navy's decision to support *Gray Lady Down* probably brought no benefit to the service. If the film did show the Navy's ability to rescue men from a disaster, it did little to improve the submarine service's image so carefully burnished in such World War II classics as *Destination Tokyo* and *Run Silent, Run Deep.* From a cinematic perspective, *Gray Lady Down* added little to the submarine-film genre and its cousin, the underwater-exploration and -rescue genre. A race against time to save trapped people, in a coal mine cave-in, in a space ship marooned in orbit, atop a burning skyscraper, in a capsized ocean liner, or in a nuclear submarine has drama inherent in its denouement. Whether the drama becomes gripping or merely diverting when brought to the screen depends on the quality of the screenplay and the ability of the director and actors to build up tension. The director did impart "a crisp professionalism," although the story was entirely predictable.[46]

Certainly, a sunken submarine provided a more authentic setting than a submerged 747 jetliner for featuring the Navy's underwater hardware. Unfortunately, the actors playing the crew seem to take their cue from the film's star, Charlton Heston, who impersonates the ship's captain with the same "agreeable stalwartness" he brings to his role in *Midway.* Although they are facing a horrible death, the sailors have a "job-oriented" air about them throughout the rescue operation. As Richard Schickel wrote in *Time,* the film's "only queasy moments occur when, for dramatic punctuation, someone is required to crack under pressure. For the most part, however, a tight rein is kept on emotion and lips are kept well stiffened against adversity."[47]

Washington Post reviewer Gary Arnold observed, "*Gray Lady Down* is by no stretch of the imagination an exemplary suspense thriller, submarine division. At best it's a tolerable exercise in stalwart hokum, a cliché snack that won't provide much nourishment but won't back up on you either. Presentably negligible may be the best term for it." Such reviews do little to stimulate interest in a film. Arnold's conclusion also did little to encourage Navy men to reenlist: "Far be it from the landlubber like me to point out the obvious, but if any movie provokes merriment among U.S. Navy personnel, it is likely to be *Gray Lady Down.*"[48]

No one in Hollywood starts a movie project with the expectation that it will receive such negative comments. If filmmakers could judge the quality of a completed work from a screenplay, studios would probably have fewer box-office failures. Likewise, the armed services have no way of telling from the script they approve how a movie will turn out. Certainly the Navy had little to gain from supporting a film that might cause laughter among its own men. However, the Pentagon does not include dramatic quality or audience appeal among its criteria for determining whether a screenplay qualifies for support. Neither do the services usually allow a bad experience to influence decisions on subsequent requests for assistance from the same filmmaker or studio. Each project that comes into the Pentagon receives the same scrutiny, to answer the one relevant question: will the proposed film in some way benefit the services providing assistance?

Using this guideline, Baruch concluded, after reading the initial script of *Raise the Titanic* in June 1977, that the Navy did not have anything to gain from supporting the production: "Gives Navy a repeat on *Airport '77*—entertaining clap trap of no great significance!! Questionable value, personally see no reason for Navy wanting to do it. . . ." Bob Manning, Baruch's counterpart in the Navy's Office of Information, agreed and recommended to the Chief of Information that the service refuse assistance.[49]

Their judgments might well have ended the Pentagon's consideration of the project. However, *Raise the Titanic* acquired a life of its own that enabled it to survive a change in directors, a requirement for at least $15,000,000 in preproduction costs, the need to find a ship to double for the *Titanic*, reservations by the Navy, and strong objections from the State Department before filming finally began in October 1979. The 1986 discovery of the *Titanic* resting in pieces on the ocean floor made any stories about raising her implausible in the same way that Apollo 11 rendered obsolete all prior fictional accounts of the first landing on the moon. At the time Clive Cussler's *Raise the Titanic* appeared in 1976, however, people suspended their disbelief enough to make the novel a best-seller. Its success prompted Marble Arch Productions to purchase the film rights for $450,000. And despite Manning's recommendation, the Navy saw another chance to show off its underwater-exploration and -rescue equipment.

During the two years four writers needed to produce a final screenplay, Marble Arch regularly sent the Navy each new version of the script, and the Navy responded with comments intended to produce an acceptable story. On 12 October 1978 Bill Graves told Marble Arch that Admiral Cooney had found in the script "a large number of technical inaccuracies" that depicted the service in ways that "are not consistent with current or even possible Navy operations and missions. For Navy cooperation, the story must portray Navy operations as they are currently executed or would be executed should the requirement exist." Graves concluded that the Navy should deny a request for support of the current script.[50]

The next May, Admiral Cooney met with director Jerry Jameson to discuss two "very substantive changes" that the Navy said Marble Arch "must" make before the service would consider helping the project. Afterward, the Office of Information told Baruch: "The Navy cannot assist unless the script is changed to remove that portion that indicates the U.S. Navy might have a high seas involvement with the Soviet Navy, and second, that section where the Navy officer is trespassing on Soviet soil without the knowledge of the Russian Government." In addition to obtaining an agreement from Jameson to have those sections rewritten, the Office said that Cooney had made "numerous minor comments and requests for change" and that Graves was working on them with the production company.[51]

Marble Arch incorporated this effort into the 27 August 1979 script submitted to the Navy for approval. In asking on 2 October for the Navy's opinion of the new version, Baruch told the Office of Information that his office and the State Department were also reviewing the screenplay. The Navy said on 15 October that it "interposes no objection to the subject screenplay as presently written" and intended to provide the requested assistance.[52]

In fact, the Pentagon's Office of International Security Affairs agreed with the State Department's concerns about the Cold War aspects of the script, telling Baruch that the story "has no relationship to any true historical event, and we find it far-fetched and unrealistic." In particular, the Office objected to the trespassing on Soviet soil and an American agent's shooting a Soviet soldier: such scenes would "play into the hands of current Soviet propaganda that it is US policies which are provocative and 'militaristic,' while Soviet policies are 'peaceloving' and truly supportive of detente."[53]

The Navy subsequently told Baruch on 22 October that Cooney had offered Marble Arch some solutions to the areas the State and Defense Departments had found problematic, but the company had ignored them. Nevertheless, the Navy repeated its 15 October position: it had "no objections to the screenplay. This position was not intended to be construed as embracing aspects of the screenplay which are beyond Navy purview and over which other departments might have objection." The Navy also said it had made clear to Marble Arch that its acceptance of the script did not represent final Pentagon approval and that some additional changes might be necessary to make the screenplay acceptable to Defense and State.[54]

The State Department refused to participate in the Pentagon's ultimate decision about assistance. Nevertheless, on 24 October the Bureau of European Affairs judged, "There are aspects of the film which could have an adverse affect on US-Soviet relations, if the Department of Defense made its resources available to support the filming, due to the manner in which the US-Soviet confrontation is depicted in the film," but also admitted, "We believe any adverse consequences given DOD cooperation in the present circumstances would in no way be serious enough to permanently damage our national interests or the US-Soviet bilateral relationship." The Bureau gratuitously concluded, "The film as projected seems to meet none of the DOD policy requirements" for assistance as spelled out in Pentagon guidelines, noting that this reality "strikes us as being more important in the consideration of DOD support than concern about the 'Cold War' aspects of the film."[55]

With this analysis in hand, the International Security Affairs Office told Baruch on the twenty-ninth that it continued "to believe that, as written, the film is not particularly helpful to our national interest" but it would defer to the

State Department's conclusion that the film would do no permanent damage to U.S. national interests or U.S.-Soviet relations. Noting that Marble Arch had agreed to change the most objectionable scene—the shooting of a Russian soldier by an American agent—Security Affairs requested that confrontations be held to a minimum and that "neither side actually be shown to bring weapons to bear." The Office also told Baruch "to determine whether the film meets the established DoD criteria for authenticity and dignity and whether previous DoD commitments and recruitment and publicity benefits to the Navy warrant Defense Department Assistance."[56] Baruch then sent Cooney's office a memo on the thirty-first, saying that he would approve the *Raise the Titanic* screenplay containing the changes Marble Arch had promised to make. He asked the Navy what assistance it would provide so that he could officially notify the company of the decision. He also requested "supportive statements" to confirm the Navy's belief that it considered the project beneficial. The service responded the same day: "The Navy position is that providing assistance is warranted and will aid in recruiting efforts by showing the public the sophisticated equipment used by the Navy to explore the ocean depths and give some insight on expertise required for undersea salvage work."[57]

Marble Arch still did not have a done deal. On 13 November Baruch told the Navy that the Pentagon had authorized assistance only for the filming of two scenes in Washington, explaining that the film company had not yet incorporated all the requested changes into the script. Unless the final version "made it clear that the so-called island 'Off Russia' is one that is under international dispute and therefore no nation has sovereignty over it, further assistance will not be approved." He also cited other "mandatory" changes, including dialogue to explain that the Soviet soldier that an American civilian shoots has no right to be on the disputed island.[58]

Without a flotilla of salvage vessels and a submersible from the Navy, Marble Arch had no way to make *Raise the Titanic*. On 16 November the company delivered to the Pentagon virtually all the script changes Baruch's office had demanded, and on the nineteenth Baruch called Horton to say that the Defense Department had approved the script for assistance, reminding him that the Navy was giving support "on a non-interference and no-additional cost to the government basis." Baruch also reiterated the DoD requirement that the company screen the completed film in Washington for Pentagon officials and said that neither the Defense Department nor the Navy desired an acknowledgment of military assistance but did not object to a screen credit for the Navy technical adviser.[59]

Despite the long and delicate negotiations that led to the script's approval and the Navy's wide-ranging support, the completed movie became a $35 million disaster for Marble Arch and a disappointment to the Navy. Although the novel was exciting, the film managed to expunge all dramatic tensions from the story. Becoming enamored with the naval hardware and the special-effects miniatures, the filmmakers failed to develop the characters. The visualization of the underwater salvage efforts does not sustain the excitement, and the film becomes a pseudo-documentary study of naval salvage techniques. Only the actual raising of the luxury liner—done with a model and reinforced with a haunting musical theme—is artistically stimulating.

Ironically, by diminishing the human elements of *Raise the Titanic*, the movie negated the Pentagon and State Department's concerns about the Cold War ramifications of the cinematic confrontation between the United States and the Soviet Union. Given the filmmakers' focus on the underwater sequences, the race between the two superpowers to acquire a rare mineral needed to create a Star Wars–like defensive shield or the most powerful bomb ever made became anticlimactic.

Raise the Titanic does show the Navy's considerable underwater-salvage equipment to full advantage, and the scenes of the flotilla at work provide strong images of the Navy's personnel and capabilities. However, Marble Arch failed to honor its apparent commitment to use Cooney's ending, written in hopes of eliminating a negative comment about the morality of the U.S. government. While such agreements have no legal weight, producers have usually honored commitments for script revisions reached through negotiations with the armed forces. The Pentagon has little leverage to enforce agreements except to threaten the withdrawal of support if the film remains in production or the withholding of assistance in the future. On those few occasions when filmmakers have used unapproved revisions, they have had sufficient resources to ignore adverse military reactions.

Cooney had had problems with the ending of *Raise the Titanic* throughout the negotiations. As written, the script had the American salvage crew discovering that the crates in the hold of the *Titanic* contain only gravel instead of the rare mineral needed to fuel a nationwide missile-defense system. Jason Robards, as the retired admiral in charge of the whole operation, tries to alleviate the disappointment of the scientist: "Look, if it will make you feel any better, I'll tell you something I didn't want to admit even to myself. If we had found the Byzantium, I'm not sure we could have hung onto it. I don't think we could have tagged it for defense only and made it stick." The scientist responds that he had the president's assurance, but Robards says, "That's right. But, presidents don't stay in office forever. And even if they did, circumstances change. . . . If a government falls in the Middle East somewhere or if they start bombing Pakistan or somewhere else, it affects all of us. . . . I am just saying that somewhere in the world, in some think tank, right now, they're figuring out a way to build a Byzantium bomb." Robards rationalizes his decision to go along with the operation anyway: "I believed in what we were trying to do. And if it didn't work defensively, if somebody *was* going to make a Byzantium bomb, I wanted it to be us." He then leaves the scientist to claim self-righteously that he would not have started the project in the first place.

In the original script, as in the book, the intelligence officer figures out where the Byzantium had actually been hidden, and the heroes track it down to a seaside English cemetery. There, the scientist finally acknowledges the intelligence officer's cynicism: the bad guys "have us outnumbered," and by implication, the American government cannot be trusted to use the mineral for defensive purposes only. United in their disillusionment, the two men leave the grave site in agreement to keep their discovery from the world.

To Cooney, who had liked the book and Cussler's ending, in which the United States does build an antimissile shield, the film's conclusion casts aspersions on military integrity and U.S. leadership. So he felt the ending would negate any benefit the film might offer the Navy. After negotiating with the producers, Cooney thought he had an agreement for them to use the ending he had written. In it, the heroes find that the crash of a World War II German bomber had obliterated the cemetery, which had been replaced by a playground and a memorial plaque.[60]

The producer did not bring the completed movie to the Pentagon for the required prerelease screening, so the Navy Chief of Information discovered that the filmmakers had not used his ending only when he requested a preview while in Los Angeles on other business. No one from the company attended the screening, and Cooney did not learn that the producer had no intention of shooting the revised conclusion until Marble Arch responded to Baruch's inquiry after the film had premiered. Then, Richard O'Connor, the company's executive in charge of production, explained that the filmmakers had understood Cooney's revisions "were to be taken as suggestions" and that his ending "was seriously taken into consideration even to the extent of writing the scene to the Admiral's specifications." In fact, O'Connor claimed that when the scene was sent to Baruch's office, it was "the intended ending to our picture."[61]

During production, however, he explained "it was decided that the ending as originally written by Adam Kennedy was creatively the better ending, and that was the scene eventually filmed." As O'Connor acknowledged, it was "unfortunate that producer Bill Frye apparently neglected to notify Admiral Cooney and you of this change but because of his many responsibilities during filming, I can understand this oversight." He also said he was "not aware" of any request for a Pentagon screening prior to release. Given the clearly stated requirement and Baruch's reminder to Horton, who had helped start the office in 1949, and a long-time studio liaison with the Pentagon, the professed ignorance has little credibility and suggests that the filmmakers knew they would have a serious problem if they screened the movie in the Pentagon before its premiere.[62]

Cooney need not have worried about the impact the ending might have on audiences since few people actually went to see the film. Made at a cost of at least $35 million, the movie returned only $6.8 million to Universal Studios. Clive Cussler, for one, observed, "The movie was so poor, it boggles the mind." *Daily Variety,* which bends over backward to support Hollywood's product, said *Raise the Titanic* "hits new depths hitherto unexplored by the worst of Lew Grade's overloaded Ark melodramas. This one wastes a potentially intriguing premise with dull scripting, a lackluster cast, laughably phony trick works, and clunky direction that makes *Voyage of the Damned* seem inspired by comparison."[63]

Judy Maslin, in the *New York Times,* observed, "Take the adventure out of an adventure movie, and what have you got? A lot of hearty he-men, barking commands or insults and offering terse congratulations on a job well done. . . . The glistening, quivering air bubbles that burst out of the ship should be readily familiar to anyone who's ever broken a thermometer. They look just like globs of mercury, and there's no mistaking the miniature TITANIC for anything truly ship-sized. Nor will anyone imagine, in the process shots near the film's ending, that a real, rusting ocean liner has actually made its appearance in New York harbor."[64]

People will accept movie magic when they can suspend their disbelief and empathize with the characters. If the characters doing the raising had seemed real, people just might have accepted the idea that the almost mythical ocean liner could reappear. But the film's producer, William Frye, probably said it best, pointing at the old freighter transformed into the raised *Titanic:* "There is the 'star' of our movie, with my apologies to the human ones. It will probably go down as the eighth wonder of the world, and upstage everyone at the same time." It didn't, and the Navy's support was for naught.[65]

The film's quick demise at the box office and the company's failure to honor its promise to Cooney did not discourage the Navy from continuing to talk with filmmakers about any script offering the potential for showing off its hardware to good advantage. Once *Midway* had rekindled Hollywood's interest in the Navy as a subject, the Office of Information usually had several major projects in various stages of development simultaneously.

The Navy even remained ready and willing to ignore the implausibility of a story about a nuclear aircraft carrier being transported back in time. After all, "The Last Countdown" would star one of the Navy's most prized ships. In their script submitted in June 1975, writers Peter Powell and Thomas Hunter used a Bermuda Triangle–type phenomenon to deposit the aircraft carrier in question off the coast of Serbia just before the assassination of Archduke Ferdinand and the outbreak of World War I. According to Hunter, the "science fiction approach in telling our story serves only as a broad canvas of a larger picture of man and his continual fight to save himself from destruction. Thus, the script is more allegorical than science fiction."[66]

He did acknowledge that during the writing "the aircraft carrier has evolved in our eyes, into the main character, the star of the film." Realizing the need for

Navy cooperation, Hunter presented the story as putting "the Navy's way of life over in a very credible and exciting way. By giving the film entertainment value in addition to technical expertise, we would hope to reach the largest possible audience in America. That includes prospective Navy volunteers and particularly men who are now serving in the Armed Forces—men who would like to see a film about what they really do and how they also really do it without the negating edge of propaganda."[67]

While the Navy had some problems with the script, it advised Baruch that the Information Office "has no objection to the story-concept." Baruch then informed Capt. C. D. Griffin, the retired Navy officer representing the writers, of the Navy's reaction and said the Navy would "be glad to discuss any story points with you whenever you wish." Submitting a revised script to Baruch's office the next May, Griffin explained that the new version "reflects the suggestions made by the Office of Naval Information."[68]

On 1 June Admiral Cooney told Baruch that "Navy cooperation in the production of the film would be in the best interests of the Navy." Baruch then told Griffin that the Navy would be able to work out support for the production, concluding, "The Navy and ourselves are looking forward to working on the production and its release bringing to the public in an intriguing way a better understanding of carrier operations." The Navy may have acted quickly for this reason. The effort was for naught since the English company holding the rights to the screenplay failed to get the project off the ground.[69]

Several months later Peter Douglas, the twenty-two-year-old son of Kirk Douglas, received a copy of "The Last Countdown" and took an immediate interest in the story "because it used a carrier and it brought up the possibility of filming on a carrier. I'm a pilot and the fantasy of flying a civilian plane is not closing your eyes, but envisioning the sound or the roar of jet engines and the thrust of your afterburners. The thought of one day being able to ride in a Navy jet and watch those planes take off and land on a carrier excited me." The fledgling producer took an option on the screenplay in early 1977 and set out to try "to make the story work" for him.[70]

He shifted the original script's time and setting because he really did not believe in the Bermuda Triangle. Likewise, he thought that "World War I is such a non-specific war. There is no one single incident. I don't think today's generation would even know Ferdinand unless they happened to be particularly well-educated in history. So, it was a question of what we could use as a catalyst and certainly Pearl Harbor was promising. Everyone knows it. Even today when you mention Pearl Harbor the immediate reaction is not the naval base in the mid-Pacific, but the disastrous sneak attack by the Japanese during WWII." With this idea in mind, the producer brought in screenwriters David Ambrose and Gerry Davis to redo the Hunter/Powell story.[71]

Douglas sent an early draft to the Pentagon to get a sense of the Navy's willingness to cooperate on the project. He recalled that the script "had certain aspects which we didn't like and which they didn't like, such as an executive officer who goes crazy." Since the human roles remained of secondary importance to the story, the producer had "little interest" in the character as written and had no "severe problem" in creatively revising the portrayal to give the proper depiction of an officer.

While not entirely enthused by the science-fiction aspect of the story, the Navy and the Pentagon made no attempt to change it. The Information Office felt "that production of this film will benefit our recruiting effort, and it will be of great assistance in familiarizing the public with the professionalism of Navy personnel." If the Navy did not concern itself with the story line, Douglas found the service a "stickler for details," changing "no" to "negative" and focusing on how an aircraft carrier's captain would have performed when confronted with a series of hypothetical situations for which he had no frame of reference. To be sure the film contained an accurate portrayal, the Navy helped Douglas locate the retiring captain of the USS *Ranger,* Doug McCrimmons, to serve as technical adviser about life aboard a carrier. Douglas found him to be "extremely knowledgeable and helpful and more specifically savvy to the needs of our industry. We used him to get the input for accuracy—what goes on a carrier."[72]

While Douglas and his writers were completing the script, the executive officer of the *Nimitz* heard through the grapevine that Douglas's production company was looking for a ship to feature in the film. Douglas recalled that the officer thought that using the ship as the location for the movie would build crew morale as well as serve the Navy in recruiting and retention. The officer contacted the producer directly and invited him to visit the *Nimitz* and meet the captain.

Once the *Nimitz* expressed willingness to allow the filmmakers aboard for an extended stay, support for the project grew within the Office of Information. Douglas said the Navy expressed an interest in creating "a more glamorous environment" and saw the movie as "a positive thrusting sword for the Navy and carrier aviation." Douglas also explained that the Navy was aware of its retention problems in the late 1970s.

The producer contributed to the authenticity of the film, not to mention fulfilling his own fantasy, by spending much of the six months from February through August of 1979 on board the *Nimitz.* He researched the script, brought out the screenwriters, and incorporated the "very complex" *Nimitz* flight schedule into his filming schedule. The production crew boarded the *Nimitz* for two months of shooting that summer. According to Douglas, his people "learned very quickly what these guys had to go through."

Douglas praised the *Nimitz*'s crew for doing "everything they could, legally within their power, to cooperate." In addition to giving recommendations and suggestions, the sailors helped during off-duty hours to make the picture technically accurate. The assistance the Navy provided over and above the filming of normal shipboard operations cost Douglas about $2 million. Unfortunately, the money did not give *The Final Countdown* box-office appeal or bring it critical acclaim, and Douglas later admitted that he did not create a high-quality film—probably the result of his inexperience. Although the movie's ad campaign in the United States did not highlight the Navy's hardware as a selling point, the Navy apparently received the benefit for which it had hoped. According to Douglas, the retention rate went up 23 or 24 percent following the release of *The Final Countdown*. Moreover, whatever problems the film had commercially, the producer felt that in the end he had captured the Navy's love of its ships: "The star of the picture was truly the *Nimitz*."

The science-fiction fantasy did provide moviegoers with a guided tour of the nuclear carrier. The *New York Times* found the ship "the only thing of interest in the movie. She's the principal character, but a chilly one." The two months Douglas's film crew spent aboard the ship did enable them to capture its essence, her men performing their assigned duties and her planes demonstrating their firepower, albeit directed against World War II Japanese Zeros. The carrier's F-14s helped create dramatic, wide-screen aerial-combat sequences with the pseudo Zeros, the same SNJ trainers rebuilt to masquerade as Japanese fighters for *Tora! Tora! Tora!*, now rented from the Confederate Air Force, which had bought them from Twentieth Century Fox. Like too many Hollywood stars, however, the *Nimitz* had to perform in a vehicle unworthy of its stature.[73]

Time-travel films require an extra suspension of disbelief, and the audience knows the climax of the story before entering the theater. If the *Nimitz,* transferred through a huge storm to Pearl Harbor the morning of the sneak attack, had ordered her planes to engage the Japanese aerial armada, she would have changed history and so would have committed suicide. Both the filmmakers and the Navy had no choice but to ignore this conundrum or they would have had no story. But, like a festering sore, it remained at the heart of the movie, dissipating any dramatic tension before it could even develop. David Ansen in *Newsweek* concluded that while *The Final Countdown* "is clunky, square filmmaking . . . it's rarely boring, and the screenwriters come up with a final mysterious twist that saves the movie at the last moment from a disastrously anti-climactic turn of events. The twist, when it comes, doesn't really explain anything that preceded it, nor does it make the least bit of sense. But after the tedium of a *Raise the Titanic!* even one crude sleight of hand can begin to look like art." The *New York Times* perhaps said it best: "*The Final Countdown* . . . looks like a 'Twilight Zone' episode produced as a Navy recruiting film." The Navy's impact on the story caused the reviewer to observe that the ship's crew "are so proper, so gung-ho, so perfectly integrated racially and so all-around sunny-natured, they seem more like members of a gigantic choir than seasoned sailors. You know it would never be necessary to show these men a training film on the perils of venereal disease."[74]

Whatever success *The Final Countdown* enjoyed at the box office, any film in the post-Vietnam era that showed well-adjusted, happy military men would satisfy the Defense Department's fondest hopes. More important, the film fulfilled the Navy's goal of advertising its hardware and showing its ships and planes well-manned. However, as presented, the sailors differ little from automatons, functioning just as predictably as the ships and planes. While the Navy was willing to show off its equipment and "perfect" sailors, it was still reluctant to show that the equipment and men sometimes fail to function as expected, as in *Tora! Tora! Tora!* or *Gray Lady Down*. The Navy also continued to have difficulty assisting a film that focused on "flawed" people, who drink, lust after women, or simply do not conform to the Navy's ideal officer or enlisted person.

★

TWELVE

A Different Image
Rehabilitation Complete

Like the Navy, the Marine Corps had been developing new guidelines for providing assistance to Hollywood in the aftermath of the Vietnam War. While denying assistance to *Coming Home,* the Marines did agree to cooperate with the television mini-series *Rumor of War* and the original effort to make *Born on the Fourth of July,* although neither story offered much benefit to the service. However, the decision to assist on production of *The Great Santini* brought the Marine Public Affairs Office into temporary conflict with the Navy and even questioned whether the Marines had truly become an independent military service.

Set in 1962–63, Pat Conroy's novel *The Great Santini* followed a year in the life of Lt. Col. "Bull" Meechum, a highly decorated Marine jet pilot. Meechum, "The Great Santini," a fictional character modeled on the author's father, remains a warrior soldier in the mold of George Patton, a man to whom a nation turns in wartime, but who has no place in peacetime. A World War II and Korea veteran, Meechum could have said, as Patton did, that he should have died with the last bullet of the last war. Instead, Santini remains a maverick, a flamboyant, fun-loving, hard-drinking officer, relegated to fighting mock combat. He loves his country, the Corps, and his family, pretty much in that order, and despite his transgressions, he remains a better officer than husband and father.

Gen. W. R. Maloney, the Marine Corps Director of Information, described the book as "an 'earthy' story which I believe will be turned into a very popular, modern movie rated R."[1] He found the story "highly authentic in detail, probably sited at Beaufort. There are several racist incidents described. The book is very upbeat towards USMC, ambivalent towards Lt Col Meechum. Some other specifics include examples of wife beating and derogatory statements concerning the USN and USNA." Maloney felt that the Pentagon was "likely" to approve cooperation, "in which case it will be in our interest to provide support."[2]

During the negotiations with Bing Crosby Productions, the Marines endeavored to improve Santini's character, particularly his drinking and abuse of his wife and children, both physically and emotionally. The Navy became involved in the discussions when BCP requested use of an aircraft carrier "moored to a dock in a location, preferably on the West Coast, where no land would be visible in one direction and where takeoffs would be feasible."[3] Having revealed its obvious lack of awareness that a carrier must be under way to launch its planes, the company showed good sense to request a technical adviser during filming.[4]

Apart from the need to explain carrier operations, the Navy had other serious problems with the script. The movie opens with Santini leading Marine jets in a victory over their Navy counterparts in a mock dogfight. In a celebration rite, Meechum, using a can of mushroom soup to create the effect, pretended to vomit in front of Navy officers and their wives and then has his fellow Marines eat up the apparent mess.

Given the request for a carrier and the Navy's brief appearance, even as a foil for Meechum's antics, Don Baruch told the Marines he had sent the screenplay to the Navy Chief of Information.[5] On 19 December 1977 Admiral Cooney informed Baruch he found the "portrayal of Navy/Marine Corps personnel is highly inaccurate and derogatory." As a result, he said the script did not meet the DoD regulations governing cooperation and so he recommended that assistance be denied.[6]

The next day Gen. V. T. Blaz, the new Marine Corps Director of Information, informed the Marines' Chief of Staff that the producers had indicated a willingness to delete some objectionable scenes, but had not removed other sequences which reflected negatively on the Navy–Marine Corps team concept. He advised the Chief of Staff that the Navy was refusing to support the film and recommended that the Marines should do the same.[7]

Nevertheless, within the Public Affairs Office, sentiment favored assistance. Art Brill, for one, recommended that the Marine Office in Los Angeles continue trying to resolve some of the problems. However, he acknowledged that the mushroom-soup scene might be "offensive to some," particularly the Navy, and said the Navy might refuse to cooperate simply because Marine pilots defeat the Navy fliers in the opening sequence.[8] Once the filmmakers indicated they would do "whatever" necessary to obtain Marine assistance, the service had to decide what script changes to require. The Navy's position on cooperation complicated negotiations since its disinterest in the project quickly became an issue. The Marine Corps considered itself a virtually autonomous military branch, while remaining under the authority of the Secretary of the Navy. In the chain of command, the Marine Director of Information and the Navy Chief of Information had the same organizational rank. However, the Chief of Information also served as Public Affairs Officer for the Secretary of the Navy, and in that capacity he outranked and so commanded the Marine Director of Information. Consequently, if the Navy Chief of Information decided he did not want the Marines to cooperate on *The Great Santini* or any other movie, he could theoretically impose his decision on the Corps.

While Cooney had "enjoyed the book," his initial comments to Baruch indicated he felt the film would contain negative references to the Navy. However, despite the unresolved problems with the script, the Marines had no intention of letting the Navy shoot down their support of the movie. According to Pat Coulter, the service saw the story "as the first realistic film about Marine aviation since *The Flying Leathernecks*" and the Corps wanted *Santini* made.[9] The situation became complicated when an officer in Cooney's office called Art Brill on 14 June 1978 to say that the Chief of Information "is dead against supporting the film primarily because of the language used."[10]

In conveying this news to General Brewer, Brill said that until the phone call, the Marines had the "impression" from the Navy people "THAT SANTINI *IS* A MARINE PROBLEM." To solve the problem, Brill suggested his office could "convince the producers to eliminate the Navy entirely or modify the two Navy scenes. With this done, it's a Marine Corps film entirely." However, he said, "Even in its present form, this is a Marine film. The Navy's role is minimal." Still, Brill acknowledged, "We do not want our sister service to look bad and I'm sure the producers will agree to modify the script accordingly." With that done, he felt the script would become solely a Marine concern.[11]

While the filmmakers refused to change the vomit scene, they agreed to add a line saying the Marines considered this behavior unacceptable and unprofessional. The company also toned down some of Meechum's abuse of his family and agreed to cut down the opening mock dogfight sequence so the Navy would not emerge humiliated. As a result, after reviewing the revised script, the Marines agreed on 10 August 1978 to provide assistance to the production. Despite his antipathy toward the script and the Navy's refusal to become involved, Admiral Cooney supported the Marine's decision to give the film limited assistance. He later explained that he had always considered the film a Marine project and "if they were comfortable with it," he had no further objections, although he recommended DoD receive no screen credit.[12] By refusing to assist, the Navy did lose an opportunity for one of its carriers to make a cameo appearance and prevented Marine aviators from taking part in carrier operations for the first time since *Devil Dogs of the Air*. Without Navy planes to provide the dogfight opposition to Meechum's Marine fliers, Pat Coulter, who served as technical adviser, had to "costume" a squadron of Marine jets as

Navy planes by putting masking tape over the word "MARINES" on the side of the fighters and then painting the word "NAVY" in its place.[13]

In any case, the Navy continued to feel more comfortable advertising its hardware and showing its ships and planes manned by clean-cut officers and enlisted personnel rather than "flawed" people, who drank, lusted after women, or simply did not conform to the Navy's ideal officer or enlisted man. Like Jack Nicholson in *The Last Detail* and James Caan in *Cinderella Liberty*, Richard Gere, as Zack Mayo in *An Officer and a Gentleman*, does not have the background and presence the Navy expects in its officers. Worse, the proposed film would contain graphic sex and portrayals of its training that the service found inaccurate. The illegitimate son of a Navy enlisted man, Zack grows up on the fringes of the sordid world of U.S. sailors stationed in the Philippines, graduates from college, and decides to enter the Naval Aviation Officer program, despite his tattoo and motorcycle. During his training he meets a local factory worker, played by Debra Winger, who frequents the Navy–base dances, looking for an officer and a husband.

Side by side with the unexceptional boy-meets-girl, boy-loses-girl, boy-wins-girl love story, Zack struggles to become a naval officer under the watchful and always demanding eye of his drill instructor, Sergeant Foley. In a role that Hollywood had made a cliché, Lou Gossett, Jr., imparts a believability worthy of Jack Webb's classic portrayal in *The D.I.* or Lee Ermey's vintage performance in *Full Metal Jacket*. Despite the torrid love scenes between Gere and Winger, Gossett becomes the focus of the movie, ultimately turning Gere into an officer and a gentleman worthy of his salute.

The story differed little from the many rite-of-passage films on which the Navy had cooperated over the years. However, the Office of Information saw it as a story of a drill instructor's physical and verbal abuse of naval officer candidates, the explicit depiction of sexual encounters, and the suicide of an officer candidate who drops out of the program.

Ironically, the initial contacts between the Navy and the filmmakers seemed to put the project on the fast track. According to Chris Baumann, then a young commander in the Navy's Los Angeles Public Affairs Office, producer Marty Elfand called in the summer of 1980, asking to discuss the story. Having gone through the aviation program as the story depicts, Baumann explained the process of becoming a Navy aviator to the producer. Elfand then gave the treatment to Baumann to read, and the officer thought "the relationship was off to a great start."[14]

Acknowledging he had no experience in dealing with the military, Elfand hired John Horton to represent him in Washington and take the script to the Pentagon. Despite Baumann's early help and Horton's great experience with the military, from the initial submission of the script the Navy voiced strong objections to the project—particularly Capt. Dale Patterson, then director of the Los

Angeles Office. He later explained he reacted so negatively "because, to be brutally honest, I didn't think it was much of a story, rather trashy, a lot of violence, sex and filthy language in it. And the characters in the script were not characteristic of Navy men."[15]

Following two months of informal discussions about the screenplay and a formal request for Navy assistance, Patterson told Elfand in July that "prior to Navy consideration for assistance the script would need re-writing or major revision." In a 16 July 1980 memorandum for the record, Patterson cited "a multitude of problem areas" just in the first twenty pages of the script. These included inaccuracies in the status of Zack's father; a Filippino gang attack on sailors that "is not an accurate portrayal of the Philippine community and their relationship with American sailors"; "atrocious" language; the harassment of female officer candidates, which is "not tolerated in any phase of training or in the Navy as a whole"; "offensive and most inaccurate" Jody calls; and references "to Mobile DEBS offensive to Mobile."[16]

When this memo reached Washington, the Navy Office of Information proposed to Baruch that the service send it to the producer in response to his request for guidance in dealing with the Navy's objections to the script. Baruch did not concur, telling Bob Manning, his counterpart in the Navy Office of Information, that the Navy needed to provide a more detailed explanation than a simple list of problem areas. He also noted that even if the filmmakers corrected the problems, the Chief of Information might still object to the project.[17]

On 7 August in a follow-up to his conversation with Manning, Baruch suggested an alternative approach. Agreeing that the Navy's comments "are well taken," he repeated his concern that even if the filmmakers corrected the objections, the Navy might still disapprove the script. So he proposed the Navy "endeavor to develop a version that could be considered acceptable, especially as the story of pilot training has not been on the screen for some time and because this is considered to be a major theatrical release." He also told the Office of Information that, at his suggestion, Elfand was coming to Washington to visit him and the Navy the next week "both for further clarification on objections and developing something more satisfactory."[18]

After the meeting, the producer spent the next several months revising the story to meet the Navy's objections. When the Navy read the second version of the script in early December, it found little difference from the original screenplay, describing it as "sordid, emphasizing the seamy side of life and featuring numerous sexually explicit scenes. Production assistance offers no benefit to the service, rather, the portrayal would be damaging to the Navy and to the recruiting effort." With the concurrence of the Los Angeles Office, the Office of Information recommended that the Navy deny the filmmakers' request for assistance on the grounds that the "Navy would suffer by association with the production."[19]

Not willing to take the turndown as a final answer, associate producer Bob Williams met with Baruch and Navy representatives on 13 January 1981. According to Baruch, the Office of Information "gave him chapter and verse" why it still found the story inaccurate. The Navy claimed the script did not present a factual account of aviation training and suggested that since the story did not involve any flying sequences, the company should consider setting it at the Navy's officer candidate school in Newport. The service also said the role of the D.I. "needs clarification as to his duties."[20] It also told Williams he would have to delete the opening montage, which shows Zack, as an eleven-year-old, coming to the Philippines to live with his father after his mother commits suicide. According to Baruch, the sequence "shows seamy-side of life there which we probably would not want to approve as it would be negative for govt.-to-govt. relations." Baruch also complained that the script had too much sex and noted that Williams "would let us know if producer will rewrite this considerably or make pix on his own." Nevertheless, the Navy Office of Information authorized a research visit to Pensacola Naval Air Station for the filmmakers "to give them an overview of the aviation program. Familiarization visit would enable them to rewrite script to more accurately reflect various aspects of basic flight training contemplated for the screenplay."[21]

In any event, the Marines first became involved in the project in February 1981 when Baumann told Pat Coulter that the Navy was about to turn down the request for cooperation. Baumann thought Coulter should "be aware" of the situation because the script included a drill instructor (the Navy used Marine D.I.s at its Pensacola flight school). He also gave Coulter a copy of the script with the admonition, "Don't tell anyone I gave you the script."[22]

Coulter thought initially that Elfand had not submitted the screenplay to the Marines because he "probably wasn't knowledgeable enough to know that he should have touched base with both services." The producer felt that he had no reason to approach the Marines directly because he considered the Corps only a branch of the Navy and *An Officer and a Gentleman* a story about naval aviation. After reading the script, Coulter concluded that the film would appeal to young people, so he was especially concerned that the Marines do what they could to protect the image of the Corps. When he took the script back to the Navy Office, he told Baumann, "You're right. This has got the potential to be a dynamite story. The Marine Corps needs to be involved, especially if you guys are going to turn it down, we need to play a key role in this thing."[23]

After calling General Brewer, still the Marine Corps Director of Information, to get permission to approach the film company, Coulter phoned Bob Williams on 19 February to "begin deliberations on what could be done to portray the Marine in the most authentic, accurate and positive manner as possible." If the Navy would not change its position, he wanted to propose turning the story into a Marine film, changing the location from preflight training to the Corps's officer candidate school at Quantico, Virginia.[24] Following the phone conversation, Williams sent the script to Coulter and confirmed the filmmakers' request for assistance, saying they were *"most anxious to meet with you to incorporate any changes or ideas that you might have regarding this project."* If the script met with Marine approval, the filmmakers would like to arrange "for an immediate survey trip to Quantico. It is anticipated that production would begin sometime in April, so you can see time is of the essence."[25]

Sending the script to Washington the next day, Coulter reported that Williams had said Elfand had been working with the Navy for more than a year on the project and had "hit an impasse in the negotiation process." Coulter found the script "well written" and "an excellent, moving story of a young man trying to find his place in the world." He explained the filmmakers would not change the story much if they made it a Marine film because they needed to begin shooting in April to complete production before the anticipated director's strike in June. Recognizing the producers wanted Marine assistance, Coulter found them "quite flexible, much more so than they were in discussions with the Navy." Explaining that he had already offered suggestions for rewriting the script, Coulter concluded that "this is a good story and will be made with or without us." He also noted that it "could be the first commercial film to feature two segments of the Corps of which we are very proud; Officer Candidate School, the transition process from carefree college days to Lieutenant of Marines and the close association that exists between members of the Air/Ground team . . . with special emphasis on the Harrier."[26]

With shooting to begin in April, Elfand met with Coulter and focused on the Navy's objections to the script. He asked if the Corps would have a problem with the suicide in a Marine-officer-candidate story. Coulter told the producer, "Anybody who can't be a Marine has every right in the world and every reason in the world to commit suicide." While Coulter made the comment "tongue in cheek," it helped break the ice: "They liked that. You know, as Marines, we can get away with being a little more colorful. We have an image that we are very proud of, one that has taken 206 years to create. We have a certain constituency we are responsible for. We aren't concerned about the propriety of a lot of things that the other services are."[27]

Coulter also said the sex, per se, did not bother the Marines as it had the Navy, particularly after it became clear that due to time constraints, Elfand was not going to be able to transform *An Officer and a Gentleman* into a Marine story. Coulter did suggest that some of the Navy's problems with the sex resulted from a failure to realize that the company could not afford to lose the "R" rating and so would have to tone down the script's explicitness.[28]

Despite his enthusiastic efforts to help the filmmakers, as late as 20 March Coulter discovered that the Navy Office of Information in Los Angeles was still "talking to the producers and maintaining the lines of communications." In describing the situation to Headquarters, he said that "the 'official' Navy response to a request for assistance, appears to be negative. As I understand it, that has never been conveyed by letter from either DOD or CHINFO to Paramount. It has all been verbal to date." Commenting on Coulter's request to assist the filmmakers, an officer in Marine Public Affairs advised the director in an undated memo that the Navy "has indicated they don't intend to support the film—'not only NO, but "Hell NO!"' As the Navy has supported films in the past, it doesn't appear to be a matter of *not* providing support to any films. I therefore feel their position is legitimate and firm."[29]

Don Baruch believed "the Navy was overly restrictive in dealing with the producer."[30] Elfant agreed, saying that the Navy had refused to even keep the door open to negotiations. While he acknowledged that the sex, the language, and the suicide formed the heart of the film, he felt the Navy may not have understood the script and so could not envision the intent of the completed film. Still, he maintained the Navy "was terrible to us."[31]

On the other hand, the Marines focused their attention on the characterization of the D.I. to ensure that the scenes depicting Sergeant Foley's verbal and physical harassment of the officer trainees would not adversely affect the Corps's image. While the Marines were considering whether to become involved in the film, two major recruit abuses had occurred: one with Pugi sticks at the recruit depot in San Diego, one in which a D.I. shot a recruit at Parris Island. Coulter said that the Commandant had made it clear that "recruit abuse was absolutely verboten. You did not do it. Of course, our job was to try to drive home the message that we don't do that."[32]

Therefore, Coulter worked with producer Elfand and director Taylor Hackford to tone down the Foley persona. The original script called for the D.I. to appear as a "rough character." From his perspective, Coulter could not have the drill instructor "be a Neanderthal, knuckle dragging, son of a bitch," which was the stereotype Lou Gossett had initially envisioned. Thanks to Coulter, the authenticity Gossett imparted to his role won him an Academy award for best supporting actor. His performance also steals the movie from the Gere-Winger fairy-tale love story, despite the explicitness of their sexual encounters.[33] The love story has a predictable climax when Zack, in his white graduation uniform, whisks away his lady to Hollywood-variety bliss as a Navy flier's wife. Far more interestingly, *An Officer and a Gentleman* details the process through which Foley turns Zack from a selfish loner, distrustful of anyone, into an officer and a gentleman. Hackford captures the change exquisitely during a scene in which Zack's unit makes a run over an obstacle course. Sergeant Foley watches from the finish line as Zack, instead of going for a record, returns to help a female classmate overcome a physical and mental wall to complete her run. With a subtle look of satisfaction, Foley's expression gives meaning to the movie and crowns Coulter's efforts: Marine D.I.s create naval aviation officers and gentlemen.

Not everyone appreciated the film, of course. Columnist Richard Cohen liked *An Officer and a Gentleman,* suggesting that if an Oscar existed for best kissing in a movie, Gere and Winger "are going to walk off with it—that is if they can still walk." However, he objected to the movie's message that brutality can turn a punk into a man: "In *Officer,* it's not the Army that does the trick but the Navy's boot camp for potential pilots. Ex-GI's will be relieved to know that the Navy has mud, too." Cohen was also disturbed that the movie "is a big, big hit—second only to *E.T.*—and that audiences that should be laughing are instead eating it up."[34]

Even without Navy assistance, *An Officer and a Gentleman* had a reasonable military ambience thanks to Chris Baumann, who had gone through aviation officer candidate school six years before. During the actual filming in Washington state, Baumann regularly provided informal assistance by giving information on uniforms, insignia to be worn, and training procedures to Bill Graves, the retired former director of the Navy's L.A. Public Affairs Office, who served as the film's technical adviser. Although DI Foley's verbal abuse of his charges may not be authentic, *An Officer and a Gentleman* contains a reasonably accurate portrayal of the daily routine of aviation officer candidates.[35]

Pat Coulter believed the objectionable scenes and portrayals "could have been brought into total compliance with current regulations and policy" if the Navy and Marines had given full cooperation. Nevertheless, he thought the film "is considerably more positive and reflects more favorably on the Marine Corps THAN IT EVER WOULD HAVE had we not become involved." Likewise, Baruch said: "The picture has many positive elements and should reflect favorably on the Navy and especially the Marine Corps through the portrayal of the D.I." He also reported that the Navy "appears pleased and surprised by the results," although "satisfied they are not officially identified with it."[36]

The failures of *Gray Lady Down, Raise the Titanic,* and *Final Countdown* had demonstrated that hardware and accuracy do not count as much as a good story about characters with whom people can empathize. *An Officer and a Gentleman* had these elements, and despite the Navy's concern about language, sex, and physical abuse, the movie most likely gave the service its biggest cinematic boost of any Hollywood film in the post-Vietnam era.

In fact, the Navy learned from *An Officer and a Gentleman* that more often than not a producer will make a movie with or without military assistance if the financiers think it will make money, and that a film will present the Navy in a more positive light if it supports the production. As important, all the armed services were learning that movies about the military in the post–Vietnam War period would most often not contain completely positive images of its men, equipment, and actions. Paradoxically, audiences accepted the portrayals as more honest, more authentic representations of the services than the sanitized stories Hollywood had produced before Vietnam.

Old habits died hard for the Navy, however, even with stories that had the potential to portray its men and equipment in the best possible light. While *The Right Stuff*, based on Tom Wolfe's book of the same name, focuses on the early years of the U.S. manned-space-flight program, the Navy became involved in the film because the producers needed a carrier and some of the astronauts had been Navy fliers. Baruch did tell the service not to concern itself over the astronauts' characterizations since the men had control over their cinematic portrayals. While the Navy did find some problems with the script including the "numerous drinking scenes of an excessive nature throughout the screenplay," the service approved the script and agreed to help with the production.[37]

In contrast to the quick approval of full assistance to *The Right Stuff*, the Navy refused to even consider cooperating in the making of *The Philadelphia Experiment*. The film had its origins in a 1977 book of the same name by William L. Moore in consultation with Charles Berlitz, the author of *The Bermuda Triangle*. The title, *The Philadelphia Experiment: Project Invisibility, An Account of a Search for a Secret Navy Wartime Project That May Have Succeeded—Too Well*, describes the author's approach and bias perfectly. Moore simply combined several accounts of an alleged Navy experiment conducted in 1943 at the Philadelphia Navy Yard. According to the stories, scientists accidentally transported a destroyer to Norfolk, Virginia, and back in less than two minutes. The resulting book had as much credibility as Berlitz's account of the Bermuda Triangle or any of the books proving the existence of UFOs. But from this myth the screenwriters concocted a time-travel story with the same level of plausibility as *The Final Countdown*. Two sailors taking part in a World War II experiment designed to make ships invisible to enemy radar find themselves transported from 1943 Philadelphia to the Utah desert in 1984. The portrayal of the "experiment" and the efforts to end its disastrous consequences remain incomprehensible.

In requesting the Navy allow the filmmakers to shoot the opening and closing scenes at the Philadelphia Navy Yard, Michele Casale, director of the Pennsylvania Bureau of Motion Picture and Television Development, acknowledged the "Navy's stance concerning the title and content of a book by the same name." While assuring the service that the screenplay "does not in any way follow the book," she acknowledged that "the idea does emanate from it." Sending the script to the Navy, the producer, Doug Curtis, claimed, "We decided long ago that the so-called 'Philadelphia Experiment' never happened. However, the basic idea that it could have happened provided us with what we think is a great premise for a *fictional* motion picture."[38]

After reading the script, Dale Patterson, then the Navy's Acting Chief of Information, told Baruch on 22 August 1983 that the Navy "does not desire to provide assistance. The position of the Navy has been that the 'Philadelphia Experiment' is a mythical event based on a fabricated story. Even though the planned film would imply the fictional character of the experiment, references are made to real-life people, places and facilities connected with the project." Without leaving the door open to further discussions, Patterson tersely concluded, "We feel that a movie of this nature would perpetuate the myth of the Philadelphia Experiment, and the role of the Navy in it. Participation or cooperation of the Navy in this project would not appear to be in its interest."[39]

When advising the producer of the Navy's decision, Baruch wrote on 26 August 1983 that he had reviewed the screenplay and agreed with the service's position that the film "probably would perpetuate the myth about such an experiment during the WW II era and the Navy's role in it. Strictly as fiction, the screenplay does not portray anything that can be considered positive or in the best interest of the Department of Defense (DOD) to qualify for approval under the criteria of the enclosed DOD Instruction."[40]

Even in the post-Vietnam period, with the military still wary of Hollywood's intentions, such an absolute refusal to assist a production was an aberration. The filmmakers themselves had provided the Navy with the basis for its decision. Curtis had stated that the "Philadelphia Experiment" "could have happened." As long as science-fiction stories remain pure fantasy, the services would usually provide the kind of limited assistance that the filmmakers were requesting for *The Philadelphia Experiment*. However, the Navy found itself in the same situation as the Air Force had when it refused to assist Steven Spielberg on *Close Encounters of the Third Kind*, released in 1977. Then the service explained that since the early 1950s it had denied flying saucers existed. The Air Force said Spielberg's film would leave "the distinct impression that UFO's [sic], in fact, do exist" and show "the government and military in a big cover up of the existence of UFOs." Since these portrayals ran counter to official policy, the government considered "support to the production inappropriate."[41]

Similarly, the Navy had regularly denied that anything like a secret experiment had occurred in Philadelphia in 1943, ever since Morris Jessup mentioned the story in his 1955 *The Case for UFOs*. Consequently, unlike *Final Countdown* whose time travel the Navy considered pure fantasy, the service could not cooperate on *The Philadelphia Experiment* it denied ever happened. Given the Navy's position, the filmmakers never pursued assistance.[42]

Instead, they used the aircraft carrier USS *Yorktown*, the "Fighting Lady" of World War II, the destroyer *Laffey*, and the submarine *Clamagore*, all berthed at the Maritime Museum in Charleston Harbor, to re-create the Philadelphia Navy Yard and to film shipboard scenes. Despite some visual authenticity, *The Philadelphia Experiment* had no believability. However, the film's hero did portray positively a Navy enlisted man and so contributed to the rehabilitation of the post-Vietnam military.

That rehabilitation reached its climax with an old-fashioned, peacetime Navy story that became the top box-office film of 1986. *Top Gun* shared with its earlier counterparts as well as the post-Vietnam Navy movies the messages that the service exists to protect the security of the nation and that its men perform with consummate professionalism. These new cinematic warriors may suffer from identity problems, self-doubts, and even rebelliousness, but they do not harbor hatreds or ambivalence toward their nation or the military, as had their counterparts in the Vietnam combat movies. The officers and men in *Top Gun* had chosen military careers out of a desire to use their talents to help ensure the survival of the United States. To them, Vietnam remained a reminder of past failures and a motivation to succeed on their watch. In portraying these contemporary fighting men, the filmmakers seemed to suggest that Vietnam served as a positive influence on the military and the nation.

In providing this message, Hollywood was only reflecting contemporary society and the revitalized armed services. The Navy, for example, had created the Navy Fighter Weapons School as a response to the mediocre performance of its pilots during the escalation of fighting in Vietnam. In contrast to kill ratios of 15:1 in World War II and 17:1 in Korea, early on in Vietnam Navy fliers enjoyed only about a 2.5:1 advantage.[43] Once the Navy had concluded that its pilots no longer knew how to dogfight, it gathered together a few crackerjack fighter instructors at Miramar, California, and started a program to train its top carrier pilots in aerial-combat techniques. The school soon became known as "Top Gun" from an annual aerial-combat competition the armed services had held in the 1940s and 1950s.[44]

In May 1983, while reading *California Magazine,* film producer Jerry Bruckheimer chanced upon Israeli writer Ehud Yonay's article capturing the excitement of "Top Gun." Bruckheimer and his partner, Don Simpson, immediately saw the possibility of making the school an "arena" in a movie featuring daring young men sweeping across the sky in aerial dogfights. The producers felt a film with such images might become another *Star Wars,* this time on earth with jet planes replacing space ships and the cream of naval aviators assuming the roles of the cute robots.[45]

Simpson recalled that both men wanted to make a movie as soon as they saw the title: "It was such a strong, unique concept, a look at the inside world of these top pilots who are really the modern equivalent of the gunslingers of the old, wild West. It was irresistible, so we immediately optioned the story and then sat down to figure out how the hell we could make the picture." However, the producers stressed they were not making a recruiting poster for the Navy. They saw themselves solely as storytellers about people: "We set them in particular environments because that is necessary to tell a story. The 'Top Gun' school was a wonderfully bright and hot venue, against which to push a character. The truth of the matter is that we could quite easily make a movie that deals with the military and goes the opposite way because it is full of human beings."[46]

At the heart of their story, Simpson and Bruckheimer saw "an exceedingly rebellious character who learns the value of winning through team effort. It was supposed to be a movie about a guy who came from the outside and learned how to play on the inside and did it for all the right reasons." Despite the perceptions of the military and the public, the producers believed that *Top Gun* "really did not have a lot to do with the Navy, per se. It had a lot more to do with a contemporary American rebel, who was not tamed, but got better through understanding that when he teamed up and played within the structure, not necessarily within the rules, he won in even a bigger way."[47]

The story dictated that the producers go to the Pentagon for assistance since *Top Gun* would need carriers and jet planes. Fortunately, they approached the Pentagon while the Navy was still ruing its failure to assist *An Officer and a Gentleman*. Moreover, Secretary of the Navy John Lehman was actively encouraging his public affairs officers to find a suitable project to support, one that would directly benefit the service.[48]

The producers had another advantage when they went to Washington. Simpson had brought the screenplay for *An Officer and a Gentleman* with him when he had become head of production at Paramount Studios. In that capacity, he had overseen the progress of the project and had gained insights on negotiating with the Pentagon from the failure of the producers to obtain assistance from the Navy. He had concluded that the filmmakers had gone to the Pentagon too far along in the production process, while disagreeing with the Navy's turn down of *An Officer and a Gentleman*: "Hey guys, are you trying to tell me that people in the Navy don't fuck, drink, and swear? Of course they do."[49]

Therefore, Simpson and Bruckheimer decided to visit Navy headquarters in Washington before they even started work on a screenplay. In fact, the producers did not intend to tell the Navy any story when they arrived at the Pentagon in early June 1983: "It was just to be a basic chat." Unfortunately, Adm. Jack Garrow, Chief of Information, liked the filmmakers' proposal: "Great. Tell us the movie you are going to make." The producers looked at each other and using their long experience spinning stories to potential backers, responded, "Okay, here's sort of the story we are going to do." While not creating the exact story, the plot they described essentially became *Top Gun*. Even in oral form, the Navy loved it, and the producers left Washington "extremely enthusiastic" about the project, and the Navy was "100 per cent receptive" to their plans.[50]

To prevent any hitches, John Horton, representing Paramount, followed up the producers' initial Pentagon meeting with a letter to Baruch on 10 June 1983. Summarizing the discussion, he wrote that the producers intended "to develop this project in close coordination with the Department of Defense and U.S. Navy to insure mutuality of interest pending the request for assistance in production." The company hoped to begin research at the Fighter Weapons School at Miramar upon the Chief of Information's approval of the producers and writers' visit to the installation during the course scheduled for 11 July

1983. Horton emphasized that the producers and the studio were "extremely enthused about the prospects of developing and producing" the film.[51]

Less than two years after *An Officer and a Gentleman,* the Navy found itself in a position "to regain some of the ground on the public relations front that it had lost." The service had a production that would feature a Navy hero, an unidentified enemy, and no scenes of an unpopular war. Apart from the *raison d'être* for the school, the only mention of Vietnam was that the hero's father, an ace pilot, had died during the war under mysterious conditions that the government remained unwilling to explain. Most important, the filmmakers were modeling the characters on the Navy's best, the top Navy carrier pilots who receive the coveted assignments to Top Gun, professional military men all, devoted to the service and its traditional lifestyle.[52]

Tom Cruise, playing the appropriately named Maverick, matures throughout *Top Gun,* becoming a team player and leader of men. The obligatory love story caused the Navy some initial discomfort, but unlike *An Officer and a Gentleman,* director Tony Scott handled the sex with restraint. More important, Maverick's relationship with Kelly McGillis's Charlie, an astrophysicist, never intrudes on the $34 million F-14 "Tomcat" jets, the carriers, and the dramatic flying sequences.

Despite the producers' initial contacts with the Pentagon and the Navy, it still took writers Jim Cash and Jack Epps Jr. more than a year to produce a screenplay. In the 15 November 1984 cover letter accompanying the script, Horton told Baruch that the producers, desiring "to present a positive patriotic film about the Navy," requested "review and comments from the Department of the [*sic*] Defense and Navy for any elements to be considered in the script revisions." The Navy needed less than two weeks to complete its review of the screenplay, and on the twenty-ninth Horton went to the Pentagon to discuss the Navy's comments.[53] Writing to Bruckheimer later in the day, Horton described the reception of the screenplay as "positive with the belief that produced with care and interpretation as a positive patriotic film that you have stated you desire, the film could be beneficial to the Navy." Horton said the Navy's primary concern centered on the producers' decision to change the female lead from a civilian to a naval officer "because of the inordinate sensitivity to the relationships in the service between male and female personnel." He did acknowledge that "romances—and marriages between male and female officers in the Navy exist but how the relationship is handled in a motion picture supported fully by the Navy puts them in the position of condoning the specific scenes." Horton also told Bruckheimer of the Navy's concern about "the portrayal of the aviators with any sophomoric characteristics—particularly with respect to hard drinking. Fighter pilots are a breed in themselves with certain traits that are identifiable. These characteristics can be captured—and are in the script—but the full dimension should be portrayed within the artistic license necessary for entertainment."[54]

The history of negotiations between filmmakers and the armed services is replete with arguments back and forth concerning the correct way to realistically portray military men and women off hours without offending the sensibilities of overly zealous public affairs officers. In developing an acceptable script for *Top Gun,* the screenwriters spent five months changing the female love interest to a civilian astrophysicist and making other revisions the Navy had requested. The new script met with more favorable response, and on 8 May 1985 Baruch notified Horton that the Navy would approve it if a scene "showing our aircraft flying after MIGs over land of the fictional foreign country" was deleted. Characterizing the production assistance to date as "friendly, cooperative," and smooth, Baruch thanked the producers "for their sincere and enthusiastic interest in bringing *Top Gun* to fruition."[55]

Top Gun differs little from Hollywood's peacetime Navy movies of the 1930s, 1940s, and 1950s, which used the service as a backdrop to a love story. The producers, however, saw Maverick as a skilled F-14 pilot who learns to function, not only in combat situations, but also in peacetime, unlike General Patton and the Great Santini: "You really want him in wartime. This is a guy who can kick ass and take names. That's his brilliance. But, we tried to take him through the emotional curves in the movie. He started out 80/20. We tried to move him to a place where he was civilized enough to where he could walk around."[56]

Simpson and Bruckheimer also saw Maverick as "emblematic of the best of the best, truly because of his abilities, his physical ability, his emotional characteristics, and his intellectual ability—this guy is an all-star." More than that, they created a character they wanted the audience to see as "a real warrior of the heart." In contrast, they considered Gere's character in *An Officer and a Gentleman* as a kid from the wrong side of the tracks "who fundamentally doesn't have any skills," describing Zack Mayo as "street scum." They believed Mayo would take a decade to reach the point from which Maverick was starting.[57]

Simpson and Bruckheimer did not see the Maverick image as fostering militarism, claiming they "understand the need for defense. It has nothing to do with being right wing, left wing, or center." They believed in the need for "eternal vigilance" and so found it "fun for us to invent a character who's not ashamed to be in the service of his country." Despite having created an idealized Navy man, the producers observed that "the military is probably never going to be safe for Hollywood again. Vietnam was a major fuck up. So the military is never going to be safe, not as long as people who lived during Vietnam are alive and are making movies."[58]

For them, however, *Top Gun* focused on Maverick, never on the Navy: "The military is a metaphor, it's true. But it's real clear that the movie is not about war. It doesn't take a position on whether war is good or bad. . . . It only takes a position regarding a particular character in his growth and frankly about ethics and commitment and about heart and about courage and teamwork." More than that, the producers thought the movie dealt with "professionalism, professionalism in any capacity, whether as a writer, moviemaker, car wash guy."[59]

Top Gun can certainly provide material to illustrate these messages. However, audiences did not flock to theaters to philosophize about its contents. The producers admitted this in trying to explain the film's success: "It is because a great majority of the audience found the picture to be totally accessible. . . . where they, for 97 minutes, got to enter into a world that is not only real but is exciting and one to which they had never been exposed and to which they never will be exposed." In a sense, they considered themselves "in the transportation business. We want to transport you. That's what we like to do."[60]

In truth, most reviews thought very little of the vehicle. *Commonweal* concluded, "*Top Gun* melds *Rambo* and *An Officer and a Gentleman*. It lacks the former's wild sincerity and the latter's raw treatment of genuine emotional needs. It also has the defects of both films, echoing the first's jingoism and the second's already familiar passage of young male hero through love and the death of a friend to greater emotional maturity. Nevertheless, it has a kind of style, in part laughable and in part visceral. The macho strutting is absurd. The casting of sultry McGillis as a flight instructor is beyond credibility. But some powerful opening and closing action sequences catapult the viewer into flight (and a kind of exhilarated vertigo) like nothing before. Sadly, the cinematic and aerial skills involved at the end serve some bad politics: combat between Navy fighters and Soviet MIGs, breezily passed over as an event of little note."[61]

David Ansen in *Newsweek* concluded, "For all its reliance on old macho clichés, *Top Gun* is devoid of a strong dramatic line. It's a disjointed movie about flying school bracketed by two arbitrary action sequences." Ansen found Cruise "simply miscast—he's not the dangerous guy everyone's talking about, but the boy next door. Nor, for all the erotic posing, is there any real spark between him and the more sophisticated McGillis. Cruise seems to think that if he stares at her hard enough chemistry will result." Ansen attributed the problem to the director and producers who "have only myth-making on their minds. Yet the effortless flyboy glamour of *Only Angels Have Wings* or *The Right Stuff* eludes them. They don't realize the importance of laconic understatement in any good macho fantasy. They're so busy inflating their characters there's no flesh and blood left to grab on to. *Top Gun* isn't boring, but it's solemnly silly. This movie has taken too many hormone shots."[62]

In *The Village Voice*, J. Hoberman not only carried the male-sexuality-in-combat thesis to hitherto unexplored depths in a review entitled "Phallus in Wonderland," but also turned *Top Gun* into a pseudo-Vietnam movie: "Sleek, fragmentary, and expertly fetishized, *Top Gun* is state of the art war-nography. It's the sort of suave, go-go propaganda you'd expect to be shown to kamikaze pilots. This teenage dating film may be devoid of 'ideas,' but it's still a conceptual leap. *Top Gun* doesn't posit sex as aggression, it reformulates aggression as sex."[63]

The reviewer thought the soundtrack gave the movie "a kind of amoral insistence and subliminal history" by establishing a direct link to Vietnam, citing Herman Rapaport's thesis, in *The 60s Without Apology*, that Vietnam became the first rock 'n' roll war: "Introjected into the technology, the libidinal impulses of rock became the lure by which some men killed with pleasure . . . putting the weapon on 'automatic fire' was called putting it on 'rock and roll.'" By recycling the music of Vietnam, *Top Gun* used rock "for militaristic ends, to evoke an utterly specious nostalgia."[64]

Hoberman also equated the thrill of war with the thrill of sexual conquest and launched into a psychosexual interpretation of *Top Gun* as "blatantly homoerotic": "Of course, as Freud is supposed to have said, sometimes a cigar is just a cigar. Still, there are moments in this movie when the screen is so packed with streamlined planes and heat-seeking missiles, wagging forefingers and upright thumbs that, had Freud lived to see it, he might be excused for thinking *Top Gun* an avant-garde representation of Saturday night at the St. Marks Bath."[65]

Neither Hoberman's deprecation nor the other less than enthusiastic reviews dissuaded people from making *Top Gun* the nation's top grossing movie of 1986. To a significant extent, this success resulted from the pure visual excitement of the film's aerial sequences, not very different from the space dogfights in *Star Wars* in form and execution, but live thanks to the Navy's assistance. In addition to allowing Tony Scott and his crew access to the *Enterprise* and *Ranger*, the Navy made available technical advisers, twenty or so fighter pilots, Miramar Naval Air Station, and a small fleet of $37 million F-14 jets, charging only for the fuel. Ultimately, Paramount paid the Navy $1.1 million for the assistance, of which $886,000 covered the cost of flight time for five types of airplanes.[66]

With this assistance, the filmmakers created some of the most dramatic flying sequences Hollywood has ever put on the screen. As a result, many people considered *Top Gun* a recruiting poster for the Navy as well as patriotic jingoism.[67] Tom Cruise recognized that "some people felt that *Top Gun* was a right-wing film to promote the Navy. And a lot of kids loved it. . . . But I want the kids to know that that's not the way war is—that *Top Gun* was just an amusement-park [*sic*] ride, a fun film with a PG-13 rating that was not supposed to be reality. That's why I didn't go on and make *Top Gun II* and *III, IV*, and *V*. That *would* have been irresponsible." Cruise simply saw the film as "a joy ride and shouldn't be looked at beyond that. *Top Gun* should be looked at as going on Space Mountain—it's like a simple fairy tale."[68]

Whether a fairy tale or transporter of people, *Top Gun* had a wide appeal. Barry London, Paramount's head of distribution, explained that this enabled him to advertise the film to many different markets: "You could make it look like an action movie. You could make it look like a love story. You could make it look like a real beefcake movie with young males. And it was a relationship picture as well as a war movie. Any kind of variation from those things."[69]

London also attributed the success of the film to changes within the country, particularly the move toward a more conservative outlook: "It got more patriotic. It became the right thing to do to wave the flag. It became a supportive issue of supporting the armed forces overseas because of the deteriorating position of the United States in the eyes of the rest of the world." *Top Gun* also told the story of an underdog and had "some terrific looking people, with some terrific music, all set in a terrifically structured movie."[70]

Whatever the reason, *Top Gun* became a huge box-office success. Its popularity also justified the assistance the Navy gave the production. The Navy's West Coast coordinator of recruiting observed, "It is a definite plus for the Navy. The feeling that we have here in recruiting is that the movie has mostly increased awareness. It is hard to put any numbers on what exactly *Top Gun* has done for the Navy, but it sure has helped." Capt. Mike Sherman, then spokesman for Secretary of the Navy John Lehman and later director of the Navy's L.A. Public Affairs Office, felt that the movie gave the Navy "a high profile, and it gives us a competitive edge with the other services." In addition, the film generated the kind of media attention the service could not get otherwise. CBS, for one, did a series about Navy pilots on the evening news.[71]

Unfortunately for the Navy, *Top Gun* apparently also had an unforeseen, less positive impact. When the Pentagon's report on the Tailhook scandal appeared in April 1992, it contained accusations from senior Navy officers that "many young officers had been influenced by the image of naval aviators portrayed in the movie *Top Gun*" and this had contributed to their "rowdy behavior" at the 1991 convention. According to the investigators, senior officers believed that "the movie fueled misconceptions on the part of junior officers as to what was expected of them and also served to increase the general awareness of naval aviation and glorify naval pilots in the eyes of many young women." Donald Mancuso, the director of the Defense Criminal Investigation Service, which produced the report, said that the senior officers had volunteered their perceptions that the younger aviators had "an impression of themselves which was built partially on the Tom Cruise image."[72] Whatever deleterious impact the film may have had on the fliers attending Tailhook, *Top Gun* certainly had a more beneficial influence on the nation's perceptions of its military and its ability to once again defend the country from any threat. Before Vietnam, Americans believed their armed services had become invincible. The post–World War II Hollywood movies contributed to that belief. To be sure, filmmakers were drawing on the U.S. victories over Germany and Japan as their models, but the movie images had merged with the historical realities in the public's consciousness. As a result, the American people had no reason to question the military leadership who promised a quick victory in Vietnam against a small, peasant nation. The North Vietnamese regular army gave lie to such arrogant predictions, and the ultimate withdrawal of American forces in defeat traumatized the nation. The manner in which the media and filmmakers subsequently portrayed the war and the returning soldiers effectively completed the destruction of the nation's unsullied perception of its military establishment.

Beginning with *Midway* and culminating with *Top Gun,* Hollywood's treatment of the Navy in war and peace significantly contributed to the rehabilitation of the military image. Consequently, when the crisis in the Persian Gulf began in August 1990, the American people once again believed its military could successfully meet any challenge, and this made it possible for President Bush to take the nation into battle again. Ironically, military leaders hung back and demanded a buildup of forces beyond anything needed to defeat the paper tiger in Iraq before willingly committing their troops to combat. Instead of responding to the images of Tom Cruise shooting down MiG fighters, they were still remembering the opprobrium the nation had heaped on the armed forces for losing in Vietnam.

★

THIRTEEN

The End of
the Cold War

The success of *Top Gun* completed the process of making Hollywood welcome at the Pentagon's doors. While each service's public affairs officers might reject scripts about the war or the military, they again considered stories on a project-by-project basis. Not all projects portrayed the services positively, but public affairs officers usually chose to negotiate the best possible image rather than turn filmmakers away, as had happened with *The Last Detail, Cinderella Liberty*, and *The Philadelphia Experiment*.

Even so, the Navy remained solicitous of the way filmmakers portrayed their men and procedures. When John Horton delivered the script for *Star Trek IV* to the Pentagon on behalf of Harve Bennett and Paramount Pictures, the Navy requested several changes. To satisfy the Navy's objection, producer/writer Bennett modified the line, "You're not one of those creeps from the military trying to teach whales to plant mines," to read, "You're not one of those military types are you, trying to teach whales to retrieve torpedoes?"[1] Bennett also assured the Navy that the entry to a base building would "not constitute a breach of Naval security. No fences will be cut, no guards overpowered. Uhura and Chekov will instead by [sic] 'beamed in' to within the center of the room they wish to enter, utilizing the internationally famous trademark of STAR TREK. Clearly, this use of STAR TREK 'magic' is something both funny and unique, and obviously no one else but our show can do it." He explained that the lead-shielded room in which Uhura and Chekov find themselves will prevent them from being beamed out. Contrary to the Navy's concerns about showing a lapse in Navy security, "it is getting *out*, not getting in, that becomes the drama."[2]

Regarding the assistance needed, Bennett told Horton that the studio would like to use Navy facilities at Long Beach. In addition, if the schedule permitted, he would like to have a second unit film Chekov and Uhura seeing the USS *Enterprise* docked at Alameda in Oakland. According to the writer/producer, having the Star Trek characters see "the carrier of today which bears the name of their Starship of the future . . . would enhance a rich tradition of public relations which has been carried on in the past between these two 'Enterprises.'"[3]

The Navy advised Baruch that it approved cooperation based on additional changes already discussed with Bennett. These included creating a different mode of escape from the carrier for Uhura. The service "recommended a scenario which would not allow her to walk off the ship during a nuclear reactor incursion alert. As written, her escape would leave the audience with the impression that naval security of nuclear reactions is lax." The Navy also required that an FBI agent rather than a naval intelligence officer interrogate Chekov: "As the character . . . would be in civilian custody in a situation like that portrayed, we have also asked that the Shore Patrol portrayed in the hospital scenes be replaced by civilian policemen."[4]

When the *Enterprise* proved unavailable, Bennett and Paramount settled for the *Ranger*. The shooting itself required three days at North Island, beginning on 25 February 1986, with the filmmakers taking both interior and external sequences, using both sailors and marines as extras aboard the ship. Even though the scenes created aboard the carrier did not show the Navy treating the space-time travelers particularly well, the Navy did get images of its supercarrier before the American people, with its crew doing its job correctly.[5]

In contrast, the Pentagon and the Navy could imagine no benefit from becoming involved with *No Way Out*. The film contained such an adverse portrayal of the Pentagon leadership that producer Mace Neufeld did not even bother to submit a script to the Defense Department. After all, how could the military assist a movie that showed the Secretary of Defense maintaining a mistress whom he ultimately murders in a jealous rage? Worse, his homosexual top aide leads the cover-up by trying to frame the decorated Navy hero assigned to solving the crime. In most instances, having Kevin Costner starring in a movie would ensure a benefit to the service, but in this case Costner's character turns out to be a deep Soviet mole.[6]

With this plot twist, *No Way Out* could have appeared any time during the Cold War. *The Hunt for Red October,* on the other hand, became the last peacetime Cold War military movie and the first post–Cold War film. If viewers allow their suspension of disbelief free rein, they may see in the story, the beginning of the end of the Soviet Union. In the double-talk vernacular of the Cold War, some people would conclude that the film's opening disclaimer, "According to repeated statements by both Soviet and American governments . . . nothing of what you are about to see . . . ever happened," is actually saying that something approximating what appears on the screen truly happened. Director John McTiernan pointed out that "this incident, or some incident like it might have been part of what shocked the Soviet hierarchy into changing."[7]

In fact, something like what appeared on the screen did occur in November 1975. Shortly before the film appeared in 1990, *Izvestia* confirmed reports that Valeri Sablin, a captain third rank in the Soviet Navy, and a dozen accomplices had put to sea aboard the Russian antisubmarine frigate *Storozhevoy* (Sentry) from their base in Riga, Latvia, in an attempt to reach Sweden. Soviet aerial bombing stopped the defection fifty miles from Swedish waters and forced the ship to return to base. The military prosecutor's office found Sablin guilty of betraying the homeland and sentenced him to death by firing squad, and his accomplices received various prison terms.[8]

Tom Clancy, the author of *The Hunt for Red October,* said he first read about the incident in a 1976 *Washington Post* article. He obtained more details in 1982 from a naval officer's master's thesis. Clancy also explained an *Izvestia* reporter told him that the imminent release of the movie gave the Soviet government a reason to acknowledge that "the incident really did take place." Admitting he had taken considerable license with events, Clancy said, "My book has a historical foundation. But it is a work of fiction."

In the novel, Ramius, the leading Soviet submariner, defects while commanding the shakedown cruise of the *Red October,* a secret, silent-running missile submarine and with his senior officers plans to turn the vessel over to the United States. The Soviet Navy gives chase, but the U.S. Navy and Jack Ryan, a CIA consultant, join forces to intervene, enabling the submarine to elude its pursuers. In the film, *Red October* makes it safely to the Maine coast, where Ryan, played by Alex Baldwin, tells Ramius, portrayed by Sean Connery, "There will be hell to pay in Moscow when the dust settles from all this." The submarine captain responds, "Perhaps some good will come of it."

Connery later said he insisted that *The Hunt for Red October* "be dated pre-Gorbachev and pre-glasnost" as a condition for his accepting the role. He "wanted the film not to be a film about the Cold War, but about an individual who would go to such an extreme to secure peace and what would make him tick." To ensure his views prevailed, he brought in writer/director John Milius to rewrite his dialogue and better focus Ramius's motivation for his actions. Connery said, "When I read the script, I wanted it to be clearer why the captain was defecting—it couldn't just be anger toward his country. Milius resolved and simplified quite a few things and events and made it easier to understand." Connery was also adamant that the film in no way undermine Gorbachev's reform efforts: "Gorbachev is undoubtedly the man of the decade, and I don't think even he could have anticipated the rapidity of the changes sweeping throughout that country."[9]

In *The Hunt for Red October,* Clancy did not provide a clear-cut explanation for Ramius's decision to defect beyond his anger over his wife's death during childbirth. In his final screenplay, Larry Ferguson inserted the idea that the Soviets had built the *Red October* as an offensive, first-strike weapon, which Ramius found unacceptable. Thanks to Connery, Milius made the motivation even clearer.[10] Nevertheless, no one loves, let alone trusts a traitor, and to create a trustworthy persona, *The Hunt for Red October* needed to make the submarine captain a selfless hero, a man who transcends national borders and takes a chance that might leave the world better off than he found it.

The film ultimately fulfills this imperative, despite some of the actions Ramius must undertake along the way, such as killing the KGB agent aboard the submarine and collaborating with the enemy. The filmmakers do spare him from destroying a pursuing Soviet submarine and its crew, as he did in the novel. Instead, the captain of the pursuing boat, one of Ramius's progenies, accidentally torpedoes his own submarine in his obsessive effort to sink the *Red October.* In the end, Ramius comes to symbolize the new world order, and his defection becomes a lone man's effort to save the world, rather than a traitorous act.

The filmmakers were to find it easier to define the intent of *The Hunt for Red October* than to come up with a suitable script. According to McTiernan, turning the lengthy, highly technical novel into a film was a difficult and time-consuming process. As he explained, "underneath everything it's a sea story, and all sea stories are in essence the same: A boy goes down to the sea in ships, and he's swept off into a weird and alien world full of colorful characters, and he eventually learns to stand up and be a man among these wild characters, and he comes home forever changed. It's the same as *Kidnapped* or *Treasure Island.*"[11]

The director and producers Mace Neufeld and Jerry Sherlock also faced the problem of keeping up with the rapidly changing international political landscape. When they acquired the rights to the best-selling novel in 1985, the Soviet Union was still the implacable enemy of the United States. During the time the filmmakers needed to develop a suitable script and put the production before the cameras, the evil empire began to disintegrate.

Sherlock and Neufeld had begun dickering for the rights before the book became a best-seller. Praise for the story from President Reagan, Lee Iacocca, and others whetted the producers' interest. Neufeld had observed, "The interesting thing about the book is that the Americans come out looking very good in it. It's a patriotic thriller and it's making the rounds in the government establishment." Apart from the President's calling it "a perfect yarn," Neufeld thought the story had two great leading-man parts—the Russian submarine captain and the American CIA investigator.[12]

Despite the obvious interest in capitalizing on the success of the novel, Sherlock said after obtaining the rights that actual production would not begin for at least a year because the producers had not yet selected a screenwriter. Nor had they found a studio willing to finance the production. Initially, Neufeld had "thought it would be an easy movie." He later explained that despite the novel's success, he needed fourteen months to secure backing because studio executives who approve projects do not read books, relying instead on reports from readers.[13] Unfortunately, according to Neufeld, *Hunt for Red October* did not "synopsize well in three or four pages. It becomes very complicated." At one point MGM stunned the producer when it rejected the project, calling the book "just another submarine story." Only after he gave the novel to Ned Tannen, a friend and production head of Paramount, to read during a thirteen-hour flight to England could Neufeld finally get a studio to consider the project. While he felt the book would "make a terrific movie," Tannen required Neufeld to secure Navy cooperation and come up with a reasonable budget before Paramount would give final approval.[14]

Ultimately, three different writers worked on the adaptation of the novel, beginning with Donald Stewart, Oscar winner for *Missing,* who received inputs from Tom Clancy on the initial version. According to Stewart, it was "a tough book to crack—there's a lot of gadgetry to it, the technology is an important part of the intrigue. And there's a lot, including characters, to boil down into two hours. Paramount's trying to get the best screenplay it can, and if it takes more than one writer to do it, that's the nature of screenwriting."[15]

On 19 February 1987 Horton sent Stewart's first screenplay to Baruch. Horton said the studio could not yet submit any detailed requirements, but the producers planned to build the interiors of two Russian and one U.S. submarine on soundstages. However, they anticipated requiring access to a carrier as well as other combat and support ships for both interior and exterior photography. Horton indicated that production would begin within six months, during which time the studio would be able to coordinate the requirements with the Navy.[16]

In fact, work continued on a final shooting script for almost two more years due to Paramount's unhappiness with Stewart's effort, a writers' strike, and problems with rights. Not until 23 November 1988 did Horton submit Larry Ferguson's final script, dated 17 November 1988, to Baruch. Horton said that "the requirements for assistance will be extensive" but also promised to produce "a motion picture that should certainly provide substantial benefits for the U.S. Navy, particularly, the Submarine Service."[17]

The huge success of *Top Gun* gave Neufeld and Sherlock every reason to expect an immediate positive reaction to their request. The submarine service itself had reason to respond affirmatively. "Frankly, we learned something from *Top Gun,*" said retired Navy Capt. J. H. Patton Jr., technical consultant for *Red October.* With *Top Gun* proving a recruiting bonanza for the carrier branch, Patton said the submarine service "had to get in this movie game for recruiting sake." In truth, submariners needed a more positive portrayal than in their last cinematic appearance, in *Gray Lady Down*.[18]

Neufeld actually did have some concern about how the Navy would react to his request for assistance. Soon after he obtained rights to *The Hunt for Red October*, while shooting *No Way Out* in Washington, the producer had gone to the Pentagon to discuss the project. As he recalled, "In the back of my mind I thought, well, if I can get permission, will they object later when they see *No Way Out* and then withdraw it. After all, we portray Costner as a spy and the Secretary of Defense as a murderer." In any case, Neufeld pursued all avenues of assistance, including trying unsuccessfully to obtain access to two nuclear submarines the United States was dismantling as part of the Salt II Treaty.[19]

After reading the final script, Adm. J. B. Finkelstein, the Navy's Chief of Information, advised Baruch on 12 December that the Navy was providing a list of changes, which "are strongly recommended to enhance the motion picture." However, he made it clear the comments were "for guidance and should not be interpreted as mandated changes to the script which the Navy requires prior to cooperation and support." The Navy was merely voicing its concern that the script "is shallow. Paramount is obviously relying heavily on visuals to carry the picture. The script does not do justice to the detailed character and plot development of Tom Clancy's novel." Nevertheless, he said the Navy was ready to support the film and awaited Paramount's requirements list.[20]

Most of the Navy's comments dealt with technical matters, such as noting that Ramius would not address a member of his crew as "Hey you!" and observing that a carrier does not "bob like a cork." More serious, the service suggested that the banter between Jonesy, the sonar operator, and the chief of the boat "must be kept very light and deferential. Remember he is the senior Chief Petty Officer on the ship and is treated with great respect. Pay close attention to this dialogue." The Navy also felt the script contained "insufficient explanation . . . to explain or justify the Soviet defection" and "insufficient development of the tremendous professional respect and admiration between Mancuso the captain of the U.S. submarine DALLAS and Ramius. This could be easily developed by a little dialogue." Most important, the Navy felt that the film's closing scene "regarding reason for Ramius' defection is vague and confusing."[21]

Capt. Mike Sherman, director of the Navy's Los Angeles Office of Information, had a more positive view, considering the script "an exciting representation of Clancy's novel that presents the U.S. Navy in a professional and realistic environment." In a memorandum to the commands that would be providing assistance, Sherman said that the filmmakers were requesting extensive assistance, including "top of the line Navy assets." He said the service expected the film to "provide the first contemporary public look at the capabilities and professionalism of our modern Navy in years. Thus it is important, within the boundaries of security and feasibility, that the public be able to see the high tech, professional quality of our personnel and equipment." However, Sherman acknowledged, "No one said it was going to be easy."[22]

Doing his best to make it easier, McTiernan wrote to Sherman on 20 December, confirming how he intended to satisfy Admiral Finkelstein and the Navy's concerns. In several instances he said he understood he was taking dramatic license, such as in using Navy dress blues "because it is more impressive looking," but said he would correct any inaccuracies. In regard to the bobbing carrier, he apologized for "the exuberance of Mr. Ferguson's description," explaining that he "was trying to say that it was stormy." He explained that the tone of banter between the sonarman and his superior "is perhaps misleading. What is intended here is that Jonesy and the COB are the closest of friends and that this dialogue is part of a long running and basically affectionate game between them. If Jonesy has overstepped here we'll try and pull it back. There is no intention for this scene to be in poor taste. The 'god damn' remark from the COB will be removed."[23]

In regard to concerns about the insufficiencies of the script, the director answered, ". . . the most candid thing I can say is that *we agree with you and share your concerns.*" He explained that the filmmakers were working to clarify the points the service had raised: "Specifically, with respect to explaining the defection, we are going to attempt to place the story in the past—prior to Gorbachev's ascension." He said they would also "strive to improve the relationship between Mancuso and Ramius in terms of their mutual professional respect and admiration for each other." Instead of being the reason for Ramius's defection, the director said his wife's death would serve merely as "a release which made defection possible." Finally, he assured the Navy that the filmmakers would revise the closing dialogue to better explain why Ramius actually defected.[24]

With McTiernan's letter in hand, Sherman sent a memorandum to Finkelstein on 20 December, advising, "I am confident that each suggestion will be acted upon and that the script will be to our satisfaction," and recommended that the Navy approve the script and agree to assist the production. Baruch met with Finkelstein on 24 December to discuss McTiernan's letter and Sherman's memorandum. Then, on 27 December, Baruch told the Chief of Information that since the director had answered all of the Navy's concerns, his office was formally approving the screenplay and assistance.[25]

The Navy did not, of course, have a Soviet submarine secreted up a Maine river. Nor had the evil empire yet been reduced to renting out its men and ships. Since the producers had only Clancy's description of the *Red October* with which to work, budgetary constraints provided the only limits the producers faced in creating the Soviet craft. For the exterior shots of the submarine running on the surface, the studio built a five hundred–foot fiberglass mock-up of *Red October* capable of submerging and surfacing, rather than taking the easier and far less costly expedient of using a model. So the giant missile boat actually seems authentic and manages to convey the huge size of the submarine, which the script describes as the length of a World War II aircraft carrier.[26]

As with all submarine films, the producers had to shoot the interiors of the *Red October,* its Soviet pursuer, and the USS *Dallas* on soundstages at Paramount Studios. There, the filmmakers built portions of each ship on hydraulically operated fifty by fifty–foot platforms that provided twenty-five degrees of pitch and roll—lending additional credibility on screen. Unconcerned with security considerations, the filmmakers created a control room for the *Red October* filled with electronic monitors and gadgets resembling the bridge of the starship *Enterprise.* In contrast, after helping McTiernan create an accurate representation of the *Dallas*'s control room, the Navy expressed the "concern that it not be too accurate. They've told us why they'd prefer that certain things not be depicted in the movie, and they help us get around those things."[27]

Nevertheless, the Navy did go out of its way to give *The Hunt for Red October* as much visual and technical authenticity as possible. The service allowed the director to film a submarine in dry dock—which it had never done before. In addition, the Navy gave the producers, director, and Alec Baldwin tours of the submarine base at New London. Neufeld, Stewart, and all the principal actors, with one exception, also took trips aboard a nuclear submarine. Sean Connery, who joined the cast late in preproduction, never went to sea. Then, beginning in late April, the Navy provided the filmmakers frigates, helicopters, three submarines, and the USS *Enterprise,* as well as off-duty personnel as extras aboard the submarines. Producer Neufeld reported that "it got to the point that rather than try to coach a crew of actors how to be like submariners, we just started using Navy instead of actors whenever possible. They were used to constantly drilling and, consequently, picked up direction better."[28]

The assistance came with a price. As it had on countless other films, the Navy was solicitous of its image. Originally, the script called for the hoist line to break as a helicopter lowers Jack Ryan onto the *Dallas.* The Navy did not want audiences to see a failure in a piece of its equipment, and in the film Ryan releases the line rather than be hauled back aboard the helicopter. As played, the scene shows Ryan's determination to reach the *Dallas,* and hoist lines seldom do break. More important, as Mike Sherman pointed out, in a previous scene a jet crashes aboard the *Enterprise*—which "doesn't make naval aviation look too safe" if combined with the broken hoist line.[29]

Cooperation clearly benefited both sides. When *The Hunt for Red October* opened in March 1990, it "pulverized the competition" by bringing in more than a third of all the money spent nationwide at the box office during its first weekend. Like *Top Gun,* however, the film received lukewarm reviews. In *Newsweek,* David Ansen observed that Clancy's book, the cast, and the director all had primed the audience "for an old-fashioned white-knuckle night at the movies. All we ask is to be kept on the edge of our seats; anything else the movie might offer—wit, interesting characters, great acting turns—will be so much gravy. But it's at the gut level that *Red October* disappoints. This smooth, impressively mounted machine is curiously ungripping. Like an overfilled kettle, it takes far too long to come to a boil."[30]

Hal Hinson in the *Washington Post* described *The Hunt for Red October* as "a leviathan relic of an age that no longer exists. It's also a leviathan bore, big, clunky and ponderously overplotted. And that it lurches into view as a Cold War anachronism is, in fact, the picture's most fascinating feature. It makes it irrelevant in an astonishingly up-to-date way." He considered *Red October* "in its own peculiar way, a disaster movie . . . though not perhaps in the way the filmmakers intended. After spending about an hour with it, you begin to feel the walls of the theater closing in. You long for wide open spaces, or even just a room with a view. Most of all, what you want is to open the hatch and escape."[31]

Not everyone reacted so negatively. Vincent Canby in the *New York Times* found the film "most peculiar, but it's not without its entertaining moments." Recognizing *Red October* had become "an elegy for those dear, dark, terrible days of the cold war," Canby considered it "the kind of movie in which the characters, like the lethal hardware, are simply functions of the plot, which in this case seems to be a lot more complex than it really is. Because everybody knows that the terrible things that might happen can't (or the movie would betray its genre), the only question is how they will be averted." He concluded, the "movie is never very convincing. Even the special effects aren't great."[32]

Despite the naysaying critics, *The Hunt for Red October* became a huge box-office success, in part because the novel had presold the film. Neufeld thought it succeeded "because it is a terrific movie," and he believed the time "was right for a submarine story, an American submarine adventure." Having Connery as the film's star helped, but most of all, Neufeld thought the film benefited from "one of the most brilliant marketing and distribution campaigns I have ever been involved with." Paramount decided that instead of releasing the film at Christmas, it would open it in March, "where you normally don't open big films like this," but then did "an incredible campaign to get audience awareness out."[33]

Moreover, since the movie delivered, the people kept coming, and so saw the Navy's hardware manned by highly competent officers and men. They also saw the professionalism of Jonesy, the young sonar expert who skillfully recognizes that he is tracking something more esoteric than a whale. Hip to music, computers, and his sonar screen, he alone on the submarine distrusts the "40 million dollar computer" and uses his own faculties to solve the mystery of the missing submarine. More important for the Navy, audiences saw in Jonesy's character how enlisted people could achieve their full potential by going to sea.

Likewise, people found in Admiral Greer, the director of the CIA's naval intelligence, whom James Earl Jones plays with his comfortable majesty, the example of how anyone regardless of race can rise through the officer corps.

Such portrayals, idealized or not, reassured audiences that the Navy was continuing to perform its mission in an exemplary manner.[34] To McTiernan, having a black admiral and a black sonar operator reinforced his belief that "in a way, the film is about immigration and integration. It's about a group of people trying to get to America." He pointed out that when Mancuso, the captain of the *Dallas* and "obviously the descendant of immigrants," reaches the *Red October,* he is the first person of authority Ramius meets. Although Frank Mancuso, chairman of Paramount Pictures, wanted McTiernan to change the captain's name, the director said he persuaded the executive to keep it, not just because five million people had read the name in the book, but because "it said something."[35]

Whatever it said, *The Hunt for Red October* marked the end of Hollywood's traditional image of the Cold War, of two implacable enemies on the verge of annihilating each other. Where else would Hollywood find enemies for the United States to fight? Iran and Iraq provided the most visible targets, along with assorted terrorist groups, and the SEALs would do the fighting. The Navy's top-secret special-forces organization, the SEALs were the direct descendants of the Underwater Demolition Teams, which Hollywood had first introduced to the American people in *Frogmen.* However, over the years, with the very minor exception of *Underwater Warrior* in 1958, the Navy has been reluctant to expose the SEALs to much publicity, for obvious reasons.

That very secrecy made the SEALs an appealing subject. It also made the screenwriter's job somewhat easier. If the Navy would not reveal much about the organization, filmmakers could create whatever story they pleased, with little worry that the service would publicly dispute its accuracy. At the same time, a producer would have little hope of obtaining extensive assistance to make a movie about the SEALs. Consequently, when Orion Pictures submitted the script for *Navy SEALs* in May 1989, it probably had little expectation of receiving a favorable response.

Mike Sherman informed Admiral Finkelstein that he could not recommend approval for full cooperation. While the filmmakers had made several changes in their story from the one submitted months before, Sherman said that "it still remains a flamboyant representation of the SEALs." He also questioned the authenticity of the final mission. Worse, he noted, "The SEALs' hallmarks, teamwork and professionalism are depicted only marginally in this script. . . . In short, this is not close to an accurate portrayal of the SEALs or their mission."[36]

Sherman did enclose, for Finkelstein's signature, a letter to Orion Pictures informing the company that the Navy could not provide assistance to *Navy SEALs.* He noted that the letter did not address the issue of limited cooperation. Sherman then reminded Admiral Finkelstein that Senator John Warner, a former Secretary of the Navy, and Virginia governor Gerald Baliles had paid an "inordinately high attention" to the script. He also reported that Michael Medavoy, the executive vice president of Orion Pictures, had called the Navy's Los Angeles public affairs office several times to ask about the status of the script and the Navy's willingness to cooperate.[37]

Sherman said he also understood that Orion had prepared itself for a rejection and was seeking assistance abroad in making the film, most likely from Spain. So he recommended that the Navy advise its commanders there "to watch for end-runs for support," and he suggested, "*We should also look very hard at providing limited cooperation, if that's possible, as damage control.*" To do that, Sherman recommended that the Navy include in its letter to Orion his office's comments on the inaccuracies in the script.[38]

Most of the observations focused on technical matters, such as correct terminology and procedures. The Navy pointed out that a Navy helicopter had a crew of two pilots and two enlisted men, not seven as in the script. In another place, the Navy pointed out that SEALs "would not fire 'make sure' rounds into each of the bodies . . . that is murder. They would not hurt or kill anyone unless 'deadly force' were authorized." Sherman's office noted that there "is no room for discussion in the Navy. When the officer in charge gives an order, that's it, ESPECIALLY in a combat situation." Acknowledging that the SEALs "are not this nation's 'most secret combat unit,'" without identifying the actual unit, the Navy suggested the filmmakers refer to the organization as the Navy's "elite special operating forces."[39]

Finkelstein agreed with Sherman's recommendation and advised Phil Strub, who had recently replaced Don Baruch as the Pentagon's liaison with Hollywood, that though "the script is exciting and well-written, we cannot recommend Navy or Department of Defense production support of a film which depicts Navy sailors on covert operations in the Middle East killing with abandon. Further, the frequent unprofessional and undisciplined conduct of the characters does not reflect the tactics or esprit of Navy SEALS." Strub agreed: "We concur with your recommendation not to support the subject film. The script contains fundamental and irresolvable inaccuracies regarding the mission and character of Navy SEALS." On 27 June Sherman told Orion Pictures that the Navy, with the full agreement of the Defense Department Public Affairs Office, could not assist.[40]

The Pentagon's decision did not end the matter. Although shooting most of the action scenes in Spain, the production company asked Sherman's office for permission to project footage from the Navy film *Be Someone Special* on television monitors. When Strub received the request, he told the Navy's Office of Information that he would not approve it, having previously concurred with the service's refusal to assist *Navy SEALs*. He did say that he would take action if "the Navy would like to reconsider its position regarding the production."[41]

In response, the Navy did modify its position, and Strub approved use of the requested footage. The Navy then agreed to provide limited cooperation "only in the form of exterior location filming at the Norfolk Naval Base. Use of Navy equipment, personnel support, technical advice and locations other than those designated . . . will not be authorized. Access to any Navy SEAL compounds or working areas is not permitted." Even this limited assistance, when combined with a script by a retired SEAL, Chuck Pfarrer, and his subsequent technical advice during the production, gave *Navy SEALs* an aura of authenticity. In particular, the film very well portrayed the rigors of the SEALs' training regime.[42]

However, limited assistance and Pfarrer's first-hand experiences could not make *Navy SEALs* different from any of Chuck Norris's special-forces movies. The heroes do a lot of shooting and killing and some romancing, a few die, but most live. The violence is so gratuitous and random and the plot so implausible that the SEALs lost little of their secret identity to the empty theater seats. Peter Rainer, in the *Los Angeles Times,* described the film as "essentially a mechanical shoot-'em-up about a bunch of hell-raising heroes." The headline for the review in the *Chicago Sun-Times* tersely summarized the whole review: "Idiotic *Navy SEALs* earns disapproval." In the *New York Times,* Caryn James asked, "What will Teen-Age Mutant Ninja Turtles be when they grow up? On the evidence of *Navy Seals,* they are perfectly suited to be members of an elite Navy commando team. The men who fight Middle Eastern terrorists in this new action film are a mere step away from the adolescent Turtles in maturity and complexity of character, though they are not likely to come near them in box-office grosses." The film quickly disappeared to cable channels.[43]

Ironically, at the very time the SEALs were going into battle in the Gulf War, Vietnam was finally becoming a subject for a straightforward movie about naval aviators. *Flight of the Intruder* does contain a brief comment about the manner in which politicians were controlling the conduct of the war, but it portrays the American fliers as brave, dedicated, and resourceful. Vietnam becomes here just the arena in which the characters perform their duties, not the controversial war that divided the nation. According to producer Neufeld, the film "is not a Vietnam movie, but it takes place during the Vietnam War."[44]

Neufeld said he became interested in the story when he read Stephen Coonts's *Flight of the Intruder* and in it "found the best, the most vivid description of bomber flying that I had ever read." He thought the novel contained "an interesting story, with a great hook, a man unraveling and then going against the Navy code, jeopardizing his own men, and then redeeming himself." Finally, as a pilot, the novel simply "appealed" to him.[45]

Flight of the Intruder does not comment on whether the United States should have been involved in Southeast Asia. Instead, it simply establishes that the war was tearing the United States apart and then focuses on the story of men in combat in much the same way as *Men of the Fighting Lady* and *Bridges at Toko-ri* did. From the Navy's perspective, the film differed not at all from any one of the stories about carrier warfare on which the service had regularly assisted before the Vietnam War temporarily ended the Hollywood-Navy relationship.

In sending the script to Baruch in April 1989, Horton asked for "review and comment" from the Pentagon and the Navy in anticipation of Paramount's request for assistance. He explained, "The missions are vividly dramatized, the characters realisticly [*sic*] portrayed, in a story destined to create extraordinary empathy and involvement of the audiences who will ultimately view the final motion picture film." The "enormous appeal" of *Top Gun* "should be recaptured in this stirring Viet Nam drama," which would "contribute positive understanding of the basic tenets of military service. The entire film should provide substantial benefits in the National interest as well as bringing gripping entertainment to the motion picture audiences worldwide."[46]

As expected, the Navy found technical and historic inaccuracies with the script, which Sherman compiled and sent back to the Chief of Information on 2 May. Among the minor problems, he noted inaccuracies in the landing signal officer's orders to returning pilots. He also noted that a conversation about body counts "is not only historically inaccurate for 1972, but would be impossible today as well. First, body count was a feature of the VN war in the South, not of the air war in the North. Second, we did not then and do not now, have the capability to count bodies immediately following an air attack conducted deep inside enemy territory in the daytime or at night." He indicated that the filmmakers would have to use some other more realistic damage assessment, such as the number of buildings or trucks destroyed.[47]

Sherman reported that the filmmakers were extensively rewriting the script and suggested the Navy wait to discuss the project "to see what the future holds." However, Paramount requested that the Navy use the February screenplay to approve assistance, with the understanding that any subsequent versions would incorporate the service's suggestions. Paramount intended to "pull out the stops" in making *Flight of the Intruder* "in an attempt to create another blockbuster 'ala' [*sic*] *Top Gun*." Stating the obvious, he noted that the A-6 Intruder "community can hardly wait to assist, and is avidly supporting this one."[48]

If the Navy agreed to assist, Sherman suggested that Puerto Rico serve as a stand-in for Vietnam, with the service flying in A-6 bombers specifically for the filmmakers. He also recommended that shooting in port and at sea aboard a carrier be done pier side and out of San Diego. He said the studio understood "that this will be wildly expensive and is prepared to foot the bill." He further explained that Paramount had agreed to hire a former Navy pilot with Vietnam combat experience as technical adviser. Given the willingness of the studio to accede to the Navy's requests, Sherman recommended that the Navy approve cooperation and inform Baruch's office of the decision.[49]

At Finkelstein's request and with Sherman's memo in hand, the Assistant Chief of Naval Operations for Air Warfare reviewed the script again and offered additional suggestions. In particular, he expressed "*the strongest possible objection . . . to the use of marijuana by the hero*. The casual use of an illegal drug by a Navy pilot sends a negative signal throughout the Navy (where it smacks of hypocrisy within the officer corps), as well as throughout a society which expects its military officer corps to maintain high standards of personal conduct." He also complained that the "vulgarity of the language used throughout the story is a bit overdone, even considering the environment and conditions of the time." Nevertheless, his office "would like to remain actively involved in the movie."[50]

Acting on the memos from Sherman and naval aviation, Finkelstein told Strub that the Navy approved cooperation to *Flight of the Intruder,* on the assumption that the filmmakers would make the suggested changes. Once Strub concurred, Sherman told the producers of the decision and indicated that his office was assuming coordination of the cooperation. On his part, Neufeld praised Paramount for committing itself to finance the film, saying it was "a very courageous decision at the time. Whether it was a wise decision when the movie comes out, we don't know. It is an expensive film. We got the green light on this about three weeks after *Casualties of War* came out and failed." He thought that to go-ahead with another Vietnam movie under the circumstances was "an extraordinary move."[51]

Both Neufeld and director John Milius saw the film primarily as an action adventure movie about men in war, not about the nature of the Vietnam War. The producer said the story "could have happened in several wars," and the director thought the film was "a celebration of valor and it is also a celebration of people having loyalties and honor and doing much for each other that they wouldn't necessarily in other situations." In contrast to *Casualties of War,* which presents "this terrible crime that is committed by American soldiers," Milius said that *Flight of the Intruder* "sympathizes with the American soldier and shows him as an honorable person."[52]

Whether the Navy liked the image or simply the opportunity to show the Intruder in action, it proceeded to provide more extensive cooperation than on any other movie about naval aviation. The Navy selected four A-6 Intruders from Whidbey Island Naval Air Station in Washington to appear in the flying sequences and began modifying them to resemble the 1972 version of the bomber. Due to political instability in the Philippines and the threat of hurricanes in Puerto Rico, Paramount chose sites in Georgia and Hawaii to recreate North Vietnam for the overland flying sequences. On 25 September the three A-6s that had completed their modifications flew East and began flying simulated missions over predesignated areas south of Savannah, completing as many as six sorties a day. The four aircrews that made the trip rotated among the two planes that flew in front of the cameras at any one time.[53]

When Milius had completed his filming in Georgia, the planes, aircrews, and support forces returned to Washington briefly before all four modified A-6s flew to Kauai, Hawaii. There the director, cast, and crew spent a month shooting additional aerial sequences and low-level flights over rice paddies to use during the hero's flight to Hanoi for the climactic air strike. Milius also filmed the rescue operation there, for which the Navy also provided helicopters stationed at Barking Sands Naval Air Station. However, since the Navy had retired the prop-driven Skyraiders twenty-one years before, private owners supplied the two A-1s that provided covering fire for the downed pilots awaiting rescue. With the filming completed, the A-6s flew back to Washington on 13 November to prepare for the final phase of their participation in the film, flying on and off the USS *Independence*.

On 27 November the bombers flew to Miramar Naval Air Station and then out to the carrier 120 miles off the coast. There the Navy supplied a second A-6 unit and other vintage fighters and bombers painted in period colors, some in flying condition and others that were not carrier operational, hoisted onto the carrier at San Diego, to serve as background on the flight deck.

Aboard the carrier for eight days, Paramount's 108-man crew filmed on a "not-to-interfere" basis while the *Independence* carried out its training mission. All the cinematic Intruder missions, except the final one, took place at night, enabling the Navy to use the deck during the day and Milius to shoot without interruption at night. The second unit crew filmed during the day to capture flight-deck operations. While Milius could have shot some of the sequences dockside or on a soundstage, he considered the cost and effort of going to sea justified: "Being on the ship puts everybody in the right mood." Moreover, it helped the director obtain the right lighting: once, to match footage taken two days earlier, the captain reversed the carrier's direction by 180 degrees, causing Milius to exclaim, "If I need backlighting, they just turn the ship around!"

The Navy did refuse to fly its planes trailing smoke, firing missiles or dropping bombs over land, and obviously having fliers eject or crash their aircraft. So the studio had to build and fly scale models of the Intruder and other planes to create those events in the film, including the attack on Hanoi, the special-effects high point of the movie. Once Milius discovered that Intruder pilots had the option of ejecting through the canopy, he had the model designers change plans so that he could film full-size dummies being ejected through a full-size canopy.

Did such special effects and the Navy's almost unlimited assistance give Paramount a fair return on its $30 million, including $1.2 million to the service for the cost of its cooperation? Paramount obtained a movie that differed little from other naval aviation stories about World War II or Korea. The hero, Jake Grafton, played by Brad Johnson, the A-6 squadron's leading pilot, complains about fighting a meaningless war, loses his original bombardier-navigator, and carries out an unauthorized bombing of People's Resistance Park in downtown Hanoi with his new crewman, Virgil Cole, played by Willem Dafoe. The clearly mutinous mission disrupts the Paris peace talks, but when President Nixon orders the military to resume bombing Hanoi, squadron commander Frank Camparelli, played by Danny Glover, informs his rebels that their mission never happened.

Grounded and denied the chance to take part in the daylight attack on Hanoi's air defenses in the opening gambit of Operation Linebacker 2, Grafton and Cole listen as Camparelli crash-lands his damaged plane while leading the squadron. Striding onto the deck like hired guns, the two fliers commandeer an Intruder—albeit with the apparent acquiescence of the carrier's commander of flight operations, who sees only "a strike preparing to launch"—and set off to provide air cover for Camparelli, who is awaiting rescue.

Arriving on station implausibly fast, their plane immediately receives fatal ground fire. Ejecting, Grafton lands near Camparelli, but Cole falls a distance away and suffers a mortal wound in a confrontation with a North Vietnamese soldier. Surrounded, he calls down bombs on his position, giving a helicopter time to rescue Grafton and Camparelli. Like Brubaker's death in *The Bridges at Toko-ri,* Cole's sacrifice does not ensure victory, any more than did the fliers' one-plane raid on Hanoi. Nor can the rescue of Grafton and Camparelli and their upbeat conversation back aboard the carrier give the film a happy ending.

★

From its perspective, the Navy did receive exciting images of its bombers in action as well as one more positive portrayal of carrier operations. To make sure no one would miss the film's intention of giving Intruder crews their due recognition, Grafton answers a fighter pilot's deprecation of his plane with "Fighter pukes make movies. Bomber pilots make history." Unfortunately, the Navy did not get the benefit it had expected from the degree of assistance it provided. *Flight of the Intruder* remained just another aviation movie. *Daily Variety* put it most succinctly: the film enjoyed "the dubious distinction of being the most boring Vietnam War picture since *The Green Berets* but lacks the benefit of the latter's political outrageousness to spark a little interest and humor." The reviewer concluded that any message Milius still might have on the Vietnam War "is lost here amid a flotilla of banalities and clichés straight out of bloated 1950s service dramas."[54]

Despite Milius's claim that he was making an apolitical war movie, reviewers still chose to offer their anti–Vietnam War commentaries. Desmond Ryan, in the *Long Beach Press-Telegram,* described the film as "a misguided missile. To pinpoint what went wrong with this picture before the cameras even started rolling, you have only to recall one of the most famous photographs taken during the Vietnam War. It showed a naked child fleeing in terror from an eruption of napalm in an image that was to be etched into the conscience of the world. In making a movie about the men who dropped the bombs, John Milius at least explains why the great Vietnam combat pictures have stayed close to the ground."[55]

Ryan acknowledged that "there is no escaping the status of the bomber as the chief symbol of the high tech, indiscriminate savagery of modern warfare."

He also noted, "Whenever the Intruder bombers touch down on their home carrier, they land on a flight deck jammed with so many war movie clichés there is scarcely room to park the planes." He observed that the film came to life only in the clash between Grafton and his superiors.[56] While Peter Rainer, in the *Los Angeles Times,* considered *Flight of the Intruder* mediocre, he felt "it comes at a time when audiences may be in the mood to see even a sub-par film about American bomber and fighter pilots braving the odds and strutting their codes of honor." He thought the film may have found "its commercial salvation. It certainly won't find salvation in its mundane script, direction, performances."[57]

Rainer felt that Milius had tried for the effect John Ford had achieved in *They Were Expendable* but concluded that the director had failed because Ford's film "was considerably darker and more complex than this straight-arrow tub-thumper. Milius attempts to recapture our feelings for the rousingly patriotic war movies of 50 years ago, but the kind of traditional, true-blue sentiments he's parading seem out of place in this Vietnam setting. That war, and our feelings about it, are far more complicated than this film allows for. It's [sic] banalities don't do justice to the war or the Americans who served in it."[58]

Unfortunately for the Navy and the filmmakers, Paramount released *Flight of the Intruder* within days of the outbreak of the Gulf War, in January 1991. Television brought flights of Intruders and smart bombs hitting their targets twenty-four hours a day almost live into the nation's living rooms. Worried about the impact the war might have on the appeal of the film and needing the money to promote *Godfather III,* Paramount let *Flight of the Intruder* quickly disappear from theater screens, much to the Navy's regret. So the real war, not Milius's rather unexceptional drama, confirmed for the American people that the images of *Top Gun* were the reality of the post-Vietnam Navy.[59]

The Navy fared far better on a film that received only courtesy assistance. *Under Siege* became a bad-news, good-news film for the Navy. Initially, the Navy saw little benefit in assisting a movie in which terrorists kidnap its most famous battleship, the USS *Missouri.* Unlike other "kidnap" movies, however, *Under Siege* offers a story with a modicum of plausibility, at least until its closing scenes, which occur with such speed that they almost mask the inaccurate, if not absurd, resolution.

For the Navy's purposes, the portrayal of a magnificent ship at sea should have triggered excitement in the public affairs offices. Unfortunately, the service could expect little benefit from such images since the *Missouri* was returning to Bremerton, Washington, and most assuredly its final retirement. The ease with which the small band of terrorists seized the ship would do little to assure taxpayers that the Navy could protect its men and equipment. Worst of all, as in *No Way Out,* the bad guys had been good guys: Tommy Lee Jones, an ex-Special Forces commander, plays the deranged terrorist leader, and Gary Busey aids and abets him from his position as the battleship's executive officer.

Nor did the hero come to the fray with particularly good credentials. Steven Seagal plays a demoted Navy SEAL, reduced to spending his final days in the Navy in relative disgrace after punching out his commander during the U.S. invasion of Panama.

Of course, Seagal had justification for his actions—the incompetence of his superior had led to the deaths of his men. More important, Seagal returns to his career specialization and almost single-handedly, with a combination of martial arts and modern weaponry, saves the ship from the terrorists who are trying to steal the ship's nuclear-tipped cruise missiles. The magnificent shots of the *Missouri* sailing under full steam create a fitting tribute to the ship. As important, Seagal's heroism provides a positive statement about the bravery of Navy personnel in the face of adversity, the image the service had been trying to put on the silver screen for more than eighty years.

$\star$

Epilogue

Where will the Navy go from here cinematically? In *A Few Good Men*, Tom Cruise, as a Navy lawyer, slays a Marine dragon in the form of Jack Nicholson, playing an arrogant, lying officer responsible for the death of one of his men. Cruise's courtroom theatrics may have served as a payback from the Great Santini's aerial defeat of his Navy counterparts, but his demolition of a Marine also constituted friendly fire on a sister service. If not another branch of the armed forces or the Soviet Union, where does the Navy find its future enemies in Hollywood movies?

Navy SEALs suggested that the military's elite forces could always fight Middle Eastern terrorists. However, neither it nor the 1993 made-for-cable-television *The Finest Hour*, its sole imitator to date, became anything more than a generic shoot-'em-up. Although *The Finest Hour* did try to establish a realistic basis in having the SEALs carry out a mission as part of Operation Desert Storm, the operation to destroy a fleet of gas-carrying missiles had no more basis in reality than did the island at the mouth of the Persian Gulf from which the Iraqis were preparing to fire the rockets. Moreover, the firefights in each movie resembled thousands of formless gun battles in war films, Westerns, or gangster movies, in which each side fires endlessly, with little direction and little effect, except to have one of the heroes suffer his obligatory fate.

Under Siege carried terrorist stories to their logical extreme. With the *Missouri* and its sister battleships consigned once again to the mothball fleet, however, what can a terrorist group hijack? A missile-firing submarine or cruiser perhaps. Still, filmmakers will have a hard time coming up with a unique plot twist to top Steven Seagal's retaking of the *Missouri* or a better visual image than a dolphin leaping into the air alongside the giant battleship plowing through the sea. More important, the Navy would undoubtedly show no more interest in helping on such a story than it did on *Under Siege* or *The Fifth Missile.*

The Navy did provide very limited help to *Patriot Games,* which featured a rogue band of IRA extremists who had targeted a member of the Royal Family, not Navy personnel or ships. To be sure, the terrorists' leader ultimately forgets his true enemy and sets out on a vendetta against former CIA operative Jack Ryan, Tom Clancy's hero from *The Hunt for Red October.* The Navy provided courtesy assistance in allowing the filmmakers to use the Naval Academy as background for two brief scenes showing Ryan, as a professor, teaching mid-shipmen and leaving campus through one of the gates. In fact, this short montage will probably remain as close as Hollywood will get to Annapolis in the near future.

Ironically, the cheating scandal that racked the Naval Academy in the early 1990s does offer some intriguing plot lines. Good drama always draws on ambiguities, conflicts of conscience, and honor codes, particularly those held more in theory than practice. As Hollywood has regularly demonstrated, film-makers have often combined such elements in an academic setting to create an interesting story. However, the Naval Academy and the Navy most likely would reject any request for assistance on a film that portrayed the Academy scandal in any way, just as West Point refused to help on the 1986 made-for-television *Dress Gray,* a story about homosexuality and murder.

On the other hand, for *Clear and Present Danger,* the Navy was willing to loan the USS *Kitty Hawk* to the filmmakers as the launch pad for an F-18A Hornet that dropped a smart bomb on a gathering of drug dealers. Given the mission, the Pentagon expressed no concern that the highly secret weapon also killed innocent women and children. More important, the Navy did not seem bothered that the scenario allowed a presidential aide to order the illegal attack without a question from the carrier's captain.

In fact, the early versions of the script portrayed the captain as not being aware of the launch. However, when the Navy objected, the filmmakers cut the scene from the script. In any case, for its assistance, the Navy did receive another portrayal of carrier flight operations and the bomb did precisely hit its target even if the key drug dealer had not yet arrived at the meeting.

In any case, if terrorists and drug dealers may serve as legitimate targets for the Navy, World War II offers few stories at this late date. Even during the nostalgia-driven fiftieth-anniversary celebration of the war, Hollywood failed to turn out one movie about the conflict on the land, sea, or air. The 1991 made-for-television *Mission of the Shark* did portray the fate of the survivors of the *Indianapolis,* the cruiser that carried the first atomic bomb to Tinian. However, the story remained only a footnote to the history of the war, and the struggle of the sailors to fend off the sharks might have been titled "Jaws Redux," particularly since the sinking of the *Indianapolis* had inspired *Jaws* in the first place.

Vietnam continues to lurk on the edges of the American psyche. Except for the POW fliers, however, virtually no naval officers or men had any firsthand contact with the enemy and so do not even offer stories of post-Vietnam stress syndrome. As *Flight of the Intruder* demonstrated, the Navy's combat experiences during the war no longer have much appeal to moviegoers, especially when competition comes from the real thing, live on television. Likewise, television coverage of peacekeeping operations, whether in Somalia, Bosnia, Rwanda, or Haiti, satisfies most people's interest in the subject. Of course, the Navy has very little involvement in these operations, except for patrolling no-fly zones and providing logistics support, neither of which provide much dramatic potential.

The Cold War ended on the screen for the Navy with *The Hunt for Red October,* although spies continue to do their work even in the Navy, as the Walker family business showed. The service did lend minimal assistance to the television account of the Walkers' misadventures in return for a trailer explaining that the Navy had tightened security following the apprehension of the spy ring. In any case, Navy preparedness in the new world order does not differ all that much from the service's training in the 1930s or during the Cold War. Consequently, Hollywood may well find action stories to set in the Navy, aboard its ships and planes. *An Officer and a Gentleman* and *Top Gun* illustrated the possibilities of combining love stories with a Navy background. Moreover, given the current instability in many parts of the world, Navy fliers may well get more opportunities to shoot down Third World planes, with relatively little risk to themselves. Nevertheless, after filmmakers get beyond Richard Gere learning to become an officer or Tom Cruise training to become a better pilot, Hollywood has about exhausted plot lines that lacked originality in the 1930s.

Spoofs such as the 1991 *Hot Shots* do not benefit the Navy and quickly become stale, anyway. The Tailhook scandal does offer some intriguing story possibilities, particularly in addressing the problems involved in the Navy's integrating the sexes into a unified fighting force. However, given the lingering stigma of the scandal and the number of careers ruined, rightly or wrongly, Hollywood would undoubtedly find little willingness from the Navy or the Pentagon to help any such story. Nor would the service find a film about the problems of women at the Naval Academy particularly beneficial, particularly if it were to show male midshipmen handcuffing female midshipmen to urinals.

Love stories set in Navy locales were a staple from the earliest days of the service's relationship with Hollywood. Given the greater sophistication of today's moviegoer, however, plots would have to contain more realistic portrayals than the service romances of the 1930s and 1940s. In light of the problems the Navy had with the explicit sex scenes of *An Officer and a Gentleman,* filmmakers would have no guarantee of receiving assistance on such stories. Nevertheless, the fact that men and women are serving together both on land and aboard all ships at sea offers many dramatic possibilities for screenwriters.

Would the Navy's refusal to provide assistance to a different approach to love among its personnel constitute censorship? The military has always emphasized that no filmmaker has to come to the Pentagon for help. This disclaimer remains disingenuous, at least in regard to the Navy. A studio can dress up actors in uniforms and even rent jet fighters in Israel, but the U.S. Navy is the only place a filmmaker can find a nuclear aircraft carrier or missile cruiser.

On the other hand, while the service might not like the idea of a love story about an enlisted man and a female officer aboard an aircraft carrier, at least the Navy might benefit from the portrayal of shipboard operations. Certainly such a film remains more plausible than helping raise the *Titanic* or having the *Nimitz* cruising off Pearl Harbor on 6 December 1941. In any event, the bottom line remains the same now as it has been for more than eighty years: the Navy wants a positive image of its personnel, equipment, and procedures and some benefit from any film on which it cooperates.

The service did not get that from the post–Cold War underwater epic *Crimson Tide*. The initial prospects did seem favorable since Don Simpson and Jerry Bruckheimer, the producers of *Top Gun,* would again be combining their talents with Tony Scott, the director of the highly positive portrayal of Navy aviation. In hopes of obtaining similar results with a peacetime nuclear submarine story, the Navy provided the filmmakers a research ride aboard the USS *Florida* at the end of 1993. Nevertheless, the service made it clear it would not consider providing cooperation until it saw a script.

When the screenplay arrived in April 1994, Cdr. Gary Shrout, the director of the Navy's Los Angeles office, found the script "extremely well written." However, he recommended that the service not cooperate since the story did not depict a "favorable interpretation of Navy operations and policies." In particular, the story portrayed a mutinous situation between the submarine's commanding officer and his executive officer. The confrontation arises after the boat receives orders to launch its missiles against a rebellious Russian unit that has seized a nuclear missile facility and threatens to attack the United States and Japan.[1]

Shrout pointed out to Navy Public Affairs and Phil Strub that despite Hollywood's need for dramatic conflict in films, the portrayal "is in direct opposition" to actual launch procedures: "In reality, the entire sequence of command and control is designed to allow for any non-concurrence to block the launch of strategic nuclear weapons." The Navy agreed and Phil Strub advised the filmmakers, on July 8, that the Pentagon had determined it could not provide assistance "due to the unrealistic portrayal of the Navy personnel assigned to the fictional ballistic missile submarine."[2]

Strub acknowledged that toning down the story "might dilute the drama." Nevertheless, he explained that "the fundamental premise of an armed mutiny, with its attendant depictions of the crewmembers' behavior, decisions, and peformance, is unacceptably unrealistic." In fact, he pointed out that the submarine-based nuclear deterrence mission "is predicated in large measure on the conviction that even during the gravest of crises, the crew would behave rationally, reasonably, and responsibly." Strub then stressed that adequate redundancies existed "in systems and safeguards in procedures to further obviate the breakdown in command authority and crisis in nuclear strike capability as depicted in the script."[3]

On their part, Simpson and Bruckheimer could not change the script and still make their film. As a result, they produced *Crimson Tide* without the Navy's assistance, telling a reasonably exciting story that would grab the attention of anyone who knew nothing about submarines and nuclear launch procedures. However, while audiences might enjoy *Crimson Tide* on a visceral level, it lacked even a modicum of authenticity. Among other things, Gene Hackman, as the submarine's captain, was at least fifteen years too old to be commanding a nuclear sub. Nor would the Navy have really ignored Hackman's bringing his pet dog aboard ship as the script's dialogue states.

Worse, the film's portrayal of the officers and men insulted submariners, their training, and their demeanor. Submarine crews simply do not run through their boats waving guns as if they were on their way to the OK corral, whatever the magnitude of the crisis. Moreover, the shouting matches between Hackman and Denzel Washington, playing the executive officer, lack any reality. Shrout acknowledged in his critique of the script that "screamers" have served in leadership positions in the Navy. Nevertheless, he pointed out that "it is a particular point of pride with submariners to accomplish the mission in a low key and quiet manner."[4]

In fact, the Navy trains its submarine officers to act with one mind. Consequently, the personality clash between Hackman and Washington, however dramatic, simply would not have occurred, the matter of a launch order aside. With such problems, who would have cared that several of the crew members were egregiously overweight, one sailor even dying of a heart attack during an early crisis.

In the end, the crew's references to such earlier undersea stories as *The Enemy Below* and *Run Silent, Run Deep* become the only real connection between *Crimson Tide* and the many submarine films which have received Navy assistance. The film simply drew on the drama inherent in any submarine story: when a sub submerges, it might not come up. However, since most nuclear submarines do reappear, the filmmakers had no choice but to hype the story, resulting in a movie which contained a false portrayal of life under the sea that provided no benefit to the Navy.

In contrast, *Apollo 13* did receive full cooperation in much the same way as had *The Right Stuff,* with the Navy providing the recovery ships needed to pick up the astronauts after their ill-fated mission. To be sure, neither NASA nor the Navy could receive much benefit from a portrayal of the near-fatal flight to the moon. Nevertheless, the film remains a model of the Navy's symbiotic relationship with the film industry compared to the ABC television movie *She Stood Alone: The Tailhook Scandal.*

Don Mancuso, the director of the Defense Criminal Investigation Service, which investigated the Tailhook Scandal, found the movie "surprisingly accurate."[5] However, the portrayal of Paula Coughlin's sexual harassment at the 1991 Tailhook convention in Las Vegas could in no way provide any benefit to the Navy. While most Navy and Marine jet pilots publicly question the veracity of Coughlin's story and its television recreation, the very quality of the production and Gail O'Grady's portrayal of the Navy flier gave the production an authentic ambience and so believability. As usually happens with film docudramas, most viewers had no way of knowing that the Navy did not cooperate on the production. As a result, most people would assume from apparent realism the uniforms, planes, and helicopters provided, courtesy of the Canadian military, that the movie had received assistance from the Pentagon.

As the Navy entered the final years of the twentieth century, the service found itself the subject of negative portrayals by filmmakers looking for dramatic stories. A Navy jet might kill a band of drug dealers or a Navy ship might help bring a disastrous space flight to a happy conclusion. But any benefit the service might gain from such positive, albeit brief, screen appearances, it would suffer negatively from cinematic images of a screaming match between two of its elite submarine officers, the sexual harassment of one of its female fliers, or the Annapolis cheating scandal.

Still, as long as the Navy protects the nation's shores from attack, it will want to maintain its positive image in motion pictures. Consequently, cooperation will continue between the Navy and the film industry, in a relationship built on mutual exploitation and mutual benefit. At the same time, with or without assistance from the Navy, Hollywood will continue to use the glamour inherent in Navy uniforms, jet planes, and esoteric ships to create exciting images that will attract audiences to the silver screen.

Appendix 1
List of Interviews

NAME	DATE(S)	POSITION
Arthur, Robert	3/7/94, 3/29/74	Producer
Bartlett, Sy	2/9/74	Producer/Writer
Baruch, Donald	3/22/73, numerous	DoD PA Official
Baumann, Cdr. Chris	8/24/88, 8/25/88	Navy PA
Beach, Capt. Edward L.	5/30/74	Author
Beebe, Capt. Marshall	3/20/74, 7/24/78	TA
Bell, Ray	4/8/75	Industry Rep.
Bellamy, Ralph	7/18/78	Actor
Bennett, Harve	8/26/87	Producer
Berman, Henry	6/28/75	Producer
Blankfort, Michael	7/19/75	Screenwriter
Bolden, Col. Charles	8/23/94	Dep. Cdr. Mids.
Booth, Capt. Blake	8/16/74	TA
Brewer, Gen. Margaret	4/4/81	Marine PA
Brown, Capt. Alan	3/27/74	Navy PA
Brown, Bill	1/9/76	TV Producer
Bruckheimer, Jerry	2/6/89	Producer
Bunting, Josiah	12/23/74	Author
Capra, Frank	9/2/82	Director
Chappell, Adm. Lucius	8/7/75	TA
Chayefsky, Paddy	5/28/64	Screenwriter

NAME	DATE(S)	POSITION
Clark, Kenneth	12/17/73, 4/3/75	MPAA Exec.
Coghlan, Lt. Cdr. Frank	3/23/74	Navy PA
Cooney, Adm. David	4/2/81, 6/27/94	Navy PA Chief
Coulter, Col. Pat	8/8/81, 1/26/89	Marine PA/TA
Cutter, Capt. Slade	7/21/75	Navy PA
Daves, Delmer	1/31/74, 2/2/74	Director/Writer
Douglas, Melvin	1/27/75	Actor
Douglas, Peter	8/3/81	Producer
Draude, Gen. Tom	5/18/93	Marine PA
Edelman, Louis	3/11/74	Producer
Ferguson, Capt. J. D.	4/5/75	TA
Ferguson, Larry	3/6/90	Screenwriter
Fleischer, Richard	6/26/75	Director
Foy, Brian	8/5/75	Producer
Garrow, Adm. Jack	4/18/90	Navy PA Chief
Gillespie, Arnold	7/14/75	Art Director
Goulding, Phil	4/4/75	ASDPA
Graves, Capt. Bill	7/19/78	Navy PA/TA
Hackford, Taylor	8/7/81	Director
Haines, William W.	3/15/74	Screenwriter
Harding, Lt. William	4/11/74	Navy PA
Harris, James	2/25/74	Director
Hendricks, Bill	3/25/74	Studio Exec.
Hetu, Capt. Herbert	4/3/75	TA
Hickey, Adm. Robert	3/19/74	Navy PA Chief
Hiller, Arthur	3/14/74	Director
Horton, John	12/18/73, 4/8/75	Studio Rep.
Hough, Stan	7/1/75	Studio Exec.
Jones, James	12/30/74	Author
Kellogg, Ray	7/3/75	Asst. Dir.
Kramer, Stanley	2/8/74	Dir./Producer
LeMay, Gen. Curtis	8/17/75	AF CoS
LeRoy, Mervyn	7/23/75	Director
Leuhman, Gen. Arno	7/1/75	AF Staff
London, Barry	2/1/89	Studio Exec.
Mackenzie, Capt. C. J.	8/28/94	TA
Maltz, Albert	7/25/75	Screenwriter
Mancuso, Donald	7/20/74	OIG, DoD
Martinson, Leslie	7/10/75, 11/23/94	Director

NAME	DATE(S)	POSITION
Marton, Andrew	7/21/75	Director
Mayes, Wendall	3/6/74	Screenwriter
McCarthy, Frank	7/31/78	Producer
McGregor, Adm. RobRoy	8/15/75	TA
Milestone, Lewis	2/7/74	Director
Milius, John	3/14/90	Director/Writer
Mirisch, Marvin	3/22/78	Producer
Mirisch, Walter W.	1/6/89	Producer
Nankin, Rick	12/14/88	Screenwriter
Neufeld, Mace	3/14/90	Producer
Nitze, Paul	4/8/75	Sec. of Navy
O'Connor, Richard	8/7/81	Producer
Parks, Adm. Lewis	12/31/74	Navy PA Chief
Poe, James	8/4/75	Screenwriter
Preminger, Otto	8/16/73	Director
Ransohoff, Martin	3/1/74	Producer
Robson, Mark	7/2/75	Director
Rosenberg, Frank	7/12/78	Producer/Writer
Rydell, Mark	9/3/75	Director
Salinger, Pierre	8/16/79, 6/29/94	WH Press Sec.
Sargent, Joseph	8/3/78	Director
Schary, Dore	12/20/73	Studio Exec.
Seaton, George	3/4/74	Producer
Shaw, Adm. James	8/17/74	TA
Sherman, Capt. Michael	3/6/88, 3/7/90, 8/30/93	Navy PA/TA
Siegel, Don	7/8/75	Director
Simpson, Don	2/6/89	Producer
Stafford, Capt. Edward	4/7/75	TA
Stevens, George, Jr.	1/9/80	Producer
Strub, Phil	3/14/90, numerous	DoD PA
Swink, Robert	7/25/78	Film Editor
Sylvester, Arthur	8/16/73, 12/23/74	ASDPA
Thompson, Adm. William	6/8/78	Navy PA Chief
Towne, Lt. Col. Clair	8/15/75	DoD PA
Trumbo, Dalton	4/10/74	Screenwriter
Valenti, Jack	11/11/76	Pres. MPAA
Warner, Jack, Jr.	4/4/74	Studio Exec.
Watkins, Capt. George	12/10/77	TA
Wayne, John	2/7/74	Actor/Producer

NAME	DATE(S)	POSITION
Wendkos, Paul	8/4/75	Director
Will, Adm. John	5/22/74	TA
Williams, Elmo	3/18/74	Producer
Winston, Gen. John	9/20/77	Marine aviator
Wise, Robert	4/10/74	Director
Zinnemann, Fred	10/12/79	Director

★
Appendix 2
List of Films

List of Films Discussed

FILM	DATE	STUDIO	DIRECTOR
Action in the North Atlantic	1943	WB	Lloyd Bacon
Airport '77	1977	Univ	Jerry Jameson
All Hands on Deck	1961	TCF	Norman Taurog
Americanization of Emily	1964	MGM	Arthur Hiller
Anchors Away	1945	MGM	George Sidney
Annapolis	1928	Pathe	Cabanne,Christy
Annapolis Farewell	1935	Par	Alexander Hall
Annapolis Salute	1937	RKO	Christy Cabanne
Annapolis Story	1955	AA	Don Siegel
Apocalypse Now	1979	UA	Francis Ford Coppola
Assault on the Wayne	1971	TV	Marvin Chomsky
Away all Boats	1956	Univ	Joseph Pevney
Battle of the Coral Sea	1959	Col	Paul Wendkos
Battle Stations	1956	Col	Lewis Seller
Bedford Incident	1965	Col	James Harris
Big Jim McLain	1952	WB	Edward Ludwig
Bridges at Toko-ri	1954	Par	Mark Robson
Caine Mutiny	1954	Col	Edward Dmytryk
Caine Mutiny Court Martial	1988	TV	Robert Altman
Cinderella Liberty	1973	TCF	Mark Rydell
Clear and Present Danger	1994	Par	Phillip Noyce

FILM	DATE	STUDIO	DIRECTOR
Convoy	1927	FN	Joseph Boyle
Crash Dive	1943	TCF	Archie Mayo
Crimson Tide	1995	Disney	Tony Scott
Destination Tokyo	1943	WB	Delmer Daves
Destroyer	1943	Col	William Seiter
Devil Dogs of the Air	1935	WB	Lloyd Bacon
Devil's Playground	1937	Col	Eric Kenton
Dirigible	1931	Col	Frank Capra
Dive Bomber	1941	WB	Michael Curtiz
Don't Give Up the Ship	1959	Par	Norman Taurog
Don't Go Near the Water	1957	MGM	Charles Walters
Enemy Below	1957	TCF	Dick Powell
Ensign Pulver	1964	WB	Joshua Logan
Eternal Sea	1955	Rep	John Auer
Few Good Men	1992	CR	Rob Reiner
Fifth Missile	1986	TV	Larry Peerce
Fighting Lady, The	1943	TCF	Henry Hathaway
Fighting Seabees	1944	Rep	Edward Ludwig
Fighting Sullivans, The	1944	TCF	Lloyd Bacon
Final Countdown	1980	UA	Don Taylor
Finest Hour, The	1991	TV	Shimon Dotan
Flat Top	1952	Mono	Lesley Selander
Fleet's In	1942	Par	Victor Schertzinger
Fleet's In, The	1928	Par	Malcolm St. Clair
Flight Command	1940	MGM	Frank Borzage
Flight of the Intruder	1991	Par	John Milius
Flying Fleet	1929	Pathe	George Hill
Flying Missile	1951	Col	Henry Levin
Follow the Fleet	1936	RKO	Mark Sandrich
Francis in the Navy	1955	Univ	Arthur Lubin
Frogmen, The	1951	TCF	Lloyd Bacon
Gallant Hours, The	1960	UA	Robert Montgomery
Girl, a Guy, and a Gob, A	1941	RKO	Richard Jones
Girl in Every Port, A	1928	TCF	Howard Hawks
Girl in Every Port, A	1951	RKO	Chester Erskine
Gray Lady Down	1978	Univ	David Greene
Great Santini, The	1982	BCP	John Lewis Carlino
Gung Ho!	1943	Univ	Walter Wagner
Hanoi Hilton	1987	Cannon	Lionel Chetwynd
Hell Below	1933	MGM	Jack Conway

FILM	DATE	STUDIO	DIRECTOR
Hellcats of the Navy	1957	Col	Nathan Juran
Hell Divers	1932	MGM	George Hill
Hell in the Pacific	1968		John Boorman
Hello Annapolis	1942	Col	Charles Barton
Here Come the Waves	1944	Par	Mark Sandrich
Here Comes the Navy	1934	WB	Lloyd Bacon
Hero of Submarine D-2	1916	Vita	Paul Scardon
Hit the Deck	1930	RKO	Luther Reed
Hold 'em Navy	1937	Par	Kurt Neuman
Hot Shots	1991	TCF	Jim Abrahams
Hunt for Red October	1990	Par	John McTiernan
Ice Station Zebra	1968	MGM	John Sturges
Inchon	1982	OWP	Terence Young
Incredible Mr. Limpet	1964	WB	Arthur Lubin
In Harm's Way	1965	Par	Otto Preminger
In Love and War	1987	TV	Paul Aaron
In the Navy	1941	Univ	Arthur Lubin
John Paul Jones	1959	WB	John Farrow
King Kong	1933	RKO	Mehan Cooper
Last Detail	1973	Col	Hal Ashby
Let It Rain	1927	Par	Eddie Cline
Let's Go Navy	1951	Mono	William Beaudine
Lieutenant Robin Crusoe, USN	1966	Disney	Byron Paul
MacArthur	1977	Univ	Joseph Sargent
Madame Butterfly	1915	FPL	Sidney Olcott
Madame Spy	1918	Univ	Douglas Gerrard
McHale's Navy	1964	Univ	Edward Montagne
Men of the Fighting Lady	1954	MGM	Andrew Marton
Men Without Women	1930	TCF	John Ford
Midshipman	1925	MGM	Christy Cabanne
Midshipman Jack	1933	MGM	Christy Cabanne
Midway	1976	Univ	Jack Smight
Minesweeper	1943	Par	William Berke
Mission of the Shark	1991	TV	Robert Iscove
Mister Roberts	1955	WB	John Ford; Meryn LeRoy
Murder in the Fleet	1935	MGM	Edward Sedgwick
Navy Blue and Gold	1937	MGM	Sam Wood
Navy Blues	1937	Rep	Ralph Staub
Navy Blues	1941	MGM	Lloyd Bacon
Navy Born	1936	Rep	Nate Watt

★

FILM	DATE	STUDIO	DIRECTOR
Navy Bound	1951	Mono	Paul Landres
Navy Comes Through	1942	RKO	A. Edward Sutherland
Navy Secrets	1939	Mono	Howard Bretherton
Navy Sets	1990	Orion	Lewis Teague
Navy Wife	1935	TCF	Allan Dwan
No Man Is an Island	1962	Univ	John Monks, Jr.
No Way Out	1987	Univ	Roger Donaldson
Officer and a Gentleman, An	1982	Par	Taylor Hackford
Okinawa	1952	UA	George Brooks
On the Beach	1959	UA	Stanley Kramer
Operation Pacific	1951	WB	George Waggner
Operation Petticoat	1959	Univ	Blake Edwards
Panama Hattie	1943	MGM	Norman McLeod
Parrish	1961	WB	Delmer Daves
Patriot Games	1992	Par	Philip Noyce
Philadelphia Experiment	1984	NWP	Stewart Raffill
Pride of the Navy	1939	Rep	Charles Lamont
Private Navy of Sergeant O'Farrell	1968	UA	Frank Tashlin
PT-109	1963	WB	Leslie Martinson
Purple Hearts	1984	WB	Sidney Furie
Raise the Titanic	1980	MAP	Jerry Jameson
Right Stuff, The	1983	WB	Philip Kaufman
Rough Riders	1927	Par	Victor Fleming
Run Silent, Run Deep	1958	UA	Robert Wise
Russians Are Coming	1966	UA	Norman Jewison
Sailor-Made Man, A	1921	Roach	Fred Newmeyer
Salute	1929	TCF	John Ford
Sea Beneath, The	1931	TCF	John Ford
Seven Days in May	1964	Par	John Frankenheimer
Seven Sinners	1940	WB	Tay Garnett
Shipmates	1931	MGM	Harry Pollard
Shipmates Forever	1935	WB	Frank Borzage
Skirts Ahoy	1952	MGM	Sidney Lanfield
South Pacific	1958	TCF	Joshua Logan
Stand By for Action	1942	MGM	Robert Leonard
Star Trek IV	1986	Par	Leonard Nimoy
Story of Dr. Wassell, The	1944	Par	Cecil B. DeMille
Submarine	1928	Col	Frank Capra
Submarine Command	1951	Par	John Farrow
Submarine D-1	1937	WB	Lloyd Bacon
Submarine Patrol	1938	TCF	John Ford

FILM	DATE	STUDIO	DIRECTOR
Submarine Pirate	1915	Tri	Syd Chaplin; Charles Avery
Submarine Raider	1942	Col	Lew Landers
Submarine Seahawk	1959	AI	Spencer Bennet
Suicide Fleet	1931	RKO	Albert Rogell
Task Force	1949	WB	Delmer Daves
They Were Expendable	1945	MGM	John Ford
Thirty Seconds Over Tokyo	1944	WB	Mervyn LeRoy
This Man's Navy	1945	MGM	William Wellman
Top Gun	1986	Par	Tony Scott
Tora! Tora! Tora!	1970	TCF	Richard Fleischer, Tashio Masuda, Kinji Fukasaku
Torpedo Alley	1953	AA	Lew Landers
Torpedo Run	1958	MGM	Joseph Peveny
Under Siege	1992	WB	Andrew Davis
Underwater Warrior	1958	MGM	Andrew Marton
Up Periscope	1959	WB	Gordon Douglas
Via Wireless	1915	Pathe	George Fitzmaurice
Wackiest Ship in the Army	1960	Col	Richard Murphy
We're in the Navy Now	1926	FPL	Edward Sutherland
When Hell Was in Session	1979	TV	Paul Crasny
Wing and a Prayer	1944	TCF	Henry Hathaway
Wings of Eagles	1956	MGM	John Ford
Wings of the Navy	1939	WB	Lloyd Bacon
Wings Over Honolulu	1937	Univ	H. C. Potter
You're in the Navy Now	1951	TCF	Henry Hathaway
Yours, Mine, and Ours	1968	UA	Mel Shavelson

KEY

Allied Artists	AA	Orion	Orion
American International	AI	Paramount	Par
Bing Crosby Productions	BCP	Pathe	Pathe
Castle Rock Productions	CR	Republic	Rep
Columbia	Col	RKO	RKO
Famous Players Lasky	FPL	Television	TV
First National	FN	Triangle Film Corporation	Tri
Hal Roach Studios	Roach	Twentieth Century Fox	TCF
Marble Arch Productions	MAP	United Artists	UA
Metro Goldwyn Mayer	MGM	Universal	Univ
Monogram	Mono	Vitagraph	Vita
New World Pictures	NWP	Walt Disney Company	Disney
One Way Productions	OWP	Warner Brothers	WB

Notes

Chapter 1. The Early Years

1. Author interviews with Naval officers who graduated from Annapolis during the 1920s and 1930s.
2. The author is indebted to Dr. Frederick Harrod for the information on the Navy's use of film before the United States' entry into World War I. In particular, see his "Managing the Medium: The Navy and Motion Pictures before World War I," in the *Velvet Light Trap*, 31 (Spring 1993): 48–58.
3. Frederick S. Harrod, *Manning the New Navy: The Development of a Modern Naval Enlisted Force, 1899–1940* (Westport, Conn.: Greenwood Press, 1978).
4. *Scientific American Supplement*, December 3, 1904, pp. 24, 180.
5. U.S. Navy Department, *Regulations for the Government of the Navy, 1913* (Washington: Government Printing Office, 1913), 78I (Instruction 714).
6. "Taking of Photographs, Passengers on Board Ships, Etc.," General Order 78, February 25, 1914.
7. Secretary of the Navy Josephus Daniels to International News Service, December 24, 1914, General Correspondence, RG 24, 5287-1259, National Archives ("National Archives" hereafter abbreviated as NA).
8. Josephus Daniels to E. B. Hatrick, International News Service, April 17, 1915, General Correspondence, RG 24, 5287-763, NA.
9. "*Via Wireless,*" *Weekly Variety*, September 24, 1915, p. 21.
10. W. S. Benson, Acting Secretary of the Navy, to Gaumont Company, July 16, 1915, General Correspondence, RG 24, 52878-865, NA.
11. Josephus Daniels to Daniel Frohman, October 12, 1915, General Correspondence, RG 24, 5287-952, NA; *New York Times*, November 8, 1915, p. 13.
12. Josephus Daniels to W. D. McGuire, Jr., Executive Secretary, National Board of Censorship, November 17, 1914, General Correspondence, RG 24, 5287-644, NA.

13. W. D. McGuire, Jr., to Josephus Daniels, January 7, 1915; Josephus Daniels to W. D. McGuire, Jr., January 11, 1915; W. D. McGuire, Jr., to Josephus Daniels, January 21, 1915. (General Correspondence, RG 24, 5287-644, NA.)

14. Elmer J. McGovern, assistant to the president of Keystone Film Company, to Josephus Daniels, July 1, 1915, General Correspondence, RG 24, 5287-644, NA.

15. R. H. Cochrane, vice-president, Universal Film Manufacturing Company, to Josephus Daniels, June 5, 1915, General Correspondence, RG 24, 5287-783, NA.

16. *Motography,* 14 (November 27, 1915): 1111; Charles Chaplin, *My Autobiography* (New York: Simon and Schuster, 1964), 160.

17. *Motography,* 14 (November 27, 1915): 1111; *New York Times,* November 15, 1915, p. 11.

18. *Weekly Variety,* March 10, 1916, p. 31.

19. Franklin Roosevelt to Hearst Pathe News, June 6, 1917, RG 24, Box 1011, NA.

20. Josephus Daniels to Admiral Coontz, July 14, 1920, RG 24, Box 1011, NA.

21. William Craft to Edwin Denby, February 16, 1922, RG 24, Box 1011, NA.

22. Ibid.

23. Edwin Denby to William Craft, March 2, 1922, RG 24, Box 1011, NA.

24. *Weekly Variety,* October 14, 1925.

25. An Alumnus to *Army Navy Journal,* May 13, 1925.

26. Arthur Barney to the Secretary of the Navy, June 18, 1925; Arthur Barney to the editor of *Army Navy Journal,* June 18, 1925. (RG 24, Box 1011, NA.)

27. Arthur Barney to the editor of *Army Navy Journal,* June 18, 1925, RG 24, Box 1011, NA.

28. *New York Times,* October 13, 1925, p. 20; *Weekly Variety,* October 14, 1925.

29. *Weekly Variety,* October 14, 1925.

30. *Weekly Variety,* February 6, 1929.

31. *Weekly Variety,* October 9, 1929.

32. Chief of Naval Operations to Commander in Chief, U.S. Fleet, August 9, 1926, RG 80, Box 433, NA.

33. Famous Players Lasky to Navy Department, October 21, 1926, RG 80, Box 433, NA; *Weekly Variety,* May 11, 1927; *New York Times,* May 9, 1927, p. 26.

34. Interview with Frank Capra, September 2, 1982; Frank Capra, *The Name Above the Title* (New York: Macmillan, 1971), 107–12; Capt. H. A. Jones to Adm. Sinclair Gannon, September 2, 1936, RG 80, Box 425, NA.

35. *Weekly Variety,* September 8, 1928, p. 26.

36. *New York Times,* February 11, 1929.

Chapter 2. The 1930s: The Golden Age of Navy Movies

1. Secretary of the Navy David S. Ingalls to All Bureaus and Offices, August 5, 1931, RG 80, Box 432, NA.

2. Ibid.

3. Commanding Officer, USS *Colorado* to CNO, August 11, 1931, RG 80, Box 432, NA.

4. Ibid.

5. Commander Battle Force to CNO, August 16, 1931; Navy Department Motion Picture Board to the CNO, August 29, 1931. (RG 80, Box 432, NA.)

6. Navy Department Motion Picture Board to the CNO, 29 August 1931, RG 80, Box 432, NA.

7. Ibid.; CNO to COMELEVEN, August 29, 1931, RG 80, Box 432, NA.

8. Samuel Goldwyn to Navy Motion Picture Board, June 3, 1932; Navy Motion Picture Board to CNO, June 8, 1932. (RG 80, Box 431, NA.)

9. Samuel Goldwyn to Navy Motion Picture Board, June 8, 1932; Navy Motion Picture Board to CNO, June 13, 1932. (RG 80, Box 431, NA.)

10. See author's *Guts & Glory* for a discussion of the making of these films.

11. *Weekly Variety,* February 4, 1931; CNO to Fox Films, September 11, 1930, RG 80, Box 432, NA.

12. CNO to Fox Films, January 30, 1931, RG 80, Box 432, NA; CNO to Commander in Chief, Battle Fleet, January 31, 1931, RG 80, Box 432, NA; *New York Times,* January 31, 1931. p. 15.

13. CNO to RKO Studios, July 3, 1931; CNO to Navy commands, July 11, 1931. (RG 80, Box 432, NA.)

14. Commander Frank Schofield to CNO, July 18, 1931, RG 80, Box 432, NA.

15. Ibid.

16. *Weekly Variety,* December 1, 1931; *New York Times,* November 26, 1931.

17. William Orr to Secretary of the Navy Charles Adams, September 28, 1931, RG 80, Box 432, NA.

18. Navy Motion Picture Board to CNO, October 17, 1931; CNO to William Orr, October 19, 1931. (RG 80, Box 432, NA.)

19. William Orr to the Chief of Naval Operations, October 28, 1931, RG 80, Box 432, NA.

20. Ibid.

21. Director of Naval Intelligence to CNO, October 31, 1931, RG 80, Box 432, NA.

22. Ibid.

23. Director, Central Division, to CNO, November 6, 1931; Acting CNO to William Orr, November 11, 1931. (RG 80, Box 432, NA.)

24. MGM to Secretary of the Navy Charles Adams, July 29, 1932, RG 80, Box 432, NA.

25. Navy Department Motion Picture Board to CNO, August 11, 1932; CNO to Louis Mayer, August 11, 1932. (RG 80, Box 432, NA.)

26. Morris Gilmore to CNO, August 12, 1932; Navy Department Motion Picture Board to CNO, August 13, 1932. (RG 80, Box 432, NA.)

27. CNO to Louis Mayer, August 20, 1932; CNO to Commanders, Battle Force, U.S. Fleet, August 20, 1932. (RG 80, Box 432, NA.)

28. Navy Department Motion Picture Board to the CNO, April 14, 1933, RG 80, Box 432, NA.

29. Ibid.

30. *New York Post,* April 26, 1933.

31. *New York Times,* April 26, 1933, p. 13.

32. Interview with Admiral John Will, May 22, 1974.

33. *Weekly Variety,* February 5, 1930.

34. Peter Bogdanovich, *John Ford,* rev. ed. (Berkeley and Los Angeles: University of California Press, 1978), 52.

35. Professional Pilots Association to CNO, September 27, 1930; CNO to Commanding Officer, Eleventh Naval District, October 2, 1930. (RG 80, Box 432, NA.)

36. Mordaunt Hall, "*Hell Divers,*" *New York Times,* December 23, 1931, p. 27.

37. CNO to MGM, July 22, 1931, RG 80, Box 432, NA.

38. William Wister Haines, "The Spig Wead Story," then titled "Eagle with Broken

Wings," January 18, 1955, MGM production files, University of Southern California Special Collections.

39. RKO Studios to the Navy Department, December 13, 1932, RG 80, Box 431, NA.

40. Ibid.; CNO to Herb Hirst, December 21, 1932, RG 80, Box 431, NA.

41. Interview with Gen. John Winston, September 20, 1977.

42. Ibid.

43. Ibid.; Orville Goldner and George Turner, *The Making of King Kong* (New York: Ballantine, 1976), 167–69.

44. Superintendent to CNO, June 5, 1933, RG 80, Box 431, NA.

45. Ibid.

46. *New York Times,* November 20, 1933, p. 18; *Weekly Variety,* November 20, 1933, p. 18.

47. *New York Times*, August 24, 1935, p. 18.

48. Ibid.

49. CNO to CinC US Fleet, July 10, 1935, RG 80, Box 432, NA; CNO to Warner Brothers, May 11, 1935, RG 80, Box 432, NA; *Weekly Variety*, October 23, 1935; *New York Times*, October 17, 1935, p. 29.

50. RKO Studios to the Secretary of the Navy, April 30, 1937, RG 80, Box 425, NA; RKO Studios to the CNO, May 18, 1937, RG 80, Box 425, NA; *New York Times*, October 2, 1937, p. 18.

51. *Weekly Variety,* November 10, 1937; Paramount Studios to the Secretary of the Navy, August 20, 1937, RG 80, Box 423, NA; CNO to Paramount Studios, August 26, 1937, RG 80, Box 423, NA.

52. William Orr to the Secretary of the Navy, July 12, 1937; Office of Naval Intelligence to the Motion Picture Board, July 12, 1937; Office of Naval Intelligence to the Motion Picture Board, July 12, 1937. (RG 80, Box 423, NA.)

53. CNO to Superintendent, Naval Academy, July 14, 1935; Superintendent to CNO, July 22, 1937. (RG 80, Box 423, NA.)

54. Superintendent to CNO, July 22, 1937, RG 80, Box 423, NA.

55. William Orr to the CNO, August 3, 1937, RG 80, Box 423, NA.

56. CNO to MGM, August 9, 1937; CNO to Superintendent, Naval Academy; CNO to MGM, November 9, 1937. (RG 80, Box 423, NA.)

57. *New York Times,* December 24, 1937, p. 21.

58. Ibid.

59. Secretary of the Navy to William Orr, October 29, 1930, RG 80, Box 432, NA.

60. CNO to CinC, October 29, 1930, RG 80, Box 432, NA.

61. CNO to MGM, January 19, 1931, RG 80, Box 432, NA; Delmer Daves to Paul Bern, January 22, 1931, Box 4, Item 12-A, Delmer Daves Papers, Stanford University Special Collections.

62. *New York Times,* May 23, 1931, p. 25.

63. William Orr to Secretary of the Navy Claude Swanson, February 8, 1935, RG 80, Box 429, NA.

64. Motion Picture Board to CNO, February 19, 1935, RG 80, Box 429, NA.

65. CNO to William Orr, March 2, 1935, RG 80, Box 429, NA.

66. Ibid.

67. William Orr to CNO, March 4, 1935, RG 80, Box 429, NA.

68. Navy Public Affairs Office to C. H. Baker, August 29, 1935, RG 80, Box 429; *New York Times,* June 3, 1935, p. 22.

69. Capt. F. E. M. Whiting to Lt. Cmd. B. L. Austin, June 25, 1940, RG 80, Box 416, NA.

Chapter 3. Hollywood Prepares for War

1. Sen. Elbert Thomas to Secretary of the Navy Claude Swanson, January 18, 1935; Secretary of the Navy Claude Swanson to Sen. Elbert Thomas, January 28, 1935. (RG 80, Box 429, NA.)
2. Secretary of the Navy Claude Swanson to Sen. Elbert Thomas, January 28, 1935, RG 80, Box 429, NA.
3. *Washington Herald,* January 22, 1935.
4. Ibid.
5. *New York Times,* February 7, 1935, p. 23.
6. Adm. W. H. Standley to Harry Cohn, 12 August 1936; Navy Department Motion Picture Board to CNO, August 12, 1936. (RG 80, Box 425, NA.)
7. *New York Times,* February 15, 1937; *Weekly Variety,* February 17, 1937, p. 12.
8. *Weekly Variety,* February 17, 1937, p. 14.
9. Interview with Jack Warner, Jr., April 4, 1974.
10. Spig Wead to Navy Department, July 28, 1936, RG 80, Box 426, NA.
11. Ibid.
12. Ibid.
13. Ibid.
14. CNO to Chief of Bureau of Construction and Repair and the Chief of Bureau of Engineering, May 14, 1937, RG 80, Box 425, NA.
15. John T. McManus, "Bringing Home the Bacon from New London," *New York Times,* 29 May 1937, p. 20; "*Submarine D-1:* Hand Book of Useful Information," Warner Brothers, n.d. [1937.]
16. McManus, "Bringing Home the Bacon," p. 20.
17. Ibid.
18. "*Submarine D-1:* Hand Book of Useful Information."
19. Ibid.; William Leahy to Warner Brothers, June 7, 1937, RG 80, Box 425, NA.
20. Frank Janata to Sen. Hamilton Lewis, December 29, 1937, RG 80, Box 425, NA.
21. Navy Department to Sen. Hamilton Lewis, January 19, 1938, RG 80, Box 425, NA.
22. Comment from Women's University Club, quoted in the Twentieth Century Fox publicity release.
23. *Weekly Variety,* November 2, 1938, p. 15; *Daily Variety,* September 29, 1938, p. 5.
24. *Variety,* April 13, 1938.
25. Capt. H. A. Badt to Navy Motion Picture Board, December 31, 1936, Box 425, NA.
26. Adm. J. J. Clark, *Carrier Admiral* (New York: David McKay, 1967), 63.
27. Clark, *Carrier Admiral,* 63; *New York Times,* May 29, 1937, p. 20.
28. Harold Turney, *Film Guide to "Wings of the Navy,"* Film Guide, Hollywood, California, 1938, cited hereafter as *Film Guide.*
29. Hal Wallis to the Secretary of the Navy Claude Swanson, September 30, 1937, RG 80, Box 423, NA; foreword to treatment of "Wings of the Navy," n.d. [before June 17, 1938], RG 80, Box 421, NA; CNO to Jack Warner, June 30, 1938, RG 80, Box 419, NA.
30. Warner Brothers Public Relations Release, n.d. [1938], *Wings of the Navy* file, Motion Picture Academy Library; *Film Guide.*
31. *New York Times,* February 4, 1939, p. 11.
32. *Weekly Variety,* January 18, 1939.
33. Robert Dana, *New York Herald Tribune,* January 17, 1941; *Weekly Variety,* December 18, 1940, p. 16.

34. Cdr. J. R. Poppen to Frank Wead, October 22, 1940, *Dive Bomber* production file, Warner Brothers Collection, USC Film Archives. Although naval records in the National Archives contain many of the same documents on the production of the film, all future citations in the discussion of *Dive Bomber* will come from the production file in the USC collection or are in the author's *Dive Bomber* file.

35. Marc Mitscher to Frank Wead, October 24, 1940.

36. Ass. Cdr. Eric Liljencrante to Frank Wead, November 19, 1940.

37. Ibid.

38. Original script, n.d. [November 1940.]

39. Ibid.

40. Walter MacEwen to Jack Warner and Hal Wallis, December 3, 1940.

41. Finlay McDermid, "Comparison of *Wings of the Navy* to 'Beyond the Blue Sky,'"December 5, 1940.

42. Ibid.

43. Ibid.

44. Walter MacEwen to Hal Wallis, December 11, 1940; Walter MacEwen to Bill Guthrie and Hal Wallis, December 17, 1940.

45. Robert Lord to Hal Wallis, February 11, 1941; Robert Lord to Hal Wallis, February 17, 1941; Robert Lord to Bill Guthrie, February 20, 1941.

46. Robert Lord to Hal Wallis, March 22, 1941; Robert Lord to Hal Wallis, March 24, 1941.

47. Robert Lord to Hal Wallis, March 24, 1941.

48. Robert Lord to Hal Wallis, May 20, 1941; CNO to Bureau of Aeronautics, June 23, 1941. (RG 80, Box 94, NA.)

49. Warner Brothers, interoffice memo on July 8, 1941; Robert Lord to Capt. Jack Poppen, July 14, 1941; Navy Motion Picture Board of Review to Robert Lord, July 29, 1941. (RG 80, Box 94, NA.)

50. Warner Brothers Press Release, n.d. [August 1941.]

51. *Daily Variety,* August 13, 1941.

52. Ibid.

53. E. C. Roworth to Secretary of the Navy Frank Knox, August 21, 1941, RG 80, Box 94, NA.

54. Ibid.

55. Arthur Keil to Frank Knox, December 1, 1941, RG 80, Box 94, NA.

56. Ens. Alan Brown to E. C. Roworth, August 26, 1941, RG 80, Box 94, NA.

57. Appendix to *Congressional Record,* Seventy-Seventh Congress, First Session, August 4, 1941, p. A3736.

58. *New York Times,* September 12, 1941, p. 2.

59. Hearings Before a Subcommittee of the Committee on Interstate Commerce, United States Senate, Seventy-Seventh Congress, First Session, pp. 339–40.

60. Interview with Ralph Bellamy, July 18, 1978.

Chapter 4. The Navy Goes to War

1. *New York Times,* November 12, 1942.

2. *New York Times,* March 12, 1943.

3. Conversation with Edward L. Beach, Captain, USN (Ret.), fall 1994.

4. It was not until the first week of July 1945 that Gene Fluckey, the captain of the

Barb, sent a raiding party ashore on the eastern coast of Karafuto to blow up a railroad bridge.

5. *New York Times,* April 29, 1943.

6. Frank Wead to Cdr. H. R. Thurber, June 9, 1941, RG 80, Box 95, NA.

7. Ibid.

8. Stuyvesant Wright to Louis Edelman, June 24, 1941, RG 80, Box 95, NA.

9. Louis Edelman to Stuyvesant Wright, July 15, 1941, RG 80, Box 95, NA.

10. Ibid.; interview with Louis Edelman, March 11, 1974.

11. Capt. F. E. M. Whiting to Cdr. Stuyvesant Wright, July 29, 1941, RG 80, Box 95, NA.

12. Stuyvesant Wright to Louis Edelman, July 30, 1941; Louis Edelman to Alan Brown, September 8, 1941. (RG 80, Box 95, NA.)

13. Alan Brown to Louis Edelman, September 12, 1941; Ens. Alan Brown to Louis Edelman, November 13, 1941. (RG 80, Box 95, NA.)

14. Ens. Alan Brown to Louis Edelman, February 6, 1942, RG 80, Box 95, NA.

15. Alan Brown to Louis Edelman, April 11, 1942, RG 80, Box 95, NA.

16. *Weekly Variety,* August 18, 1943; *New York Times,* September 2, 1943, p. 15.

17. Script of May 13, 1943, Delmer Daves papers; *Life,* January 24, 1944, p. 38.

18. Script of May 13, 1943. Unless otherwise noted, all citations to scripts, letters, memos, and other documents come from the *Destination Tokyo* file in the USC Film Archives.

19. Ibid.

20. Ibid.

21. Ibid.

22. Clair Blair, Jr., *Silent Victory,* 2 vols. (New York: J. B. Lippincott, 1973), 1:298–98.

23. Ibid., 299; Stanton Delaplane, "Via U.S. Sub to Japan and Back," *Liberty,* December 12 and 19, 1942; John Field, "West to Japan," *Life,* March 15, 1943, pp. 38–43; Irwin Shaw, "Faith at Sea," *New Yorker,* May 15, 1943; *Readers Digest,* August 1943; Robert Kent to Jerry Wald, interoffice communication, March 2, 1943; Finlay McDermid to Geller-Hanline, interoffice communication, July 28, 1943.

24. Daves interview, January 31, 1974; Delmer Daves to Steve Trilling, May 20, 1943, interoffice communication, Box 20, Daves Collection, Stanford University; interview with Albert Maltz, July 25, 1975.

25. Jack Warner to Jerry Wald, June 19, 1943, interoffice communication; Jack Warner to Delmer Daves, June 21, 1943, interoffice communication, *Destination Tokyo* file.

26. Joseph Breen to Jack Warner, 22 June 1943.

27. J. W. Coe, "Suggested Constructive Criticisms of Temporary Script—*Destination Tokyo* (From a Submariner's standpoint)."

28. Howell M. Forgy, cited in *Bartlett's Familiar Quotations.*

29. For the story of the involvement of the *Thresher* in Doolittle's raid, see Blair, *Silent Victory,* pp. 191–92. Life was to ultimately imitate art, since later in the war, American submarines did enter Tokyo Bay. Blair, *Silent Victory,* pp. 799–801; interview with Capt. Slade Cutter, June 21, 1975.

30. Daves Memo, May 20, 1943, Delmer Daves Papers; interview with Delmer Daves, January 31, 1974.

31. Bosley Crowther, *New York Times,* January 1, 1944, p. 9.

32. Steve Trilling to Jack Warner, November 19, 1943; Jack Warner to Secretary of Navy Frank Knox, November 24, 1943; Alan Brown to Bill Guthrie, November 25, 1943.

33. *Life,* January 24, 1944; *New York Times,* January 1, 1944.

34. Nathaniel Clik to Warner Brothers, 23 January 1944; Austin Day to Jack Warner, 15 March 1944.
35. Lt. Cdr. Alan Brown to Bill Guthrie, March 27, 1944.
36. Blair, *Silent Victory,* p. 851. While Hollywood would portray the sinking of American submarines in postwar movies, none received a direct hit, on screen, from a depth charge, setting loose a torrent of water on the crew, as happened to innumerable German and Japanese undersea craft.
37. Interview with John Wayne, February 7, 1974.
38. Bosley Crowther, *New York Times,* March 26, 1944; Wayne interview.
39. Wayne interview.
40. Ibid.
41. Philip Hartung, "*The Fighting Seabees,*" *Commonweal,* February 25, 1944, p. 471.
42. Bosley Crowther, *New York Times,* February 10, 1944.
43. Alvin Sunseri and Kenneth Lyftogt, "The Sullivan Family of Waterloo." This account comes from a pamphlet that the Friends of the Waterloo Public Library published in 1988; Dan Kuzman, *Left to Die: The Tragedy of the USS Juneau* (New York: Pocket Books, 1994).
44. Ibid.
45. Ibid.

46. Sidney L. James, "Torpedo Squadron 8," November 20, 1942, and Mortimer Braus, "Torpedo Squadron 8," January 8, 1943, *Wing and a Prayer* file, Twentieth Century Fox Collection, USC Film Archives. Unless otherwise indicated, all subsequent scripts, meeting notes, and other documents come from this file. *New York Times,* February 6, 1944, sec. 2, p. 3; Samuel Eliot Morison, *The Two-Ocean War* (Boston: Little, Brown, 1963, 156.
47. Jerry Cady, "Wing and a Prayer," October 26, 1943; *New York Times,* February 6, 1944, sec. 2, p. 3; Clark Reynolds, *The Fighting Lady* (Missoula, Mont.: Pictorial Histories Publishing, 1986), 14, 17.
48. Minutes of November 19, 1943, meeting.
49. Ibid.
50. Ibid.
51. Jerry Cady, *Wing and a Prayer,* temporary script, December 14, 1943; minutes of meeting, December 16, 1943; final script, December 27, 1943; revised final script, January 3, 1944; minutes of meeting, January 20, 1944; minutes of meeting, January 24, 1944.
52. Minutes of meeting, January 24, 1944.
53. Ibid.
54. *New York Times,* February 6, 1944, sec. 2, p. 3.
55. Morison, *Two-Ocean War,* 139–47.
56. The Navy tried to launch a plane from the hangar deck perhaps four times. Three ended in crashes. There is no way to determine if this was the successful launch.
57. Lars-Erik Nelson, "Where Did Reagan Hear That One?," *Washington Post,* January 1, 1984, p. H5.
58. *New York Times,* August 31, 1944.
59. Preface to *Thirty Seconds Over Tokyo* script, June 18, 1943.
60. Stan Cohen, *Destination Tokyo* (Missoula, Mont.: Pictorial Histories, 1983) 3–4.
61. Interview with Mervyn LeRoy, July 23, 1975; interview with Dore Schary, December 20, 1973; interview with Arnold Gillespie, July 14, 1975.
62. Gillespie interview; Bosley Crowther, *New York Times,* November 16, 1944, p. 19.

63. *Motion Picture Herald*, January 6, 1945.

64. *Daily Variety*, January 18, 1945.

65. "The New School," program notes by William K. Everson, February 23, 1973, Museum of Modern Art.

66. Ibid.

67. Ibid.; program notes, "Cinema Texas," October 26, 1978; interview with Ernie Saftig, March 15, 1974.

68. Bosley Crowther, *New York Times*, December 21, 1945, p. 25.

Chapter 5. Preparing for the Cold War

1. The information on the creation and operation of Donald Baruch's office comes from the author's several interviews and on-going discussions with Mr. Baruch for more than eighteen years, beginning in March 1973.

2. Original idea titled "Carrier Story," from Max Miller, March 11, 1944; *Task Force* file, USC Film Archives (unless otherwise noted, all letters, notes, memos, scripts, and other documents related to the making of *Task Force* are from this file); Delmer Daves, "Washington Interviews," n.d. [before March 17, 1944], Item 35 F, Box 26, Daves Collection, Stanford Library; Delmer Daves, "History of the Preparation and Making of the Film 'Task Force,'" Item 6, Box 33, Daves Collection, cited hereafter as "Making of *Task Force*." The author's interviews with Delmer Daves on January 31 and February 2, 1974, covered all aspects of the making of *Task Force*. The interviews will be cited only when quoting Daves directly.

3. Daves, "Washington Interviews."

4. Ibid.

5. Making of *Task Force*.

6. Jerry Wald, notes on meeting, February 1, 1945.

7. Ibid.; Jerry Wald to Gene Markey, February 22, 1945; George Boggs to Jerry Wald, May 22, 1945, Box 26, Item 11, Daves Collection.

8. Jerry Wald to Bill Guthrie, March 23, 1945; Jerry Wald to Bill Guthrie, March 23, 1945.

9. Foreword and story outline for "Task Force," June 11, 1945.

10. Ibid.

11. David Hopkins to Jerry Wald, June 25, 1945, Item 12, Box 26, Daves Collection.

12. Ibid.; interview with Capt. Alan Brown, March 27, 1974; Jerry Wald and Delmer Daves interstudio memo to Steve Trilling, July 31, 1945.

13. Jerry Wald, interstudio memo, August 23, 1945; Delmer Daves, "General Notes," September 19, 1945, Item 12, Box 33, Daves Collection.

14. J. S. Thach, "Comments," September 28, 1945, Item 27, Box 27, Daves Collection.

15. "For Spacious Skys" ("Task Force"), October 27, 1945, Item 14, Box 33, Daves Collection; *New York Times*, October 17, 1948, sec. 2, p. 5.

16. "Making of *Task Force*"; Delmer Daves, temporary script, July 9, 1948; E. M. Eller to George Dorsey, July 26, 1948, Item 38, Box 33, Daves Collection.

17. Harry Sears to Bill Guthrie, September 14, 1948, Box 33, Item 51, Daves Collection.

18. Warner Brothers' "Cast and Credits for *Task Force*," n.d. [September 1949.]

19. Ibid.

20. *New York Times*, September 4, 1949, p. 32; *Daily Variety*, September 28, 1949, p. 3.

21. Bosley Crowther, *New York Times*, October 1, 1949, p. 8.

22. Ibid. In fact, Twentieth Century Fox conceived the documentary while Henry Hathaway was aboard the *Yorktown*, shooting footage for *Wing and a Prayer*. However good a documentary *The Fighting Lady* became, it had its own share of inaccuracies and distortions.

23. Comments by J. S. Thach on script for *Task Force*, Item 27, Box 27, Daves Collection.

24. *New York Times*, December 25, 1950, p. 25.

25. Walter Mirisch to Office of the CNO, July 21, 1950, Department of Defense files (hereafter cited as DoD; see also note on sources).

26. Maj. Clair Towne to Walter Mirisch, August 2, 1950, Towne files (unless otherwise noted, all correspondence to and from Clair Towne is from Towne's personal files; see note on sources).

27. Ibid.

28. Walter Mirisch to Clair Towne, August 15, 1950.

29. Clair Towne to Walter Mirisch, September 25, 1950; Capt. R. G. Benson to Don Baruch, September 28, 1950. (DoD).

30. Clair Towne to Walter Mirisch, October 2, 1950; Walter Mirisch to Clair Towne, October 20, 1950; Walter Mirisch to Clair Towne, December 26, 1950; Clair Towne to R. G. Benson, January 3, 1951.

31. R. T. Swenson to Alan Brown, January 18, 1951, DoD.

32. Alan Brown to Clair Towne, January 19, 1951; Clair Towne to Walter Mirisch, January 22, 1951; Walter Mirisch to Clair Towne, January 26, 1951.

33. Walter Mirisch to Clair Towne, October 25, 1951; Clair Towne to Walter Mirisch, November 2, 1951; Walter Mirisch to Clair Towne, November 14, 1951; Adm. Thomas Dykers to Clair Towne, December 4, 1951.

34. Walter Mirisch to Clair Towne, December 4, 1951; Clair Towne to Walter Mirisch, January 5, 1952.

35. Richard Heermance to Donald Baruch, February 21, 1952, DoD.

36. Donald Baruch, memorandum for the record, March 13, 1952, DoD; Richard Heer-mance to Clair Towne, July 7, 1952; Clair Towne to Walter Mirisch, September 5, 1952.

37. *Hollywood Reporter*, November 13, 1952.

38. *Daily Variety*, November 13, 1952, p. 3.

Chapter 6. The Navy and Korea

1. In fact, from the end of World War II to the present day, no American submarin has launched a torpedo in anger.

2. *Time*, February 18, 1952, p. 88.

3. Lowell Redelings, "*Submarine Command* Deals with Crucial Decisions of War," *Hollywood Citizen-News*, December 7, 1951.

4. Bosley Crowther, "*Submarine Command*," *New York Times*, January 19, 1952, p. 9.

5. Ibid.

6. James Michener, "The Forgotten Heroes of Korea," *Saturday Evening Post*, May 10, 1952, p. 19.

7. Ibid., pp. 20–21, 124, 126.

8. Ibid., p. 128.

9. Orville Crouch to Clair Towne, June 19, 1952; Clair Towne to Orville Crouch, June 19, 1952.

10. Orville Crouch to Clair Towne, 18 February 1953; Cdr. Harry Burns, "The Case of the Blind Pilot," *Saturday Evening Post,* November 29, 1952; Clair Towne to Orville Crouch, 20 February 1953.

11. Clair Towne to Orville Crouch, March 11, 1953.

12. Orville Crouch to Clair Towne, March 26, 1953; Clair Towne to Orville Crouch, May 5, 1953; Orville Crouch to Clair Towne, June 4, 1953; Clair Towne to Orville Crouch, June 8, 1953.

13. Robert Denton to Clair Towne, July 7, 1953; Robert Denton to Clair Towne, July 7, 1953.

14. Conference Notes, July 8, 1953, DoD.

15. Memorandum for the record, July 8, 1953, DoD.

16. Memorandum for the record, July 10, 1953, DoD.

17. *Variety,* July 15, 1953.

18. Memorandum for the record, July 29, 1953, DoD.

19. Ibid.

20. Ibid.

21. Ibid.

22. Russell Holman to Clair Towne, July 30, 1953.

23. E. J. Mannix to Y. Frank Freeman, August 5, 1953, DoD.

24. Navy Office of Information to Donald Baruch, July 15, 1953, DoD.

25. Clair Towne to Orville Crouch, September 15, 1953.

26. Joanne D'Antonio, *Andrew Marton* (Metuchen, N.J.: Scarecrow Press, 1991), 243–44, 250, 254; interview with Andrew Marton, July 21, 1975; interview with Henry Berman, June 28, 1975.

27. Ibid.; Gladwin Hill, *New York Times,* November 1, 1953, sec. 2, p. 5.

28. D'Antonio, *Andrew Marton,* 254.

29. Bosley Crowther, *New York Times,* May 8, 1954, p. 54.

30. John Scott, *Los Angeles Times,* June 18, 1954; Hal Morris, *Los Angeles Mirror,* June 17, 1954.

31. Interview with George Seaton, March 4, 1974.

32. Ibid.

33. Clair Towne to Russell Holman, August 5, 1953.

34. Seaton interview; notes on first draft screenplay of *Bridges at Toko-ri,* July 22, 1953, DoD; *Daily Variety,* August 12, 1953; *Daily Variety,* September 9, 1953.

35. Robert Denton to Clair Towne, October 14, 1953.

36. Ibid.

37. Ibid.; Frank Caffey, "Requirements for the First Pre-Production Phase," October 9, 1953, accompanying Denton's letter.

38. Caffey, "Requirements."

39. Ibid.; Seaton interview; interview with Capt. Marshall Beebe, March 20, 1974.

40. Ibid.

41. Ibid.

42. Ibid.

43. Clair Towne to Navy Chief of Information, October 16, 1953.

44. Ibid.

45. Robert Denton to Clair Towne, October 22, 1953.

46. Robert Denton to Clair Towne, October 27, 1953; MGM to Clair Towne, October 29, 1953.

47. Clair Towne to Robert Denton, November 2, 1953.
48. Ibid.
49. Ibid.
50. Enclosure to Ibid.
51. Clair Towne to Robert Denton, November 2, 1953.
52. Ibid.
53. Robert Denton to Clair Towne, November 12, 1953; Clair Towne to Marshall Beebe, December 4, 1954.
54. James Michener, "The Writer's War," *Saturday Review*, January 22, 1955.
55. *Saturday Review,* January 22, 1955.
56. Ibid.
57. Ibid.
58. Walter Mirisch to Clair Towne, August 29, 1952, with attached treatment.
59. Clair Towne to Walter Mirisch, September 5, 1952; Walter Mirisch to Donald Baruch, September 24, 1954, DoD; Lewis Parks to Walter Mirisch, November 20, 1952, with attached comments from C. T. Joy, n.d., DoD.
60. Interview with Don Siegel, July 8, 1975.
61. *New York Times*, April 9, 1955.
62. Ibid.

Chapter 7. On the Surface in World War II

1. Robert Fellows to Clair Towne, July 3, 1952.
2. Clair Towne to Robert Fellows, July 16, 1952.
3. Capt. E. B. Dexter to E. L. Hinton, January 3, 1949.
4. John Horton to Leo Morrison, July 12, 1949; Leo Morrison to John Horton, July 19, 1949; John Horton, memo for the record, n.d. [around August 16, 1949]; Leo Morrison to John Horton, September 2, 1949; John Horton, memorandum for the record, November 21, 1949; John Horton to Tony Muto, December 2, 1949; James Cross, treatment of December 12, 1949, *Frogmen* file. (DoD).
5. Clair Towne, memorandum for the record, February 20, 1950.
6. H. E. Sears to Public Information Officer, Eleventh Naval District, May 1, 1950, DoD.
7. Darryl Zanuck to Sam Engle, July 1, 1950, *Frogmen* file, DoD.
8. Ibid.
9. Ibid.
10. Scripts in *Frogmen* file; Clair Towne, memorandum for the record, May 15, 1950; September 25, 1950, studio conference on revised outline, *Frogmen* file; Tony Muto to Clair Towne, November 6, 1950; Clair Towne, memorandum for the record, November 6, 1950; Clair Towne, memorandum for the record, November 8, 1950.
11. "Vital Statistics," Twentieth Century Fox, 1951.
12. *Saturday Review,* July 21, 1951.
13. *New York Times,* June 30, 1951.
14. *Weekly Variety,* February 27, 1952.
15. Clair Towne to George Dorsey, April 25, 1951.
16. Ibid.
17. Ibid.
18. Consensus of naval officers interviewed.
19. Letter from Adm. James Shaw to author, March 28, 1977; interview with Adm.

James Shaw, August 17, 1974; interview with Adm. Robert Hickey, March 19, 1974.

20. In fact, the sensational affair did have a positive effect, producing national support for a formal training program to replace the traditional method of educating midshipmen aboard ship. Although previous efforts to do this had failed, the *Somers* affair resulted in a mandate to the new Secretary of the Navy George Bancroft, one of America's leading historians, to establish the Naval Academy at Annapolis, in order to ensure high-caliber education for future naval officers. Shaw interview; Felix Riessenberg, *The Story of the Naval Academy* (New York: Random House, 1958), 40–41; Leonard F. Guttridge, *Mutiny* (Annapolis, Md.: Naval Institute Press, 1992), 87–116.

21. Interview with Col. Bill Call, January 13, 1976.

22. Hickey interview.

23. Interview with Stanley Kramer, February 8, 1974.

24. For a discussion of the making of *From Here to Eternity,* see author's *Guts & Glory.*

25. Kramer interview; Slade Cutter to author, June 13, 1974.

26. Slade Cutter to author, June 13, 1974.

27. Ray Bell to author, January 13, 1976.

28. Kramer interview.

29. Herman Wouk to author, undated, in reply to questions submitted December 20, 1975; Kramer interview.

30. Slade Cutter to author, June 13, 1974.

31. Kramer interview.

32. Interview with Ray Bell, April 8, 1975.

33. *Daily Variety,* November 25, 1952; Kramer interview.

34. *Christian Science Monitor,* July 21, 1953, p. 4; *Daily Variety,* November 26, 1952, pp. 1, 11; Cutter to author; interview with Capt. Slade Cutter, July 21, 1975; Shaw interview.

35. Interview with Adm. Lewis Parks, December 31, 1974; Kramer interview; *Daily Variety,* December 2, 1952, pp. 1, 4; *Daily Variety,* December 19, 1952, pp. 1, 8. Although Admiral Parks did not recall the meeting with Secretary of the Navy Kimball and Kramer, the producer remembers it in vivid detail and believes it was responsible for his obtaining cooperation.

36. Interview with Michael Blankfort, July 19, 1975; Shaw interview. Shaw, a highly decorated officer during the war, had later worked with Samuel Eliot Morrison on the writing of the Navy's official history of World War II.

37. Kramer interview; Shaw interview.

38. Adm. Lewis Parks to Ray Bell, n.d. [after September 1953.]

39. *Daily Variety,* January 21, 1954, p. 4.

40. Wouk to author.

41. Interview with Josiah Bunting, December 23, 1974.

42. Kramer interview; *Newsweek,* October 17, 1960.

43. Interview with James Jones, December 30, 1974.

44. Don Baruch, memorandum for the record, September 23, 1953, DoD; Clair Towne, memorandum for the record, n.d. [September 1953.]

45. Clair Towne to George Dorsey, September 30, 1953.

46. A. J. Bolton to DoD Public Information Office, May 3, 1954; George Dorsey to Donald Baruch, May 25, 1954; Donald Baruch, memorandum for the record, June 3, 1954. (DoD).

47. A. H. Weiler, *New York Times,* July 15, 1955.
48. *Time,* August 27, 1956.
49. Interview with Wendall Mayes, March 6, 1974.
50. Ibid.; interview with Capt. Herbert Hetu, April 3, 1975.
51. Ibid.
52. *Time,* January 13, 1958; Stanley Kaufman, *New Republic*; Edwin Schallert, *Los Angeles Times,* January 1, 1958.
53. Navy Office of Information to Donald Baruch, March 6, 1957; Donald Baruch to Ellen McDonnell, March 8, 1957. (DoD).
54. Richard Dyer MacCann, "Hollywood Letter," *New York Times,* 1960.
55. *Newsweek,* May 23, 1960.
56. Philip Scheuer, "Cagney Describes Two Adm. Halseys," *Los Angeles Times,* June 10, 1960.
57. MacCann, "Hollywood Letter."
58. Jesse Zunser, *Cue,* June 18, 1960.

Chapter 8. Submarines versus Aircraft Carriers

1. Clair Towne, memorandum for the record, July 29, 1952.
2. John Horton to George Waggner, November 18, 1949; John Wayne to John Horton, November 25, 1949. (DoD).
3. Draft screenplay, dated April 21, 1950, *Operation Pacific* file, USC Film Library.
4. Clair Towne to George Dorsey, May 22, 1950.
5. Ibid.
6. Ibid.
7. Interstudio memo from Charles Lockwood to Bill Guthrie, June 8, 1950, DoD.
8. Scripts in *Operation Pacific* file; George Dorsey to Clair Towne, August 2, 1950; Navy Director of Public Relations to Donald Baruch, August 10, 1950. (DoD).
9. Navy Director of Public Relations to Donald Baruch, August 10, 1950, DoD.
10. Clair Towne to George Dorsey, August 11, 1950.
11. George Dorsey to Bill Guthrie, August 11, 1950; excerpts from telephone conversation between Lou Edelman and Clair Towne, August 11, 1950, *Operation Pacific* file.
12. Ibid.; Clair Towne to Navy Office of Public Relations, August 16, 1950; Clair Towne to Charles Lockwood, August 18, 1950.
13. *New Yorker,* February 10, 1951.
14. *Weekly Variety,* May 5, 1957.
15. Charles S. Aaronson, "Submarines 'come alive' for visitor at New London *Hellcats* Premiere," *Motion Picture Herald,* April 20, 1957.
16. Ibid.
17. Delmer Daves, "Notes on *Run Silent, Run Deep,*" n.d. [1955?], Daves Collection.
18. Interview with Robert Wise, April 10, 1974.
19. Interview with Capt. Edward L. Beach, May 30, 1974. In fact, the commander who perfected the technique later disappeared on a combat cruise.
20. Bosley Crowther, "*Run Silent, Run Deep,*" *New York Times,* March 28, 1958, p. 29.
21. Bosley Crowther, *New York Times,* October 25, 1958, p. 16.
22. *Submarine Seahawk,* January 28, 1959.
23. Jack Moffitt, *Hollywood Reporter,* February 11, 1959; A. H. Weiler, *New York Times,* March 5, 1959, p. 35.

24. Columbia Studios, "Production Notes, *Battle of the Coral Sea,*" n.d.; interview with Paul Wendkos, August 4, 1975; *Weekly Variety,* October 14, 1959.

25. George Dorsey to Donald Baruch, January 8, 1957, DoD.

26. Navy Office of Information to Donald Baruch, January 23, 1957; Wallace Marley to George Dorsey, January 25, 1957. (DoD).

27. Blair, *Silent Victory,* pp. 111, 148, 172–74; *Los Angeles Times,* December 5, 1959; obituary for Rear Adm. J. C. Dempsey, *Washington Post,* July 12, 1979, p. B6; Robert Arthur to George Dorsey, June 6, 1958. (DoD).

28. *Los Angeles Mirror-News,* February 23, 1959; interviews with Robert Arthur, March 7 and 29, 1974; interview with Adm. Lucius Chappell, August 7, 1975.

29. Robert Arthur to George Dorsey, June 6, 1958; Arthur interviews.

30. Army Technical Liaison Office to Army Chief of Information, July 14, 1958.

31. Wallace Marley to George Dorsey, July 21, 1958; Donald Baruch to Robert Arthur, September 16, 1959.

32. Bosley Crowther, *New York Times,* December 6, 1959, p. 38.

33. Quotes from *Wings of Eagles.*

34. Biography of Commander Frank W. Wead, Naval Historical Center.

35. Frank Wead biography, Columbia Pictures, August 1941, Motion Picture Academy Library.

36. MGM biographical information, June 2, 1944.

37. Kenneth MacKenna to Donald Baruch, November 2, 1954, DoD.

38. "Comments on the Spig Wead Story," n.d. [September 1955]; Motion Picture Section, DoD Public Affairs, to Chief, Navy Public Information Division, October 14, 1955; Navy Chief of Information to Donald Baruch, November 1, 1955. (DoD).

39. Donald Baruch to Orville Crouch, November 4, 1955, DoD.

40. Navy Chief of Information to Adm. John Dale Price, March 23, 1956; Navy Chief of Information to Donald Baruch, March 29, 1956. (DoD).

41. Adm. John Dale Price to Office of Chief of Information, May 10, 1956; Office of the Chief of Information to Adm. John Dale Price, May 18, 1956. (DoD).

42. *New York Times,* September 9, 1956, sec. 2, p. 7.

43. J. A. Place, *The Non-Western Films of John Ford* (Secaucus, N.J.: Citadel Press, 1979), 136–37.

44. *Newsweek,* February 11, 1957, p. 89; Bosley Crowther, *New York Times,* February 1, 1957, p. 28.

45. Dick French to Office of Secretary of Defense, n.d. [April 9, 1957.]

46. Donald Baruch to Dick French, April 24, 1957, DoD.

Chapter 9. World War II Again and the Bomb

1. *Congressional Record,* September 8, 1961, pp. 18733–735.

2. Ibid., pp. 18733–736; *Time,* September 8, 1961.

3. *Daily Variety,* September 20, 1961, p. 7. For a detailed discussion of controversy over the making of *The Longest Day* and the changes in regulations governing cooperation, see the author's *Guts & Glory,* chapters 8 and 9. Interviews with Arthur Sylvester on August 16, 1973, and December 23, 1974, provided insights into the secretary's thinking on cooperation.

4. *Daily Variety,* January 30, 1962, pp. 1, 15.

5. Charles Greenlow to Bill Hendricks, Warner Brothers interoffice communication,

April 11, 1960; DoD Office of News Services to Warner Brothers, July 19, 1960. See author's *Guts & Glory,* chapter 8, for a full discussion of the cooperation Darryl Zanuck received from the Defense Department in making *The Longest Day.*

6. Bertram Kalish, "Premise for Considering Approval of *No Man is an Island,*" n.d. [February 1962.]

7. Navy Office of Information to Donald Baruch, August 8, 1961, DoD.

8. E. A. Dougherty to Richard Goldstone and John Monks, Jr., August 11, 1961, DoD.

9. John Monks, Jr., and Richard Goldstone to E. A. Dougherty, August 16, 1961.

10. Navy Office of Information to Donald Baruch, September 19, 1961; E. A. Dougherty to Richard Goldstone and John Monks, Jr., September 25, 1961. (DoD).

11. Richard Goldstone and John Monks, Jr., to E. A. Dougherty, September 28, 1961; E. A. Dougherty to Richard Goldstone and John Monks, Jr., October 18, 1961; Navy Chief of Information to Chief, Audio-Visual Division, Department of Defense, July 23, 1962; Chief, Audio-Visual Division, memo for the record, July 30, 1962. (DoD).

12. Hubert Humphrey to Arthur Sylvester, June 14, 1962; Arthur Sylvester to Hubert Humphrey, June 30, 1962. (DoD).

13. Interview with Sy Bartlett, February 9, 1974; interview with Gen. Arno Leuhman, July 1, 1975; interview with Gen. Curtis LeMay, August 17, 1975; Baruch interviews.

14. *Newsweek,* July 23, 1962, p. 72; interview with Leslie Martinson, July 10, 1975; phone conversation with Leslie Martinson, November 23, 1994.

15. Interview with Jack Warner, Jr., April 4, 1974; *New York Times,* March 9, 1961; Pierre Salinger to Secretary of the Navy Fred Korth, January 6, 1962; interview with Pierre Salinger, August 16, 1979.

16. Interview with George Stevens, Jr., January 9, 1980.

17. Ibid.

18. Ibid.; Pierre Salinger, *With Kennedy* (Garden City, N.Y.: Doubleday, 1966), 103–4.

19. Ibid.; George Stevens, Jr., to Pierre Salinger, March 1, 1962, DoD.

20. Stevens to Salinger, March 1, 1962, DoD; interview with Fred Zinnemann, October 12, 1979; letter from Fred Zinnemann to author, June 30, 1994; Salinger, *With Kennedy,* 104.

21. Jack Warner to John Kennedy, March 22, 1962; Salinger interview; Salinger, *With Kennedy,* 104; Bill Davidson, "President Kennedy Casts a Movie," *Saturday Evening Post,* September 8, 1962, p. 26.

22. Salinger, *With Kennedy,* 104; Davidson, "President Kennedy Casts a Movie," 26.

23. Jack Warner to John Kennedy, June 11, 1962, DoD; *Newsweek,* July 23, 1962.

24. Salinger, *With Kennedy,* 104–05; Martinson interview; Salinger interview; *Newsweek,* July 23, 1962; Martinson phone conversation.

25. Martinson interview; Martinson phone conversation.

26. *Newsweek,* July 23, 1962.

27. Ibid.; Martinson phone conversation.

28. *New York Times,* October 2, 1962; Martinson phone conversation.

29. *Wall Street Journal,* July 12, 1962, p. 1; *Time,* July 13, 1962, p. 54; Davidson, "President Kennedy Casts a Movie," 26–27.

30. Interview with Pierre Salinger, June 29, 1994.

31. Kenneth Clark to Charles Boren, August 8, 1962, DoD.

32. *New York Times,* October 2, 1962.

33. Sylvester interview, August 16, 1973.

34. Jack Hirschberg, "Preminger Invades Hawaii," *New York Times,* September 6, 1964, sec. 2, p. 5.

35. Otto Preminger, "Keeping out of Harm's Way," *Films and Filming,* 1965, p. 6; interview with Otto Preminger, August 16, 1973.

36. Preminger interview.

37. Interview with Capt. Blake Booth, August 16, 1974; letter from Capt. C. J. Mackenzie to author, August 8, 1975; interview with Capt. C. J. Mackenzie, August 28, 1994.

38. Ibid. In fact, Preminger did more for Wayne in the movie than Wayne did for the Navy. When the director completed the production ahead of schedule, the actor had a chance to have a complete physical, which revealed he had lung cancer. Preminger claimed therefore that he saved Wayne's life.

39. *Weekly Variety,* March 31, 1965.

40. *Time,* April 9, 1965, pp. 102–3; *Los Angeles Times,* April 9, 1965, pt. 5, p. 15.

41. *Cleveland Plain Dealer,* June 2, 1965; Preminger interview.

42. Stanley Kramer, "*On the Beach*: A Renewed Interest," 117; Nevil Shute, *On the Beach* (New York: William Morrow, 1957), 67–71.

43. Rudolph Sternad to Donald Baruch, May 28, 1958, DoD.

44. Navy Office of Information to Donald Baruch, June 9, 1958, DoD.

45. Director, Motion Picture Service, USIA, to Donald Baruch, June 24, 1958, DoD.

46. Donald Baruch to Rudolph Sternad, July 1, 1958, DoD.

47. Rudolph Sternad to Donald Baruch, July 17, 1958; Donald Baruch to Rudolph Sternad. (DoD).

48. Bertam Kalisch, memo for the record, August 27, 1958.

49. Ibid.

50. Ibid.; C. C. Kirkpatrick to Donald Baruch, October 20, 1958, DoD.

51. C. C. Kirkpatrick to Donald Baruch, October 29, 1958; Donald Baruch to Stanley Kramer, November 4, 1958. (DoD).

52. Baruch to Kramer, November 4, 1958, DoD.

53. Ibid.

54. U. S. G. Sharp, Office of Chief of Naval Operations, to Chief of Information, December 5, 1958, DoD.

55. Ibid.

56. Donald Baruch to DoD Office of Plans and Programs, December 8, 1959, DoD.

57. Shute, *On the Beach,* 238.

58. Ironically, looking back, Kramer wondered if the closing statement "offered enough hope." Kramer, "*On the Beach*: A Renewed Interest," 118.

59. One of the few changes that Kramer made in transferring novel to the screen was having the lovers consummate their relationship. Although Shute complained, Kramer believed it was realistic: "Peck's memory of wife and children was not damaged: they were dead. It was sacrifice enough that Peck finally took the submarine home from Australia to satisfy his crew and left Gardner behind." Kramer, "*On the Beach*: A Renewed Interest," 118.

60. Donald Baruch to Myer Beck, September 18, 1959, DoD.

61. Baruch to DoD Office of Plans and Programs, December 8, 1959, DoD; *Chicago Tribune,* February 4, 1959; Kramer interview.

62. *Newsweek,* October 17, 1960.

63. Bell interview.

64. Ibid.

65. Ibid.; *Variety,* October 17, 1962, p. 5.
66. Ted Sorenson, *Kennedy* (New York: Harper & Row, 1965), 606–7; Gerald Pratly, *The Cinema of John Rankenheimer* (New York: A. S. Barnes, 1969), 114.
67. Pratly, *The Cinema of John Rankenheimer,* 114.
68. Donald Baruch to Kenneth Clark, Vice President, Motion Picture Association, August 16, 1963, DoD; *Washington Post,* November 3, 1963, p. G2.
69. Ibid.
70. Donald Baruch to the Motion Picture Association of America, August 16, 1963, DoD.
71. Edward Lewis to author, October 25, 1976.
72. Interview with James Harris, February 25, 1974; interview with James Poe, August 4, 1975.
73. James Poe to Ray Bell, Richard Widmark, and James Harris, June 14, 1964, James Poe Papers, UCLA Special Collections.
74. Ibid.; *Daily Variety,* August 3, 1964, p. 4.
75. Ibid.; Harris interview; interview with Capt. J. D. Ferguson, April 5, 1975.
76. Ferguson interview.
77. Ibid.; Harris interview.
78. Ferguson interview.
79. Ibid.
80. Bell interview; Ferguson interview.
81. Harris interview.
82. Howard Horton to Donald Baruch, March 5, 1965, DoD.
83. *Daily Variety,* April 9, 1965, p. 2.
84. Louella Parsons, "*Zebra* Has Navy Trouble," *Los Angeles Herald-Examiner,* April 19, 1965, p. D7; Howard Horton to Donald Baruch, May 7, 1965, DoD.
85. Howard Horton to Orville Crouch, June 2, 1965, DoD.
86. *Daily Variety,* August 4, 1967; *Hollywood Reporter,* October 2, 1967; MGM, "Facts Book for Editorial Reference," n.d. [1969.]

Chapter 10. *Tora! Tora! Tora!* and Vietnam

1. Navy Public Affairs Office to Alexander Jacobs, November 17, 1967; John Beck to Department of the Navy, August 28, 1967. (DoD).
2. *New York Times,* October 4, 1970, sec. 2, p. 1.
3. Vincent Canby, "The Last Tycoon," *New York Times Magazine,* March 17, 1968, p. 33; *New York Times,* June 16, 1969, p. A24; *Washington Post,* June 16, 1969, p. 10.
4. *Los Angeles Times Calendar,* June 15, 1969, p. 22.
5. Interview with Elmo Williams, March 18, 1974.
6. Ibid.
7. Ibid.
8. Ibid.
9. Ibid.; "Final Information Guide," Twentieth Century Fox, n.d. [1970.]
10. Ibid.
11. *Air Classics,* February, 1969, pp. 15, 20, 62, 66; interview with Capt. George Watkins, December 10, 1977.
12. Williams interview; "Department of Defense Assistance to Twentieth Century Fox Corporation in the Production of *Tora! Tora! Tora!,*" 1969.
13. Williams interview; interview with Richard Fleischer, June 26, 1975.

14. Navy memo, August 9, 1967, DoD.

15. Confidential Navy memo, October 15, 1968, DoD; Fleischer interview.

16. Navy memo, August 9, 1967, DoD; "Review of Support Provided by the Department of Defense to the Twentieth Century Fox Film Corporation for the Film *Tora! Tora! Tora!* by the Comptroller General of the United States, February 17, 1970."

17. Daniel Henkin to Twentieth Century Fox, February 2, 1968, DoD.

18. Twentieth Century Fox to Department of Defense, August 1, 1968; Department of Defense to Twentieth Century Fox, August 27, 1968, DoD.

19. Department of Defense to Twentieth Century Fox, August 27, 1968, DoD.

20. Williams interview; Watkins interview; interview with Phil Goulding, April 4, 1975.

21. Navy memo to Phil Goulding, October 11, 1968, DoD.

22. Goulding interview; interoffice memo to Phil Goulding, October 8, 1968, DoD.

23. Confidential Navy memo, October 15, 1968, DoD.

24. Jack Valenti to Phil Goulding and to Clark Clifford, October 3, 1968, DoD.

25. Jack Valenti to Clark Clifford, October 23, 1968, DoD; interview with Jack Valenti, November 11, 1976.

26. Phil Goulding to Clark Clifford, October 24, 1968, DoD.

27. Interview with Paul Nitze, April 8, 1975; *Sixty Minutes,* May 13, 1969.

28. Department of Defense Project Officer's Final Report, July 1969, DoD.

29. Interview with Capt. Edward Stafford, April 7, 1975; Watkins interview; Fleischer interview.

30. Vincent Canby, *New York Times,* October 4, 1970, sec. 2, pp. 1, 7.

31. Ibid.

32. Fleischer interview; Stafford interview; *Sixty Minutes,* May 13, 1969.

33. Interview with Bill Brown, January 9, 1976.

34. Interview with Bill Brown; Phil Goulding to the Navy Department, November 27, 1968, DoD; Twentieth Century Fox to Department of Defense, November 29, 1968, DoD; *Navy Times,* October 7, 1970, p. 29; *Honolulu Star-Bulletin,* December 13, 1968, p. B1; *Navy Times,* December 13, 1968. As part of its response to Bill Brown's request for research information in preparing his *60 Minutes* feature, the Department of Defense Office of General Counsel ruled on April 2, 1969, that the correspondence between Twentieth Century Fox and the Pentagon could be made available to CBS under the Freedom of Information Act. Ironically, CBS had a television van aboard the *Yorktown* to cover the Apollo landing. Stafford interview; Baruch interviews; Department of Defense file on *Tora! Tora! Tora!*; GAO Report of February 17, 1970; Military Operations Subcommittee staff memorandum of Committee on Government Operations, House of Representatives, December, 1969, DoD.

35. *Hollywood Citizen-News,* December 30, 1964.

36. Arthur Hiller, *Los Angeles Times Calendar,* January 3, 1965, p. 7.

37. *Newsweek,* November 2, 1964, p. 96; interview with Paddy Chayefsky, May 28, 1964; interview with Arthur Hiller, March 14, 1974.

38. Hiller, *Los Angeles Times Calendar,* p. 7.

39. Ibid.

40. Ibid.

41. Interview with Martin Ransohoff, March 1, 1974; Drew Pearson, *Washington Post,* January 27, 1965, p. D15.

42. *New York Times,* October 28, 1964, p. 51.

43. Hiller interview.

44. Bosley Crowther, "*The Sand Pebbles,*" *New York Times,* December 21, 1966, p. 48.

45. Ibid.

46. Interview with Lt. William Harding, April 11, 1974; interview with Mark Rydell, September 3, 1975; interview with Donald Baruch, August 16, 1976; interview with Adm. Jack Garrow, April 18, 1990.

47. Baruch interviews.

48. Rydell interview; Valenti interview.

49. Baruch interview; Valenti interview; Garrow interview.

50. Rydell interview.

51. Gerald Ayres to Donald Baruch, August 17, 1972, DoD.

52. Baruch memo for the record, August 24, 1972; Defense Department memo to the Navy, August 25, 1972; Gerald Ayres to Don Baruch, n.d. [before August 28, 1972.] (DoD).

53. Navy memo to DoD Public Affairs Office, September 7, 1972; Gerald Ayres to the Navy Department, October 2, 1972. (DoD).

54. Ayres to the Navy, October 2, 1972, DoD.

55. Ibid.

56. Cdr. Jack Garrow to Gerald Ayres, October 19, 1972, DoD.

57. Ibid.

58. *New York Times,* September 5, 1976, sec. 2, p. 9; *New York Times,* December 5, 1976, sec. 2, p. 13.

59. Interview with Adm. John Will, May 22, 1974.

60. Garrow interview.

61. The voluminous DoD file on *Apocalypse Now* contains no request for Navy assistance; Francis Coppola to President Jimmy Carter, February 12, 1977, DoD.

62. *Daily Variety,* February 27, 1987, pp. 73, 86; Donald Baruch to Assistant Secretary of Defense for Public Affairs Robert Sims, April 16, 1986, DoD. The Navy had had a similar problem in 1983 responding to a request for assistance in making *The Philadelphia Experiment.* The service had refused to cooperate in the production, arguing it could not associate itself with an occurrence it claimed had never happened. See chapter 13.

63. Donald Baruch to Robert Sims, April 16, 1986, DoD.

64. Ibid.

65. Donald Baruch to Jonathan Avnet, April 30, 1986; Donald Baruch to Col. O'Brien, Internal Security, May 28, 1986; Jonathan Avnet to Defense Information Agency, August 4, 1986. (DoD).

66. Jonathan Avnet to Robert Sims, August 15, 1986; Robert Sims to Jonathan Avnet, September 9, 1986. (DoD).

67. Interview with Rick Nankin, December 14, 1988.

Chapter 11. A Return to Normalcy

1. Cdr. Bill Graves to Navy Chief of Information, November 20, 1974.

2. Ibid.; Donald Baruch to Director, Defense Information, August 15, 1974, DoD.

3. Emerson Batdorff, "Gun Camera Movies Intensify *Midway,*" *Cleveland Plain Dealer,* January 25, 1976, sec. 4, pp. 1–2.

4. John Horton to Donald Baruch, November 6, 1974; Donald Baruch to Norm Hatch, November 19, 1974. (DoD).

5. Navy memorandum, December 19, 1974; *Lexington* to *Cnaira,* Corpus Christi, Texas, December 26, 1974; Navy memorandum, December 30, 1974. (DoD).

6. Ibid.; *After the Battle,* Number 15, 1977, pp. 34–35.

7. *After the Battle,* p. 35; interview with Robert Swink, July 25, 1978.

8. Vincent Canby, *New York Times,* June 19, 1976, p. 11.

9. Interview with William W. Mirisch, January 6, 1989.

10. Canby, *New York Times,* June 19, 1976, p. 11.

11. Interview with Frank McCarthy, July 31, 1978.

12. Adm. David Cooney to Frank McCarthy, July 27, 1976, DoD.

13. Ibid.

14. *MacArthur* production notes; after-action report to the Navy Chief of Information, June 22, 1977, DoD; *Daily Variety,* August 24, 1976.

15. After-action report to Navy Chief of Information, June 22, 1977, DoD.

16. Universal production notes, February 1, 1977; interview with Frank Rosenberg, July 12, 1978.

17. Universal production notes, February 1, 1977; Rosenberg interview.

18. BCP to Donald Baruch, February 12, 1973; Don Baruch, memo for the record, March 1973; Don Baruch, memo for the record, July 25, 1973; Don Baruch, memo for the record, August 21, 1973. (DoD).

19. Chief of Information to Don Baruch, n.d. [mid-August 1973.]

20. Ibid.

21. Don Baruch, memo for the record, August 21, 1973; Frank Rosenberg to Navy Office of Information, August 23, 1973; Navy Chief of Information to Don Baruch, September 18, 1973. (DoD).

22. Donald Baruch to Frank Rosenberg, September 20, 1973, DoD.

23. Frank Rosenberg to Don Baruch, November 7, 1974, DoD.

24. Norm Hatch to Navy, November 12, 1974; Navy Office of Information to Donald Baruch, December 2, 1974; Donald Baruch to Frank Rosenberg, December 4, 1974. (DoD).

25. Interview with Capt. Bill Graves, July 19, 1978; Robert Aldrich to Donald Baruch, November 4, 1975, DoD; Aldrich to Baruch, November 4, 1975, DoD; Navy Operations Office to Chief of Information, November 18, 1975, DoD; Don Baruch to Chief of Information, November 18, 1975, DoD; Navy Office of Information to Donald Baruch, December 9, 1975, DoD.

26. Telephone interview with Marvin Mirisch, March 22, 1978.

27. Ibid.; John Horton to Donald Baruch, January 13, 1976.

28. Ibid.; Donald Baruch to Marshall Green, January 16, 1976, DoD.

29. Navy Office of Information, "Special News Items of Interest," January 19, 1976; Don Baruch intraoffice memorandum, January 20, 1976. (DoD).

30. Navy memorandum for the record, January 26, 1976; Marvin Mirisch interview, March 22, 1978.

31. Donald Baruch, memo for the record, January 28 and 29, 1976; Rosenberg interview.

32. Memorandum for the Chief of Information, May 10, 1976, DoD.

33. Navy Memo for the Chief of Information, May 21, 1976, DoD.

34. David Cooney to Walter Mirisch, May 25, 1976, DoD.

35. Ibid.

36. Bill Graves to David Cooney, June 15, 1976, DoD.

37. Ibid.

38. Ibid.

39. Assistant Deputy Chief of Naval Operations (Submarine Warfare)(OP-02B) to Chief of Information, July 15, 1976, DoD.

40. David Cooney to Donald Baruch, July 16, 1976, DoD.

41. Don Baruch to John Horton, November 23, 1977, DoD.

42. Conversation with Lt. Cdr. Mel Sundin and author, at Pearl Harbor, June 15, 1983.

43. "TV Week," *Washington Post,* March 1, 1986, p. 9.

44. Charles Champlin, "Delayed Horror in *Gray Lady,*" *Los Angeles Times*, March 10, 1978, sec. 4, p. 21.

45. Graves interview.

46. Richard Schickel, *Time,* March 27, 1978, p. 81.

47. Ibid.

48. Gary Arnold, "*Gray Lady Down*: The Intrigue of Technology," *Washington Post,* March 11, 1980, p. B8.

49. Don Baruch's comment on Adam Kennedy's "Raise the Titanic" screenplay, n.d. [June 1977]; Charles Schreger, "Preproduction: A Titanic Task," *Los Angeles Times*, October 20, 1979, pt. 2, p. 6.

50. Bill Graves to Marble Arch Productions, October 12, 1978, DoD.

51. Navy Office of Information to Don Baruch, May 16, 1979, DoD.

52. Donald Baruch to Navy Office of Information, October 2, 1979; Navy Office of Information to Donald Baruch, October 15, 1979. (DoD.)

53. George Bader for Secretary James Siena to Donald Baruch, October 17, 1979, DoD.

54. Navy Office of Information to Donald Baruch, October 22, 1979, DoD.

55. State Department Bureau of European Affairs to State Department Office of Public Communications, October 24, 1979, DoD.

56. George Bader to Donald Baruch, October 29, 1979, DoD.

57. Donald Baruch to Navy Office of Information, October 31, 1979; Navy Office of Information to Don Baruch, October 31, 1979. (DoD.)

58. Donald Baruch to Navy Office of Information, November 13, 1979, DoD.

59. Don Baruch to John Horton, November 20, 1979, DoD.

60. Interview with Adm. David Cooney, April 2, 1981.

61. Richard O'Connor to Donald Baruch, August 20, 1980; interview with Richard O'Connor, August 7, 1981.

62. Ibid.

63. *Time,* March 30, 1981, p. 71; *Daily Variety,* August 1, 1980.

64. Judy Maslin, *New York Times,* August 1, 1980, B1.

65. *Raise the Titanic,* "Production Information," DoD.

66. Donald Baruch to Navy Office of Information, June 17, 1975.

67. Thomas Hunter to Donald Baruch, n.d. [Summer 1975.] (DoD).

68. Navy Office of Information to Donald Baruch, June 30, 1975; Don Baruch to Capt. C. D. Griffin, July 2, 1975; C. D. Griffin to Don Baruch, May 21, 1976. (DoD.)

69. Don Baruch to C. D. Griffin, June 3, 1976; C. D. Griffin to Don Baruch, August 30, 1976. (DoD).

70. Interview with Peter Douglas, August 3, 1981. Unless otherwise noted, all information about Douglas's production of *The Final Countdown* comes from this interview. A small file exists in DoD on "The Last Countdown," the story which Douglas acquired; however, the file on *The Final Countdown* is missing. Donald Baruch believes the Justice Department acquired it for use during the trial of the film's tech-

nical adviser, Cdr. Emory W. Brown, Jr., who was convicted of illegally accepting a payment from the film producers for understating the hours Navy planes flew during the filming of the story aboard the USS *Nimitz*. *Daily Variety*, September 11, 1986.

71. Charles Champlin, "Launching a New Genre—Sea-Fi," *Los Angeles Times*, August 1, 1980, pt. 6, pp. 1, 6.
72. The author took this quote from the DoD *Final Countdown* file while researching a newspaper article, before the file was removed.
73. *New York Times*, August 4, 1980; United Artists production notes for *The Final Countdown*.
74. *Newsweek*, August 18, 1980, p. 85; *New York Times*, August 4, 1980.

Chapter 12. A Different Image: Rehabilitation Complete

1. W. R. Maloney to Marine Corps Chief of Staff, March 24, 1976, DoD.
2. W. R. Maloney, memorandum for the record, March 24, 1976, DoD.
3. John Pommer to Donald Baruch, October 5, 1977.
4. Ibid.
5. Donald Baruch to Marine Corps Public Affairs, October 14, 1977, DoD.
6. David Cooney to DoD Public Affairs, December 19, 1977.
7. V. T. Braz to Marine Corps Chief of Staff, December 20, 1977.
8. Art Brill to Director of Information, n.d. [May 1977].
9. Interview with Pat Coulter, August 8, 1981.
10. Art Brill to Margaret Brewer, June 14, 1978.
11. Ibid.
12. David Cooney to Donald Baruch, August 17, 1978.
13. Coulter interview, August 8, 1981.
14. Baumann's note on a draft of the manuscript, n.d. [1989.]
15. Phone conversation with Marty Elfand, July 7, 1989; Dennis Anstine, "Paramount Film Doesn't 'Reflect Navy's Mission,'" *Port Townsend Leader*, April 22, 1981, p. A1.
16. Memorandum for the record, July 16, 1980, DoD. Baumann himself did not agree with Patterson that the portrayal of the Mobile Debs was inaccurate, Baumann note on author's manuscript.
17. Navy Office of Information to Don Baruch, July 18, 1980, and Baruch's undated handwritten notations on memo, DoD.
18. Don Baruch to Chief, Production Services Division, CHINFO, August 7, 1980.
19. Navy Office of Information memo for Deputy Chief of Information, December 12, 1980; draft memo to Don Baruch, n.d. [December 12, 1980.] (DoD).
20. Navy Office of Information to Don Baruch, n.d. [January 1981], on which Don Baruch recorded his recollection of meeting, n.d. [after January 13, 1981], DoD.
21. Ibid.; Navy Chief of Information to Pensacola Naval Air Station, January 29, 1981, DoD.
22. Interview with Cdr. Chris Baumann, August 25, 1988; interview with Col. Pat Coulter, January 26, 1989.
23. Ibid.; phone conversation with Marty Elfand.
24. Coulter interview, January 26, 1989; Gen. J. T. Hagen, Director of Public Affairs to Commandant of the Marines, July 27, 1982. (DoD).
25. Bob Williams to Maj. Pat Coulter, February 19, 1981; phone conversation with Marty Elfand.

26. Pat Coulter to Media Branch, Division of Public Affairs, February 20, 1981, DoD.

27. Interview with Pat Coulter, August 8, 1981; Coulter interview, January 26, 1989.

28. Ibid.

29. Pat Coulter to Marine Corps Public Affairs Office, February 20, 1981; Pat Coulter to Public Affairs Office, March 21, 1981; J. L. Schilling to Director of Public Affairs, n.d. [after March 21, 1981.] (DoD).

30. Donald Baruch to Col. Robert O'Brien, July 30, 1982, DoD.

31. Donald Baruch to Col. Robert O'Brien on *An Officer and a Gentleman,* July 30, 1982, DoD; Pat Coulter in a speech to the Marine Combat Correspondents Convention, in Long Beach, California, September 28, 1982, DoD; phone conversation with Marty Elfand.

32. Ibid.

33. Coulter interview, August 8, 1981.

34. Richard Cohen, "Brutality Wrong Tool for Making a Man," *Los Angeles Times,* September 8, 1982.

35. Baumann, note on author's manuscript.

36. Pat Coulter to Marine Director of Public Affairs, July 22, 1982, DoD; Don Baruch to Col. Robert O'Brien, July 30, 1982, DoD; Chris Baumann, note on manuscript.

37. Navy Office of Information to Donald Baruch, October 16, 1980, DoD.

38. Michele Casale, Director, Pennsylvania Bureau of Motion Picture and Television Development, to Navy Chief of Information, June 20, 1983; Doug Curtis to Navy Chief of Information, June 27, 1983. (DoD).

39. Dale Patterson to Donald Baruch, August 22, 1983, DoD.

40. Donald Baruch to Doug Curtis, August 26, 1983, DoD.

41. Air Force Office of Information to Office of Public Affairs, National Guard Bureau, May 3, 1976, DoD.

42. Office of Naval Research, "Information Sheet, Philadelphia Experiment; UFO's sic," n.d. The Naval Historical Center Library, in the Washington Navy Yard, has an extensive file on the "Philadelphia Experiment," which refutes the story that the Navy performed any experiments of the nature described in Moore's book.

43. Figures vary by source. In the source of the film, Ehud Yonay's "Top Guns," *California Magazine* (May 1983): 95–102, 144–47, the author writes: "The navy was losing one Phantom for every two MiGs it bagged." Jim Farmer, in "The Making of *Top Gun,*" in *Air Classics* (July 1986), writes: "In the first years of the Vietnam War, the kill ratio was a disappointing three kills for every American planes destroyed in the air-to-air arena" (24). In "The Selling of *Top Gun,* in *American Film* (June 1986), Alexander Cockburn writes: "By 1968, U.S. fighter pilots were having an unexpectedly hard time of it in the skies over Vietnam. The 'exchange ratio' was one to three, meaning that the U.S. Navy and U.S. Air Force were losing one plane for every three enemy downed" (30). In "The Jet Set," in *Rolling Stone Summer '86,* Fred Schruers writes, "When the first bunch of Top Gun-trained F-4 jocks came off the carriers in 1972, they upped their kill ratio from barely even to twelve to one" (132). The Paramount "Handbook or Production Information" for *Top Gun* cites a three to one ratio before the Top Gun School. The 2.5 to 1 ratio comes to the author from Top Gun pilots themselves who say that is the one the school cites.

44. Les Paul Robey, "Flying High with *Top Gun*", *American Cinematographer* (May 1986): 50, hereafter cited as Robey; Ehud Yonay, "Top Guns", *California Magazine* (May 1983): 95, hereafter cited as Yonay.

45. Interview with Don Simpson and Jerry Bruckheimer, February 6, 1989. As a joint interview, the men spoke as one voice unless otherwise identified.

46. Ibid.; Iain Blair, "Team Behind *Top Gun* Brings Back Creative Producing," *Chicago Tribune,* May 11, 1986, sec. 13, p. 2.

47. Simpson-Bruckheimer interview.

48. Interview with Cdr. Chris Baumann, August 24, 1988; interview with Capt. Michael Sherman, January 1989.

49. Ibid.; Simpson-Bruckheimer interview. In critiquing the author's manuscript, Marine Maj. Bill Miles, a former Top Gun instructor, commented on Simpson's remark, "And we do!!"

50. Simpson-Bruckheimer interview; *20/20,* March 26, 1987; Don Simpson and Jerry Bruckheimer to Donald Baruch, June 14, 1983, DoD; interview with Adm. Jack Garrow, April 18, 1990.

51. John Horton to Donald Baruch, June 10, 1983, DoD.

52. In fact, the Marine Corps sends twelve of its top carrier pilots to Top Gun every year, approximately twenty-five percent of the students at the school.

53. John Horton to Donald Baruch, November 15, 1984, DoD.

54. John Horton to Jerry Bruckheimer, November 29, 1984, DoD.

55. Don Baruch to John Horton, May 8, 1985, DoD.

56. Simpson-Bruckheimer interview.

57. Ibid.

58. Ibid.

59. Ibid.

60. Ibid.

61. *Commonweal,* June 20, 1986.

62. David Ansen, "Macho Myth-Making," *Newsweek,* May 19, 1986.

63. J. Hoberman, "Phallus in Wonderland," *Village Voice,* May 27, 1986, p. 59.

64. Ibid.; Alexander Cockburn, "The Selling of the Pentagon," *American Film* (June 1986): 52.

65. Hoberman, "Phallus in Wonderland." Hoberman demonstrated his knowledge of things military by describing the F-4 fighter as a "bomber."

66. *Top Gun* press book, Paramount Pictures; Richard Halloran, "Guardians of the Screen Image," *New York Times,* August 18, 1986, p. 12.

67. For account of the making of *Wings,* see *Guts & Glory,* chapter 2.

68. Tom Cruise interview, *Playboy* (December 1989).

69. Interview with Barry London, February 1, 1989.

70. Ibid.

71. *Washington Post,* July 16, 1986, p. D6.

72. "Tailhook 91" Report, DoD, April 1992, pt. 2, X2.

Chapter 13. The End of the Cold War

1. John Horton to Donald Baruch, December 2, 1985; Harve Bennett to John Horton, December 18, 1985. (DoD).

2. Harve Bennett to John Horton, December 18, 1985, DoD.

3. Ibid.

4. Director, Production Services Division, to Donald Baruch, February 7, 1986, DoD.

5. Harve Bennett to Donald Baruch, February 14, 1986, DoD; *Star Trek IV* press kit.

6. Interview with Mace Neufeld, March 14, 1990.

7. William Honan, "Can the Cold War Be a Hot Topic for a Movie?" *New York Times,* February 25, 1990, sec. 2, p. 15.

8. *Time,* March 12, 1990, p. 81; *Washington Post,* March 19, 1990, p. A28; *Parade,* June 24, 1990, p. 2.

9. *Village View,* March 2–8, 1990, p. 19; interview with John Milius, March 14, 1990.

10. Interview with Larry Ferguson, March 6, 1990; Milius interview; Neufeld interview.

11. *Washington Post,* March 17, 1989, p. D7.

12. *Daily Variety,* May 29, 1985, pp. 1, 18; *Hollywood Reporter,* July 3, 1985, pp. 1, 12.

13. *Daily Variety,* May 29, 1985, p. 1; Neufeld interview; *Los Angeles Times,* September 21, 1988, "Calendar," pt. 6, p. 1.

14. Neufeld interview; *Los Angeles Times,* September 21, 1988, "Calendar," pt. 6, p. 1.

15. *Los Angeles Times,* November 8, 1987.

16. John Horton to Donald Baruch, February 19, 1987, DoD.

17. *Los Angeles Times,* September 21, 1988, "Calendar," pt. 6, p. 1; John Horton to Donald Baruch, November 23, 1988, DoD.

18. Jim Stewart, "Navy Goes Hollywood," *Press-Telegram,* March 3, 1990.

19. Neufeld interview; *Los Angeles Times,* June 1, 1986.

20. Chief of Information to Donald Baruch, December 12, 1988, DoD.

21. Ibid.

22. Memorandum for the record, Capt. Mike Sherman, December 15, 1988, DoD.

23. John McTiernan to Mike Sherman, December 20, 1988, DoD.

24. Ibid.

25. Mike Sherman to the Chief of Information, after December 20, 1988; Donald Baruch to Chief of Information, December 27, 1988. (DoD). Sherman's letter is dated December 12, 1988. However, he had not received McTiernan's letter until December 20. While Baruch gives a December 20 date in his memorandum, Sherman's memorandum has a fax date of 22 December.

26. Capt. J. H. Patton, Jr., "The Making of *Hunt for Red October,*" U.S. Naval Institute *Proceedings* (January 1990): 10–11.

27. Ibid.; "The Shoot of *Red October,*" *Washington Post,* March 17, 1989, p. D7.

28. Ibid.; Navy Chief of Information to CINCLANTFLT, Norfolk, February 28, 1989, DoD; *Press-Telegram,* March 3, 1990, p. C3; Neufeld interview.

29. Cathryn Donohoe, "Navy Action Starring Real McCoy," *Insight,* March 26, 1990, p. 55.

30. *Washington Post,* March 9, 1990, p. D7; David Ansen, *Newsweek,* March 5, 1990, p. 63.

31. Hal Hinson, "*Red October,* Full Speed Astern," *Washington Post,* March 2, 1990, pp. D1, D7.

32. Vincent Canby, *New York Times,* March 2, 1990, p. C13.

33. Neufeld interview.

34. Honan, *New York Times,* February 25, 1990, sec. 2, p. 18.

35. Ibid.

36. Mike Sherman to Chief of Information, May 30, 1989, DoD.

37. Ibid.

38. Ibid.

39. Ibid.

40. Adm. J. B. Finkelstein to Phil Strub, June 20, 1989; Phil Strub to Adm. J. B.

Finkelstein, June 20, 1989; Capt. Mike Sherman to Mike Medavoy, Orion Pictures, June 27, 1989. (DoD).

41. Navy Seal Production to Navy Office of Information, Los Angeles, September 1, 1989; Phil Strub to Navy Office of Information, September 19, 1989. (DoD).

42. Memo from Navy Chief of Information to Commander in Chief, Atlantic Fleet, Norfolk, September 26, 1989, DoD; Phil Strub to Chief of Information, October 2, 1989, DoD; David Scheiderer, "This Screenwriter Trained the 'Navy SEALS' Way," *Los Angeles Times,* August 6, 1990, p. F6.

43. Peter Rainer, "*Navy SEALS*: It's Dirty Dozen with Flippers," *Los Angeles Times,* July 20, 1990, p. F18; *Chicago Sun Times,* July 20, 1990, p. 35; *New York Times,* July 20, 1990, p. C9.

44. Neufeld interview.

45. Ibid.

46. John Horton to Donald Baruch, April 10, 1989, DoD.

47. Mike Sherman to Navy Office of Information, May 2, 1989, DoD.

48. Ibid.; Mike Sherman to Chief of Information, May 16, 1989, DoD.

49. Mike Sherman to Chief of Information, May 16, 1989, DoD.

50. Assistant Chief of Information to Chief of Information, May 26, 1989, DoD.

51. J. B. Finkelstein to Phil Strub, June 22, 1989, DoD; Phil Strub to Chief of Information, June 23, 1989, DoD; Mike Sherman to Lance Young, June 27, 1989, DoD; Neufeld interview.

52. Neufeld interview; Milius interview.

53. James Farmer, "Making *Flight of the Intruder,*" *Air Classics* (August 1990): 30–32, 36–38, 64–70. In a lengthy article, Farmer details the filming of the aerial sequences in Georgia, Hawaii, and aboard the USS *Independence,* as well as at Paramount Studios. Other sources for the discussion of Navy cooperation include a memo from the Chief of Naval Operations to various commands about the assistance being provided to the film, n.d. [after September 2, 1989], DoD; Penny Smith, "On Location: *Flight of the Intruder,*" *Hollywood Reporter,* 1989 Hawaii Special Report, November 21, 1989, pp. 5–8, 9; Lt. Cdr. R. O. McHurg, *The Hook* (Summer 1990): 84–87; Ralph Rugoff, "It's Not Just an Adventure, It's a Job," *Premiere,* 2 (August 1990): 39–40; *Daily Variety,* November 6, 1989. Unless otherwise cited, the discussion is based on a synthesis of all these sources.

54. *Daily Variety,* January 18, 1991.

55. Desmond Ryan, "Misguided Missile," *Long Beach Press-Telegram,* January 18, 1991.

56. Ibid.

57. Ibid.; Peter Rainer, "*Flight of the Intruder* Takes to the Air at the Right Time," *Los Angeles Times,* January 18, 1991, p. F12.

58. Rainer, "*Flight of the Intruder,*" F12.

59. Interview with Mike Sherman, August 30, 1993.

Epilogue

1. Cmd. Gary Shrout to Navy Public Affairs, April 26, 1994, DoD.

2. Ibid.; Phil Strub to the Walt Disney Company, July 8, 1994, DoD.

3. Strub to Disney, July 8, 1994, DoD.

4. Shrout to Navy Information and Phil Strub, April 26, 1994, DoD.

5. Author's phone conversation with Don Mancuso, May 20, 1995.

Sources

As indicated in the preface, I have based *Sailing on the Silver Screen* on original sources, primary documents, and oral interviews. I have cited published books only as they supply general information on some aspect of the subject, such as my own *Guts & Glory*, Samuel Eliot Morison's *The Two-Ocean War*, and Clay Blair's *Silent Victory*. For the most part, I have used magazine and newspaper articles either for specific information such as first-person quotes, data on the production of motion pictures, or historical facts. I have used film reviews as documents supporting my own observations about a movie, not for their artistic judgments. Both the *New York Times* and *Weekly Variety* have collected and published their entire sets of reviews, and they can be found in most major research libraries.

The primary documents come from many sources, both public and private. The National Archives in Washington, D.C., contain Navy records relating to cooperation with the film industry from before World War I into the early 1950s. The John F. Kennedy Library contains material about the making of *PT-109*. The Stanford University Special Collections Library contains the papers of Delmer Daves. The UCLA Special Collections Library contains the James Poe Papers. By far the greatest source of original documents is the Department of Defense files.

Although Don Baruch's office retired the early records of its operation to the National Archives, it retained virtually all its files on cooperation from 1960 onward, at least as of when I moved to Washington in 1976. In the course of events, Mr. Baruch allowed me access to this material for my research in writing *Guts & Glory*. In turn, I agreed to show him my manuscript to ensure I had not violated the confidentiality of corporate information. However, at no time did Mr. Baruch or his office refuse permission for me to use the material.

Even after I completed my book, Mr. Baruch allowed me to keep my research current—which helped particularly in the writing of my Ph.D. dissertation, *The Film Industry and the Vietnam War* (Case Western Reserve, 1980). Phil Strub, who replaced Mr. Baruch in 1989, has continued to give me access to the files on a need-to-know, freedom-of-information basis, which was invaluable during the writing of this book. He has continued to provide information and advice informally, with the understanding that they would read the results of my writing to ensure accuracy of content, *not* of my analysis or interpretation.

In Los Angeles, the Motion Picture Academy Library contains files on virtually every film ever made. These files include reviews, production notes, and articles relating to the films. The library also has collections of filmmakers' documents and papers. As important, the University of Southern California Film Cinema and Television Library contains production files from Warner Brothers, Twentieth Century Fox, and MGM, among others. The files include scripts and correspondence relating to the making of many of the films I have discussed.

In addition, over the years I have acquired documents from many people. In some cases the material might consist of a few letters or official memoranda. However, two collections particularly enriched my work. Cdr. Edward Stafford, the technical adviser for *Tora! Tora! Tora!,* happened to mention during our interview that he had saved all his correspondence pertaining to his assignment to the film. He kindly loaned the material to me, and it was the basis for my account of the making of the movie. (In contrast, the film's producer, Elmo Williams, told me he had destroyed all his material when he could not obtain a tax break for donating the records to a library.)

Although not containing the depth of material on any one film as Stafford's documents, Lt. Col. Clair Towne's contribution covered a four-year period in the early 1950s. Towne had served as Baruch's assistant and had saved all his own correspondence to filmmakers and much of the responses. He kindly loaned the material to me for copying, without which my discussions of *Men of the Fighting Lady* and *Bridges at Toko-ri*, for example, would lack the substance they now have.

Unless otherwise noted, I have placed all the documents and printed material used in *Sailing on the Silver Screen* in individual files on each film and deposited them at the Georgetown University Special Collections Library, where they will remain available for inspection. The folders containing material from the National Archives include citations to the record group and box number. I have labeled the documents obtained from the office of Donald Baruch and Phil Strub as DoD files. Documents obtained from Clair Towne are listed as Towne papers. (Where there was duplication of material, I simply included the clearest document.)

In Appendix 1 I have listed all the interviews used in writing the book. I have quoted directly only from those transcripts for which I received approval from the interviewee. However, I have cited the interviews of all those involved with a particular production since the information itself provided the framework in which to tell my story. All transcripts as well as the original tapes are also on deposit at the Georgetown Library. The transcripts are available for research. With permission, a researcher may listen to the tapes, but they may not be used without permission from me and the interviewee.

I am fully aware that many historians question the validity of oral interviews. They challenge the interviewee's veracity, memory, and self-serving recollections. For example, an interview I did with Theodore Sorensen was questioned on the ground that he was serving as gatekeeper for Camelot. In truth, Mr. Sorensen had refused to meet with me for more than a year before finally agreeing to talk about President Kennedy's decision to send astronauts to the moon. In contrast to wanting to burnish the image of the president, I realized that he was reluctant to give the interview because it hurt him too much to talk about the past.

In fact, I have treated the oral interviews as an historian should treat any primary document: with caution. In almost all cases I have used the information from the interviews in combination with other primary and secondary material. In the course of more than one thousand interviews, I believe I have had only one person deliberately lie to me. Going into the interview, I knew he was going to lie and knew why he was going to lie. Even though I later told him I could not corroborate his information, he continued to claim he was telling the truth. Naturally, I did not use the interview.

For the most part, however, the interviews provide valuable insights and information not otherwise obtainable. To be sure, questions must be asked carefully to avoid putting words in a person's mouth, while still stirring up old memories. Even then, information must always be reexamined in the light of new material. Adm. John Will, for example, told me that he had ruined a shot during the filming of *Men Without Women* because he blurted out in surprise at the realism of the flooding of the submarine. When I first screened the film at the Library of Congress, I found it was silent. Was Admiral Will padding the story? One book on John Ford said that only silent versions of the film remained extant. At least that suggested that a sound version had once existed and that Will might well be remembering correctly. In fact, the Museum of Modern Art did have the sound version of the movie.

In any case, the use of interviews does add to the richness of the story when they are treated as simply another source. However, they must be combined with traditional sources to produce as accurate a recreation of events as possible. In *Sailing on the Silver Screen* I believe I have done this and so given my book a uniqueness.

Finally, though I have written a military and institutional history, the movies I have discussed remain important components of the story. They help confirm the accuracy of both the documents and the oral recollections. As recently as when I wrote *Guts & Glory* in the late 1970s, most of the films I discussed could be seen only on television or in the Library of Congress. Since the arrival of the VCR, video-rental stores, and cable television, almost all the sound movies I have included in this book have become readily available. The Library of Congress and the Museum of Modern Art contain most of the few films not on tape, such as *Submarine Pirate, Men Without Women,* and *Hell Divers.* If *Sailing on the Silver Screen* serves no other purpose, perhaps it will stimulate the release of some of the early movies. Most of them are at least as interesting as the more recent *Final Countdown* and *Raise the Titanic.*

In this book, of course, I do not discuss the films as entertainment. As a military history, *Sailing on the Silver Screen* does not provide a theory of film analysis in discussing any of the movies included in this study. The book does not consider the cinematic quality of the individual motion pictures except where a lack of redeeming filmmaking resulted in no audience appeal. Only to the extent that the book chronicles the release and content of the movies does it provide a history of film. In any case, *Sailing on the Silver Screen* uses the motion pictures only as primary documents that the author analyzes in the same way as he uses the traditional paper documents also cited in the discussions. They are simply primary documents containing the image that the Navy wanted to show the American people, that it tried hard to change to a better portrayal, or that it tried to stop from appearing. This interaction between the Navy and the film industry remains the focus of my book. The many sources upon which I drew provide credibility to my story.

★

Index

ABOUT THE AUTHOR

Lawrence Suid is the author of *Guts & Glory: Great American War Movies, Film and Propaganda in America: A Documentary History*, and numerous other publications on military and film history. A frequent lecturer, he has provided commentary for such television news shows as *20/20*. He also served as a consultant to the PBS series *Vietnam: A Television History*. He holds a Ph.D. in American Studies from Case Western Reserve University and currently resides in Washington, D.C.

The **Naval Institute Press** is the book-publishing arm of the U.S. Naval Institute, a private, nonprofit society for sea service professionals and others who share an interest in naval and maritime affairs. Established in 1873 at the U.S. Naval Academy in Annapolis, Maryland, where its offices remain, today the Naval Institute has more than 85,000 members worldwide.

Members of the Naval Institute receive the influential monthly magazine *Proceedings* and discounts on fine nautical prints and on ship and aircraft photos. They also have access to the transcripts of the Institute's Oral History Program and get discounted admission to any of the Institute-sponsored seminars offered around the country.

The Naval Institute also publishes *Naval History* magazine. This colorful bimonthly is filled with entertaining and thought-provoking articles, first-person reminiscences, and dramatic art and photography. Members receive a discount on *Naval History* subscriptions.

The Naval Institute's book-publishing program, begun in 1898 with basic guides to naval practices, has broadened its scope in recent years to include books of more general interest. Now the Naval Institute Press publishes about 100 titles each year, ranging from how-to books on boating and navigation to battle histories, biographies, ship and aircraft guides, and novels. Institute members receive discounts of 20 to 50 percent on the Press's nearly 600 books in print.

For a free catalog describing Naval Institute Press books currently available, and for further information about subscribing to *Naval History* magazine or about joining the U.S. Naval Institute, please write to:

Membership Department
U.S. Naval Institute
118 Maryland Avenue
Annapolis, Maryland 21402-5035

Telephone: (800) 233-8764
Fax: (410) 269-7940

LAWRENCE SUID is the author of *Guts & Glory: Great American War Movies*, *Film and Propaganda in America: A Documentary History*, and numerous other publications on military and film history. A frequent lecturer, he has served as a consultant to the PBS series *Vietnam: A Television History* and provided commentary for such television news shows as *20/20*. He holds a Ph.D. in American Studies from Case Western Reserve University and currently resides in Washington, D.C.